Politics in GERMANY

Attitudes and Processes

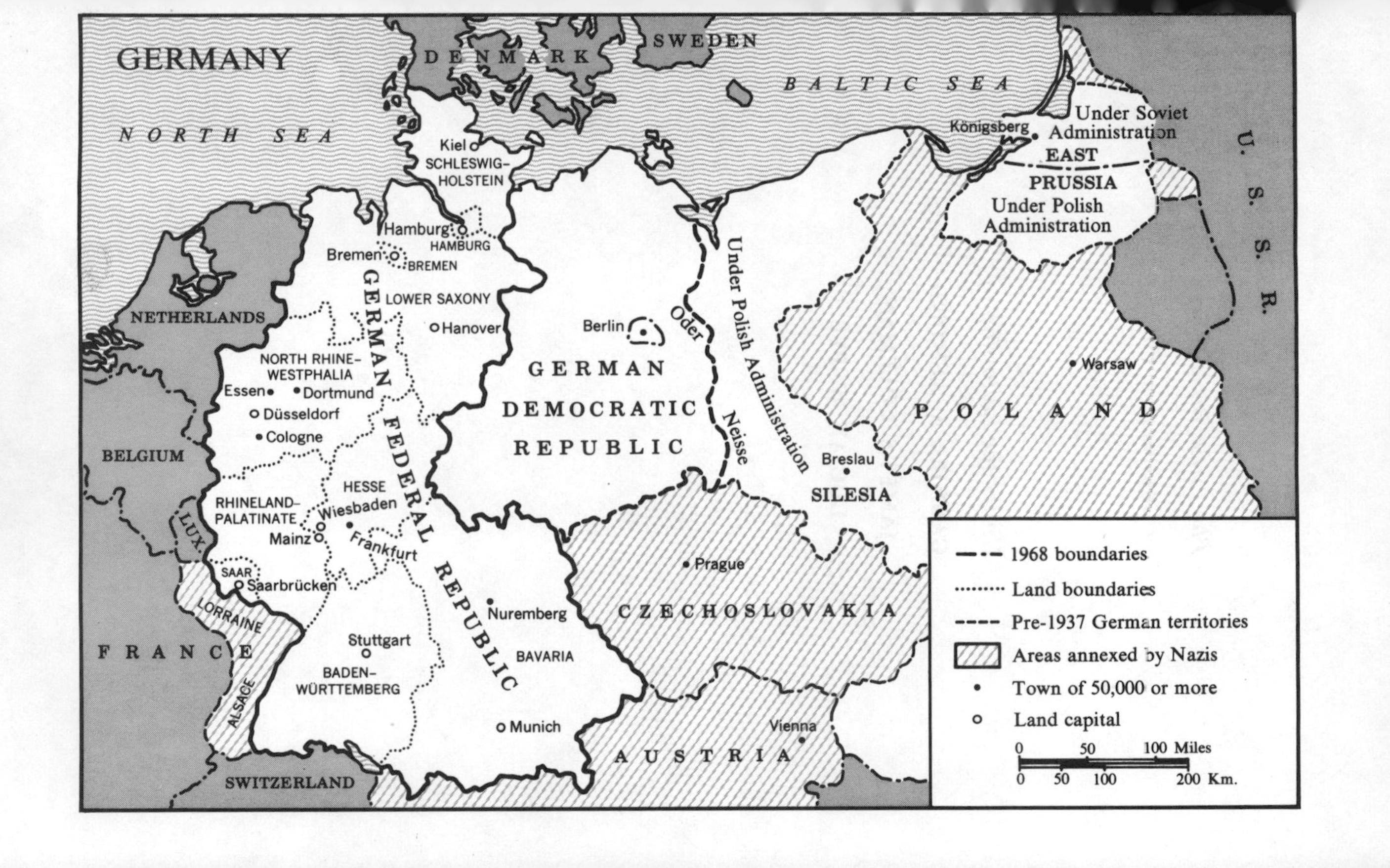
GERMANY
NORTH SEA
BALTIC SEA
DENMARK
SWEDEN
U. S. S. R.
Königsberg
Under Soviet Administration
EAST PRUSSIA
Under Polish Administration
Kiel
SCHLESWIG-HOLSTEIN
Hamburg
HAMBURG
Bremen
BREMEN
LOWER SAXONY
Hanover
NETHERLANDS
NORTH RHINE-WESTPHALIA
Essen
Dortmund
Düsseldorf
Cologne
BELGIUM
HESSE
RHINELAND-PALATINATE
Wiesbaden
Mainz
Frankfurt
LUX.
SAAR
Saarbrücken
LORRAINE
FRANCE
ALSACE
Stuttgart
BADEN-WÜRTTEMBERG
SWITZERLAND
Munich
BAVARIA
Nuremberg
GERMAN FEDERAL REPUBLIC
Berlin
GERMAN DEMOCRATIC REPUBLIC
Oder
Neisse
Under Polish Administration
Breslau
SILESIA
Warsaw
POLAND
Prague
CZECHOSLOVAKIA
Vienna
AUSTRIA
1968 boundaries
Land boundaries
Pre-1937 German territories
Areas annexed by Nazis
Town of 50,000 or more
Land capital
0 50 100 Miles
0 50 100 200 Km.

The Little, Brown Series

in Comparative Politics

Politics in GERMANY

Attitudes and Processes

Lewis J. Edinger

Columbia University

Boston

LITTLE, BROWN AND COMPANY

LIBRARY OF CONGRESS CATALOG CARD NO. 68-31592

FIRST PRINTING

Published simultaneously in Canada
by Little, Brown & Company (Canada) Limited

PRINTED IN THE UNITED STATES OF AMERICA

To

MONICA AND SUSAN

Foreword

The Little, Brown Series in Comparative Politics has three main objectives. First, it will meet the need of teachers to deal with both Western and non-Western countries in their introductory course offerings. Second, by following a common approach in analyzing individual political systems, it will make it possible for teachers to compare these countries systematically and cumulatively. And third, it will contribute toward re-establishing the classic relationship between comparative politics and political theory, a relationship which has been neglected in recent decades. In brief, the series seeks to be global in scope, genuinely introductory and comparative in character, and concerned with broadening and deepening our understanding of the nature and variety of political systems.

The series has two parts: the Country Studies and the Analytic Studies. The Country Studies deal with problems and processes deriving from a functional, as compared with a purely structural, approach to the study of political systems. We are gratified that the participants, all mature scholars with original insights, were willing to organize their discussions around a common set of functional topics in the interest of furthering comparisons. At the same time, each author has been urged to adapt the common framework to the special problems of the country he is discussing and to express his own theoretical point of view.

An introductory book, *Comparative Politics: A Developmental Approach,* written by Gabriel A. Almond and G.

Bingham Powell, provides an analytic supplement to the Country Studies. It also opens our set of Analytic Studies, which offers basic discussions of such topics as political change in the emerging nations, comparative analyses of interest groups, political socialization, political communication, political culture, and the like. We hope these books will prove to be useful and stimulating supplements to the Country Studies as well as points of departure in more advanced courses.

Lewis Edinger's *Politics in Germany* is the first full-length study of Germany's political and governmental processes to employ a system-functional approach. It draws together historical, anthropological, sociological, psychological, and political theory and data in a coherent description and explanation of the German political system. Certain themes of great importance in forecasting future trends in German politics (*e.g.*, postwar changes in German social structure and culture, contemporary patterns of political socialization, and recruitment into and participation in politics) receive their first treatment in depth in a book intended for classroom use.

Gabriel A. Almond
James S. Coleman
Lucian W. Pye

Acknowledgments

The information and insights on which the following study is based are the products of research, teaching, and personal observations extending over more than two decades. Directly and indirectly I am deeply indebted to the work and stimulation of far too many persons to be named here. They include professional colleagues in the United States and Europe, German leaders who were generous enough to allow me to interview them on a number of trips to the Federal Republic, my co-workers in the United States Department of Defense during the years 1953 to 1956, and my students. I am indebted to legions of librarians who valiantly sought to cope with my demands for books and documents, to a number of research assistants who struggled with complex assignments, and to all too many secretaries who typed various portions and versions of the manuscript.

Some of the opinion survey data utilized in this study were made available by the Inter-University Consortium for Political Research and originally collected by Gabriel A. Almond and Sidney Verba. Other data were provided through the Yale University Political Data Library, by the Press and Information Office of the German Federal Government, and by Professor Dr. Elisabeth Noelle-Neumann of the Institut für Demoskopie in Allensbach. Neither the original collectors of these data, nor those who made them available, bear any responsibility for the analysis or interpretations presented here. Similarly, while the manuscript greatly profited from the reading of various portions by Professors Karl Dietrich Bracher, Gerard Braunthal, Richard Dawson, John Kautsky, Juan Linz, Richard Rose, Stanley Rothman, Donald D. Searing, Roberta Sigel, and Steven Warnecke, none of these can be blamed for my errors of commission and omission. I am grateful to Donald R. Hammonds of Little, Brown and to the editors of this series for waiting long and patiently for the completion of this study.

This book would not have been written had it not been for financial support from the United States Educational Commission in the Federal Republic, from Washington University (St. Louis), and from the European Institute of Columbia University. To Washington University and its Chancellor, Thomas Elliot, I owe a very special debt for lightening the load of academic citizenship duties while this study was in progress and for allowing me to spend a year in the Federal Republic.

Lewis J. Edinger

Table of Contents

Tables and Illustrations

Politics in

GERMANY

Attitudes and Processes

CHAPTER I

Introduction

INTERPRETING GERMAN POLITICS

This book has two major objectives. One is to provide an introductory survey of the political system of the German Federal Republic (West Germany), the second is to offer a contribution to the comparative study of politics in various countries during various periods. I have sought neither to make Germany's role in contemporary international politics the heart of my presentation nor to concentrate on the major issues of current politics. Although these matters are basic ingredients for a book such as this, our principal subject is the nature and operation of a political system within which demands for public policymaking arise, are processed, and are converted into decisions that to a greater or lesser extent affect the entire population. I have therefore, on the one hand, deliberately slighted certain specific aspects of German politics to gain breadth of focus and, on the other, included features which might ordinarily not be looked for in a book about politics in Germany.

An endeavor of this sort calls above all for perspective. When we seek to understand a political system we are interested not only in the formal governmental institutions, political parties, and pressure groups, but also in the less evident and more elusive aspects of political life – such as the sociological and psychological characteristics of the citizenry and of its formal and informal leaders insofar as they impinge upon the political system. We thus cast our nets wider than is customary in studies of German government and politics, and, for this reason, we must be especially careful to identify what we consider relevant and significant for political developments and why, to distinguish between political and nonpolitical actors, and to look beyond evident political attitudes and behavior patterns for implicit ones. As in photography, a true picture requires the establishment and maintenance of clear boundary lines between the relevant and the irrelevant and a proper balance between simplicity and detail and between breadth and depth of focus.

The need for perspective is basic to all studies of political systems, but in the German Federal Republic it is particularly important. First, we are confronted with an enormous number of books, articles, and reports by German and non-German observers which provide us with a great deal of detailed information – particularly about developments in recent decades – but all too little synthesis.[1] The interested student who immerses himself in this vast accumulation of data needs perspective so he will not lose sight of the wood for the trees. Second, we are dealing with a highly complex political system in which traditional and modern components, political and nonpolitical relationships, and domestic and international factors are closely enmeshed. More than in a less sophisticated system – or one about which we have less information – the complexity of the German polity poses difficulties when we try to identify its general features and patterns. Here too, a clear focus can help us gain perspective.

A third problem that confronts us in studying the German political system arises from the dynamics of its development. Whereas in the United States, Britain, and other countries more or less stable political patterns have prevailed for many decades, in Germany five regimes have succeeded each other in

[1] Among the very best recent surveys of German government and politics in English are Arnold J. Heidenheimer, *The Governments of Germany*, rev. ed. (New York: Crowell, 1966); Alfred Grosser, *The Federal Republic of Germany* (New York: Praeger, 1964); and Elmer Plischke, *Contemporary Government of Germany* (Boston: Houghton Mifflin, 1961). In German: Thomas Ellwein, *Das Regierungsystem der Bundesrepublik Deutschland* (Köln-Opladen: Westdeutscher Verlag, 1965) and Theodor Eschenburg, *Staat und Gesellschaft in Deutschland*, 5th ed. (Stuttgart: Curt E. Schwab, 1962).

less than a hundred years, and at times the transition from one to another was radical and drastic. The present regime was established in 1949, too recently to allow us to be certain about the direction of its development.

A number of political analysts have sought to explain the present system and to predict its future by relying heavily on earlier German political experiences, but such efforts run the risk of slighting or distorting perpetually changing conditions that distinguish contemporary German politics from those of the past. When we view these political developments primarily in historical perspective, we run the danger of slighting dynamic contemporaneous factors which may be significantly altering political patterns. Thus, characteristics associated on historical evidence with the "German national character" need to be carefully reconsidered because of radically changed environmental conditions for politics in Germany. Without conclusive supporting evidence we cannot simply assume that the evidence of the past provides us with sufficient clues to understand present developments and evaluate future trends. At the same time, it would undoubtedly be a grave mistake to ignore the past entirely. As learned and experienced history, it affects present political attitudes and behavior in Germany. The crucial questions are how much and in what manner? For example, how solidly are traditional values entrenched and to what extent are they giving way to new ways of perceiving and participating in political processes?

Finally, Germany's Nazi past presents a very special problem for the analyst of contemporary German politics seeking an objective picture. Almost twenty-five years after the destruction of the Hitler regime, memories of its deeds still provoke intense emotions that complicate efforts to analyze the present political system dispassionately. The black eagle, for example, is a symbol of national identification which arouses conflicting reactions among Germans and non-Germans. The founders of the Federal Republic chose the coat of arms of the medieval German emperors as a symbol of national unity in a divided country; the chicken-like creature in a frying pan, which the German novelist Günther Grass drew in 1964 for a cover of the British periodical *Encounter* seemed to symbolize impotence; emblazoned on the cover of the American magazine, *Holiday,* at about the same time, a mighty eagle with wings of bolted steel conveyed the image of the surging power of German recovery – frightening to many who recall the past. Particularly among non-German observers, the black eagle still evokes memories of aggression, destruction, and mass murder by German soldiers – memories which color foreign interpretations of political development in contemporary Germany.

Stereotyped images of Germany and the Germans based on memories of the past thus threaten to distort and obscure the present and future patterns of the political system of the Federal Republic. Perhaps it is impossible for German as well as non-German observers who still retain vivid memories of the Nazi era to study contemporary German politics with the same detachment with which they might investigate the Nepalese political system – or German politics in the middle ages. But we can consciously strive for – even if we cannot hope to realize entirely – an objective approach which balances special insights derived from a familiarity with German politics with the detachment that empirical political science demands.

For all these reasons, perspective is our most important problem. To help us achieve it, we have employed a conceptual model developed by Gabriel Almond.[2] Such a model allows us to determine what information is to be included in our study for an analysis which is neither too detailed nor too diffuse. By proceeding in this manner, we may succeed in our efforts to facilitate objective comparisons between the contemporary German political system and others – German as well as non-German.

THE POLITICAL SYSTEM AND ITS ENVIRONMENT

Any discussion about the German political system confronts us with the question of what we mean by "German" and what

[2] See Gabriel A. Almond's Introduction to Almond and James S. Coleman, *The Politics of Developing Areas* (Princeton: Princeton University Press, 1960); Gabriel Almond and G. Bingham Powell, *Comparative Politics: A Developmental Approach* (Boston: Little, Brown, 1966); and Gabriel Almond, "A Developmental Approach to Political Systems," *World Politics,* XVII (1965), 183–214. I am also indebted to David Easton, *A Systems Analysis of Political Life* (New York: Wiley, 1965).

by "political system." To answer these questions is to define the boundaries of our subject, but this is no easy task. Let us first consider the concept "political system." Following Max Weber, Gabriel Almond and others have associated it with the use of legitimate physical force in societies.[3] That is to say, a political system is separated from its environment by two types of boundaries: (1) those which divide it from other subsystems within a society, such as the economic system, and (2) those which divide it from political systems associated with other societies. Beyond these boundaries we find the environment of the political system, intrasocietal on the one hand and extrasocietal on the other.

The first type of boundaries are analytical constructs postulated by our comparative model. That is, they serve as guidelines for identifying and delineating attitudes and processes which are "political" because they concern the authoritative distribution of public benefits and obligations through governmental agencies. In this sense, politics in Germany involves not only formal governmental processes, but also nongovernmental structures and functions which influence and are influenced by the rules and regulations of the official decisionmakers in the state.

As we shall see, these analytical boundaries are flexible and porous in West Germany. Political and nonpolitical orientations, roles, and activities are not always easily distinguished, particularly in implicit rather than explicit political attitudes and processes. Manifestly nonpolitical relationships may, upon closer inspection, appear to be politically significant and political issues may have an impact on matters ostensibly unrelated to public policymaking. For instance, a priest's appeal to the Christian conscience of his parishioners may induce them to vote for or against a party, a politician's divorce may ruin his career, and a governmental regulation for jailing intoxicated drivers may cause a citizen to sell his car.

Politics "in Germany," however, also implies another and more familiar type of boundary, that dividing this polity from those subject to the authoritative decisions of a different gov-

[3] See Almond, "A Developmental Approach to Political Systems," pp. 191–192 and the sources cited there.

ernment. In general, this is the boundary commonly thought of as dividing one sovereign state from another, but in divided Germany the matter is more complicated. According to the official position of the West German government the German state — and therefore "domestic" German politics — extends beyond the boundaries of the Federal Republic. Germany, as every school child in Munich or Bonn, Hamburg or Heidelberg learns, is the old prewar Reich, the Germany for which television announcers forecast each night tomorrow's weather, the Germany "within the borders of 1937" which appears on every official map. In this view, the entire city of Berlin is legitimately a part of Germany under "temporary" foreign occupation, the "German Democratic Republic" is "The Soviet Zone in Central Germany," and territories in "Eastern Germany" are merely under Polish and Russian "administration." Accordingly, all German "citizens" inside and outside the Federal Republic are said to be legitimately subject to the authority of the only "freely elected" German government — that in Bonn — and a Federal Ministry for All-German Affairs exists primarily to give emphasis to this claim.

Our definition of a political system implies a more restricted conception of Germany. We shall consider all individuals not directly subject to the authoritative decisions of the government of the German Federal Republic outside the boundaries of the West German state and society. Therefore, relations with the German Democratic Republic and its population will be treated in the same fashion as other extrasocietal "foreign" relations with political systems normally identified with sovereign states. This distinction serves to facilitate objective comparative analysis under present conditions and deliberately avoids the normative issues posed by the division of Germany. Thus, the question of whether the German Democratic Republic and the annexation of East German territories by Poland and the Soviet Union are legal or illegal, moral or immoral, does not concern us here — except insofar as they involve attitudes and behavior in the West German polity.

CHAPTER II

The Setting for German Politics

IN THE ALMOST TWO DECADES since its establishment in 1949, the German Federal Republic has shown great political stability, a stability which has impressed observers particularly because of past political turmoil in Germany and the instability of new regimes in other parts of the world. Some commentators have given West German leaders much of the credit, others have attributed political stability to formal constitutional and legal arrangements, but in the last analysis favorable environmental conditions seem to have been most responsible. Recognition of this fact has led to the fear, inside as well as outside Western Germany, that under less favorable conditions in the future latent elements of political instability might emerge and put the political system to far more severe tests than it has yet had to face. In this view, a severe economic crisis might place such strains on the system as to bring about a repetition of the conditions which in the 1930's brought Hitler to power.

These fears may be entirely unjustified, but they are not unreasonable. Formal constitutional arrangements and "great leaders" by themselves give no assurance of political stability but may, if they become too rigid, prevent necessary political adjustments to a dynamic environment. The young West German polity is still evolving, and, until its structures have become more solidly established within the society, its future will depend much more on intrasocietal and extrasocietal environmental factors than do political systems with institutionalized features backed by custom and tradition.

Any political system consists essentially of interlocking roles played by major and minor participating actors on a stage with shifting scenery. The players are the leaders and citizens of the country while the background which influences their political behavior is the domestic and international environment. In a stable system the political actors are more or less in agreement on the rules of the game, on what political behavior and which goals are "legitimate." Political roles and norms endorsed by popular consensus tend to structure political relationship; leaders as well as followers know what is expected of them and what they may expect as "responsible rulers" and "good citizens." In a less stable system what may be done and what needs to be done legitimately cause disputes which may deeply divide society, role expectations are less congruent, and the interaction between the polity and its environment proceeds less smoothly.

The fathers of the constitution of the Federal Republic sought to ensure future political stability by giving very precise formal structure to the new polity through the legal arrangements which they incorporated in the "Basic Law" of 1949. Determined to prevent the recurrence of political developments which they believed had led to the destruction of German democracy in the 1930's and uncertain about the future of what they described as a temporary political community pending the reunification of Germany, they thought it necessary to spell out in great detail how the new political system was to work. In 146 articles, divided into many subsections, the constituent assembly of 1948–49 laid down a formal framework for the relationship between the component parts of the polity, between polity and society, and for the behavior of political actors.

These structural components, under the impact of internal and external environmental factors, have in the last nineteen years given the West German political system its present form. Its future stability will depend on the functional adequacy and adaptability of its political structures in meeting and processing demands for authoritative governmental action arising from a dynamic environment. The more stable the environment and the greater the capacity of the system to process such demands to the satisfaction of the actors involved, the greater will be its stability. Relative stability in the domestic and international environment will require comparatively little adaptability and changes in established political structures and functions. On the other hand, radically changing environmental conditions, which produce greater and more intense demands for authoritative action by the public policymakers, will place correspondingly greater strains on the capacity of the system to process such demands. In time and under relatively stable environmental conditions the new political system is likely to become more resilient to external pressure. For the present it seems still highly sensitive to such pressures and, therefore, potentially unstable.

INVOLVEMENT AND POLYCENTRISM

Among the major countries of the world the Federal Republic in some respects resembles Britain most closely. About equal in area and in the size and structure of their populations, both are densely settled, highly industrial countries which depend for their economic well-being principally on external trade. But geographic and historical factors have also produced important differences between the two countries. Whereas centuries of insularity have decisively shaped British society and politics,[1] two thousand years of intensive involvement with their neighbors have led to rather different political attitudes and patterns among the German-speaking peoples living roughly between the Rhine and Elbe rivers.

Wide open frontiers unencumbered by major geographic obstacles made this area a thoroughfare for soldiers, merchants, scholars, and artists moving across the European continent. This geographic factor has been one of the most important environmental elements shaping the political attitudes and relationships of the German population from ancient times to the present. The ravages of the Thirty Years' War in the

[1] See Richard Rose, *Politics in England* (Boston: Little, Brown, 1964), p. 7.

seventeenth century, the French invasions of the eighteenth and early nineteenth century, and the experiences of the two world wars in the twentieth have resulted in an enduring feeling that West Germans live in a land exposed to attack by more powerful neighbors. In the age of thermonuclear weapons – a few of which would suffice to wipe out most of the population of Western Germany – memories of past wars and destruction combined with fears of future cataclysms have made most West Germans very anxious about the stability of the international environment. A feeling of dependence on their Western allies – above all, the United States – against a perceived threat of overt or covert aggression from the Communist East is today basic in West German domestic and foreign political relations. To the West German people, assurance of security against Soviet invasion and Communist subversion is all important.

The division of Germany largely severed once intimate contacts between West Germans and their eastern neighbors. Mutual suspicions, fear, and hostility have patterned relations between the West German government and that of the Communist German state across the Elbe and its East European allies. West Germans' relations with their European and American allies on the other hand have been intimate since the establishment of the Federal Republic in 1949. Military and economic ties have forged bonds which may prove insoluble in the future. American and British troops stand guard with German soldiers on the eastern frontiers of the country, and American nuclear deterrent power seems to West Germans an indispensable shield against an attack from the East. The economy depends heavily on trade with the Western nations, the new European Economic Community has established particularly close ties with France, Italy, and the Low Countries, and two decades of intimate relations with the United States have Americanized West German society more than probably any other in the world. Over a million Italians, Spaniards, Greeks, and Turks have come to work in the Federal Republic, while hundreds of thousands of West Germans take to the road each summer to visit the countries of Western and Southern Europe.

The absence of a firmly established sense of national identity is another characteristic which distinguishes West Germans from Englishmen and from citizens of other long established political communities, such as France, the United States, and Japan. Since the decline of the loosely organized medieval German empire in the thirteenth century, Germans have been united in a national community for only a relatively short time.

Until 1871 the present territory of the Federal Republic was divided into numerous small principalities, kingdoms, and city-states enjoying a rather precarious existence between more powerful neighbors. Cut off from the oceans which allowed Britain, France, and the United States to become world powers, these states vegetated for centuries as small provincial entities dependent for political and economic survival on others. They participated in the religious wars of the sixteenth and seventeenth centuries and the European power struggles of the eighteenth and nineteenth – now as allies of one side, now of another – striving to preserve their own independence with varying success. After the northern regions were gradually absorbed by the expanding Prussian state, the entire area in 1871 became part of the Second German Empire ruled from Berlin. But for the seventy-four years of the new Reich the southern regions in particular retained a strong sense of regional identity, which even the radical centralization efforts of the Hitler regime were unable to eradicate.

The destruction of the Reich in 1945 again left West Germany without a cohesive political community and political system. For some years American, British, and French military governments ruled over different parts of West Germany more or less independently. In 1949 the Western occupation zones were transformed into the Federal Republic while, soon thereafter, the Soviet Union established the German Democratic Republic across the Elbe. Within a few years two very dissimilar social systems emerged in these two German states, both different from the society of pre-1945 Germany. Two highly antagonistic regimes and the eastward orientation of the one and the westward orientation of the other accentuated the disruption of the former German political community.

The brief but intense experience in national unity before World War II left Germans living in the Federal Republic with rather ambivalent emotions about a political community established ostensibly only as an interim *provisorium* until national unity could be restored. The question "What is the German's Fatherland?" which the patriotic poet Ernst Moritz Arndt had posed before the unification of 1871, once again confronts West Germans. Whether this fatherland is the Federal Republic, undivided Germany, a united Europe, or an Atlantic Community, remains for most of them an open question.

A related feature of West German society is that it lacks a metropolitan center – such as Berlin had been and London, Paris, Buenos Aires, Stockholm, and Tokyo still are. Postwar development produced a polycentric society in Western Germany in which political, economic, and cultural activities are decentralized to an extent quite exceptional in advanced industrial societies. Cut off from Berlin, divided into almost entirely new political entities by the occupying powers, and compelled to organize under physical conditions that favored decentralization, West German society developed in the crucial early postwar years around numerous geographic centers, scattered from Hamburg in the north to Munich in the south. In the years that followed, the supposed provisional aspects of the new political community and hopes for a reunited Germany ruled from Berlin, as well as the prospects of a greater European community, helped to maintain these polycentric features and slowed if they did not check countervailing centripetal pressures.

The capital, Bonn – an old university town favored in the past by civil servants and businessmen as a place to retire and chosen almost accidentally in 1949 as the provisional seat of the federal government – lies largely outside the mainstream of West German society. Many West Germans refer to it rather contemptuously as the *"Bundesdorf,"* a provincial hick town that lacks the attractions of a real capital city. Those German leaders who don't have to live there avoid Bonn, and most of those who do have to live there make no secret of their contempt for the town and its native population. The great bank-

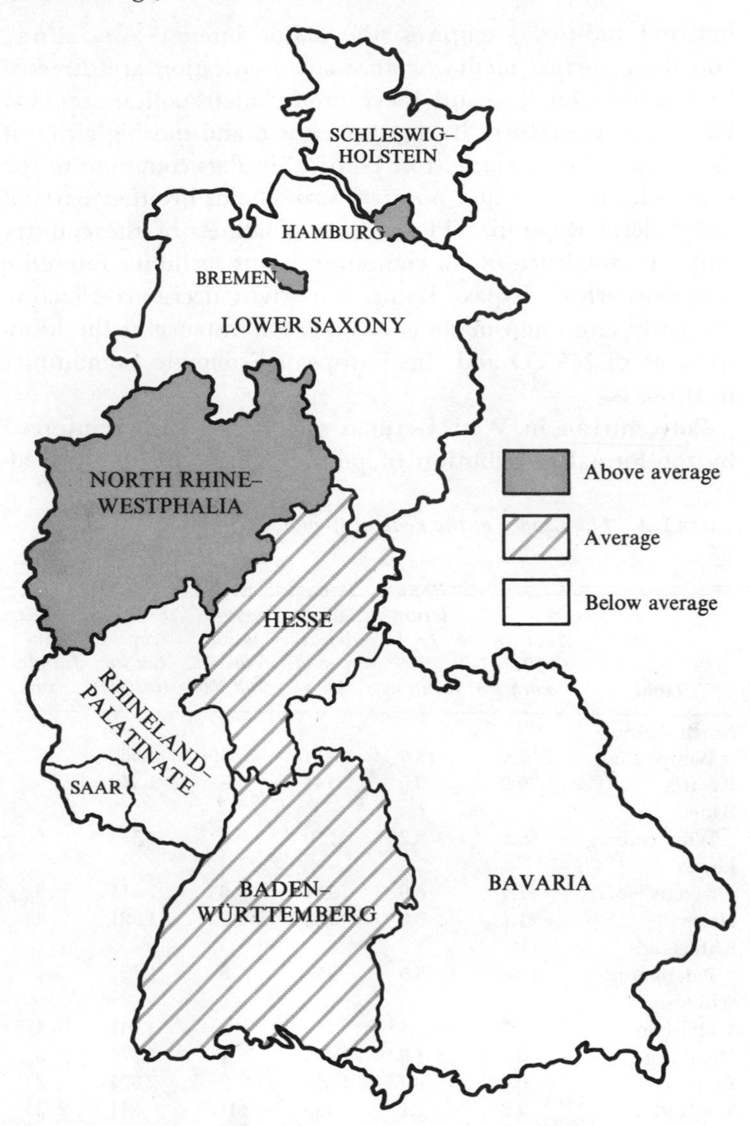

FIGURE II.1 *Per Capita Tax Income, by Länder, 1963*

ing and industrial empires, the major interest associations, and the principal media of mass communication are directed by leaders who live and meet in the metropolitan centers: Hamburg, Frankfurt, Stuttgart, Munich, and the big cities of the Rhine-Ruhr region. Most political leaders commute to the capital from homes and political strongholds in other parts of the Federal Republic. The relative smallness of the country and the excellence of its communications facilitate interelite relations, which bypass Bonn. Important decisions affecting the polity are often made elsewhere, for instance at the headquarters of NATO and the European Economic Community in Brussels.

Polycentrism in West German society has been reinforced by the formal distribution of political authority in the Fed-

TABLE II.1 *The Länder of the Federal Republic*

Land	*Area (in 1,000 sq. km.)*	*Population, 1964 (in millions)*	*Population density (per sq. km.)*	*Cities with population over 100,000*	*1963 per capita tax inc. (in DM)*	*Seats in Bundesrat*
North Rhine-Westphalia	33.95	16.5	484	34	1,666	5
Bavaria	70.5	9.9	141	5	1,248	5
Baden-Württemberg	35.8	8.2	230	5	1,539	5
Lower Saxony	47.4	6.8	144	6	1,211	5
Hesse	21.1	5.0	239	5	1,521	4
Rhineland-Palatinate	19.8	3.5	178	3	1,151	4
Schleswig-Holstein	15.7	2.4	153	2	1,191	4
Hamburg	0.7	1.9	2,485	1	4,674	3
Bremen	0.4	0.7	1,805	2	2,624	3
Saarland	2.6	1.1	433	1	941	3
Federal Republic	247.97	56.0	218	64	1,558 [a]	41

[a] Includes West Berlin.

Source: Statistisches Jahrbuch für die Bundesrepublik Deutschland 1964, 1965.

eral Republic. The Basic Law of 1949 reversed the trend toward centralization in Germany (which had culminated in the Hitler regime) and granted considerable powers to constituent Länder, already strongly established as political and administrative entities when the Federal Republic was created. Under the present federal system – irrevocable under the Basic Law – the ten Länder control most of the public administration, the educational system, and the disbursement of public funds to local authorities. They also participate in political decisionmaking at the federal level through the Bundesrat, the upper house of the federal legislature representing the Länder. The distribution of seats in that chamber grants the smaller and poorer states disproportionate influence and allows them to outvote the more populous and wealthier Länder (see Fig. II.1 and Table II.1). Together with the disappearance of Prussia – which had included two-thirds of the population of the old Reich and dominated it – this arrangement has in effect dispersed public authority far more extensively than before 1945.

AN URBAN SOCIETY

Among the larger world powers the Federal Republic is one of the most densely settled and urban.[2] Fifty-six million West Germans, crowded into an area the size of Oregon, live mostly in or around the great urban areas. In 1963 one-third of them

TABLE II.2 *Area and Population of the Major Countries of the World*

	G.F.R.	*U.K.*	*France*	*U.S.*	*U.S.S.R.*	*China*	*Japan*	*India*
Area (in 1,000 sq. km.)	248	244	551	9,363	22,402	9,561	337	3,046
Population, 1964 (in millions)	56.1	54.2	48.4	192.1	227.7	690.0	96.9	471.6
Population density (per sq. km.)	226	222	89	21	10	72	262	155

2 Most of the data cited in this chapter are taken or calculated from the *United Nations Statistical Yearbook, 1965,* the *Statistisches Jahrbuch für die Bundesrepublik Deutschland 1964, Das Bulletin der Bundesregierung 1960–1964,* and various newspaper and periodical articles, monographs, and opinion surveys. Unless specifically noted, these data do not include West Berlin. Because almost all the sources used are German, extensive footnotes have been omitted. Some of the most important ones are cited in the bibliography as a guide to further study.

resided in the sixty-four cities with a population over 100,000, two-thirds in towns and cities with a population over 5,000, and of the rest a considerable number worked in the urban centers. Each weekday morning hundreds of thousands of commuters pour into the larger cities from surrounding smaller towns and villages. In the Rhenish-Westphalian region – where one-fifth of the population is concentrated and population density averages about 1,200 per square kilometer – streets and highways are choked with traffic and pastoral scenes are to be found only in pictures on museum walls. Here and in the great metropolitan regions to the south and north one can pass from the jurisdiction of one municipality to that of another without leaving built-up areas.

The urbanization of Western Germany began with the industrial revolution of the nineteenth century, but it was enormously accelerated by the postwar migration of twelve million Germans to the west. Constituting about one-fifth of the population of the Federal Republic today, the majority of them had fled or were expelled from east of the Oder-Neisse line, territory presently under Polish and Russian control, and from other parts of Eastern and Southeastern Europe. Many of them former farmers and agricultural laborers, they found employment in West German cities and settled in urban areas. So did most of another three million refugees from the present German Democratic Republic who provided much needed additions to the West German labor force before the Communist regime sealed the borders in 1961 to stop the exodus. In 1964, a proportionately larger number of these so-called "expellees" and refugees than native West Germans lived in urban areas and worked in urban occupations.[3]

The farmer and the village dweller are a rapidly vanishing breed. While the total population increased 24 per cent between 1939 and 1958, the rural population declined from 18 to 11 per cent. Its birth rate is higher than that of the urban

[3] Data from *Die Neubürger: Bericht über die Flüchtlinge und Heimatvertriebenen in der Bundesrepublik* (Allensbach: Institut für Demoskopie, 1964); "Jeder Vierte Vertriebener," *Frankfurter Allgemeine Zeitung*, October 13, 1959 (reporting on a study by Professors Eugen Lemberg and Friedrich Edding, *Die Vertriebenen in Westdeutschland* (Kiel: Hirt Verlag, 1959); *Statistisches Jahrbuch 1964*.

dwellers, but the younger people around such industrial regions as those of the Rhineland and Westphalia are leaving in increasing numbers for well-paying jobs in the cities. As agricultural imports grow in volume, farming is becoming increasingly unprofitable for the large number of small, marginal producers. Full-time employment in agriculture, forestry, and fishing declined over a third from 1950 to 1961, and today farmers and farm laborers constitute at best 12 per cent of the labor force. The federal government has encouraged the flight from the land by lowering tariff barriers on agricultural imports and by subsidies designed to bring about the consolidation of farm lands and the rationalization of domestic agricultural production.

In politics these developments are gradually reducing the once predominant influence of the farmer, but only slowly. Especially in the southern and northern regions of the Federal Republic the political influence of the farmers has been disproportionately greater than their actual voting power, in part because the federal system lends strength to the demands of the rural areas, in part because agricultural interests are represented by highly effective interest associations, and in part because the rest of the population has acquiesced. Quite a number of industrial and service workers are still five o'clock farmers who after hours and on weekends work small parcels of land and raise chickens. To them and to many former farmers among the urban population the preservation of German agriculture remains an important political task, because of direct economic interest or because traditional sentiments still cause them to look upon the farmer as the mainstay of noble virtues in an advanced industrial society.

An aging population appears to be another product of urbanization. In 1963 the Federal Republic had proportionately fewer children under fifteen than almost any country in the world, and demographic projections indicate that the annual birth rate will drop from about 7 per cent in recent years to less than 3 per cent over the next decade or two. On the other hand, the proportion of West Germans sixty-five years and older is expected to increase by 40 per cent until 1980, at which time they are likely to make up 14 per cent of the population and a considerably larger proportion of the electorate.[4]

These demographic projections suggest several politically relevant implications. First, a comparatively stable adult population also implies relatively stable political orientation patterns. What we can learn about values and role perceptions in the present political system may thus identify the orientations of the participants in the system for some time to come. Second, numerous studies have suggested that an aging population tends to be on the whole more conservative in its political orientations than a younger population, particularly when a prosperous, satisfied people feel they have more to lose than to gain by innovations and experiments. Demographic trends in Western Germany may thus help to maintain the stability of the present political system and further the institutionalization of social structures, roles, and values. Finally, as older voters form an increasingly large proportion of the electorate, their demands are likely to be correspondingly greater in West German politics. Demands for job security, adequate pensions, social services for the aged, and the protection of fixed retirement incomes have great political relevance in a society with an aging electorate. Insofar as public policymakers feel it necessary to accommodate such demands, an increasing proportion of the society's capabilities will have to be devoted to their satisfaction rather than to other activities.

In general, the combination of urbanization and polycentrism appears to have produced considerable sense of rootlessness among West Germans. The average urban dweller or commuter doesn't feel especially attached to the town or city where he lives or works and takes little interest in civic affairs. A survey in 1964 found that no more than one-third to one-half of the residents of seven representative urban centers had been born there and that newcomers lacked a sense of identification with their city.[5] Except perhaps in Bavaria and some of the

[4] Calculated from data of the Plat-Woerman projection, reported in *Das Bulletin der Bundesregierung,* October 12, 1962, and from estimates reported in Hans Meenzen, "Keine Angst vor Überalterung," *Die Zeit,* February 2, 1964, p. 15.

[5] Institut für angewandte Sozialwissenschaft, *Ifas Report: Sonderheft Kassel* (Bad Godesberg, July, 1964).

northern Länder, traditional civic and regional loyalties seem to have greatly weakened; at the same time West Germans lack a strong sense of identification with the larger political community of the Federal Republic. In the urban society of Western Germany social relationships and attitudes revolve around work groups and families which function in an urban environment but lack strong associations with any particular geographic component unit of society.

THE ECONOMIC SETTING

The new political system has developed during an explosion of national and individual prosperity in Western Germany. Never in history has a country risen as rapidly from rags to riches as has the Federal Republic since its establishment, and undoubtedly the most significant element in the domestic environment for its political system has been dynamic collective economic growth and rapidly increasing individual affluence. It is most unlikely that the new political system would have established itself as quickly and as smoothly on the basis of a broad popular consensus had it not been for the so-called "economic miracle" of the 1950's which transformed a war-devastated country into one of the most prosperous and economically powerful in the world (see Table II.3). Between 1950 and 1961 the gross national product increased 123 per cent, industrial production expanded 162 per cent, and the per capita national income grew by 152 per cent. By mid-1960 the German Federal Republic had become the third largest industrial power in the world, the second largest trading nation, and enjoyed one of the world's strongest currencies and highest per capita incomes (1967: $2,000).

Tangible evidence of this new affluence is to be found everywhere. Wartime destruction wreckage and slums have practically disappeared, there are no beggars in the streets, farmers as well as business executives drive Mercedes limousines, and overnourishment has become a major health problem. In 1962 almost nine out of ten homes contained a radio, six out of ten a vacuum cleaner and washing machine, five out of ten a refrigerator, and four out of ten a television set; in 1967 every

TABLE II.3 *The Economies of Selected Major Industrial Powers*

	G.F.R.	*U.K.*	*France*	*U.S.*
GNP, 1964 (in billion dollars at current exchange) [a]	99.1	117.3	88.1	638.8
Percentage growth of GNP, 1960–64 (in 1958 prices) [a]	4.9%	3.4%	5.4%	4.3%
Index of industrial production, 1964 (1958 = 100) [a]	149	128	136	141
Percentage of labor force employment, 1960–64 [b]				
Agriculture, hunting, and fishing	12.8%	4.1%	20.7%	8.8%
Mining, manufacturing, and construction	48.4%	46.4%	38.9%	31.9%
Trade, utilities, finance, and services	38.7%	49.7%	40.4%	59.0%
Total labor force	99.9%	100.2%	100.0%	99.7%
Percentage output by industrial divisions, 1960–64 [b]				
Agriculture, forestry, and fishing	5.2%	3.8%	8.7%	3.7%
Mining, manufacturing, and construction	51.2%	44.6%	46.1%	36.2%
Trade, utilities, services, and transportation	43.6%	51.6%	45.2%	60.2%
Total output	100.0%	100.0%	100.0%	100.0%
Percentage of 1964 GNP from [a]				
exports	20%	19%	14%	5%
imports	18%	21%	14%	4%
Total trade percentage	38%	40%	28%	9%

Sources: [a] *United Nations Statistical Yearbook, 1965*
[b] United States Department of Commerce: *Long Term Economic Growth, 1860–1965: A Statistical Compendium,* October, 1966.

fifth West German owned an automobile. A British newspaper correspondent observed five years ago:

> This is a country where building never ceases – half a million homes every year, towering office-blocks, ultramodern factories; where a tremendously ambitious autobahn network is about 70 per cent completed; where an affluent society supports the best

system of social services in the Old World. It is a country where there seems to be a perpetual spending spree, where second-hand goods have no market, where trade union officials wear the same clothes as employers and the average worker probably takes his holiday abroad and drives there in his own car.[6]

The principal basis of West German economic growth and prosperity has been trade, particularly industrial exports, and the well-being of the economy depends heavily on the continued fortuitous competitive conditions in the world market which made possible the economic expansion of the 1950's. At that time relatively low public expenditures and domestic consumption, as well as extensive American financial assistance, facilitated the rapid growth of industrial exports. Trade union restraint, the influx of millions of often highly skilled from Eastern Germany, and governmental regulations kept domestic wages, salaries, consumer prices, and taxes on business down and, together with comparatively low overhead expenditures, allowed the export industry to exploit fully the favorable conditions in the world market. Low-priced raw material imports were transformed into high-priced industrial exports that found ready buyers abroad. Potential competitors, such as the United States, Britain, and France had to devote a considerable proportion of their national productive capacity and income to international military commitments whereas disarmed Germany was free to devote its economic capacities to expanding exports. The ubiquitous Volkswagen became symbolic of the expanding volume of German automotive and electrotechnical products, machinery, steel, and synthetic fibers pouring into the world market. By 1968 an export surplus of over four billion dollars gave the Federal Republic a favorable balance of payments not equaled in size by any other country in the world, and a gold and foreign exchange hoard surpassed only by the rapidly diminishing one of the United States.

The economic environment for German politics in the

[6] Terence Prittie, "Sixteen Years in Germany," *The Guardian* (Manchester), May 10, 1963. According to the Federal Minister for Housing, new residential construction since the end of World War II had reached 10 million units by late 1967, about one new unit for every five Germans, with close to 600,000 units built in 1967 alone.

1960's is the direct outgrowth of the tremendous expansion of the preceding decade and the socioeconomic changes it wrought. But the demands which influence the relationship between the economic and political systems have changed. A rearmed Germany is committed to large military expenditures. The economy now depends heavily on an expanding market at home as well as abroad. Domestic politics are conditioned by the expectations of an affluent society whose members have become accustomed to prosperity and a continually rising standard of living.

The developing patterns of West German trade in goods and services have reinforced the bonds between the Federal Republic and the Western nations – particularly the ties with its partners in the European Economic Community (Common

TABLE II.4 *The Direction of West German Trade, 1960–1965 (in Percentages of Total Trade)*

Countries	*Imports from* 1960	1962	1965	*Exports to* 1960	1962	1965
EEC [a]	29.0	31.7	38.1	28.9	33.5	35.5
EFTA [b]	19.2	18.6	17.0	27.5	27.4	27.6
Other non-Communist European [c]	3.2	3.0	3.3	3.3	4.4	4.3
Non-European industrial [d]	18.4	18.8	17.7	13.2	12.2	12.3
(U.S.)	(13.6)	(13.9)	(13.1)	(7.7)	(7.1)	(8.0)
Eastern European Communist [e]	6.8	6.2	3.8	6.5	5.1	4.7
(East Germany)	(2.5)	(1.8)	(1.7)	(1.9)	(1.6)	(1.7)
Other countries	23.5	21.6	22.0	20.5	17.4	15.5
Total	100.1	99.9	100.3	99.9	100.0	99.9

[a] *European Economic Community:* France, Italy, Belgium, Netherlands, Luxembourg.

[b] *European Free Trade Association:* Britain, Denmark, Norway, Austria, Sweden, Portugal, Switzerland.

[c] Finland, Spain, Greece.

[d] Australia, Canada, Japan, Israel, New Zealand, South Africa, United States.

[e] Czechoslovakia, East Germany, Hungary, Poland, Romania, U.S.S.R., Yugoslavia.

Source: United Nations Yearbook of International Trade Statistics, 1966.

Market). Trade with the Communist countries other than the German Democratic Republic, on the other hand, has thus far remained relatively insignificant (see Table II.4). In 1964 55 per cent of the West German imports and 67 per cent of exports involved trade with other non-Communist countries of Europe, 13 per cent of imports and 7 per cent of exports involved trade with the United States. Western countries — notably the United States — have invested heavily in key German industries, and German capital exports to these countries have risen as well. Of 1.1 billion DM invested by Germans in 1964 in foreign countries, close to 868 million flowed into the economies of non-Communist European nations — mostly members of the Common Market — and over 100 million were invested in the United States and Canada. Commercial ties with the EEC countries have been expanding rapidly and this development is likely to accelerate with the elimination of trade barriers in the Common Market and the introduction of a common tariff policy on imports.

The unpredictable variable in future German trade and, therefore, economic development, is essentially a political quantity. Former German markets in Eastern and Southeastern Europe, shut off by international political developments after the war, are once again attracting the interest of business leaders. West German industrialists and investment bankers have found Communist leaders in East-Central Europe receptive to their overtures and, sensing the prospect of lucrative profits, have not hesitated to bypass official channels in initiating new trade relations in this area. In the long run, however, the expansion of such relations calls for political measures. The federal government has therefore come under increasing pressure from the business community to underwrite private loans and investments in Communist countries and establish more cordial relations with them. Until the mid-1960's West German governmental leaders were rather reluctant to yield to such pressures. They feared that the establishment of diplomatic relations with the East European governments would make it a great deal more difficult to assert their claim to "legal" jurisdiction over the territory of the German Democratic Republic and former German lands under Polish "administration." Counterpressures from refugee and expellee associations were also important. More recently, however, economic considerations appear to have become more persuasive in this respect. A mild recession in the mid-1960's apparently contributed to the decision of the federal government to establish diplomatic relations with Romania, re-establish them with Yugoslavia, and encourage closer trade relations with other Communist states which recognize the German Democratic Republic's and Poland's claims to former German territories.

In general, changing economic conditions have led to greater governmental intervention and controls. Whereas in the 1950's the problem was primarily the maximal utilization of resources in the private sector of the economy, in the 1960's West German leaders seek ways for mobilizing new capabilities for producing goods and services through the public sector. They have to achieve a better balance between imports and exports and between governmental revenues and expenditures. Fiscal policies must provide for continuing economic growth and price stability in the domestic market as well for a high rate of reinvestment of the national income that will promote trade expansion.

The mobilization of skilled new manpower resources has been complicated by a tight labor market in key industrial sectors. The number of gainfully employed West Germans increased by a third between 1950 and 1963, and in 1968 more than half the adult population was working full time. Though technological changes have created some pockets of temporary unemployment, especially among coalminers, on the whole the number of positions available has persistently exceeded the number of persons seeking jobs by a large ratio. Real wages and salaries rose 115 per cent between 1949 and 1964 – three times as much as in the United States and twice as much as in Britain, Italy, and Canada – while, with the reduction of the regular work week from 50 to 45 hours and less, overtime pay and "moonlighting" provided additional sources of income for West German wage earners. Today the German worker earns more and spends less time at his regular job than any of his European colleagues. Though only about one-fourth of the labor force is organized in trade unions, prospering employers, anxious to maintain and expand production, have made substantial concessions to trade union demands in recent years that benefited nonunion labor as well. While in the United States, Britain, France, Italy, and other industrial countries millions of man-hours were lost through strikes, West German labor obtained higher wages, shorter hours, and generous fringe benefits without resorting to this weapon. In 1964 less than 17,000 man-hours – an infinitesimal proportion – were lost through strikes in the Federal Republic; employers and trade unions usually achieve agreement quickly through collective bargaining. To prevent inflation and maintain economic growth in this tight labor market, the federal government has encouraged, through fiscal and other measures, increased rationalization of production and the importation of more goods and services. More than one million foreign workers in the Federal Republic have helped to fill the gap left by the sudden end of the influx of refugee labor from Eastern Germany, and a growing volume of imported manufactured products has aided government efforts to check inflationary pressures and maintain price stability.

The economic problems facing West German society today are far less critical than in many other countries. However, the intimate relationship between economic recovery and stability and the development of the new polity established since 1949 has made West German political decisionmakers extremely sensitive to the possibility of more intensive demands for government action to protect the new prosperity. To those West German leaders who recall vividly that economic catastrophe helped to bring Hitler to power in 1933, the preservation and institutionalization of the new political structures and norms require that the political system possess a strong latent capacity to provide instant authoritative action should developments at home or abroad threaten economic stability.[7]

[7] Here and elsewhere in this volume I am relying heavily on information collected in interviews with 173 West German leaders in 1964 under the auspices of the Yale University Arms Control and Disarmament Project. For a summary see Karl W. Deutsch, Lewis J. Edinger, Roy C. Macridis, and Richard Merritt, *Arms Control and European Unity* (New Haven: Yale University Political Science Research Library, 1966) and, by the same authors, *France, Germany, and the Western Alliance* (New York: Scribner, 1967).

MODERNIZING GERMAN SOCIETY

The political system of the Federal Republic has been evolving against a background of dynamic social change, and in many respects the contemporary social system differs radically from those which previously blocked the development of modern political institutions in Germany. Roughly one-third of the population and close to a third of those over eighteen were born in the last three decades, an era which extensively transformed the structures and values of society – in this sense we must beware of superficial judgments based on "the lessons of the past." Where these social changes will lead and what their ultimate influence will be on the emerging political system is by no means clear, but their extent suggests that society and polity may resemble less and less those of the past.

Influenced by industrialization and urbanization, German society experienced during the last century a "persistent movement toward modernity and away from the traditional structures of pre-Enlightenment and pre-industrial days." [8] Until Nazi totalitarianism and post-totalitarian developments greatly accelerated social change, this transformation had been slow, painful, and sporadic because of the resilience of traditional social structures and values. The division of Germany, the dissolution of Prussia, and other socioeconomic and political transformations sponsored by the victors in both parts of Germany completed the destruction of a society once dominated by an alliance between East German landed aristocrats and West German industrialists and characterized by deep ideological, class, and status cleavages. A pluralistic and achievement oriented society has emerged in West Germany, very different from its predecessors as well as from the new society developing simultaneously in the Communist German state across the Elbe. The modernization process in West Germany has been hastened by what has been referred to as a second industrial revolution. But it is not alone a more rapid socioeconomic transformation than that of the first, but a far less

[8] Ralf Dahrendorf, "The New Germanies: Restoration, Revolution, Reconstruction," *Encounter,* XXII (1964), 50–58.

painful and upsetting process for the mass of the population.

Opportunities for upward mobility and material advancement softened the impact of dynamic social change and facilitated the stabilization of a new political system lacking as yet the sustaining support of institutionalized structures and norms. In this respect, the conjunction of social fluidity and amorphousness with rapid economic recovery proved to be a particularly fortunate combination. The openness of an increasingly affluent society greatly facilitated the remarkably smooth development of a new consensus on social norms and roles and the assimilation of groups uprooted by postwar socioeconomic and political changes. The millions of penniless refugees who had to leave their native homes, and the once independent farmers, artisans, and shopkeepers who became wage and salary earners, did not coalesce into encapsulated subcultures divided from and hostile to the new socioeconomic and political structures. An open society without rigid social strata or barriers readily integrated them by offering them incentives and possibilities for material and social advancement on a basis of equality with its other members. For the average West German the opportunity to partake in rising national prosperity – only a hope when the new political system was established – had become a reality by the 1960's. His rising material aspirations were not merely aroused but he believed himself better off than in the past and looked forward to an even higher standard of living in the future.

The magnitude of the structural changes which have taken place in West German society since the establishment of the Federal Republic is indicated by the shifts in the distribution of incomes and in the occupational structure. Not only have personal incomes increased in general much faster than the cost of living, but the gap between the high and low income groups has greatly diminished (see Table II.5).

Between 1954 and 1963, moreover, income from employment increased 135 per cent; income from property 100 per cent. The tax structure, which in the early years of the Federal Republic strongly favored the high income groups, in recent years has become more equitable, and the lower income groups

TABLE II.5 *Shift in West German Income Distribution*

	1951	*1963*
Index of consumer prices (1958-100)	91	112
Distribution of individual monthly net income (in rounded-off %)		
Under 250 DM [a]	56	5
250–399 DM	33	12
400–599 DM		34
600–799 DM	11	27
800–999 DM		12
1,000 DM and more		10

[a] Four DM in 1963 was one dollar at the official rate of exchange but bought the equivalent of about $1.60 in most domestic goods and services.

Source: Elisabeth Noelle and Erich Peter Neumann, *Jahrbuch der öffentlichen Meinung, 1958–64,* p. 4.

have also benefited from increased social service benefits, public assistance for home construction and dependent children, and larger pension payments.

Shifts in the occupational structure, as shown in Table II.6, are leading to a labor force distribution closely resembling that

TABLE II.6 *Shifts in the Occupational Structure (in Percentages of Total Labor Force)*

	West Germany			*United States*
	1939	*1950*	*1961*	*1954*
Self-employed (business and professional)	13.5	13.5	10.6	7.4
Farmers	14.9	12.5	8.7	5.9
Farm workers	3.9	5.0	1.6	4.1
Manual workers	46.7	47.1	48.2	51.7
Salaried employees and officials	19.3	21.9	30.4	30.8
Unclassifiable	1.8	—	—	—
Total	100.1	100.0	100.0	100.0

Sources: For 1939 (survey data) and 1954 United States census data, Morris Janowitz, "Social Stratification and Mobility in West Germany," *American Journal of Sociology* LXIV (July, 1958), 6–24; for 1950 and 1961 census data, *Jahrbuch der öffentlichen Meinung, 1958–64,* p. 4.

of the United States. The number of independent farmers has been rapidly declining, as we saw earlier, as has the proportion of self-employed small entrepreneurs. On the other hand, the proportion of salaried white-collar employees in private and public service occupations is steadily increasing. These shifts are characteristic of an advanced industrial society, as is the changing social position of the salaried employees in relation to the manual workers. As in the United States, differences in status between wage and salary earners are diminishing because of technological developments and the rising income of industrial workers. In a society where income, skills, and conspicuous consumption have become important criteria of social status, the fact that the wages of blue-collared industrial workers have risen much faster than those of white-collared office workers and officials has meant that social distinctions between these occupational groups have waned. The earnings of West German skilled industrial workers on the average today exceed those of lower civil servants and clerical workers, and many a wage earner can afford a higher standard of living than an accountant or army officer.

In 1955 a study by an American sociologist found social mobility to be very high in West Germany, particularly among skilled industrial workers between the generations of fathers and sons.[9] A German sociologist spoke at the time of a "standardization of social designs," a "far advanced breakdown of social distinctions," and of the emergence of "a relatively equal and uniform social class." [10] More recent data indicate that the expectation for upward mobility through increased incomes remains high among the children of industrial workers and other young Germans from comparatively low income families. In the view of 72 per cent of respondents in a 1958 opinion poll a capable child of poor parents faced no serious obstacle to social advancement in the Federal Republic. Contemporary developments seemed to lend credence to these expectations. A 1959 survey revealed that young West Germans between 18

[9] See Morris Janowitz, "Social Stratification and Mobility in West Germany," *American Journal of Sociology*, LXIV (July, 1958), 6–24.

[10] Helmut Schelsky, "Elements of Social Stability," in *German Social Science Digest* (Hamburg: Claasens Verlag, 1955), p. 115.

and 25 years of age included a significantly higher proportion of individuals earning a thousand DM and more a month than almost any other age group.[11]

Out of the leveling of the early postwar era a new social structure based primarily on occupational skills and earned income has emerged. At the apex of a broad-based socioeconomic pyramid stands a new aristocracy whose members have been increasingly recruited on the basis of achievement rather than social background or inherited wealth. In a comparatively open society providing extensive opportunities for upward mobility to qualified men, rigid social barriers no longer bar the road to social advancement to the extent that they once did in Germany; a man's status today is determined more by the size than the source of his income. A title of nobility is no longer an open sesame to high positions, and religious discrimination in employment has largely disappeared. In all sectors of society, but above all in the business community, highly paid managers and technocratic experts now control vast economic enterprises and mass organizations on the strength of individual accomplishments, rather than race, breeding, or birth.

The modernization of the social context for German politics is also evident in the changing position of women, who in 1964 constituted 54 per cent of the adult population and 39 per cent of the employed. As in the United States and other countries, persistent traditional norms about their "proper" roles have slowed social change in the relationship between the sexes – particularly in rural areas. But under accelerated urbanization and industrialization the gap between social norms and the principles of equality between the sexes stipulated in the new constitution and various laws is clearly diminishing. In the words of a German psychiatrist, West German society is

[11] Calculated from data collected for Gabriel A. Almond and Sidney Verba, *The Civic Culture* (Boston: Little, Brown, 1965). However, a study based on another 1959 opinion survey found that there was still a considerable difference in the income of "workers and middle-class groups" (with the latter having a decisive edge) and in the type and quality of consumer goods and services sought. See Richard F. Hamilton, "Affluence and the Worker: The West German Case," *American Journal of Sociology*, LXXI (1965), 144–151.

moving along "the road toward a fatherless society," radically different from the paternalist order of the past.[12]

The position of women in German society began to change radically with World War II. The exigencies of total mobilization compelled the Nazi regime to abandon its efforts to maintain women in their traditional roles as housewives and mothers in a paternalistic family; as the men marched off to war their roles in the economy and the family were taken over by women. After the war, in millions of families in which the father had died or did not return for many years from prison camps, the mother remained the principal source of income and authority. In others the wife became the husband's peer in earning a living and raising the children under severe social and economic dislocation – a sharp contrast to prewar family patterns. At the same time single women, confronted by the shortage of eligible bachelors which wartime casualties had caused, had to strike out on their own in far larger numbers. New laws and the development of a tight labor market accelerated the trend toward a new relationship between the sexes because they offered women greater opportunities for social and economic independence. More jobs at higher pay and the lure of consumer goods and services kept married women at work and drew more unmarried ones into the labor market. In 1964, 42 per cent of employed women were working in industry, where a more rapid increase in their pay in recent years has narrowed the gap between the wages of men and women – especially in those rapidly expanding sectors of industrial production that do not demand labor, such as the manufacture of synthetic and electrical products. Employers have encouraged women to take full-time or part-time jobs requiring few skills. Guarantees of job security and seniority rights and the chance to increase the family's purchasing power in an expanding consumer market have induced more and more women to remain at their jobs after marriage, to delay having children, and to return to work as soon as possible after delivery. (Under law, new mothers are entitled to six weeks of paid vacation after delivery.) The contemporary trend was indicated by a 1965

[12] Alexander Mitscherlisch, *Auf dem Weg zur vaterlosen Gesellschaft* (Munich: Piper, 1963).

survey which showed that the number of married mothers in nonagricultural occupations had tripled since 1950.

However, modernization in West German society has not yet reached a point where the formal legal provisions for absolute equality between the sexes have become generally accepted normative standards. As in the United States and other advanced industrial societies, traditional discriminatory practices assigning an inferior social and economic role to women still persist. They are encouraged to seek employment but, especially in nonindustrial occupations, they are largely barred from higher income and higher status positions and receive lower pay than men for equal work. In 1957, 79 per cent of all low-grade positions and 65 per cent of medium-grade positions were held by women, but only 6 per cent of top managerial jobs. In 1964, only 6 per cent of skilled workers were women and only 3 per cent of employed women held leading salaried positions, compared to 51 per cent and 22 per cent respectively of employed men. Only 1 per cent of top civil service positions were occupied by women – none of them at the apex of the administrative pyramid; less than 3 per cent of judges and state attorneys were women; and of 3,203 professorships in German universities only 26 (0.8 per cent) were held by women. In status, women and foreign workers constitute the social proletariat of semiskilled and unskilled industrial workers in the Federal Republic, last to be hired and first to be fired.

The change in the role of German women is only gradually becoming evident in economic and public life. Male-imposed as well as self-imposed limitations based on traditional orientations have slowed women's emancipation, and their quantitative weight as members of the labor force and the electorate has as yet not been translated into significant qualitative influences. There are no important women's civic or interest associations – as in the United States – and women who openly voice demands for greater social equality are still looked upon as oddities even by members of their own sex. However, for the first time in German history a woman became a cabinet minister in 1961, and prominent female politicians have here and there raised their voices on behalf of greater real equality. Unorganized though it is, the women's vote is a strong influence in political life. Potentially most important of all, however, is the changed position of women in the German family. This has led one German journalist to claim that "mom" rules the new Germany.[13]

The passing of the traditional paternalistic German family structure may be producing far-reaching changes in the social and psychological basis of German political life. According to numerous studies of past German "national character," most authoritarian features in society and polity were rooted in traditional family patterns which accustomed Germans at an early age to obey their paternal "superiors" and lord it over their "inferiors." The family is today the most solidly established traditional institution in a changing society, but its structure and functions bear increasingly less resemblance to those of the past.

Family solidarity and affective ties, weakened by the Nazi regime and the war, were greatly strengthened after 1945. The disappearance of groups which had previously competed with the family for the loyalty of its members, such as the Hitler Youth and the armed forces, and postwar social dislocation established the family as the center of primary interpersonal relations in the emerging pluralist society. It was the one collectivity from which one could not be expelled, purged, or fired, and thus the family provided a haven of emotional security in a period when everything else was in flux. The family has maintained this position in a society characterized by geographic and social mobility and the disappearance of strong class and national loyalties. Political parties, religious organizations, interest associations, and the state – none are any longer its serious rivals.

A new, tightly knit, nuclear family unit has been emerging in place of the paternalistic, extended family of the past – particularly in the urban areas and among Germans who grew to adulthood after 1945. It is a family based on partnership between husband and wife – both of whom are likely to be working – and united by personal, emotional, and pragmatic bonds rather than traditional social and religious ties. The strength

[13] See Hans Georg von Stadnitz, "Die Bundesrepublik – Ein Mutti Staat?" *Der Spiegel,* September 23, 1965, p. 55.

of the family is reflected in the fact that the number of divorces in Western Germany declined by 50 per cent between 1950 and 1961, and its changed structure by studies indicating that, more and more, decisions are made jointly by both partners and that children enjoy greater autonomy from parental control. In a 1959 survey only 14 per cent of the respondents stated that in their families decisions were made by the husband alone — mostly families where the man was over forty — but 30 per cent of the respondents recalled that when they were children, father had ruled alone.[14] New laws have deprived the husband of his former legal right to govern the family and control its property and have given the wife an equal voice. The unity of the new family has probably been strengthened by its smallness and economic viability. In 1962 more than half of the families had only one child living with the parents and only a sixteenth four or more, and in 1966 barely 12 per cent of the family units included three generations — most of them in rural areas. Increasing pensions and security benefits for the aged and extensive public assistance for minor children have eased the financial strain of dependent support for the family. At the same time, family income has risen, allowing it to share fully in the rising living standards of an affluent society.

A special federal ministry for family and youth affairs and other public bodies reflect the importance which political leaders attach to the needs of the family and its position as an element of stability in West German society. Highly sensitive to demands for increased public expenditures for the family, they have vied with each other for popular support in sponsoring legislation designed to satisfy such demands. Implicitly and explicitly, the family thus is an important social influence in shaping the structure of the political system.

AMBIVALENT SOCIAL VALUE PATTERNS

Contemporary West German society and culture is a mixture of traditional and modern elements, which gives rise to

[14] My information here is based on data collected for Almond and Verba, *op. cit.* See also Max Wingen, "Erster Bericht der Bundesregierung über die Lage der Familien," *Bulletin des Presse- und Informationsamt der Bundesregierung,* March 1, 1968, pp. 213–220.

ambiguities and latent tensions between the old and the new. As in any transitional society — particularly one undergoing rapid structural change — traditional social and cultural patterns have by no means been entirely eradicated. What anthropologists refer to as a "cultural lag" between changed social structures and persistent traditional orientations manifests itself in German society in the clash between demands for new innovations and demands that traditional goals and values be preserved. This conflict prevails on two levels: (1) the open interpersonal and intergroup contest between innovators and traditionalists, and (2) the psychological intrapersonal tension between conflicting old and new orientations and values which sporadically manifests itself in West German attitudes and behavior. The need to maintain congruence at both levels between old and new social structures and cultural values may be one of the most critical problems for the continuing stability of the political system.

German social critics and foreign visitors to the Federal Republic are frequently appalled by the climate of hedonistic materialism, pragmatic egocentrism, and ruthless competitiveness which seems to characterize the spirit of the new mass-consumption and achievement oriented society. "The most striking quality about every German, regardless of social position or occupation," a young Israeli visitor observed, "is that he always and constantly wants something." [15] Whereas the German stereotype was once known for his *Arbeitswut,* an obsessive compulsion to work for the emotional satisfaction it gave him, today's West German seems to be motivated by a frenetic acquisitive drive to give himself and his immediate family material security through saving and the very best in goods and services his rising income will buy. Some Germans describe it as a *Nachholbedürfnis* of the older generations, a desire to compensate for years of economic deprivation and insecurity, but the phenomenon is even more evident among younger Germans. It is, in fact, the product of rapid modernization in an open society. With the disappearance of the clearly defined and relatively closed social strata of the past with ac-

[15] Vera Elyashiv, *Deutschland: Kein Wintermärchen* (Düsseldorf: Econ Verlag, 1964), p. 37.

cepted status symbols — aristocratic and official titles, military rank, and so forth — not only the size of one's income, but its conspicuous consumption has become the principal measure of achievement and status.

These new values induce the contemporary German not merely to keep up with the Joneses, but ahead of them — as anyone driving a car on the autobahn can observe. The affluent German is not a satiated German. He no longer aspires just to a home, but to a home of his own; he demands not merely the necessities of life but its amenities — and he expects to get them. Rising expendable incomes and more leisure time are allowing more and more citizens of the Federal Republic to taste the luxuries and pleasures which not very long ago were reserved for the privileged few, and thus stimulating their appetites for even more. Never before in German history have so many spent so much for cars, appliances, leisure-time activities, and travel to foreign countries. And probably never have so many Germans apparently cared so little about the welfare of others and the needs of the community.

Today's West German, particularly if he is male and under fifty, seems far more self-centered, materialistic, and pragmatic in outlook than his father and grandfather. Like Voltaire's Candide, he has learned to concentrate his interests and energies on improving his own garden so he may enjoy its fruits and is little moved by appeals for collective action on behalf of class, community, or nation. Apart from members of his immediate family the average West German feels little responsibility and affinity toward his fellow men and tends to distrust them. He is likely to belong to a number of the many formal organizations in the Federal Republic — partly because membership is often required by law, partly because they promote his material interests — but beyond paying his dues he tends in general to take little part in their activities and to confine himself to sporadic and peripheral involvement in their affairs.

The break with the past, both literally and figuratively, appears especially pronounced in the postwar generation which experienced the full effect of the dramatic transformation of social structures and values at a more impressionable age than its elders. These Germans, raised in an era which witnessed a decline of paternal authority in the home and in society and, at the same time, offered young people unprecedented opportunities for social advancement and material independence at an early age, have emphatically rejected the old norms demanding discipline, obedience, and dedicated service, and embraced wholeheartedly the values of the achievement oriented age of materialism. Ambitions and expectations for upward economic mobility run high and traditional status occupations in the civil service, for instance, are rejected in favor of those promising better incomes and, therefore, higher living standards. According to the prevalent view of these young Germans, diligence, hard work, and the acquisition of new skills make sense only if they serve to put more money in the hands of the individual and his family. Numerous studies have shown this to be on the whole a highly pragmatic and rootless generation, critical of the romantic notions of the past, independent in its choice of occupations and marriage partners, and skeptical — if not cynical — about the value of formal organizations and collective action. Its members are in no way represented by a tiny minority of vocal and rebellious university students. Its affections are reserved for members of the immediate family and its emotions are aroused only when personal, family, or material interests are involved. For them alone, and not for class, party, or fatherland, are these young Germans under thirty willing to make real sacrifices. In many respects, the American way of life, as they understand it, rather than German or even European traditions, sets the standard for their social and economic values. They strive to live, dress, and even talk like Americans, but in their political orientations they are still far from Americanized, and differ little from their older countrymen.

These social value patterns seem to represent a radical break with the orientations identified with the past stereotype of the German "national character." Now the traditional ideal roles of the meticulous and disciplined German artisan, soldier, or official achieving self-expression and self-development through dutiful labor in a calling assigned to him by some superior authority — father, employer, state — appear irrelevant, and the traditional norms of self-denying, dedicated service on behalf of a large collectivity or an abstract ideology no longer valid. Outwardly, the contemporary West Germans seem to be symbolized by the vacation-bound families hurtling along the superhighways at the top speed their new streamlined cars will command, hermetically sealed off from communication with their fellows, and intent on reaching their goal as rapidly as possible no matter how dense the traffic.

But such an image is superficial. The streamlined car and the facades of the ultramodern office and university buildings, factories, and churches conceal social values and orientations which are incongruent with those of the modern mass consumption and achievement oriented society. Opinion surveys reflect extensive ambivalence and uncertainty about the validity of the new social values as guiding norms and a lack of confidence in the new social orientations.

We have already seen how traditional attitudes toward women's role persist. An international survey found in 1957 that equality for women was rejected by a third of a cross-section of German adults – a higher proportion than in ten of the twelve industrialized societies studied. Only 9 per cent of the German respondents approved of married women with children holding jobs. More and more women work outside the home so the family can afford more of the amenities of the affluent society, but a 1964 poll showed that 72 per cent of German men and 68 per cent of German women believe it "abnormal" and at best a "necessary evil" for women to take office and factory jobs. In the opinion of the majority – including three-fourths of the women with only an eight-year primary education – a German woman's place is in the home, especially if she is married and has children. Other polls have shown that most German men, regardless of age, want their wives to play the traditional role of the hardworking, good housewife who does not spend too much of their money.

Germans are enjoying more and more leisure but still see themselves as a very hardworking people. The skilled artisan is still held in much higher esteem than the industrial worker. The educated man is highly respected, though the average German does not seek a university education for himself or his children. He believes that material achievements are the measure of success in contemporary society but retains his traditional respect for those bearing formal titles even if their income does not fall within the top brackets. A 1959 survey, as we saw, showed that most West Germans were highly suspicious of their fellow men and convinced that they must look out for themselves first and foremost, but the same survey also found that a majority believed that people were fundamentally cooperative and named as the qualities they most admired generosity, considerateness, thrift, and the willingness to do one's job well.

Such ambivalent social orientations seem to reflect ambiguities and unresolved tensions between traditional and modern elements in West German society and a cultural dualism which manifests itself in political attitudes and behavior, as we shall see. The sudden transition from the very tightly structured social patterns and orientations of a totalitarian society to a new era characterized by a comparatively dynamic social environment has confronted West Germans, individually and collectively, with difficult adaptive problems.

Opinion polls and private conversations in Germany reflect a vague sense of uneasiness about the validity and permanence of the modern features of the postwar society. In public this manifests itself in a clash between the traditional German formalism and a new antiformalism in cultural life, between a desire to conform and a rejection of traditional caste orientations and structures, and between particularistic subcultural norms and the culturally diffuse values of an open society. The ostentatious display of new wealth finds its most articulate critics among some university students, intellectuals, and clergymen who insist that affluence threatens to destroy the moral vitality of the German people. But beyond a common revulsion against the "materialistic" amoralism and hedonism they denounce in contemporary German society, these social critics find little to agree upon. Some admonish their countrymen to embrace the "higher" goals of a collectivity and to abandon the single-minded pursuit of purely material and personal objectives, others voice their alienation from the "bourgeois" values of a mass consumption society; some call for a return to the traditions of dedicated German idealism, others want to have no part of the past and reject all ideologies.

These tensions produced by the clash between demands for modern innovations and demands for the preservation of traditionalist structures and values are most evident in two areas, religion and education. Both are of great importance for the future development of the polity since, directly and indirectly, the churches and the schools are key elements in the socialization process through which role perceptions, social norms, and other orientations influencing political behavior are formed, maintained, and altered over time. And both are strongholds of traditionalist components in contemporary German society.

THE RELIGIOUS SYSTEM

Formally and informally, religion is significant in West German society. The population is about equally divided into two major religious groups: in 1964, 50 per cent were listed as Protestant — mostly members of the United Evangelical Lutheran Church (VELKD) — and 47 per cent as Roman Catholics, while merely 3 per cent belonged to some other faith or to none. Separation of church and state, such as prevails in the United States, exists neither in form nor in fact. By law every citizen is required to belong to a church and to pay about a 10 per cent surcharge on his regular income tax to support its activities, unless he goes through difficult and socially disapproved legal procedures to "opt out." This provides the major churches with a guaranteed annual income from government-collected taxes of about 3 billion DM in addition to income derived from extensive property holdings, and enables them to engage in far-flung public functions for which they are accountable neither to political authorities nor to their members. In addition to strictly religious functions, they are engaged in youth activities, family counseling, and other social services, as well as educational and political tasks. Their representatives participate in the control of the public education system and sit on the boards supervising the publicly owned radio and television networks.

According to survey research data about a third of the adults attend religious services at least once a week, and only a tenth never go to church at all. Roman Catholics, women over forty-

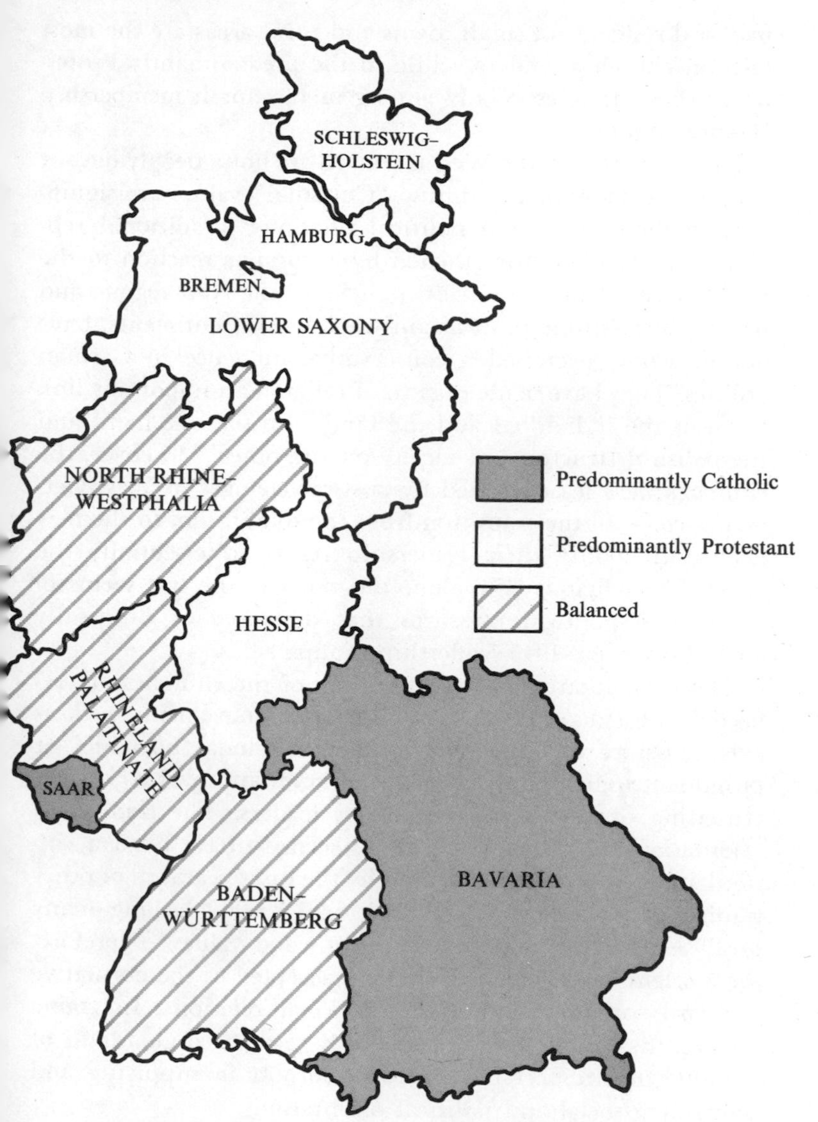

FIGURE II.2 *Religious Distribution, by Länder, 1961*

five, and residents of small towns and rural areas are the most faithful church attenders, while in the predominantly Protestant urban areas, especially among men, church membership is more nominal.

For the most part the West Germans are not a deeply devout people, but more or less diffuse "Christian" values are significant in their social and political relations. Traditional religious orientations, strengthened by a popular reaction to the irreligiousness and anticlerical policies of the Nazi regime and by extremely strong postwar anti-Communist sentiments, have on the whole exercised a conservative influence in German politics. They have made organized religion an important link between the individual and the family on the one hand and the political structures of society on the other. Moreover, the churches were least affected by postwar changes in West German society. In the transition from the totalitarian to the new democratic polity their leadership remained essentially the same. The religious elite alone did not feel the full socioeconomic and political pressures that destroyed or drastically altered other pre-1945 leadership groups.

The present strength and influence of the churches are reflected in the disappearance of anticlerical movements, such as existed before 1945, and by the fact that today no major or prominent individual dares risk public disapproval by openly criticizing organized religion or its leaders. The traditional orientations which they propound seem to have filled a cultural and emotional void created by the disappearance of other traditional structures in a transitional society lacking many firmly established modern institutions and values. Therefore, these orientations have been widely accepted as the normative standards of propriety in interpersonal relations. In consequence, the churches, as the generally recognized guardians of morality and respectability, are important in supplying and controlling social and political orientations.

On the one hand, these orientations have exercised a stabilizing influence by helping to form and maintain the broad popular consensus which sustains present social and political structures. On the other hand, however, they have contributed to the preservation of religious cleavages and cultural ambivalence, which remain sources of tensions in the German society. The churches' conservative influence may prove an obstacle to fulfilling demands for further social innovations and cultural change which emerge from a dynamic environment. Urbanization, the requirements for economic growth, changes in the structure and function of the German family and in women's role, and de-ideologizing political life confront the social and political systems in general and the churches in particular with adjustment problems which threaten the traditional religious orientations that at present are so important in maintaining stability. Because of the intimate relationship between religion and politics this need for adaptation to changing conditions has both an actual and a latent political significance.

In both major churches demands have been voiced for modernization so that congruence can be maintained between the religious system and other elements of German society. But thus far little concrete action has been taken in this direction. Those who demand major reforms going beyond the strictly theological sphere see themselves as a small deviant minority without real influence in the councils of the church leaders. Many of the latter insist that, on the contrary, rootlessness and social ambivalence in German society require the stricter preservation of traditional religious ideals (*Leitbilder*). For the political system this poses a special problem since persistent cleavages because of religious ideologies complicate the process of the consensus formation required for the stability of the polity and institutionalization of its secular structures. Although the disappearance of traditional differences in other areas of German society has facilitated this process, the preservation of such cleavages between Protestant and Catholics has not. Though opinion surveys suggest that in general public sentiment vaguely favors closer relations – if not fusion – between the two major religious groups, centuries of open and covert conflict reaching back to the Reformation of the sixteenth century struck wounds which continue to fester. These antipathies have traditionally been most intense in those regions where devoted adherents of one or the other faith have been on the defensive as a minority that considered itself victimized. In prewar united Germany, with a Protestant majority of about 66 per cent of the population, the Roman Catholic Church had become very sensitive to threats and inroads against its rights and privileges. This attitude was continued into postwar Germany in spite of the fact that now Roman Catholics enjoy equality with the Protestants. The latter, for their part, conscious that a more rapidly rising Roman Catholic birth rate may before long reduce them to a minority, fear or resent the Catholic church's militancy – especially in education.

Of the two major churches, the Roman Catholic has the better organization, commands a larger devoted following – particularly outside the urban areas – and is more active and effective in obtaining satisfaction of its political demands. The most important of these has been the demand for publicly supported denominational schools, and, in response to strong pressure from the Church, these have become the norm at the primary level of education in the predominantly Roman Catholic Länder: Bavaria, Rhineland-Westphalia, Rhineland-Palatinate, and the Saarland. In the rest of the country, "Christian," nondenominational schools prevail in which religious instruction forms part of the curriculum but is taught to children of different faiths separately. The decision as to what type of primary school a community is to have usually rests with the majority of the parents. Although survey data indicate that privately even most Roman Catholics may prefer the nondenominational school because they think it offers better instruction, the influence of the Roman Catholic church has been powerful enough to maintain its educational prerogatives. Its leaders insist that it is of the greatest importance to educate Roman Catholic children in strict accordance with the Church's dogma and have fought bitter and usually successful battles to maintain this principle of "separate but equal" education. A noticeable decline of Roman Catholic students attending secondary schools and universities in the last decade and a decided preponderance of Protestants in the increasingly important technical and scientific professions has led some of them to urge the extension of this principle into the universities and the greater consolidation of a separate Roman Catholic educational system.

THE EDUCATIONAL SYSTEM

Educational levels in the Federal Republic are exceptionally low for an advanced industrial society, and educational opportunities for social advancement remain restricted by traditional structures and orientations. The educational system is highly stratified and conforms closely to long-established elitist patterns which provide a comparatively brief "popular education" for the masses and rigidly restrict entry to higher education to a small minority. After four or at most six years of primary education in an elementary school (*Grundschule*), a child must take an examination to determine the nature and extent of his pre-occupational secondary education. Once the decision has been made it is exceedingly difficult to alter or modify it because subsequent schooling is specifically designed to equip the student for his future station in life.

In accordance with the traditional educational pattern, a rigid distinction is maintained between the students, teachers, and curriculum in the three principal types of secondary schools: the four- or five-year people's school (*Volksschule*), the four- or six-year intermediate school (*Mittelschule*), and the seven- or nine-year high school (*Oberschule*). Some modifications in these rigid structures have recently been introduced in some of the Länder, but it requires exceptional ability and effort for a student to take advantage of very limited opportunities to achieve a higher education than was originally chosen for him by his parents and by the educational authorities.

In 1962, 82 per cent of the adult population had completed only eight years of required basic education, designed for low-grade clerical and service employees, farmers, housewives, and manual workers. An almost equal proportion of school-age children is being educated today to enter these occupations, either as unskilled labor or – provided they follow a lengthy, poorly paid apprenticeship – as skilled workers and minor salaried employees. A mere 13 per cent of the adult population had completed the ten years of middle-range education required for most middle-grade, white-collar occupations — such as minor civil service positions — and only 9 per cent of children in the corresponding age groups were receiving the more advanced education. Finally, 5 per cent of adults had had the equivalent of a junior college education in the United States and had passed the coveted *Abitur* — the examination necessary to enter a university and most professional schools, practically all top positions in German society. In 1963 and 1964 only 7 per cent of the same age group achieved the *Abitur,* most of them boys, while a higher proportion had earlier dropped out of the university oriented high schools. Less than half (44 per cent) of the students who seven years earlier had been registered in such schools completed the course of study. They alone could gain admission to *Hochschulen,* universities, professional schools, and institutes of technology, which train the future elite.

The public universities stand at the apex of this highly stratified educational system. Today, as in the past, a university degree or its equivalent, is not only required for admission to the professions and all higher-grade positions in public administration, education, and the judiciary, but also represents an important achievement symbol facilitating entry into the top executive positions in the business community. A law degree is preferable; it requires a long course of study, at least two years of internship, and the passing of two state examinations. For example, a civil servant, who wants to rise above a medium-grade position, no matter what his task will be, must usually have a degree in law. A 1964 study of a representative cross-section of German leaders showed that two-thirds had received a university type of education and that such an education has become more rather than less important in the last five years for entry into an elite position in the emerging new social hierarchy.

Whereas most traditional status symbols have vanished in the postwar modernization, a university education has retained its prestigious value. Most respondents to opinion surveys have consistently placed the university professor at the top of the social status scale, ahead of clergymen, businessmen, civil servants, military officers, and government ministers. Therefore, it is not surprising that an honorary or part-time professorship is much sought after by nonacademic leaders, such as the members of the new economic and political managerial elite.

The structure of higher education and the orientation of those who control it maintain the traditional patterns of recruitment and instruction in the entire educational system. The public universities and professional schools are the recruiting ground for future teachers, scientists, and clergymen, and also directly and indirectly set educational standards for secondary and primary schools and thus influence the mobilization of intellectual resources and opportunities for access to top positions in the German social system. According to their critics they are "the single most formidable internal obstacle to innovation." [16] Founded in the sociopolitical environment of an absolute monarchy and in an era when great scholastic achievements were the works of individuals rather than teams, as the German journalist Rudolf Walter Leonhardt has pointed out, they have preserved in fact the traditional, self-perpetuating, paternalistic and authoritarian patterns and outlook of the medieval guild system. About 2,500 full professors (*Ordinarien*) rule as independent masters of their craft over about 300,000 students and assistants who, like the apprentices and journeymen in the medieval guild, must conform to the professional value system and render faithful service to pass the examinations for a career in education, the professions, or the public services. "Our academic institutions," according to Leonhardt, "resemble minuscule solar systems – with satellites and planets revolving around an all-illuminating star." [17]

The traditional practices and social orientations in the German educational system – supported by professors who have guarded their independence against outside interference all the more vehemently since the days of the totalitarian Nazi regime – are reflected in the comparatively small number of

[16] Ralf Dahrendorf, *op. cit.*

[17] Rudolf Walter Leonhardt, "In Lieu of Robbins," *Encounter,* XXII (1964), 82.

university students, the even smaller number who complete their course of study (about 65 per cent), and the neglect of such modern subjects as applied science and economics in their training. While in the United States 3 per cent of the 1962 population attended institutions of higher learning, only 0.4 per cent did so in the Federal Republic and of these only 16 per cent studied applied sciences and 14 per cent economics. University-imposed standards compel the young university student to extend his studies until he is thirty or more. Thus, if he completes his education at all, he begins his career when others of his age are already well established in a job, are earning a good income, and are enjoying a far more comfortable standard of living.

Women and young men from the lower income groups, facing great obstacles in this respect, either do not attempt to enter a university or tend to drop out before passing their examinations. High costs, comparatively few generous scholarships or grants (particularly in the physical and social sciences), and the discriminatory secondary school system combine with social pressures to bar them access to positions requiring university training. Today only 22 per cent of the university students are women and more than half of these never finish. Every second employed German is a manual worker, but only one out of ten university students is a child of a worker – compared to one in five in France, one in three in Britain and Sweden, and one in two in the United States. Nine per cent of the working population are farmers, but only 2 per cent of university students are children of farmers. On the other hand, whereas less than 5 per cent of employed Germans are civil servants, a third of university students are children of civil servants.

Traditional orientations, endorsed by the clergy and professors, are reflected not only in the structure but in the curricula of the educational institutions and the consequent training of the students. A limited "three R" education, along with religious instruction, suffices for the eight out of ten students receiving only a basic education – often in a small denominational village school in which a harassed, overworked teacher must instruct four or more grades simultaneously. The textbooks he uses are likely to be full of stories, poems, and pictures which idealize life in a rapidly vanishing rural society and hold up the anachronistic roles of the small farmer, independent artisan, and housewife-mother as normative models for the children. In the denominational schools these are further colored by traditional religious motives that set off one faith from another and de-emphasize the modern aspects of the urbanized industrial society into which most children are ejected at the age of fourteen or fifteen.

In most university preparatory schools the humanities, rather than the physical and social sciences, are still heavily stressed, on the grounds that the future elite needs primarily a broad humanistic education in history, German grammar and literature, and the arts. This curriculum reflects the preferences of the so-called "philologists" who control it and who, for their part, reflect the educational values they inherited from their university professors – including contempt for the primary school teachers and opposition to less rigid barriers in the hierarchic educational system.

The universities, for their part, seem unable to adjust to the demands of the modernizing society as rapidly as necessary. There are not enough institutions or professors to provide proper guidance and adequate instruction to students who have not learned to shift for themselves in the vast university communities – a major reason for the many dropouts and the long course of study. In 1938 the average had been one professor for every 34 students; in 1964 the ratio was 1 to 120 and vastly higher in such fields as pharmacy, engineering, and economics. Partly because of the preuniversity training in the secondary schools, partly because of the overcrowded facilities – particularly in the biological and physical sciences – and partly because of the emphasis on the law degree for government positions, the supply of qualified engineers, scientists, and teachers for modern society has not kept up with rapidly increasing demands. The lagging development of intellectual resources in a country once known for its international scientific leadership is indicated by the emigration of young scientists in search of better research opportunities than those available to them at German universities and by increasing expenditures for foreign patents and licenses in the Federal

Republic. According to a recent report of the German Research Association (*Deutsche Forschungsgemeinschaft*), German science in many fields is "disturbingly" backward.

A 1965 poll showing that a majority of West German adults oppose a longer period of compulsory education, reflects a general apathy toward demands for educational reform. Parents who usually themselves had only eight years of primary education but nonetheless measurably increased their income in the last decade, see no reason why their children need more – especially since (1) most youngsters have little trouble finding a job under full employment and (2) girls in any case are expected to become housewives and mothers who need no more education. A child in school is seen as a drain on the family pocketbook, particularly in lower-income families. A child with a job, however, is a financial asset and helps to pay for a new house or car.

Young people, for their part, are only too glad to escape the drudgery and demanding standards of formal education as soon as possible and easily succumb to the lures of relatively high pay in the tight labor market of a consumption oriented society. The proportion of failing students and dropouts is high. Employers needing unskilled workers are not interested in extending compulsory education; it would only increase competitive pressures for scarce labor. Public officials find other needs more pressing and point out that a shortage of teachers and the need to restrict financial expenditures make it impossible to institute major educational reforms.

In 1964, 37,000 primary school teachers were needed but could not be found – not least, as studies show, because the traditional educational status system and social orientations discourage qualified young people from entering the profession. A young woman sent to teach in a village or small town school finds herself socially isolated and without the freedom and leisure time opportunities available either in urban areas or in other occupations. The demand of primary school teachers for better training and higher status has found little support among their colleagues in secondary schools and universities. Public indifference and even opposition to higher public educational expenditures have resulted in a relative decline in the proportion of the national product invested in educational services.

The conditions we have described have been the despair of student advisers and educational reformers, some of whom have gone so far as to claim that German society faces an educational catastrophe. Their demands that a "national educational emergency" be proclaimed and that major reforms be instituted in the entire educational system have, however, met with very limited concrete government action thus far. Lack of public interest, general acceptance of the traditional patterns and orientations, the cultural autonomy of the Länder, and opposition by such influential groups as the Roman Catholic church weaken minority demands for better schools, less rigid barriers between the different educational subsystems, more centralized direction by agencies of the national government and the "enlightenment" of parents.

Present educational practices and norms may not lead to the imminent cultural and social catastrophe, but they do seem to contain one more source of latent tensions threatening German social and political stability. Postwar socioeconomic changes and the proclamation of new democratic political norms have fostered the popular expectation that "careers are open to all talents" in the Federal Republic – that everyone should and can have a chance to improve his social and material position. In the early 1950's a scarcity of labor and exceptional opportunities for upward social mobility and material betterment allowed many Germans to overcome the traditional barriers of a limited education with hard work and native ability. But the new social structure based on earned income and the greater need for acquired skills and expertise, particularly in the higher-income and higher-status occupations, are giving formal educational achievements a new importance.

Traditional orientations as well as affluence, however, obscure the potential threat of lagging educational growth to popular expectations of continuing unlimited economic growth and ever higher standards of living. If present trends persevere, they are likely to be increasingly at variance with pressures arising from modernization at home and from international economic and political developments. Present restrictive educational practices and orientations appear to pose major obstacles to the mobilization of latent intellectual resources – which numerous studies have shown exist – and to a wider acquisition of scientific and technical skills. But the greater development of such resources is a prime requisite for individual and social growth in a period of rapid scientific and technological advances – especially in a social system which has undergone as rapid a transition as has the German and which is as dependent for its stability on a balance between its traditional and modern components and between domestic and foreign demands. For these reasons the need to reform an educational system which is almost entirely public is an urgent problem facing authoritative German political decisionmakers. However, the apparent strength of resisting forces makes it a difficult if inescapable political task.

CHAPTER III

Foundations of the Political Culture

THE LEGACY OF THE PAST

A story making the rounds in West Germany these days tells of a minor collision between two cars. A crowd gathers and the driver of the first car jumps out, runs over to the other, and inquires: "Are you a Jew?" Upon receiving a negative reply, he instantly unleashes a flood of abusive comments about the other man's driving skills – uninhibited by fears that he might be charged with anti-Semitism, a politically sensitive issue in present-day Germany. Thirty years earlier, however, anti-Semitism was generally accepted as a respectable and legitimate civic virtue and the identification of the other driver as a Jew would, by this very fact, have put him "subjectively" in the wrong in the eyes of the onlookers – regardless of the "objective" circumstances surrounding the collision. When Hans Schmitt scolds his wife for running up a high telephone bill, politics do not enter the argument. But if he also speaks of the high rates charged by the state-owned telephone system, Schmitt introduces a public policy issue which lends a political coloration to his argument. The distinction is neither always easy nor explicit, but when we speak of collective beliefs, values, and emotions relating to political issues and objects, we deal with attitudes which constitute the political culture of a people.[1]

[1] See Lucian Pye and Sidney Verba (eds.), *Political Culture and Political*

Remember the story of the three little pigs and the houses they built to keep the wolf out? Appearances proved to be misleading when their structures were put to the test. The strength of political structures is also tested in time of crisis and at such times their capacity for survival depends on how solidly they are embedded in the political culture. The present regime of the German Federal Republic is like a new house — seemingly well-built, structurally sound, and equipped with modern devices to provide efficient services for the inhabitants. But if we consider past German political developments, here, too, appearances may be deceptive if the foundations are weak.

We must, therefore, probe beneath the structures of government and politics and examine the political culture. Are these structures supported by a popular consensus strong enough to withstand the buffeting winds of either a severe economic crisis or an increase in international tensions in Central Europe? How extensive and intensive are the elite and mass attitudes supporting the legitimacy of the prevailing political system and its component structures? How far are the new norms and roles established by law congruent with the unwritten rules of the political culture, and to what extent have the new structures already become institutionalized in the minds of the public and its leaders?

The stability, adaptability, and resilience of any political system depend very largely on the degree of congruence between the functions performed by its component structures and the attitudinal patterns of the underlying political culture. This congruence may be put to the test by sudden and far-reaching changes in governmental policies which arouse popular opposition because they run counter to established cultural norms. It may also be tested by strong pressures upon the system calling for a redistribution of political functions among existing structures — for example, demands for stronger executive leadership in time of crisis — or for the introduction of entirely new political structures. These pressures may result from changes in the international environment, such as threat

---

Development (Princeton: Princeton University Press, 1965), *passim,* and especially pp. 6–11, 516 ff., and 550–55.

of war or defeat in war, or from shifts in mass attitudes toward established structures or toward prevailing policies, as in the French Revolution of 1789.

Public opinion displays varying degrees of fluidity in these respects. It may be very stable and, therefore, highly resistant to changes in the political environment or it may be highly unstable and characterized by sudden and unpredictable shifts in political orientations.[2] A third possibility lies between these two extremes: moderate fluidity and a corresponding flexibility of opinion which permits relatively easy adaptation to policy changes and to more profound structural and functional transformations in the political system.

What Germans believe about political developments, what concerns them, how they feel about and judge political actors, structures, and relationships in domestic and foreign affairs, and what they expect, demand, and accept in public policy-making can therefore tell us a great deal about the stability of the present system.

In the last hundred years the German people have experienced periods of great prosperity and abject poverty, domestic tranquility and bitter strife, military victory and immense world prestige, and catastrophic defeat in two world wars. Within twenty-seven years three German regimes came to grief because they were not equal to the demands they faced in major crisis: the Hohenzollern Empire (1871–1918), the Weimar Republic (1918–1933), and Hitler's Third Reich (1933–1945). The political transitions which such changes involved were often dramatic, abrupt, and sweeping, requiring major and difficult reorientations in mass opinion. Usually Germans displayed a decided propensity to cling to established attitudes, even when the pressure to change them was very strong — as in World War II — and a great tolerance for sudden policy changes by those they accepted as their legitimate rulers. But there were also times when the mobilization of previously dormant emotions sharply restricted such tolerance and undermined established attitudes, producing behavior which threatened the stability of the political system. At such times the

[2] V. O. Key, *Public Opinion and American Democracy* (New York: Knopf, 1962), p. 235.

basic congruence between political orientations and the performance of fundamental political structures proved critical for the survival of the regime.

At least twice in recent German history, in 1933 and in 1945, sudden and major changes in the political environment were followed by equally sharp transformations in the patterns of mass opinion, displaying evidence of a high psychological capacity to adopt to new conditions. Generally, the extent of change in political orientations depended on the one hand on the resilience of established attitudes and on the other on the strength of the pressures demanding reorientation. The stability of the readjustment rested on the ability of the political system to translate input demands into policy outputs which did not sharply conflict with the norms of the political culture.

Memories play an important part in shaping any political culture. Like other people, Germans perceive and react to contemporary political developments on the basis of personal experiences and transmitted history. These lessons learned from the past provide clues and guidelines for the formation of attitudes about their own political roles and goals and those of other actors – German and non-German. Opinions about political practices, which are not necessarily well articulated or even consciously perceived, represent, to a greater or lesser extent, negative or positive reactions to such past experiences among different individuals and groups. In some cases they are but vague pictures in the mind, in others they are sharply engraved memories that resist alteration and lead to rigid behavioral reactions that disregard changed environmental conditions. The legacy of their past furnishes contemporary Germans in many respects with rather ambiguous and even contradictory images of what to do and what to expect.

The constitutional and legal norms embodied in the present form of government establish rather explicit perimeters for the political system, but the citizens of the Federal Republic can derive from the past only a rather diffuse image of the proper boundaries and linkages between society and polity, between the private and the public spheres, and between their political and nonpolitical roles.

The picture of the evolution of German society which Germans derive from their history books is that of a people d vided for centuries by intense cultural cleavages and oscillating between fratricidal conflict and precarious unity enforced by stern paternalistic authority. The Reformation gave rise to profound religious cleavages; particularism stood in the way of national unity; economic development created intense friction between rural and urban interests and between workers and employers; and the commitment of political factions to sharply conflicting, exclusive ideologies confronted Germans with irreconcilable demands for their loyalties.

The function of governmental structures under these circumstances came to be seen as maintaining harmony by suppressing domestic conflict rather than by absorbing competing beliefs and values, and by compelling compliance with formalistic rules and regulations imposed from above rather than facilitating far-reaching consensus through compromise. The authoritative structures, roles, and norms which developed aimed at maintaining stability on the basis of a subject culture rather than a participant culture, but failed in an emerging industrial society to provide adequate stabilizing and integrating links between the input of domestic demands for interest satisfaction and governmental policy output.[3]

THE PROSAIC AND THE ROMANTIC GERMAN

The new stress on materialism, empiricism, and individualism in contemporary German society and the liberal-democratic norms embodied in the present regime in many respects represent a rather sharp break with past German cultural patterns. These have combined rather uneasily the steady diligence and skill of the medieval craftsman with the admiration for the military prowess and apparent romantic daring of the medieval knight, while the mercantile traditions of empiricism, rationality, adaptability, and ease of compromise were markedly underrepresented.[4] Political traditions, in turn, reflected a more

[3] For the difference between a subject and a participant political culture, see Gabriel Almond and Sidney Verba, *The Civic Culture* (Boston: Little, Brown, 1964), pp. 19–25.

[4] The following discussion is based in part on Karl W. Deutsch and Lewis J. Edinger, *Germany Rejoins the Powers* (Stanford: Stanford University Press, 1959), pp. 11–19 and also is indebted to Ralf Dahrendorf, "Wand-

ral dualism between two quite different orienta-
which Germans could never entirely reconcile
t century.

...se patterns incorporated the social role of the hard-working, persevering, and methodical German willing to put up with personal discomforts and deprivations in order to execute with maximum efficiency self-assigned tasks or those assigned to him by a superior authority. It emphasized discipline, orderliness, and sobriety in personal conduct and in the public sphere expressed itself in a strong stress on highly formalized role relationships and respect for the authority of acknowledged experts. This pattern was reflected in the relationship between master craftsmen and their apprentices, the prevalence of legalized monopolistic organizations (such as guilds, trusts, and cartels) in the economic system, the normative role perceptions, and the relationship between teacher and student in the highly stratified educational system.

In politics this propensity for the "juridification of human relations" tended to formalize and depersonalize relationships.[5] Deeply ingrained habits of voluntary compliance with formalized rules laid down by accepted public authorities maintained domestic stability over long periods, and militated against the development of revolutionary movements or less radical expressions of civil disobedience. This compliance allowed Hitler to seize power "legally" after he had failed to do so earlier by revolutionary action, and even induced his Jewish victims to obey faithfully the decrees of his government. The principle of the *Rechtsstaat* in German law implied a strong faith in "constitutional engineering" rather than in trial and error experimentation, and a high degree of popular dependence on very explicit and detailed, as well as comprehensive, authoritative instructions as formal guides to legitimate political behavior.[6] The incumbents of public offices, from the

lungen der Deutschaft Gesellschaft der Nachkriegszeit," in Dahrendorf, *Gesellschaft und Freiheit* (Munich: Piper, 1961) as well as the sources cited in both these works and in the bibliography.

[5] Otto Kirchheimer, "German Democracy in the 1950s," *World Politics*, XIII (1961), pp. 254–266.

[6] See Herbert Spiro, *Government by Constitution* (New York: Random House, 1959), p. 181.

ruler down to the lowliest civil servant, were accordingly perceived, respected, and obeyed as the administrators of legal norms which bound those who had made them as much as any other citizen.

The second pattern in German cultural traditions incorporated the role of the romantic knight and his intellectual cousin, the daring demonic magician, who sought to mold rather than submissively accept their destinies. This has been reflected in modern German history by individual and collective attempts to escape from difficult, real life situations which seemed beyond the mastery of ordinary men – such as economic dislocation or overwhelming enemy power – into a more congenial twilight world composed less of fact than of fancy. In this world the outwardly weak – but pure and virtuous – vanquished wicked giants and man-eating dragons, the possessor of magic powers bested hosts of enemies, and heroic leaders performed miraculous feats. Goethe's Faust contracts with the devil to achieve his desires, but divine intervention saves him from living up to the terms of his contract. Parsifal, the "pure fool" in Wagner's mystical opera, triumphs over Klingsor, the wicked magician. Gretel's cunning saves her and Hansel from paying the penalty for violating the property rights of the witch in one of the most popular German fairy tales. Professing to be bands of loyal comrades who rejected the alleged philistinism and materialism of an industrializing society, the members of the German youth movements gathered in the early twentieth century about flickering campfires to invoke in song and story romantic visions of semifictitious military heroes, pirates, and robber knights who defied the conventions and laws of ordinary men.

Such flights of fancy beyond the formalistic pattern at times led to bold excursions into uncharted philosophical, scientific, and political areas. The idealist philosophies of a Kant or Hegel and the social science of a Karl Marx and Max Weber originated from the intuition of creative imaginations. But, frequently, such bold, imaginative ventures also terminated in intolerant and categorical, all-or-nothing ideologies which implicitly or explicitly allowed no compromise. Particularly in politics, this emphasis on firmly held, fundamental ideological principles led to sharp divisions and efforts to silence nonbelievers by force, if need be.

The antiformalistic, romantic orientation toward politics and its emphasis on wonder-working, heroic leaders, became identified with German nationalism and autocracy in the course of modern German history and as such proved to be both a stabilizing and an unstabilizing element in the political system. The leaders of the Hohenzollern Empire, particularly Chancellor Otto von Bismarck and Emperor William the Second, invoked this mystique to lend stability to its regime — the former more successfully than the latter. During the Weimar Republic the romantic orientation proved to be highly unstabilizing as it clashed with the attempts of democratic leaders to create a political culture congruent with the liberal, rational norms and structures promulgated by the new constitution. The impact of a catastrophic military defeat in World War I and two major economic crises provoked strong romantic escapist sentiments among large portions of the German people, which Hitler ultimately integrated successfully by assuming the role of a charismatic leader. By promising magic escape from national humiliation and economic chaos through the destruction of the enemies of the German people whom he held responsible, the *Führer* became a symbol of salvation to millions of Germans alienated from an increasingly urbanized and industrialized environment, particularly young people and impoverished small farmers, artisans, and shopkeepers.

Once in power, Hitler exploited these romantic attitudes to give stability to his "Third Reich" through a political culture built around the notion of a mystical, affective union between *Volk* and *Führer* from which Jews, Slavs, and other "inferior non-Germanic races" were permanently excluded. Magic symbols and the myth of the leader's unfailing intuition performed important integrative functions in the political community of Nazi Germany to the very last. "Magic weapons" and miraculous developments remained the hope for salvation for fervent believers even while enemy armies occupied Germany. But once Hitler committed suicide the hangover of the morning after took effect, and mass opinion swung sharply away from romanticism to embrace wholeheartedly the role of the prosaic, hard-working German.

THE QUIESCENT AND THE ACTIVIST VIEWS OF POLITICS

Directly related to these more general and historical orientations toward politics have been specific political role orientations. The past offers contemporary Germans few clues about how to play and evaluate participant roles in a pluralist democracy sanctioned by constitutional-legal norms of the present regime. Neither of the two major orientations for the role of the citizen offered by political tradition provide for the participation of the "little man" in public policymaking.

One of these orientations provided for a quiescent role. It conceived of politics as evil, to be shunned by virtuous men who feared the demons of power, thereby consigning power to rulers whom God or destiny had mandated to act on behalf of the apolitical multitude. This image of politics, propagated by German intellectual leaders from Martin Luther in the sixteenth century to Thomas Mann in the twentieth, embodied a fatalistic perception of the German masses as submissive, loyal subjects of "statesmen" wrestling with problems beyond general understanding. Those who accepted this role believed it best to direct their creative energies into what they conceived to be the private sphere. As housewives, peasants, artists, and scholars, they strove to live apart from or "above" politics and neither sought nor would accept responsibility for the actions of their government.

A contrasting but related orientation embraced the demons of power and embodied activist, though very different, roles in politics for the masses as well as their leaders. This orientation gained ascendancy in the nineteenth century as Prussia became the focus of the German industrial revolution and of the national unification movement, and it was inspired by the example of the collaboration between the "enlightened despots" of Brandenburg-Prussia and their disciplined soldiers and civil servants in promoting the military expansion and internal consolidation of that state in the seventeenth and eighteenth centuries. It was also part of the reaction of German political and intellectual leaders to the French Revolution and the Napoleonic invasions. This view assumed that in a world of hostile forces, locked in bitter conflict, politics was an unavoidable evil and that force and cunning were the only realistic methods of advancing personal and group goals. In its idealized version, this orientation maintained that a great and worthy goal which promoted the interests of state, nation, and class justified the means which had to be employed to attain it.[7] The Machiavellian and Social Darwinist variations maintained that politics was simply a struggle for the survival of the fittest. In both its versions, this orientation recognized no boundaries between society and polity. The entire community was seen as permanently involved in political action, and the distribution of roles provided for the direction of the politicized masses by enlightened governmental elites or astute, heroic leaders.

THE EVOLUTION OF POLITICAL ORIENTATIONS FROM BISMARCK TO HITLER

When unification grafted the autocratic Prussian political system onto German society in 1871 under the direction of Otto von Bismarck, the "Iron Chancellor," the quiescent and the activist orientations were largely fused by formal law and political practice. The relationship between the *Obrigkeit,* the authoritative organs of the political community, and the *Untertan,* the obedient subject, was deeply embedded in the political culture of the Hohenzollern Empire and retained its legitimacy for large sections of the public after the Empire's fall in 1918. The fusion was based on an orientation which identified the German state as the only organization that could safeguard the survival of the national community and provide for the welfare of its members in a world of enemies. In oppo-

[7] It was no accident that the Hegelian glorification of the state, the Marxist doctrine of the revolutionary class struggle for control of the state, and the integral nationalism of Hitler had their origins in nineteenth-century German political thought. All three ideologies assumed that it was the supreme duty, not the free choice, of the individual to serve the collectivity to which history had assigned him. All reflected an inability to accept the possibility of a peaceful compromise of conflicting interests.

sition to the liberal democratic principles of nonconformist elements, the dominant schools in German political and legal philosophy placed the needs and interests of a personified, anthropomorphic state above those of any of its component parts – particularly parties and interest groups – and asserted the overarching identity of private and public values in the German nation-state. Liberty was identified with the freedom of the state from external restraints and not with the freedom of the individual from control by the state – or rather those acting in its name. The principal duty of all citizens was to serve the national community, and political structures intervening between its primary unit, the family, and its highest, the state, tended to be viewed as essentially unimportant, if not disruptive, elements in the task of preserving and expanding the unity and strength of the German people.

By integrating traditional beliefs with rising nationalist emotions and important social values, this political orientation effectively upheld the legitimacy of the established authorities in Hohenzollern Germany. For the most part the growing industrial middle class accepted and even embraced it with enthusiasm. In return for a form of state capitalism promoting their economic interests, the financial and industrial upper middle class submitted to the continuing rule of the traditional Prussian rural aristocracy which held key political positions in Imperial Germany. The rapidly expanding working class was "negatively integrated" into the system, partly by becoming the beneficiary of the most advanced public social security system in the contemporary world, partly because its political and economic organizations developed largely into nonrevolutionary interest associations whose members on the whole accepted passive roles in the system.[8] The peasantry, bound by traditionally strong affective and economic ties to the ruling aristocracy – especially in Protestant Prussia – and fearful of the changes caused by industrialization, provided the ruling groups with some of their most reliable soldiers and voters. Most of

[8] See Günther Roth, *The Social Democrats in Imperial Germany* (Totowa, N.J.: Bedminister Press, 1963), *passim*. Also, Carl Schorske, *German Social Democracy* (Cambridge, Mass.: Harvard University Press, 1955), *passim*.

the intellectuals, deeply committed emotionally to national unity and integration, accepted the system and frequently employed their talents to propagate its conservation, like the influential historian Heinrich von Treitschke and the highly popular composer Richard Wagner. Only a comparatively small number became alienated from the political system and sought escape through political aloofness or, more rarely, exhausted themselves in bitter, largely negative political criticism which frequently was misunderstood by their readers – as in the case of the philosopher Friedrich Nietzsche.

These political orientations which supported the Imperial regime obscured for almost fifty years the fundamental structural weaknesses which most of its citizens could not see or would not see until defeat in war brought about its collapse. Although Germany's newly won unity, world prestige, and rapidly rising prosperity seemed sufficient proof that the system was working well, actually it failed to facilitate the smooth integration of traditionalist patterns with those produced by industrialization. Bismarck's political design – tailored to suit his needs when the regime was established – worked reasonably well while he was in charge of its execution, from 1871 to 1890. But the effort to fuse traditional Prussian conservatism with modern integral nationalism in the form of a thinly disguised autocracy was increasingly unequal to the demands placed upon the political system, particularly, but by no means exclusively, in international affairs.

The Imperial regime underwent no substantial changes, though its decisionmaking structures became more and more unequal to the tasks confronting them both at home and abroad. The demands of various domestic groups were inadequately integrated and satisfied, and, in the realm of foreign policy orientations, affective orientations – particularly toward Austria, France, Russia, and Britain – led to commitments on the part of the autocratic leadership which exceeded the system's capabilities when put to the test in World War I.

After close to three million lives had been lost and the country drained of its resources, the Imperial regime collapsed. Responsibility for making peace and establishing a new regime was suddenly thrust upon political party leaders inexperienced in the art of government; key positions in the army, the judiciary, and the public administration remained in the hands of supporters of the old regime and its political culture. The so-called "Revolution of 1918" was no radical political transformation, like the American and French Revolutions, nor the beginning of a gradual democratization, like the English Revolution of 1688. Instead of marking a new, democratic beginning, the Revolution of 1918 and the ensuing Weimar Republic proved to be but a stormy interlude between two autocracies.

The Weimar Republic has been called a democracy without democrats, which is an exaggeration. But during its brief existence, from a third to more than half the German voters refused to acknowledge the legitimacy of this attempt to provide their political community with a democratic form of government. The regime was an unsuccessful compromise between traditional and new political concepts, between a unitary and a federal state, between a parliamentary and a presidential form of government, and between a plebiscitary and a representative democracy. Its complex and greatly formalized structures failed to function as intended in its highly fragmented political culture, and conflicting demands from inside and outside the political community could not be satisfied by the decisionmakers in a manner congruent with the diverse beliefs, values, and emotions of its various subcultures.

Friction between religious, socioeconomic, and political groups, which had existed in a more latent form under the Imperial regime, became more virulent under a liberal democratic form of government based on the theoretical assumption that consensus could be achieved through compromise between conflicting goals. Innumerable political parties and interest associations – ideologically deeply divided over the scope, form, and functions of state and government – were unwilling or unable to achieve the stable agreement on fundamental issues which was necessary to establish a consensus on legitimate political roles and norms. Instead of being supported by an integrated political culture, the Weimar regime rested shakily on an unstable standoff between various forces representing traditionalism and modernization in a compartmentalized pluralist society, until it too disintegrated in the face of demands exceeding the capacity of its political structures. Attempts to adjust these structures to accommodate new or different functions during the economic crisis of the early 1930's created chaotic conditions and a power vacuum which facilitated the regime's destruction by Hitler and his witting or unwitting allies.

Thus the German people's first brief experience with a democratic form of government did not establish firm new political role perspectives, but rather produced an anarchic cultural mix between the older quiescent and activist orientations. Perhaps, as has been maintained by some historians, more time and fewer critical pressures might have allowed the formation of a new political culture, but a growing sense of abject fatalism and a lack of confidence undermined the determination of the defenders of the regime and played into the hands of its opponents. "We were at the mercy of events," the leaders of the Social Democratic Party argued when Hitler seized power in 1933.

Only a comparatively small minority sought to influence the course of political developments in the Weimar Republic. The average German shunned the participant role which its democratic constitution assigned him, except when he was mobilized by the political activists to exercise his voting rights in plebiscites and elections. A high turnout invariably benefited the parties opposing the regime, reflecting the limited support which it enjoyed in mass opinion.

Among those who played a more activist role in politics were many intent on replacing the regime with an entirely different one. The Communist leaders, who in November, 1932 received the backing of 17 per cent of the electorate, sought a "proletarian dictatorship" and, like the Nazis, promoted political instability, expecting that chaos would bring them into power. Hitler and his cohorts mobilized increasing support for the establishment of a National Socialist dictatorship, endorsed in November, 1932 by 33 per cent of the voters. Overtly and covertly the still extremely powerful remnants of the preindustrial feudal elites, entrenched in the army and the civil service, sought to restore princely particularism, especially in Bavaria, or the autocratic regime of the Hohenzollern Empire. The financial and industrial elites increasingly favored a nationalist autocracy that would suppress the interest associations of the industrial workers and promote German economic imperialism. Leaders of numerous groups representing the lower middle class of salaried employees, farmers, artisans, and small shopkeepers wanted a strong government which would save their clientele from the economic and social impact of industrialization. Many of the intellectuals who occupied strategic positions in the political communications and socialization systems – such as journalists, teachers, and religious leaders – either were opposed to the Weimar regime from its inception or became alienated because it failed to live up to their expectations and perfectionist standards of performance. Their frequently savage and destructive criticism implied or declared openly that another more or less democratic regime could do a better job in meeting its responsibilities for the welfare of the state, the nation, or the masses. The alleged neglect of such abstractions was commonly advanced by the self-appointed spokesmen for the army, the judiciary, public administration, and other governmental and nongovernmental groups to justify their opposition to the Weimar regime and their frequent defiance of its elected leaders.

Mass and elite dissatisfaction with the Weimar regime came to a head in the severe economic crisis that made millions unemployed and destitute and paved the way for Hitler's "legal" accession in 1933. He was carried to power largely on the strength of his promise that he could provide full employment, stability, unity, and order, and satisfy conflicting values through authoritative decisions far more adequately than had the Weimar leadership. His confident cry "Give me four years and you won't recognize Germany" inspired among very heterogeneous elements the idea that the "new" Germany would correspond to their particular image of what it should be like.

Very quickly, a leader who had never managed to obtain the endorsement of a majority of the voters in a free election effected a dramatic shift in political opinions and obtained the enthusiastic support of most Germans, primarily on the strength of negative memories of the Weimar regime and utopian expectations about the future. The Protestant Prussian aristocracy had visions of a return to the "glorious times" of the Hohenzollern Empire, while the leaders of the Roman Catholic church were encouraged to accept the Nazi regime by a treaty made with the Vatican, granting their church privileges which they had sought in vain from Weimar governments. The paramilitary storm troopers who had fought Hitler's street battles expected to take control of the army, while the old military elite looked forward to building a new military establishment unencumbered by the "fetters" placed on German rearmament under the Weimar regime. Industrialists were cheered by the abolition of trade unions, while the lower middle class expected that its interests would be served by the elimination of "Jewish capitalists" from German economic life. Nationalists were stirred by Hitler's spectacular successes in foreign policy, and anti-Communists applauded his destruction of the left wing parties. Senior civil servants welcomed the elimination of parliamentary controls and the concentration of executive power in one hand, while youngsters looked to Hitler to realize their romantic dreams of a new German society released from the formalistic restraints of the past.

Hitler skillfully exploited this euphoria in his efforts to create a political culture which would support the Nazi regime. His work was greatly facilitated by the destruction of most formal interest articulation structures of the past, such as the political parties, and by established political role orientations toward the state. Respected official government structures like the public administration and the judicial system, as well as the "unofficial" terror and propaganda apparatus of the Nazi movement, were employed to eliminate or gravely weaken competing groups, such as the churches and the aristocratic officer corps, which might deny the leader the absolute loyalty of his subjects. In the new, totalitarian "leader-state" (*Führerstaat*) all boundaries between polity and society and between political and nonpolitical roles were to be eradicated, and beliefs, emotions, and values were to reflect solely the spirit of the national collectivity as articulated by its embodiment, the omnipotent leader. "Hitler is Germany and Germany is Hitler" was the slogan chanted in unison by the uniformly dressed thousands at carefully staged monster rallies and echoed all over the country from millions of loudspeakers. Belligerent nationalism, anti-Semitism, and radical romanticism were incorporated in a rather diffuse National Socialist philosophy based on Hitler's *Mein Kampf,* which was to be the ideological substance for integrating state and society, government and Nazi movement, in a new cultural mix.

Twelve years of intensive political socialization – in schools and in mass organizations, in the army and in the conscript labor service, in prisons and in concentration camps – established or reinforced the role relationships based on command and absolute obedience which sustained the Nazi regime until it disintegrated in 1945. Studies of German civilian and military morale during World War II indicate that positive support for the regime, as well as acquiescent compliance, enabled it to maintain domestic stability even under extreme external pressure. A mass revolutionary potential never developed; the few conspiracies to overthrow Hitler – most notably that of July, 1944 – did not actively involve more than a handful of individuals.

But this overt cultural homogeneity also concealed elements in the political system which in effect weakened Nazi efforts to establish a new political culture. The Hitler regime incorporated features which did not permit it to follow up the atomization of pre-Nazi German society with the institutionalization of new patterns of stable role orientations and relationships. Essentially, the Nazi system sought to manage the problems of Germany's continuing transition from a preindustrial traditional society to an advanced industrial society through the agency of a charismatic leader. But Hitler's erratic and intuitive style of government, as well as the organization of the totalitarian state, introduced destabilizing tensions into the political system which accentuated rather than resolved incongruities between the cultural norms propagated by the Nazi regime and the actual operation of the totalitarian system.

The one-sidedness of political communications in a hierarchic regime resting on command and obedience and the dualism of governmental and Nazi party structures produced far-reaching uncertainties about expected role behavior, bitter jurisdictional disputes, and inefficient performance. These reduced the adaptability of the system when it faced its most critical test in the last years of World War II. In every sphere of social action decisionmaking power formally descended from the dictator, in his dual capacity as chief of the government and leader of the Nazi movement, to thousands of subordinate Nazi potentates, military commanders, and public administrators, but formal lines of command were deliberately obscured and often bypassed by Hitler, and previous decisions were unexpectedly reversed. The nature of the regime encouraged not only blind obedience to commands from the top, but "buck-passing" by subordinates unwilling to accept responsibility for decisions which might be disapproved of by their superiors. Even Hitler's closest associates labored under the constant threat of sudden disgrace in a regime marked by arbitrary decisions affecting life, property, and status. The irrational, affective, and antiformalistic elements that were the basic ingredients of the Nazi political culture precluded the predictable, rational procedures that are the requisite of a stable modern social system. "The Revolution of Nihilism" described by one perceptive observer at an early stage of Hitler's rule led eventually to anarchic conditions in the conduct of government and culminated in complete disintegration in 1945.[9]

POST-NAZI POLITICAL RECONSTRUCTION

Determined efforts to engineer a radical transformation of German political orientations after the fall of the Nazi regime began after total defeat had brought about the virtual collapse of previous socioeconomic and political structures. Under the occupation regime American, British, and French military governments assumed authoritative control over what was to become, four years later, the territory of the Federal Republic and outlawed the articulation of opinions which they identified with the Nazi regime. Remnants of the totali-

[9] Hermann Rauschning, *The Revolution of Nihilism* (New York: Longmans, Green, 1939).

tarian structures were shattered by measures aimed at the complete eradication of German authoritarian traditions and the permanent elimination from positions of status and power of groups and individuals believed to have been prominent in the Nazi regime or indirectly responsible for it. Not only Nazi party leaders, but civil and military officials, business leaders, journalists, and educators identified by the occupation authorities as members of the old authoritarian elites, were purged. The destruction of the preindustrial elites initiated by the Nazis was completed with the dissolution of Prussia, the division of Germany, and the complete disarmament of Germany. On the other hand, ostensible anti-Nazis and non-Nazis were to be encouraged to participate in the political reconstruction of Germany, and the former socioeconomic and political structures were to be changed radically so that democratic orientations might develop under foreign tutelage.

The political roles assigned the Germans, regardless of their political orientation during this period of deliberate denazification and democratization, were to receive commands issued by foreign decisionmakers, a relationship quite congruent with the role expectations Germans had been taught in the past. What Germans wanted, whether they were evident anti-Nazis or not, was of no great importance; cooperative acquiescence was all that was expected of them. On the one hand the victor's authoritative decisions were based on a punitive policy toward a people held collectively responsible for the actions of the Nazi regime, on the other they reflected a tutelary "enlightened despotism" aimed at preventing future German aggression. War crimes trials, denazification proceedings, educational reforms, dismantling of industrial plants for reparation payments, and the carefully controlled reconstruction of political structures were the means used by the three occupation powers to implement these policies.

Most Germans apparently accepted these role assignments and political lessons readily and with alacrity, though a few anti-Nazi leaders demanded a more active role in political reconstruction for themselves. Among the masses a mood of despair and political anomie prevailed in the wake of the Nazi regime's collapse. Past beliefs had been proven wrong, former values had lost their meaning, and expectations about the future were gloomy. More than four million Germans had lost their lives in World War II, about two million had been orphaned, and at least a million and a half crippled. Starvation was widespread, shelter in the bombed out cities was entirely inadequate, and employment was hard to find. The once propertied urban middle class had suffered severe financial losses in the war, and many used up the money they had left in the chaotic postwar years. Social leveling was increased by allied purges and by the influx of millions of refugees from the East, most of them former farmers and bourgeois who had lost their status as well as their property.

As noted in the preceding chapter, economic recovery and social reorganization began about 1948 and developed rapidly in the following decade, hand in hand with the recovery of German political influence. As tensions between Western and Soviet leaders increased, foreign supervision and intervention in German political affairs decreased. The establishment of the Federal Republic in 1949 terminated Western punitive and tutelary efforts, war crimes trials came to an end, and political decisionmaking was gradually handed over entirely to German leaders. The new policy was to woo the West Germans into a voluntary and intimate partnership against the Soviet bloc by providing them with economic assistance and military protection, and by encouraging political opinions and behavior which appeared to conform to Western intentions to turn the Federal Republic into a democratic bulwark against Soviet aggression. West Germans now learned that they could expect very tangible rewards – such as complete sovereignty, achieved in 1955 – in return for demonstrations of their reliability as anti-Communist partners of the West and of the stability of their new political system. Such lessons, combined with the impact of socioeconomic recovery, enormously strengthened the position of leaders who took over the authoritative direction of political reconstruction from the Western military governments – above all, Konrad Adenauer, Chancellor of the Federal Republic from its inception until 1963. They rallied elite and mass opinion behind their efforts to stabilize the new regime and gave it legitimacy at home as well as abroad.

THE PAST IN PERSPECTIVE

French politics to this day reflect deep cleavages which date back to the revolution of 1789, and Americans are still trying to come to terms with the legacy of a civil war which occurred more than a century ago. West Germans, however, are ostensibly an ahistorical people without memories linking past experiences to contemporary political orientations. What is popularly referred to as "The Year Zero," the collapse of the Nazi regime in 1945, is said to mark the beginning of an entirely new era, having no connection with past experiences. The "lessons of history" allegedly offer no guidance to present and future problems facing the citizens of the Federal Republic. On the contrary, the average West German maintains that evocations of former political orientations are not merely a waste of time but a hindrance in dealing with the pressing tasks at hand. Except for relatively few deviant intellectuals, opinion leaders and other elite groups have increasingly conformed to this climate of "here and now." Even former anti-Nazis more or less reluctantly agreed to bury memories which appear to inhibit the building of a new political culture in support of the new regime, and the incorporation of its norms and role assignments in the political orientations of West Germans.

The old Germany seems dead and forgotten and with it the political orientations of the past. On the face of it these orientations appear to have no bearing on present attitudes and behavior; but, as we shall see, less explicitly and consciously they remain ingredients of the contemporary political culture. Not merely in their specific statements about the past but even more in their implicit political orientations, West Germans give evidence of the survival of attitudes rooted in historical memories and learning experiences going back more than two decades.

The vast and dynamic changes which characterize West Germans' individual and collective experiences in recent years have undoubtedly helped to erase conscious recollections of the past. Perceptions of a satisfying present and of an even more satisfactory future have dimmed memories of former triumphs and disasters and weakened both positive and negative recollections of earlier regimes. In 1951, shortly after the establishment of the Federal Republic, as much as 45 per cent of a representative cross-section asserted that Germany had fared better before 1914, under the Hohenzollern empire, while 42 per cent thought it had been better off under the prewar Nazi regime. By 1963 only 16 and 10 per cent, respectively, maintained that Germany had been better off under the peacetime Empire or Third Reich, whereas two-thirds said their country had never fared better in this century than at the present time.[10] The younger the respondents and the less they therefore knew about previous regimes from personal experience the more likely they were to declare Germany better off now, while satisfaction with the present was lowest among the oldest groups. This suggests that explicit and implicit postwar learning experiences on the part of the younger generation and the dying-off of the older generation have significantly influenced this shift in opinion favoring the present regime.

The hope and/or belief that German influence in world politics might be restored to its former state appear to have faded with the growing acceptance of the present political system. Though their country is today one of the mightiest economic powers in the world, most Germans seem content, resigned, or even eager to have it play the role of a second- or even third-rate power in international politics. In 1954 almost as many believed as did not believe that Germany would again be one of the most powerful states in the world but by 1964 this view was expressed by less than a fifth; the vast majority gave voice to no such expectations, 53 per cent expressing outright disbelief. In 1955, 60 per cent thought West Germans more "competent" than other people, but by 1960 only 42 per cent expressed this view.

Germany's shattering defeat in World War II with its consequences appear to constitute a traumatic learning experience

[10] Very few, either in 1951 or 1963, remembered the era of the Weimar Republic as the best period.

Unless otherwise indicated, all opinion data cited apply to representative samples of Germans over 18 years of age and are derived from published and unpublished reports of leading German survey organizations and Almond and Verba's *The Civic Culture*.

that left a deep, or even buried, impression very different in its political repercussions from that which followed defeat in 1918. Increasingly, Germans have come to accept Germany's sole responsibility for a catastrophic war, rather than to put the blame on others as did so many after World War I. In 1951 only a third of the respondents in a survey would accept such exclusive responsibility, but by 1963 a majority did. What is of interest here is not the objective validity of such beliefs about the causes of World War I or II, but that, this time, war and defeat are attributed directly to the shortcomings of the preceding regime and its leaders, whereas in the Weimar Republic millions of Germans continued to hold the Hohenzollern regime in high esteem to the detriment of its successor. The present regime labors under no such handicap and has profited by the negative image left by its totalitarian predecessor.

The "great men" of the past have similarly suffered an increasing loss of esteem in comparison with leaders of the Federal Republic. Imperial Chancellor Bismarck's popularity as the man who had "done most for Germany" dropped from 35 per cent in 1950 to 21 per cent in 1963, while that of Chancellor of the Federal Republic Konrad Adenauer increased from less than 1 per cent to 28 per cent in the same interval.[11]

Hitler's reputation as a great German leader has all but vanished. He was named as the man who had done most for Germany by only 10 per cent in 1950 and by merely 5 per cent in 1963. But for many his regime retains an aura of legitimacy as a duly constituted form of government. In a 1962 poll more than half the respondents considered the men who sought to overthrow the Hitler regime in July, 1944 subversive traitors, and merely a fifth thought this effort to end a catastrophic war was justified. Another fifth said they knew nothing about it.

With the passage of time the images of Hitler and his regime

[11] However, a study of young Germans born between 1940 and 1946 and educated after the war revealed Bismarck as the most admired figure among German leaders of the last two hundred years. Fifty-eight per cent of these young Germans singled him out as the greatest leader from a large list that included Frederick the Great, Hitler, and Marx — the last two being least admired. See Walter Jaide, *Das Verhältnis der Jugend zur Politik: Empirische Untersuchungen zur politischen Anteilnahme und Meinungsbildung junger Menschen der Geburtsjahrgänge 1940–1946* (Neuwied: Luchterband, 1964), pp. 82–88.

have become more diffuse rather than more explicitly negative. The Third Reich appears to many West Germans today to have been an unsuccessful rather than an oppressive form of government. Its *Führer* is seen more as a fallible leader – who foolishly started and lost a war he could not win – than as a brutal German dictator. In the frank opinion of more than a third of the respondents in a 1964 opinion survey, had it not been for the war Hitler might have become one of the greatest German statesmen. This was a smaller proportion than expressed the same view in earlier polls, but between 1955 and 1964 the proportion who professed no opinion on the subject increased almost twice as much as the percentage who explicitly rejected Hitler's potential greatness. Similarly, while the proportion of those who said they would vote for "a man like Hitler" declined from 12 to 3 per cent between 1953 and 1962, the proportion of those who claimed to have no opinion declined to a much smaller extent. Moreover, the latter group included a disproportionate number of young adults educated after 1945 and, therefore, exposed to intensive "re-education" efforts.

Significant for present political orientations is the fact that numerous surveys and studies indicate that the potential learning experiences of the intervening years have failed to teach a large proportion of contemporary West German adults a clear differentiation between the norms and roles which prevailed under the Nazi regime and those which are stipulated by the new constitutional order. Particularly among those 80 per cent of West German adults who have had only an eight-year education and among the postwar generation educated after 1945, the passage of time has obscured rather than sharpened such understanding and confused rather than clarified images of the past.[12]

The average West German, in learning to play the role of responsible citizen assigned to him by the new constitution, is inclined to dismiss the past, rather than consciously apply it.

[12] See DIVO-Institut, *Basic Orientation and Political Thinking of West German Youth and Their Leaders: Report on a Nationwide Survey* (Frankfurt am Main – Bad Godesberg: 1965), and "Beliefs of Youth on Nazis Studied," *The New York Times*, February 16, 1961.

This is conspicuously demonstrated by mass attitudes toward crimes committed in the name of the German people by their Nazi leaders. Such crimes are generally condemned but at the same time dismissed as matters for which present Germans bear no responsibility. Poll after poll has indicated that the older generations who were actively or passively involved in the totalitarian regime are extremely eager to forget a past which evokes unpleasant memories for them and resent efforts by German and non-German groups to prevent such psychological burial through oblivion. Younger Germans, who profess no responsibility for the sins of their fathers, tend to share their elders' objections to keeping the issue alive.

All sorts of psychological tensions involving the stability of the family, the educational system, political relations, and personal peace of mind come into play here; the general inclination is to resolve them by letting bygones be bygones and by placing the blame on the dead Hitler and his immediate subordinates and thereby to be done with it. Thus, three-fourths of the respondents in a 1961 poll agreed that Adolf Eichmann should be severely punished by the Israelis for his crimes against the Jews, but nine out of ten also asserted that they did not feel personally involved or responsible, and most said they wanted to hear no more of such matters. Such evocations of the past were said to injure Germany's prestige in the world and create domestic disharmony. Moral issues in this respect appear to have little relevance to present issues, and most West Germans think it far better to concentrate exclusively on problems facing them now and in the future than to harp on the past. German juries have been conspicuously lenient in trials of former Nazis, and when the federal parliament in 1965 deliberated on and eventually passed a bill to extend the statute of limitations for trials of Nazi murders, two-thirds of the German men and three-fourths of the women in a poll demanded that to the contrary there be no further prosecutions.

Only a comparatively small number of West Germans today are prepared to confront the past and learn from its lessons. Some of these are young trade unionists and university students. But most are men between forty and sixty who remember the Nazi regime from personal experience and it is from their ranks that the present politically active leadership is largely recruited. In public statements and private conversations, members of the politically relevant elites in West German society frequently point to past experiences as lessons for the present and future. Some invoke history in calling for a return to forgotten civic virtues. Others, particularly former anti-Nazis, cite lessons of the past in warning of future dangers for the present system. Memories of the fate of the Weimar Republic are invoked by them in efforts to guard against the erosion or even the destruction of the new democratic system by antidemocratic forces, especially if there should be once again a major economic crisis. In such an event, it is feared mass unemployment might well produce widespread hysteria among a people who have become too accustomed to ever greater prosperity to accept economic deprivation quietly. Once again, it is feared, radical demagogues intent on destroying the existing regime might turn mass opinion successfully against moderate, democratic leaders.

But for most West German leaders, too, the past seems remote and not very relevant today. Many are not certain how the masses would react to a new economic crisis or how effectively in such an event the present political system could cope with strong pressures to change its fundamental structures. But most also believe that the lessons of history offer little or no guidance for dealing with such a possibility and trust that effective contemporary leadership would find the solution. Few fear a Nazi revival. However, in the view of leaders who lack faith in the stability of mass opinion and its firm adherence to the present system, a more authoritarian form of government might become necessary in time of crisis.

In a very real sense, political stability in Western Germany has been sought and promoted by an implicit consensus to forget the divisive issues of the past in the common task of socioeconomic and political reconstruction. Historical memories are evoked, as in the persistent, though limited, image of a united *Reich* and in quasi-governmental and governmental efforts to strengthen allegiances to the present regime by impressing upon the public its superiority over those of the past. But, generally, explicit memories of German political orientations and experiences before 1945 are not notable in the contemporary political culture.

The desire for harmony and the necessity for cooperation among individuals and groups who not so long ago were associated with bitterly antagonistic camps have caused a perceptual curtain to be dropped upon the past, a curtain which is becoming ever more impenetrable. Large gaps in the official biographies of many prominent West Germans bear witness to deliberate efforts to veil the past, while less deliberate and conscious feats of repression are evident in replies to surveys of mass and elite opinion. Moreover, formal and informal restrictions inhibit the frank articulation of opinions that are not congruent with the political norms proclaimed in the constitution and by law. For example, social and political considerations make it appear "improper" to give voice to extreme nationalistic sentiments or to endorse "antidemocratic" causes openly. Nazi and Communist organizations have been officially outlawed, and the electoral system restricts opportunities to express effective support for groups opposing the regime. It may well be that few West Germans consciously embrace opinions which conflict with the formal norms of the contemporary system, but such inhibitions on their expression of such opinions leave the question in doubt.

However, as we probe deeper into political orientation and behavior patterns, it will become evident that role and norm perceptions rooted in German historical experiences have not in fact suddenly been eradicated. Implicitly and often indirectly, learning experiences under earlier regimes still influence orientations toward political objects and relationships among large sections of the West German public and its leaders. Undigested and ambiguous memories seem to complicate the reconciliation of the innovative features of the present system with older elements of the political culture. But the survival of older orientations may also be facilitating a stable adjustment in orientations to political conditions which are very different from those West Germans have been accustomed to in the past and which demand new perspectives and responses. Insofar as diffuse memories and implicit learning experiences of the past in fact maintain moderate fluidity of elite and mass opinion, a gradual process of adaptation to a new political environment may safeguard the present system against the destabilizing effect of extremely high or extremely low opinion fluidity.[13]

[13] See pp. 54 ff., 114 ff. above on the relationship between various forms of opinion fluidity on the one hand and political stability and change on the other.

CHAPTER IV

The Contemporary Political Culture

CONSTITUTIONAL NORMS AND POLITICAL ORIENTATIONS

The Basic Law of the German Federal Republic was not an expression of prevailing political norms in Western Germany but was superimposed upon the political culture in 1949; its popular acceptance was never put to a direct test in a referendum. The framers, representatives of the occupation powers and those German political leaders acceptable to them, were primarily concerned with the stabilizing function of the constitution – the political community and regime which they thereby established remained to be "bought" by the mass of West Germans. The document was a compromise between various constitutional theories derived from German and non-German political philosophies and experiences, and its intended purpose was to reshape popular political orientations inherited from previous regimes. By establishing exemplary norms and roles sanctioned by constitutional law and by endeavoring to prestructure future relationships, the framers sought to reshape the political culture in conformity with *their* image of a stable and democratic political order.

As stated in its preamble, the Basic Law was to be but *a temporary instrument* of government pending the reunification of Germany and, eventually, the incorporation of the country in a European state. The form of the regime which was ultimately to prevail and the scope of the political community to which it was to apply were thus left open to question. At the same time, however, the constitution was designed to guarantee long-range political stability under the regime and in the political community formally established with the creation of the Federal Republic of (Western) Germany. To smooth what was expected to be a difficult road of transition to a firmly established democratic regime in a pluralist society, the framers drafted rational rules that were to govern political conduct and relationships. In doing so they expressed, as well as appealed to, the conservative formal legal tradition in German political culture and repudiated the radical romantic orientations of the past. But the roles assigned to the citizens of the new state called for *involvement and participation* in the political process and in this sense repudiated the quiescent citizenship orientations of the past.

The roles assigned to rulers and ruled made the Basic Law a far more democratic instrument than those which governed such relationships in Germany before 1914 and under the Nazi regime, but it was also far more conservative than the Weimar Constitution. Its provisions reflected the belief of its authors, based on past experiences, that too much "direct" democracy was likely to prove destabilizing in Germany. The average citizen of the new Federal Republic was not trusted to play more than an intermittent and indirect role in public policymaking as a participant in a "representative" democratic system. Implied in the norms and structures which were established was the assumption that it would require strong governmental leadership to assure the efficient operation of the new system and to create popular orientations which would give it legitimacy. An educative function of the constitution was thus linked to its stabilizing function by the assumption of its fathers that a smoothly functioning system would accustom West Germans to accept the role assignments and norms of the Basic Law.

Liberal democratic norms are incorporated in the constitution in the form of a large number of "fundamental rights" of man and the citizen.[1] The dignity of man is declared to be inviolable, all public authority is said to emanate from the people, and the state is to serve rather than dominate its members. The Federal Republic is identified as a "democratic and social state," a community of free men governed by democratically elected representatives and subject to laws which assure social justice and equality for all. Less explicitly, the constitution also incorporates elements of more traditional German political theory. Pluralist group interests are strictly subordinated to the interests of the state; for example, the collective needs of the political community are placed firmly above the desires of its individual members. Responsible citizenship, according to the Basic Law, implies respect for established public authorities and the duty to obey their decisions.

By far the largest part of the Basic Law concerns the intended operation of the political system and spells out in considerable detail how it is supposed to work. These instrumental provisions seek to assure stability as well as flexibility by qualifying the underlying theoretical principles, or leaving their interpretation in the hands of executive, legislative, and judicial authorities. Accordingly, parliamentary acts, administrative rulings, and court decisions over the years have amplified or modified the "fundamental" principles of the constitution to maintain congruence between political theory and political practice under conditions of socioeconomic and political change. Article 21, for instance, permits restrictions on the right of free association by stipulating that only political parties which support the community and the regime established under the constitution are legal. This has allowed the federal government to ban the Communist and a neo-Nazi party and to prosecute groups and individuals suspected of supporting "subversive" causes. Article 2 provides that the right to life and the inviolability of personal freedoms may be curbed by law in the public interest; such restrictions have been imposed by formal legislation as well as by administrative and judicial

[1] The text may be found in James K. Pollock and John C. Lane (eds.), *Source Materials on the Government and Politics of Germany* (Ann Arbor: Wahrs Publishing Co., 1964), pp. 11–37.

interpretations. Thus, the provisions of the old criminal code, drafted in the Hohenzollern Empire and maintained under the Weimar and Nazi regimes, have been used to impose authoritative restraints on the exercise of fundamental individual rights proclaimed in the constitution. On the other hand, the abolition of the death penalty by the Basic Law has saved the lives of many former Nazi officials convicted of the murder of hundreds of thousands of victims, while the constitutional principle of equal justice for all has prevented the prosecution of others under the statute of limitations on "manslaughter" in the old criminal code. To cite a final example, Article 18 of the constitution bars the "misuse" of the freedom of expression. This has permitted governmental authorities to confiscate "seditious" literature and to censor those publications believed to corrupt "public morals" and threaten the sanctity of marriage and the family.

Insofar as it was the intention of the fathers of the Basic Law to provide a stabilizing element in a period of dynamic change, the formal constitutional framework they established has served this purpose well.[2] It allowed Chancellor Adenauer to exercise strong authoritative leadership and, at the same time, permitted adequate opportunities for the expression and satisfaction of key interests in society. It has been flexible enough to accommodate modifications of political structures and functions and appears to have provided almost all political actors with roles which they can accept. In striking contrast to past German political experiences, today most leading as well as supporting players have assented to constitutional rules for political conduct that seem to rest on a broad popular consensus.

It is less clear whether the Basic Law as yet has been as effective in fulfilling its intended educative function. Earlier we noted a gap between West German social behavior and surviving traditional attitudes. A gap that may be even greater seems to prevail in the political sphere. Compliance with the rules of

[2] In contrast to the bitter constitutional controversies which have characterized recent French politics, for example, West Germans have been quite contented with a Basic Law which has undergone only minor modifications in two decades. None of the thirteen amendments to the constitution significantly altered the original document.

the constitution, overwhelming electoral support for the parties identified with the present regime, and other behavioral evidence of congruence between political regime and political culture, seem to conceal popular attitudes which may contribute to the stabilization of the system but do not conform to norms which were intended to give supportive legitimacy to the new regime and community.

FEDERAL REPUBLICANS

A sense of political community involves feelings of unity, common political identity, and pride in membership, reinforced by strong emotional attachments to symbols of communality such as the monarchy in England and the star-spangled banner in the United States. The Federal Republic has many of the formal appurtenances of a political community, but to many of its inhabitants West Germany seems more a geographic expression — or, as a current saying puts it, an economic system — than a national community. They recognize and accept their status as citizens of an explicitly provisional state, but they take little pride in its political institutions and only in the most formal terms consider the Federal Republic their fatherland. In 1959, a mass opinion survey in Western Germany, Britain, and the United States asked a representative cross-section of adults what things they were most proud of in their country. West Germans, as indicated in Table IV.1, professed comparatively little pride in present political institutions or in their performance. They singled out instead attributes which did not focus on the political community or regime, particularly the economic system, the sociocultural characteristics generally attributed to the German people (e.g., cleanliness, diligence, efficiency, frugality), and the physical endowment of the country. The lack of emotional loyalties toward the new German fatherland was reflected in a 1964 survey which asked West German adults whether there was anything on earth for which they were ready to lay down their lives. Fifty-one per cent of the male and 45 per cent of the female respondents declared there was nothing worth dying for; 29 per cent of the men and 42 per cent of the women declared that the family was the only group for which they were prepared to die; only 3 per

TABLE IV.1 *Attributes Perceived with Pride (1959 Poll; Figures are Rounded-off Percentages)*

	G.F.R.	U.S.	U.K.
Political objects			
Government, political institutions	7	85	46
Social legislation	6	13	18
Position in international affairs	5	5	11
Subtotal	18	103 [a]	75
Nonpolitical objects			
Characteristics of the people	36	7	18
Economic system	33	23	10
Physical attributes of country	17	5	10
Contributions to science	12	3	7
Contribution to the arts	11	1	6
Spiritual virtues and religion	3	3	1
Subtotal	112	42	52
No objects perceived with pride			
Nothing or don't know	15	4	10
Total percentage of responses	145 [a]	151 [a]	137 [a]

[a] Totals exceed 100 per cent because multiple responses were possible.
Source: Almond and Verba, *The Civic Culture* (Boston: Little, Brown, 1964), p. 102.

cent of the men and 1 per cent of the women singled out "the fatherland."

The Federal Republic and its political institutions appear to be objects of neither profound feelings of positive emotional support — such as the Second Reich of the Hohenzollern regime and the Third of the Nazi regime had enjoyed — nor strongly negative sentiments such as the Weimar regime had experienced. Most West Germans have come to evaluate the present political system as one "with which one can live," according to a 1961 opinion study.[3] They are, on the whole, satisfied with a form of government which has evolved simultaneously with unprecedented economic growth and rapid recovery of German world prestige, but their attitudes toward

[3] Viggo Graf Blücher (ed.), *Der Prozess der Meinungsbildung: dargestellt am Beispiel der Bundestagswahl 1961* (Bielefeld: EMNID, 1962), p. 15.

regime and state for the most part do not reflect a sense of positive emotional involvement and affective identification.

Conceived as an artificial creation imposed upon West Germans, the Federal Republic is widely looked upon as "a provisional polity, created *ad hoc,* derived neither from the grace of God, nor the will of the people, nor the ineluctable workings of history, nor as an emanation of the folk soul." [4] Insofar as its citizens are not simply content to consider themselves German-speaking beneficiaries of a thriving economy, or West German residents of the European continent, they identify themselves, rather ironically and without much pride, as *Bundesrepublikaner* – Federal Republicans – as the young German journalist Klaus Boelling recently wrote in a book he called *Republic in Suspense*. According to Rudolf Leonardt, another prominent commentator, the only common goal of the citizens of the Federal Republic is the desire to preserve prosperity.

West Germans have conspicuously ignored or rejected official efforts to create a sense of common identity at the symbolic level. The black eagle emblem may provoke negative reactions abroad, but it has thus far failed to serve as a positive symbol of national unity in the Federal Republic. The national holidays proclaimed by the federal government are not "holy" days to West Germans – as are religious holidays for many of them – but simply opportunities to engage in the conspicuous mass consumption of leisure time and display of symbols of personal affluence. They take to the roads in their new cars rather than parade with drum and fife, as of old, and ski in the mountains or camp on the beaches rather than listen to patriotic oratory and songs. President Heinrich Lübke was ridiculed when in 1964 he called on young West Germans to sing patriotic tunes, and Chancellor Adenauer was ignored when he appealed for a new sense of German unity focused on the Federal Republic. In 1961 an opinion survey showed that less than a third of a cross-section of West German adults could identify the first line of the official national anthem – the third verse of the old *Deutschland über alles* – and less than

[4] P. G. J. Pulzer, "West Germany and the Three Party System," *Political Quarterly* XV (1962), 681–705.

half professed to be moved by the sight of the official flag bearing the black, red, and golden colors of the medieval German empire.

An emotional vacuum seems to have taken the place of the affective, integrative ties which previously had linked national community with political culture in Germany. Some West German observers attribute this to the abuse of national sentiments and symbols in the past. Thus, the theologian Helmuth Thielcke has spoken of "paralyzing complexes" that have led West Germans neither to seek nor to find a new sense of community because they have not as yet come to terms with latently divisive historical memories. Such symbols as the word "fatherland" or the tune of the old national anthem, he holds, invoke unpleasant memories at home and abroad from which West Germans have deliberately sought to dissociate themselves. Others assert that the fragmentation of their former national community prevents West Germans from finding a new common identity in the Federal Republic. The existence of two rival regimes – each alleged by its leaders to represent the "real" Germany – has deprived the concept of nationhood of any meaning for West Germans, according to the young writer Hans Magnus Enzensberger. "Phantom-like we live in two parts of a whole which does not exist," he maintains, and although his passport might identify him as a "German," for him the Federal Republic was not "Germany." One of the paternalistic Prussian kings is said to have sought to beat his subjects into loving him; but, according to Enzensberger, "love cannot be commanded . . . and identity determined administratively" by the actions of authoritative decisionmakers in either the Federal Republic or the (East) German Democratic Republic.[5]

Ostensibly it is above all the hope and desire for reunification which militate against the development of a sense of community in the Federal Republic. The latter is portrayed as the provisional nucleus of a free and democratic Germany in official government statements; ultimately the political commu-

[5] See Hans Magnus Enzensberger, "Gespenstisch aber wirklich: Eine Frage der deutschen Nätionalität," *Die Zeit*, November 1, 1963, p. 8. See also "Broken Symbols," *Time* (November 1, 1963), p. 34.

nity is supposed to incorporate "all of Germany." *"Das ganze Deutschland muss es sein"* as the slogan of the semiofficial Association for an Indivisible Germany puts it. Every major West German political leader is a member of this association and stands pledged to do his utmost to bring about early reunification. In foreign affairs, friends are distinguished from foes by the degree of their symbolic reassurance on this issue. Foreign leaders who fail to profess periodically their firm commitment to the restoration of German unity are suspect and when they visit the Federal Republic are expected to demand reunification before they depart. Opinion polls suggest that this goal has become of increasing importance for West Germans and that domestic economic issues, the preservation of peace, the furtherance of European unity, and other issues seem of far smaller significance in comparison (see Table IV.2).

TABLE IV.2 *The Most Important Question Demanding the Attention of the West German People (Opinion Survey Data in Rounded-off Percentages)*

	October 1951	*Average 1951–57*	*Average 1959–64*	*January 1965*
Reunification	18	32	34	47
Domestic economy and welfare	45	27	23	33
Preservation of peace and security	29	26	21	13
European unity	—	1	4	3
Other issues	17	21	26	7
D.K., N.A.	5	6	7	8
Total [a]	114	113	113	111

[a] Totals exceed 100 per cent because multiple responses were possible. Absolute numbers not available.

Source: Institut für Demoskopie, *Informationen,* June 1965.

However, while the satisfaction of other wants – such as economic improvement and adequate housing – has apparently helped to move reunification to the top of the goals professed by most West Germans, such quantitative figures do not seem to tell the whole story. Above all, they fail to reveal the low intensity of reunification sentiments and the extent to which they appear to reflect a pious wish rather than a surpassing desire. When asked in December, 1964 what was their greatest wish for the year 1965, only 3 per cent of a cross-section of West German adults mentioned a reunited Germany. Other desires, such as good health (55 per cent), peace and freedom (26 per cent), personal wealth and welfare (6 per cent), and occupational success (5 per cent) were felt to be more important. Perceived Communist threats against the safety of Berlin – such as the building of the Wall in August, 1961 – may temporarily reveal some residues of national sentiments associated with the symbol of the former capital, but these reactions appear to be sporadic rather than durable, anti-Communist rather than patriotic, and restricted to Berlin rather than extending to the entire old Reich. Especially among native West Germans and, particularly in southern Germany, on closer inspection mass opinion reveals a rather cold enthusiasm for reunification.

The same sober and nonemotional, evaluative outlook which seems to characterize attitudes toward the Federal Republic appears to govern present West German views toward reunification. Studies of both elite and mass opinion reflect increasing disbelief that a reunited national community is feasible. In 1955, 26 per cent of the respondents in an opinion survey declared chances for reunification were good or even excellent, 18 per cent thought they were bad, and 3 per cent that they were very bad; three years later no one thought such chances were excellent, only 7 per cent thought them good, while the proportion of pessimists had grown to more than two-thirds of the respondents. In December, 1957, 47 per cent of a representative cross-section of West German adults claimed to have no idea when Germany would be reunified, by February, 1959 this figure had increased to 61 per cent. A 1964 survey of elite opinion found that only one out of ten West German leaders insisted that Germany would be reunified in the next twenty-five years, whereas four out of ten expressed serious doubts, and three out of ten considered it highly unlikely or entirely out of the question. Younger leaders proved to be no more optimistic on this point than older ones, and a sober evaluation of world conditions seemed to persuade most that the status quo was likely to persist.

Neither responsible West German leaders nor the average "man in the street" appears willing to endanger personal security or political stability for the sake of German unity. Thus, although 80 per cent of the respondents in a 1960 poll said that "everything" should be done to promote reunification, only a third were prepared to do all they could do personally to bring it about and to accept the risks which might be involved. Above all, there appears to be no strong desire to risk the loss of economic prosperity and American military protection against a Soviet attack by pushing for German unity. Given the choice of a reunified neutral Germany or a divided Germany with its western portions included in NATO, five out of ten West German leaders in a 1961 survey chose the latter alternative and only three out of ten the former. In a 1964 mass opinion poll 44 per cent rejected the suggestion that to facilitate reunification the Federal Republic should leave NATO if the Democratic Republic quit the Warsaw Pact, only 23 per cent approved of it. Both instances reflected the waning attraction of a neutral united Germany, the only form of reunification which seems even remotely feasible to most West Germans.

The weakening of sentiments of national community encompassing Germans living in the Communist German Democratic Republic has apparently been furthered by a growing estrangement between East and West Germans. Those living beyond the Berlin wall and the barbed wire barriers dividing the old Reich seem increasingly remote in their attitudes and behavior to West Germans. Revealingly, a group of journalists who inspected the Democratic Republic in 1963 entitled the report on their visit *Journey to a Distant Land.* They found there a Germany which bore little resemblance to the Federal Republic, not only in its form of government but also in prevailing social norms and behavior. The novelist Uwe Johnson, himself a refugee from the Democratic Republic, has written a series of novels on the theme that although Germans on either side may speak the same language, they no longer understand each other. Since their respective worlds seem more and more different, they talk *about* each other and *at* each other, but less and less *with* each other. Apart from aged visitors from the Democratic Republic – who seem to find the Federal Republic a "distant" land – the ordinary West German sees little or nothing of his supposed "brothers" living across the Elbe. Officialdom on both sides has tended to discourage informal contacts, particularly between young people who have no direct memories of a single national community. The dying out of the older groups, with memories of a united Germany and of life in its eastern portions, and the virtual end of migration in either direction, has accelerated the breakdown of personal ties. Thus, whereas in 1954, 44 per cent of the Germans in the Federal Republic still claimed to have friends and relatives in the Democratic Republic, by 1962 only 27 per cent did. In 1954, 39 per cent of West Germans reported sending letters to East Germans; by 1964 this had dropped to 25 per cent.

The strong anti-Communist sentiments which today provide the principal emotional bond among West Germans appear at the same time to have produced negative, even hostile, sentiments toward Germans in the Communist-controlled state across the Elbe. Not only formal encounters between governmental officials of the two states but athletic contests between West and East German teams are seen as political confrontations between Communists and anti-Communists. A recent study by a psychologist at the University of Hamburg revealed that the vast majority of a cross-section of the citizens of the Federal Republic identified "good Germans" with West Germans and "bad Germans" with East Germans. Whereas West Germans were credited with such positive attributes as "peaceful," East Germans were collectively associated with negative attributes, such as "aggressive." Significantly, West German respondents who had close relatives in East Germany had the same unfriendly image of East Germans as those who did not.[6]

In sum, it appears that today neither the Federal Republic

[6] See David Binder, "West Germans see themselves as 'good,' Easterners as 'bad,'" *The New York Times*, February 5, 1967, and Kai Hermann, "Die Deutschen in Gänsefüsschen: Wie sicht der Bundesbürger den Bruder in der DDR?" *Die Zeit*, January 17, 1967.

nor the severed remnants of the old Reich represents a strong focus for mass sentiments of political community and national identity. This has led some observers, especially in the United States, to conclude that West Germans have been transferring their loyalties to larger collectivities, such as a European or a North Atlantic community. They see a society of sober and materialistic West Germans embracing liberal and cosmopolitan *Weltbürgertum* orientations in place of the narrower loyalties focused on the *Nationalstaat*. But the absence of one type of loyalty does not necessarily allow us to infer the presence of another. Rather vaguely perceived, a European and even North Atlantic superstate seem attractive to most West Germans and get massive support in both elite and mass opinion surveys. However, there is little evidence that such evaluative endorsements of supranational communities and institutions also carry emotional support. On the contrary, in recent years enthusiasm for European unity seems to have waned under the corrosive effect of disputes within the European Common Market and NATO.

It may be that some day the lack of emotional identification with the Federal Republic will prove to have facilitated its incorporation in a larger political community, whether this be a united Germany or a united Europe. The maintenance of the present regime and the legitimization of its norms, however, demand more than evaluative acceptance on the part of the citizens of the Federal Republic. A supportive political culture must also encompass positive emotional commitments and sentiments of collective national identity that go beyond parochial loyalty to subcultures, such as the family, but stop short of disintegrative attachments to supranational ideologies promoting divisive "higher loyalties." As of now, this task of communal integration has not yet been accomplished in the Federal Republic.

PERCEPTIONS OF THE STATE

The formal, legal norms concerning the relationship between society and polity in the Federal Republic as well as popular perceptions of the role of the state, its government, and its citizens reflect the transitional character of the German political culture. The effect of the social and economic changes and of the new learning experiences of the last two decades is clearly evident in political orientation, as is the survival of older perspectives rooted in the cultural patterns of the past. The stability of the present political system has to a very large extent been due to its ability to reconcile new and old orientations in the performance of its functions.

The constitutional norms, despite the specificity of the Basic Law, present West Germans with ambiguities and contradictions concerning the proper relationship between state, political authority, and citizens. Though a prime example of the traditional German propensity for formalizing political relationships through legal engineering, the constitution bears the marks of differences and compromises among its framers regarding the roles to be played in the system. It includes liberal democratic principles largely alien to German political cultures of the past, which call for extensive individual freedom and initiative and for competition and compromise between political actors in a pluralist society. In this respect, the state is but an arena for legitimate conflict between competing elites and interest groups, none of which are strong enough to exercise absolute control over the conversion of political input demands into authoritative public policy outputs. At the same time, the Basic Law incorporates elements of the traditional German view of the state as a supreme arbiter of conflicting interests and an authoritative guardian of the needs of the collectivity. In this respect it lifts the state and its interests above its citizens and their individual values and associates the new political system with the tradition of popular compliance to the commands of public authorities acting in the name of the state.

In fact, politics in Western Germany involve extensive competition and intensive bargaining between diverse elites and interest groups, and authoritative policy outputs reflect the negotiations and compromise between such groups. In this sense the state sets the boundaries of the political system and for most West German adults under forty it no longer represents anything else. A 1959 poll asked whether an individual owed his first duty to the state or himself; for 41 per cent of the respondents – including 57 per cent of the men between 51 and 60 who were questioned – duty to the state came ahead of personal welfare, for 45 per cent – particularly young adults under forty – it did not. And yet it seems quite clear from other studies and polls that the view that the state is more than its parts and constitutes a supreme, impartial force in maintaining societal stability and harmony is still a strong element in the contemporary political culture.

German political leaders may act as representatives of heterogeneous interests, but they will insist that the citizen's first duty is toward the state. Many, if not most Germans belong to interest associations, but public opinion surveys reflect widespread antagonism toward a *Verbändestaat,* a state dominated by interest groups. In elections close to 90 per cent of the voters in effect endorse the *"Parteienstaat,"* a state controlled by political parties, but large numbers of them oppose it in opinion surveys. Young Germans may be preoccupied with the pursuit of their private interests and maintain that these take precedence over those of the state, but like their elders they look to the state to assure them their proper share in the distribution of goods and values. A "free enterprise" economy is widely given credit for the present prosperity, but this prevents neither German businessmen from demanding that the state protect them against "unfair" competition nor trade union and employer organizations from calling upon it to guarantee wages and prices.

Such ambiguities exist in other political cultures, including that of the United States, but to comprehend many of the apparent contradictions in West German political attitudes it is essential to recognize the persistence of the old orientations relating to the state and its functions. Elite as well as mass opinion studies indicate that West Germans have not yet become accustomed to the politics of pluralism and that the maintenance of political stability is largely viewed as a function of state control rather than of voluntary group compromise. Not only is there a widespread inclination to look upon political bargaining as a nasty and sordid business demeaning to the state, but sustained political controversy is viewed as unnecessary because the impartial state should regulate and arbitrate. In view of legal anarchy and arbitrariness experienced under the Nazi regime, a well ordered *Rechtsstaat* – a state under law – seems all the more desirable to those who remember them. Such orientations give rise to a desire for highly formalized rules for regulating political relations – above all those between state and citizen – and to efforts to provide definitive, explicit, and substantive *solutions* to outstanding problems rather than settle for more informal, tentative, and ambiguous *arrangements* between competing interests.[7]

What the state "does" is more or less vaguely perceived by most West Germans not as an expression of their will, but as the action of a formalized legal abstraction that seems to them something above the political system and apart from society. They neither love nor hate it but see it rather as something like a giant corporation with its managers (government), board of directors (parliament), and administrative staff (civil service). The ordinary citizen appears in this view as a common stockholder who may vote for the board of directors, who expects efficient services, and who gets whatever share of the profits board and management deem his due; the elites appear to be preferred stockholders who have disproportionately greater influence and, therefore, receive a larger share of corporate profits and services. The input flow of demands into the polity and the output flow of the authoritative distribution of values is accordingly perceived as the state distributing goods and services for payments rendered – such as taxes and other citizenship duties – with some citizens getting more and some paying more than others.

Though such perspectives retain elements of the earlier concept of the state as a supreme governor, guardian, and provider, they also reflect the new pragmatic outlook which we noted in present German society. The contemporary view of a state under law implies a contractual relationship between state and citizens based on reciprocal obligations. West Germans accept the formal principle of the supremacy of public over private interests but in return they expect the state to

[7] On this point see Ralf Dahrendorf, "The Social Structure of German Politics," *British Journal of Sociology,* XIV, no. 3 (1966), 197–211.

provide for domestic harmony and stability, for continuing economic prosperity and extensive social security, and, above all, for their physical security against external threats. Upheld by contemporary jurisprudence and administrative practices as an institution above individual interests and group conflicts, the state is generally expected to provide for the society's welfare, to enforce conformity with dominant social norms, and to safeguard primary social units such as the family. The manner in which this is done and the structures involved seem far less important to most citizens of the Federal Republic than having the functions attributed to the state performed satisfactorily.

PERCEPTIONS OF POLITICAL AUTHORITY

The prevailing image of the relationship between state and society influences popular perceptions of political roles in the polity and more particularly attitudes toward the legitimate relationship between public authorities and the citizens. These perceptions and attitudes strikingly demonstrate the extent of the prevailing lack of congruence between the new social and constitutional norms on the one hand and popular political orientations on the other. West Germans may believe that they live in an achievement oriented society in which everyone has an opportunity to advance his social and economic status, and the Basic Law may proclaim that the present regime rests on the equality and political participation of all citizens, but both elite and mass opinion reflect a preponderant conviction that political relationships in the Federal Republic are rigidly structured and sharply divide the rulers from the ruled.

The social and economic changes of the last two decades and civic education efforts, intended to give legitimacy to a democratic regime, seem to have had little effect on the accepted notion that the impotent multitude is governed by a few men at the top. Thus far democratic political norms appear to have been embraced more in form than in fact, and most of the citizens of the Federal Republic think of themselves as passive objects of a political system controlled by forces beyond their influence.

West Germans complain of too many bureaucrats and too

much bureaucracy in the Federal Republic, and they grumble about governmental regulations which seem to restrict the full enjoyment of their new affluence and personal freedom. Obvious governmental violations of individual liberties and arbitrary interference in spheres which are believed to be outside the jurisdiction of the state may provoke resentment against particular officials on the part of individuals and groups who feel themselves affected.

But most citizens of the Federal Republic respect and trust the governmental executive elite, the judiciary, and the administrative bureaucracy which they identify with formal and legitimate political authority in their state more than they do each other or those who claim to be their spokesmen in parties, interest associations, and legislative bodies. According to the prevailing view the management of the state is legitimately vested in the hands of a small group of formal decisionmakers who are qualified to make and enforce public policy. Just as specialists in the management of huge industrial enterprises are seen as authoritative leaders in their domain and members of the academic and religious elites in theirs, so these assumed experts in government are perceived by themselves and by most of the public as holding positions which entitle them to direct the affairs of the state without interference from "outsiders." But this does not mean that there is unqualified trust in their authority or skills. West Germans expect their public officials to live up to very exacting standards of performance and to see to it that the state fulfills the regulative functions which they assign to it.

Though the contemporary German political system reflects the politics of bargaining and compromise between manifold mass organizations and pluralist elites, most citizens of the Federal Republic do not yet see it that way. They perceive the proper function of the system primarily as authoritative outputs from a small governmental elite acting on behalf of the state rather than as the satisfaction of competing demands for public policy arising from political inputs from society into the polity.

Politics, in this view, appears to be, above all, formal management and administration, rather than the conversion of many interests into feasible compromise solutions by the elected representatives of the people. This focus carries with it sharp qualitative distinctions between the stereotyped roles of "the statesman" and "the politician" and between those of the functionary of the state and the functionary of parties and interest groups. The roles of the statesman and government administrator are endowed with high prestige by virtue of their association with the efficient management of the state; the roles of the party politician and "pressure group" representative, on the other hand, are widely identified with behavior that at best does little to advance one's claims upon the state and at worst is a threat to the satisfaction of such demands. It seems that Germans find the traditional images of the statesman and public servant, who are expected to be "above" politics, a satisfying answer to the clash of competing interests – which is, in fact, a characteristic of politics in their pluralist society – but these images conflict with the prevalent desire for stability and harmony in the state.

These qualitative and dichotomous distinctions between the idealized roles of the managers and administrators of the state and the less esteemed roles of special interest spokesmen were illustrated by a 1956 poll in which respondents in eight countries were asked which group of leaders was "doing the most" for their country. In the Federal Republic, 36 per cent singled out "the statesmen," a group which enjoyed a proportionately (slightly) higher prestige only in Mexico and a lower prestige in Britain, Italy, Sweden, Denmark, the Netherlands, and Japan.[8]

Other poll data reflect a sharp evaluative distinction in popular attitudes between parliamentarians and civil servants. West Germans are prone to be rather cynical about their elected lawmakers and to doubt whether they play the roles assigned to them by the constitution, as "representatives of the whole people, not bound by orders and instructions and subject only to their own conscience." Though respect for the

[8] Trade union leaders were named by only 12 per cent of the West Germans questioned as doing the most for the country, 20 per cent said they did the least; 9 per cent singled out the clergy as doing the most, 14 per cent thought they did the least; 7 per cent mentioned the industrialists, 11 per cent said these did the least.

ability of the democratically elected deputies and belief in their responsiveness to the wishes of their constituents have decidedly grown since the establishment of the Federal Republic, they are still far from enjoying the confidence which Germans place in their appointed public officials as expert, politically neutral, and devoted servants of the state. At both the national and the subnational levels of government, political authority is primarily identified with the executive and judicial organs of the state. Opinion polls indicate that most Germans are rather vague about what their elected legislative representatives do and tend to look upon them either as the tools of special interests or the pliant instruments of governmental leaders.

On the other hand, members of state bureaucracy – including the police – are thought to know their job and to execute it without discrimination. This is particularly the view of those strata of the population closest to these appointed public officials in social background but whose commitment to the present political system as a whole is often quite shallow. Thus, as one moves from the more poorly educated income and status groups to the better educated higher status and income groups – such as professional men, businessmen, and higher administrators in public and private institutions – the belief increases that the civil servant (*Beamte*) can be expected to consider and to provide fair and equal treatment of one's interests.

The German civil servant may still deal rather brusquely with "the little man," and his record under the Nazi regime may not have been as "clean" as some West Germans wish it had been, but his reputation as a dedicated, carefully selected, and strictly law-abiding administrator of the state's interest has in fact increased. There have been a few instances of corruption among high civil servants and some widely publicized criticisms in the press of arbitrary action by public administrators, as well as some charges that the bureaucracy is being subverted by special interest groups. However, whereas in 1950 only 21 per cent of a representative cross-section of citizens of the Federal Republic expressed trust in their civil servants, by 1965, 50 per cent believed that civil servants could neither be influenced nor corrupted, and only 29 per cent expressed explicit doubts on this score. Another study, in 1960, found that 70 per cent of adult West Germans could not imagine a strike by their civil servants, and this included 73 per cent of the government bureaucrats in the sample. On the basis of survey research findings in a 1959 cross-national investigation, Almond and Verba concluded that in the Federal Republic, in contrast to the United States and Britain, the proportion of "administrative competents" who expected fair treatment from their civil servants was much higher than the proportion of "citizen competents" who considered themselves able to *influence* the conduct of public administrators. Most Germans, it appeared, felt that they were able to appeal to regular and orderly formal rules in their dealings with civil servants and policemen and believed that they could expect fair treatment and consideration from officials seen as subject to the same rules.[9]

Most citizens of the Federal Republic – especially women over thirty – feel they have no real influence over public policymaking. But they generally do trust their governmental leaders to provide for their needs and they accept the regime.

A 1964 study of German elite attitudes found that a majority of the 173 opinion leaders, business executives, top administrators, political and interest group leaders interviewed professed to be satisfied with the way in which the state was being run – though few expressed real enthusiasm about the regime. Most did not think that any particular interest group had significantly increased its influence in the state in recent years and most expected the distribution of political authority to continue unchanged. Surveys of mass opinion, like those of elite opinion, reflect some ambiguity toward strong governmental leadership, but reservations tend to focus on the way particular actors wield political power rather than on the principle of strong executive authority.

Learning experiences and at least the formal acceptance of the constitutional norms of democratic leadership and party competition in the state seem to be reflected in various mass opinion surveys. These indicate that about two-thirds of the

[9] Almond and Verba, *op. cit.,* chap. 8.

TABLE IV.3 *Preferred Form of Government (Mass Opinion Data in Rounded-off Percentages)*

	1953	*1955*	*1957*	*1960*	*1962*
Democracy	57	70	69	74	67
Monarchy	11	10	5	5	2
Authoritarian	8	4	2	2	1
Other form, indifferent	1	3	3	1	4
No opinion	23	13	21	18	26

Source: EMNID, *Informationen,* No. 31/1962.

citizens of the Federal Republic explicitly prefer a democratic regime to other forms of government (see Table IV.3), that about an equal proportion believe that it is better to vest political authority in more than one man so as to prevent its abuse, and that about three-fourths think it better to have several parties rather than just one. Pressed to be more specific, in a 1959 survey, a larger proportion agreed than disagreed with the traditional view that a few strong leaders could do more for the country than a lot of "laws and talk."

However, such interpretations of democracy, or total lack of commitment to its formal aspects, seem to characterize the views of people over fifty – particularly women – who constitute a declining proportion of the adult population, rather than those of younger groups. The first group is made up mainly of widows and pensioners who have been least affected by the learning experiences of the last decades and who have fared comparatively poorly in the new era of affluence, whereas the second encompasses those who associate the contemporary democratic form of government with highly satisfying social and economic developments. This appears to be most true for young men. Close to a majority of those between 18 and 30 years of age in 1959 rejected the view that a few strong leaders working together were "better" than a lot of laws and talk, possibly indicating that at least formal commitments to the present system will continue to grow if that system remains associated with the satisfactory performance of its perceived functions.

Not trusting themselves or most other Germans to play active political roles – above all in positions of public authority – citizens of the Federal Republic seem to have confidence only in those who approximate their image of ideal political behavior. Since involvement in politics is considered corrupting for the ordinary citizen he should, in his own opinion and those of many of his leaders, keep out of it. In this view the ideal political activist appears to be either the man who as a statesman can be trusted with power or the one who has no real power. Thus Bismarck and Adenauer are widely esteemed as tough, but skillful and successful statesmen who knew how to manage political authority – in contrast to opponents who did not. Professor Carlo Schmid and Eugen Gerstenmaier, presiding officer of the Bundestag, were judged the most sympathetic of contemporary politicians in a 1965 poll, apparently because they were seen as honest, but politically powerless and, therefore, nonthreatening figures. Men like Hitler and, among contemporary political actors, the aggressive Bavarian Franz Josef Strauss, on the other hand, are perceived negatively by many Germans today, apparently because their image does not fit the ideal role of the political activist and political authority in such hands seems misplaced and dangerous.[10]

In sum, the greater the congruence between the idealization of the roles of public officials and the public performance by the incumbents, the greater seems to be the support which these receive as legitimate wielders of authority. Thus Adenauer's paternalistic rule as chancellor of the Federal Republic and the sometimes rather arbitrary actions of his administrative deputies were endorsed at the polls, from 1949 to 1961, by increasing numbers of German voters because they seemed an efficient exercise of political authority. Toward the end of the Adenauer administration, however, its reputation for effective, authoritative leadership began to decline, since it appeared to many voters to fail to meet its responsibilities to the state.

Just before the 1961 election, when the building of the Berlin Wall suddenly aroused a highly sharpened sense of insecurity among many West Germans, the Adenauer administration seemed uncertain of its course and unable to still the fears of the alarmed public. Public sentiment turned sharply

[10] See the INFRATEST survey reported in *Der Spiegel,* July 14, 1965, pp. 28–29.

against it and, though by the time the election was held four weeks later, Adenauer's party had recovered sufficient support to win a plurality (though a reduced one), this crisis of confidence in his fitness to exercise political authority was the beginning of the end of the chancellor's long rule. A second crisis of confidence in November, 1962, provoked by the partly high-handed, partly inept behavior of his subordinates in attempting to silence *Der Spiegel* (a magazine highly critical of the Adenauer administration), led to Adenauer's retirement a year later. His successor, Ludwig Erhard, was unable to claim the prestige which Adenauer had commanded at the height of his popularity as a statesman. He appeared honest enough to many Germans, but not decisive enough to fill the idealized role of the authoritative leader satisfactorily. Erhard's electoral victory in 1965 seemed due less to popular respect for him as a strong leader than to an even greater lack of confidence in his opponent's ability to play the role of statesman and authority figure.

Since under the present form of government it is the voter who ultimately decides who is to exercise political authority, public officials in the Federal Republic feel it necessary to show that they conform to the popular perceptions. The incumbents of political roles, as well as those who aspire to exercise them, in trying to appear qualified to meet the high standards which West Germans expect of leaders of the state, feel constrained in their freedom of political action. But the need to accommodate and reconcile many conflicting demands from outside the polity – particularly from its international environment – makes it difficult for these leaders to maintain such popular images at all times. This dilemma leads to efforts to conceal government operations from public view, and to the labeling of criticism, as disruptive interference and as injurious to the interests of the state. It also tends to induce governmental leaders and officials to encourage political passivity on the part of the citizenry, to reinforce traditional orientations of respect for legitimate political authority, and to portray themselves as the defenders of the state's interests against the onslaught of various interest groups. Chancellor Erhard, for example, sought to strengthen his position by calling himself a plebiscitary *Volkskanzler,* as the representative of the interests of all Germans valiantly fending off the demands of special interests. Though such endeavors may reduce popular pressure restricting the governmental elite's freedom of action, they also seem to preserve the incongruence between the traditional elements in the political culture and the politics of a modern, pluralist society.

PERCEPTIONS OF THE CITIZEN'S ROLE

The average West German's image of his role in the political system relates directly to his views of the state and political authority. It, too, reflects the mingling of the past orientations of the quiescent citizen with the modern, pragmatic orientations of the passive consumer in the political marketplace. The prevailing emphasis on privatization has carried with it social norms focused on nonpolitical objects and nonpolitical roles, for example in the economy and the family. Thus, in 1959, only 4 per cent of a representative cross-section singled out interest in politics and participation in public affairs as the qualities they most admired in a person. And a 1964 survey of married people found that more than three-fourths of the respondents, especially women, were unwilling to encourage their spouses to participate in public affairs. Although the German, preoccupied with his private problems, may see it as his duty to fulfill the public functions which he identifies with the legitimate role of the citizen, he looks upon these largely as formal obligations that involve him only peripherally in the political process and do not demand more than sporadic participation (see Table IV.4).

German cultural values place a high premium on knowledge and most West Germans assert that they are informed citizens in the realm of political affairs. Almond and Verba's cross-national survey of 1959 found that more Germans claimed to follow political developments more or less closely and considered themselves competent to evaluate political input processes and role performances than did respondents in the four other countries studied: the United States, Britain, Italy, and Mexico. Forty-eight per cent of the Germans claimed to understand political issues either very well (13 per cent) or pretty well (34

TABLE IV.4 *Perception of Obligations of Citizenship, 1959 (Mass Opinion Data in Rounded-off Percentages)*

To do one's job well, raise one's children properly; to be honest, helpful, and have a sense of responsibility in one's conduct	31
To vote	31
To pay taxes	30
To obey the laws; to respect public authorities	23
To love one's country; to be loyal and faithful to it; to speak well of it; to be a good representative of it in foreign lands	21
To defend one's country, if necessary; to serve in the armed forces	12
To participate in public and political affairs, in political discussions; to speak one's mind; to criticize the government, if necessary	4
To endeavor to understand public affairs and keep abreast of political developments	3
Other answers	7
No obligations specified, no response to question	9
Total	171[a]

[a] Total exceeds 100 per cent because multiple responses were possible.
Source: DIVO, *Umfragen* III/IV. 112.

per cent), 16 per cent said their competence varied with the issues, and merely 24 per cent admitted to having only an imperfect understanding and 15 per cent to no understanding of such matters. Though very few said they frequently discussed politics with others, far more claimed to closely follow political developments reported by the mass media, in private, than would admit that they rarely or never did so. In a 1965 survey 72 per cent claimed to be interested in politics and only 28 per cent said they were not.

But a closer analysis of these responses, and the findings of other surveys (such as the 1959 poll reported in Table IV.4), indicate that most Germans in fact do not consider the need to be well informed about public affairs a particularly important responsibility of citizenship. German women, especially, appear to feel that they must profess their conformity with what they take to be the respectable role of the cognitively well-informed and evaluatively competent citizen. But such attitudes evidently represent more a commitment to the form than to the actual exercise of this political role.

Various studies have shown that the average citizen of the Federal Republic is rather poorly informed about political matters which he feels do not involve him directly and that, as long as he considers his immediate interests are taken care of, he is not particularly concerned about more general public issues. In 1965, for example, only a minority of respondents in a survey knew what the Basic Law was – and many of these were extremely vague about its contents – and in 1962 only 38 per cent knew that the Federal Republic was not a member of the United Nations. Numerous other opinion surveys have shown that most West Germans have only the vaguest knowledge of the structures of their political system – especially its representative bodies – and that, in most cases, extensive exposure to political communications does not carry with it a clear comprehension of public affairs. To justify such shortcomings in the performance of their citizen role, many will claim that political problems are really too complex for the average person to understand. But when pressed they will admit that it is not so much that as that "people" don't care about matters that do not seem to matter very much because their own interests are not really involved.

The dichotomy between formal adherence to democratic norms and citizenship roles on the one hand and a sense of effective participation on the other is strikingly revealed by the way in which most West Germans look at the voting franchise which their constitution bestows upon them.

Most citizens of the Federal Republic profess to believe that theirs is a government of, by, and for the people – as the Basic Law provides. Thus, 79 per cent of the respondents in a 1959 opinion survey agreed that "the way people vote is the main thing that decides how things are run in this country" and merely 12 per cent explicitly denied it. Compared to other regimes that provide for representative government and entirely voluntary participation by the voters, the turnout in West German general elections is exceptionally high. Whereas, for example, at best two-thirds of those eligible cast their ballots in American national elections, over the last decade, 87 per cent or more of the qualified Germans have done so. Such a turnout is unprecedented in the history of German elections and, on the face of it, seems to indicate a high sense of involvement in politics and of influence over the composition and policies of the government.

But numerous studies have shown that in fact most Germans

neither believe that their vote matters very much nor that this lack of influence is very important. In the same 1959 survey, 68 per cent of the Germans held that they had no real influence over rulemaking and rulemakers, a belief frequently expressed by the observation that, whether they voted or not, "those on top will do with us as they please anyway." (*Die da oben machen ja doch mit uns was sie wollen.*) Whereas 75 per cent of the Americans and 62 per cent of the British respondents in this survey felt competent to influence their national government, only 38 per cent of the Germans did.

Voting is generally considered a formal citizenship obligation rather than a means of control over the government. Asked why they went to the polls, 45 per cent of the West German respondents in the 1959 survey cited said it was their duty, 32 per cent claimed that it gave them a sense of personal satisfaction, and the rest could give only rather ambivalent explanations or none. The 31 per cent who, in 1959, cited voting as one of the principal obligations of citizenship (see Table IV.4), represented a higher proportion of respondents who did so than in the other four countries where this question was asked. Moreover, as one of the principal investigators in this study remarked, many of the Germans "explicitly stated that their obligation to participate in politics is exhausted by their voting obligation." [11]

Although the rate of voter turnout for federal elections in Germany is even higher than the previous crest in the last years of the Weimar Republic, the motivation of most voters appears to be very different. Whereas then a high degree of dissatisfaction with the prevailing regime enabled the antiregime, extremist parties to mobilize on their behalf voters who had previously not gone to the polls, the increasing turnout since the establishment of the Federal Republic has on the whole served to enhance rather than weaken the combined strength

[11] See Sidney Verba, "The Remaking of Political Culture," in Lucian Pye and Sidney Verba (eds.), *Political Culture and Political Development* (Princeton: Princeton University Press, 1965), p. 148. See also Karl A. Deutsch, *et al.*, *Arms Control and European Unity*, Chap. 9, and Wolfgang Hartenstein and Günther Schubert, *Mitlaufen oder Mitbestimmen: Untersuchungen zum demokratischen Bewusstsein und zur politischen Tradition* (Frankfurt: Europäische Verlagsanstalt, 1961), pp. 36 ff., 49 ff.

of the parties supporting the present regime. Moreover, neither the elites nor the average voter believe that the election outcome really matters very much. The major parties appear to them to have become increasingly alike in the policies they support and political decisionmakers seem in any case to have little choice about what they can do in domestic and foreign affairs. Perhaps 2 per cent of the electorate may cast invalid ballots as a form of protest vote, but even these voters manifest their conformity with the socially approved role of the citizen in this manner rather than stay away from the polls entirely.[12] The pressure to conform is rather great – particularly in smaller communities – whereas the cost is not. Since elections always fall on Sundays there is no loss of income, and since legal residence and age automatically entitle every citizen to vote, there is no need to register, pay a poll tax, or take a qualifying test.[13]

In short, an electorate which believes that voting has no real influence on policy outcomes is extensively but not intensively involved in elections. Dissatisfaction with some political leaders may produce some shifts among parties at election time; but such shifts reflect comparatively mild protest votes directed against particular actors rather than against the regime and the operation of the political system. In general, the attitudes of the voters in West Germany reflect a sense of sporadic, rather than constant, involvement in the political input process and of political passivity rather than effective influence.

The image of the citizen's role prevailing among present-day West Germans reflects the highly formalized perceptions of political relations and objects. For the mass of relatively poorly educated Germans it incorporates a low sense of voluntary commitment to political controversy and collective action on the input side, but a high sense of involuntary commitment to the formal rules derived from the political outputs of gov-

[12] See Rodney P. Stiefbold, "The Significance of Void Ballots in West German Elections," *American Political Science Review,* LIX (June, 1965), 404 ff.

[13] Only in the cases of criminals convicted of major offenses may the privilege be withdrawn by court action.

ernmental authorities. The average citizen of the Federal Republic feels he "ought" to be interested in and to know what his governors are doing because this is a mark of respectability, but that he "must" vote and obey the laws because this "duty" is formally required of him. The "little man's" distrust of his fellow citizens and his dislike of pressure groups combine with a sense of futility about his ability to influence the course of political events to make him shun active participation in collective political action. When he sees his interests conflicting with those of other political actors he tends either to confine himself to passive grumbling or to have recourse to formal legal appeals to established authorities. Thus, only 38 per cent of Germans in the 1959 survey made by Almond and Verba said they could personally do something about a national law they believed to be unjust or harmful, compared to 75 per cent of the American and 62 per cent of the British respondents. A larger proportion, 62 per cent, felt they could do something about a local regulation of this sort compared to 77 per cent in the United States and 78 per cent in Britain. But of those Germans who claimed they could do something, 41 per cent opted for individual action through established channels of communication – such as taking their complaints to administrative officials – rather than joint action with their fellow citizens. To this group, personal access to political decisionmakers evidently represented a better way to get action than a more indirect approach through some formal or informal citizen organization. In any case, whether local or national regulations were involved, to most of the respondents it seemed unlikely that any action on their part would really be effective, and few thought they were likely to become politically active in such a case.

Such orientations do not apply equally to all West German adults today. A low sense of political efficacy and involvement prevails particularly among those who were born before 1930, among women, among residents of nonurban areas, and among the mass of West Germans who had only a basic eight-year education. At present, no more than about 10 per cent can be considered firmly committed supporters of the regime who also feel politically involved and influential as participants in its input structures. This 10 per cent is usually found among better-educated males in urban areas who were born between 1930 and 1940 and thus obtained most of their citizenship education in the period immediately following the fall of the Nazi regime. This might suggest that increased urbanization, better education, and the gradual dying off of the older generation will establish broader and more profound public support for the prevailing system, and, indeed, this may be true. However, studies of the generation of incoming citizens, those born after 1940, provide no such assurances.

Sociologists and political scientists in the Federal Republic have devoted considerable attention to the political orientation of university students and of the more poorly educated West German representatives of the incoming generation. Their findings indicate that the formal rights and duties of citizenship under a democratic regime are generally accepted and outright alienation from the system is relatively rare among the generation most intensively exposed to postwar political learning processes. But although this generation acknowledges the obligation to serve in the armed forces more so than does the older generation, it is not distinguished by its participation in the political input processes nor by its more than formal acceptance of democratic norms and structures. A large majority professes no deep loyalty for the political community or regime, and close to half are either uncertain whether an authoritarian form of government might be better, or actually prefer it. Most are totally uninterested in political issues and quite willing to let others tell them what is required of them as citizens. About a third are "enlightened subjects," who feel it their duty to take some interest in politics but lack a sense of personal involvement. No more than a fifth appear to feel deeply involved, and of these somewhat more than half firmly identify with the present regime and somewhat less than half are more or less opposed to it.

Generally, feelings of involvement in politics appear to increase with the educational level of young Germans. Though most university students remain quite apathetic and indifferent about public affairs, protest movements similar to the "New Left" in the United States have of late attracted the support of a more active, if small, minority. But whereas for the young supporters of the contemporary political system involvement implies the responsibility of participating actively in the maintenance and strengthening of its structures, among the alienated a sense of involvement is coupled with bitter contempt and cynicism. Regime-supporting political associations draw their recruits from the former group for positions of eventual leadership at the middle and top levels. The latter group remains for the present largely unorganized and politically inactive, but in the view of a number of astute observers it may represent a reservoir of potential support for radical anti-democratic movements in Germany.[14]

Thus, most of the younger and older adult citizens of the German Federal Republic consider it neither possible nor really necessary to play the roles of active participants in the making of public policy. The average West German is content to be a *Staatsbürger* — by fulfilling the formal obligations of citizenship he can concentrate his emotions and energies in nonpolitical spheres, particularly his job and his family. He is motivated to take an interest in political issues only when they appear clearly pertinent to his own interests and those of his family. As long as these interests seem to be adequately taken care of, he is satisfied with a passive role which allows him to remain aloof from active involvement in political affairs and conflicts.

The traditional German dictum that the citizen's principal duty is to be a quiescent subject (*Ruhe ist die erste Bürgerpflicht*) still seems to prevail in the Federal Republic, though in a version rather different from those of the past. In an

[14] The above analysis is based on extensive survey research data, including a secondary analysis of some of the materials collected for Almond and Verba, *op. cit.* A brief report on contemporary attitudes among young Germans may be found in Walter Jaide, "Not Interested in Politics," in Walter Stahl (ed.), *The Politics of Postwar Germany* (New York: Praeger, 1963), pp. 361–376. Whereas the study of Helmut Schelsky, *Die skeptische Generation* (Düsseldorf: Diederichs Verlag, 1957) is already rather dated, the interested reader familiar with German will find more pertinent and recent data reported in Jürgen Habermas, *et al.*, *Student und Politik* (Neuwied: Luchterhand Verlag, 1961), and Walter Jaide, *Das Verhältnis der Jugend zur Politik: Empirische Untersuchungen zur politischen Anteilnahme und Meinungsbildung junger Menschen der Geburtsjahrgänge 1940–1946* (Neuwied: Luchterhand Verlag, 1964).

affluent society in which middle-class norms are dominant, the preservation of domestic tranquility is highly valued and political symbols of quiescence carry particular weight. Efforts to articulate political demands — or, for that matter, any demands — through other than established, formal channels, tend to be looked upon as illegitimate by elites and masses alike. Political life in the Federal Republic has not been troubled by continuous riots, and mass demonstrations organized by interest groups have been rare. Sporadic student demonstrations for better educational facilities or against "antidemocratic" trends in German politics have been either ignored or strongly condemned by most of the public. The most telling criticism which political leaders have directed against dissenters has been the charge that disagreement threatens to disrupt the necessary harmony of the state.

This prevailing desire for stability and political conformity and the general passivity of the citizenry in an affluent society has had two noteworthy effects on the operation of the political system. First, the participant roles in public policy-making have been largely left to the comparatively few leading actors identified with various elites, such as party leaders, government officials, interest group spokesmen, and religious and mass media opinion leaders. Second, the political elite's task in making and enforcing authoritative rules has remained relatively unencumbered by mass pressures for the satisfaction of conflicting demands. There has been less need to respond to public sentiment than under the Weimar Republic, for instance, and less need to resort to the actual application rather than the threat of authoritative sanctions against dissident political elements.[15]

THE CULTURAL MIX

A new mix in the political culture appears to be evolving in Germany from the interaction of recent learning experiences with strongly established orientations. Memories linked to

[15] The extent of prevailing conservatism and political disengagement among the public has led observers of German politics to believe that the outlawing of the Communist Party was a superfluous concession to legal niceties, since the Party's political influence was, in any case, insignificant.

earlier forms of the political culture sometimes reinforce, sometimes weaken, the effect of new socio-economic and political developments on the formation of attitude patterns. Although cleavages between political subcultures have enormously diminished in recent years, an integrated national political culture has not emerged, and traditional loyalties associated with family and religion appear to be stronger than loyalty to the new regime and political community. In short, the attitudes which have thus far emerged from a century of sharp political discontinuities and repeated shifts in dominant political norms contain too many ambiguities to allow us to speak with certainty about the stability of popular orientation.

The prevailing climate of political opinion in the Federal Republic indicates that the new political system is based more on a permissive than a supportive mass consensus.[16] This suggests that the system's roots in the political culture are still fragile and their future growth uncertain. Mass and elite opinion reveal neither a very high degree of stability that can block the development of new attitudes nor an especially low degree of susceptibility to sudden changes in the political environment. While the manifest conservative climate of German opinion might suggest strong resistance to attitude changes in response to such developments, the extent of the transformation of political orientations over the last two decades also indicates a considerable adaptive capacity. A moderate degree of fluidity appears to characterize West German political opinions, allowing for comparatively easy and smooth attitudinal adjustments to changes in the political system imposed by developments within as well as without West German society.

At the most conspicuous level of political opinion it seems that we are witnessing an adjustment to new environmental conditions that reflects the growing influence on political perspectives of new social norms and role perceptions resulting from the accelerated modernization of Western Germany since

[16] For the functional distinction between a supportive and a permissive consensus see V. O. Key, *Public Opinion and American Democracy* (New York: Knopf, 1962), pp. 28–29.

1945. In place of the exclusive ideological commitments and the identifications with national or subnational collectivities of the past, political orientations today focus on the satisfaction of private goals. Elements of the prosaic and quiescent, passive view of politics inherited from the past appear to have been absorbed into a new pragmatic empiricism to produce popular attitudes that show neither strong attachment for nor strong opposition to the contemporary political system. Compared to the destabilizing political orientations which rocked the Weimar Republic and still plague many other countries today, harmony seems to typify German political attitudes. There are no deep cleavages between generations, subcultures, and various social groupings to interfere with the development of a popular consensus to support the system. Contemporary German political opinion seems bland, political controversy pedestrian, and the comparatively few actors continuously involved in politics on the whole appear to find it relatively easy to achieve agreement on rather mundane policy differences.

On the whole, opinion surveys and election results have shown very little fluctuation over the last decade in West German political opinion. Short-term and superficial fluctuations have invariably been succeeded by very rapid returns to established patterns of generalized political orientations, and long-term changes in attitude have been extremely moderate and gradual.

Such stable orientations seem to be due to a number of causes. First, Germans have been satisfied with the performance of their economic system. Second, they have been content with the performance of the political system. It seems to most that both systems have functioned well in providing for the satisfaction of dominant social values, particularly when compared to past experiences and developments in other countries.

Positive evaluations of the economic and political systems' performance relate to a third source of opinion stability: an underlying mood of insecurity in a world seen by many Germans as fraught with potential dangers. West Germans want continued smooth sailing for a ship of state traveling on seas which experience has taught them can suddenly turn into raging waters. The threat of an economic crisis or of another war lurks in the back of their minds, though such fears are not often explicitly articulated or even consciously recognized.

Finally, opinion stability seems to be the product of a sustained conservative mood following a catastrophic experience with radical political romanticism. It is the disillusioned morning-after feeling of a people burned by repressed, but not forgotten, experiences that all but destroyed them. Thus, to the distress of a small minority longing for a livelier political climate and greater mass participation, an intense popular desire for stability, harmony, and privacy typifies the prevalent opinion in the Federal Republic.

The new mix in the political culture includes both traditional and modern norms and role perceptions. The former are reflected in the great importance attached to the family's sanctity and welfare, to male dominance in politics, and, to a lesser extent, to the preservation of traditional religious and educational structures. These play an important part in determining political attitudes and involvement by the average citizen and certain elite groups, such as leading clergymen and educators. Traditional political orientations significantly influence prevalent perceptions of the political system's regulative functions. But the more pragmatically instrumental and functionally specific norms of an achievement oriented, pluralist, mass consumption society are reflected in modern orientations that focus on the distributive capabilities of the political system, rather than on the search for a collective national identity or feelings of secondary group solidarity. Feelings of attachment to exclusive and contending secondary subcultures (and their emotion evoking symbols) have waned, but a sense of deep loyalty to a particular political community and/or form of government has not taken their place. However, the formal legitimation of the constitutional norms identified with the present regime and its structures and roles has gained acceptance, boosted by affluence and by the rapid replacement of ascriptive criteria by achievement criteria for evaluating the eligibility and performance of the incumbents of political and other positions in German society.

In short, it seems that a broad, diffuse, and stable mass and elite consensus supports present political structures and practices in the Federal Republic. The political system and its role assignments are evaluated positively by instrumental standards based on efficient output performance, particularly in matters relating to economic welfare and external security. This legitimizing consensus is reinforced by efforts to conform to roles identified with the norms of the prevailing political system. Organized interest groups and public administrators vie with each other in advertising their skills in satisfying the demands of their clienteles. Political leaders present themselves as stabilizing agents in converting interest inputs into authoritative public policy output. The major political parties compete for the voters' favors by promising all things to all men, but at the same time appeal to the prevailing mood of public conservatism with such symbolic slogans of reassurance as "no experiments" and "let's play it safe." Such activities reflect and reinforce prevalent orientations that pragmatically consider the political system analogous to the economic system: services must be provided for payments rendered, and contractual obligations between active and passive actors in the system must be honored at all cost.

The present democratic form of government has thus become identified primarily with the pursuit of self-interest, subject to certain formal legal restrictions and obligations. To some observers this seems a rather precarious foundation for future political stability. What disturbs them is the great stress which most West Germans place on harmony and efficient performance in the operation of the political system and the apparent lack of a deep emotional commitment to its support. These observers fear that excessively high expectations combined with low system affect might very well result in seriously destabilizing political repercussions should a major economic or foreign policy crisis suddenly greatly increase the input load of demands on the system. In the view of leading participants in the present regime the supportive psychological resources which could be mobilized in such an event may well be inadequate to guarantee the survival of a democratic form of government.

A 1964 study of West German elite opinion indicated widespread uncertainty about the staying power of the present system should less favorable environmental conditions put its popular acceptance to the test. A majority of a cross-section of the most prominent leaders of the Federal Republic seemed far from confident of the latent support potential in the political culture and uncertain whether the contemporary system could survive a crisis without major changes in its structures. Most of those who were interviewed either professed not to know what might happen if West Germans should suddenly be faced with the threat of economic deprivation or war, or held that such threats would arouse intense popular opposition to the present regime and its representatives. Popular loyalty to the Federal Republic, as presently constituted, seemed as yet only skin deep to many of its staunchest supporters, whereas sentiments incongruent with the contemporary political system seemed still solidly entrenched in the political culture.

These aspects of the political culture which we re-examined in the preceding sections give credence to such appraisals. They suggest that neither positive system affect nor tolerance for less satisfactory system outputs are as yet high enough to give assurances of continued stability. Most West Germans are presently willing to accept the distribution of roles between rulers and ruled which they identify with the contemporary regime, but they tend to see themselves primarily in the roles of passive consumers of output flows, rather than active participants in the production of input demands. They are, on the whole, content to have "those on top" see to it that they get what they want, but are less concerned with the how means of getting it. A sense of formal rather than active commitment to the present form of government appears to be accompanied by an inclination to withhold affective loyalties and to suspend really firm evaluative support of the system. Influential as well as noninfluential West German political opinion reflects a sense of caution regarding the durability of a regime which has as yet not been solidly institutionalized in the political culture. Memories of the fate of earlier forms of government and of the consequences of past political commitments seem to play an important part in this reluctance to become too closely identified with the present regime.

The mix in the political culture reflects the ambivalent values and latent tensions observed in West German society as a whole. Though their journey from a traditional to a modern culture has already taken a century or more, West Germans have yet to come to terms with the world into which industrialization and international developments have thrust them. In that sense we are dealing here with a transitional political culture in which long established orientations toward state, authority, and citizenship are confronted by political conditions and norms very different from those which formed such political orientations in the past.

The ambivalence and paradoxes in contemporary West German political attitudes appear to be not so much the product of deliberate equivocation as the reflection of unresolved contradictions and tensions in a changing political culture. The wish to avoid political involvement and evade the role of the participating citizen, and the propensity to saddle the state and public authorities with responsibility for the collective welfare, seem to point to an attempt to escape the uncertainties and complexities of a political reality which appears incomprehensible and even frightening to many West Germans. This is the political aspect of the ambivalent social value patterns — the mutual distrust, the desire for privatization, the self-centered materialistic callousness — examined in our discussion on the social setting of German politics. Outwardly self-assured and brash, West Germans are at bottom a frightened and anxious people seeking to escape from forces which they consider beyond their control, one of their journalists tells us. Their egocentricity, he maintains, constitutes an attempt to shield themselves from the disturbing impression that their personal security is not really assured and that they are in fact living at the brink of a volcano that can erupt at any time.[17]

[17] "The defense is put up to hide an excess of anxiety, a sense of insecurity and an awareness of the dubious quality of all existence. One withdraws into oneself like a snail. . . . It is the result of an overconsumption of disturbing experiences. We are dealing with the boisterous whistle of the frightened boy walking through the woods in the black and ominous night pretending courage, with dancing at the rim of a volcano, with the attitude 'after us the deluge,' with petrification as a reaction to fear — not well-being." Johannes Gaitanides, "A Word on the Impotence of German

Such fears and anxieties and the consequent desire to avoid commitment through political involvement may seem pathological amid the economic affluence and political stability which prevail in the Federal Republic today. But apart from the fact that invasion and nuclear war still seem real threats to West Germans, the far-reaching changes which have taken place within their country appear to have been too sudden and too numerous to be absorbed as readily as the stability of mass opinion suggests.

In the political as in the social sphere changes in subjective attitudes have not kept pace with objective developments. Memories of the past – especially the trauma of the Nazi regime – have not been laid to rest, and surviving traditional political orientations have not been properly integrated with the norms and role perceptions associated with the present political system. New, emotionally satisfying political ideals and reference symbols have not developed to take the place of the discredited nationalism and charismatic leader-mass relationship of the Third Reich. Neither the Federal Republic nor any of its political groups and leaders have thus far provided strong affective links between political system and political culture. The average West German lacks a clear understanding of the stable relationship between citizen and government in a pluralist society. The boundaries between political and nonpolitical roles and values are not distinct for him because the realities of political life obscure the formal, legal separation of state, society, and self which he seeks. Because the perimeters of the political system are diffuse, he is uncertain about what political behavior he may expect from others and what others expect from him, and he finds it correspondingly difficult to establish congruence between personal desires and public obligations. Finally, the average West German is torn between his search for personal freedom in an increasingly complex and bureaucratized society and his wish for absolute security against economic deprivation and physical destruction. In the contemporary version of this well-

---

Literature," in Walter Stahl (ed.), *Education for Democracy in West Germany* (New York: Praeger, 1961), pp. 349 ff.

known conflict between liberty and welfare the new sense of freedom from authoritarian controls clashes with the demand for peace, domestic harmony, and collective security under the auspices of the state. Thus the individualism promoted by postwar developments encounters vivid memories of past insecurity and fears of new catastrophes leaving most West Germans uncertain as to exactly what they want their political system to do.

The background and the characteristics of the political culture of Western Germany should make the political system's operation a good deal clearer now. The fragility of its cultural roots, the lack of system affect among the population, and the ambivalence of evaluative political orientations suggest that the structures of the political system and the functions they perform have not yet been firmly embedded in the political role and norm perceptions of the majority of citizens of the Federal Republic. Their legitimacy is backed by a diffuse rather than a profound popular consensus, and the system's stability, adaptability, and resilience depends to a far greater extent on highly efficient performance than it would in a country where the political superstructure rests on firmer cultural foundations.

In contemporary German politics collective beliefs, values, and emotions, examined in the preceding three chapters, impose restrictions upon the activities of the leading actors. Under present circumstances the elites who largely "run" the system enjoy a lot of latitude in what they can do but they need to be highly sensitive to the climate of mass opinion in an evolving political culture. This, however, confronts political leaders with the difficult task of striving to anticipate and satisfy diverse demands, which are not always manifest, while remaining keenly aware of latent values and emotions in German society which might suddenly be mobilized against them.

As various investigations have indicated, such mass values and emotions are rooted in very deep anxieties about the security of the self and the family. The more public issues appear to involve such particularist components of the political culture the greater the usually passive citizen's emotional concern in the outcome. Thus, fears of economic deprivation or war not only tend to arouse profound emotional reactions in

Western Germany but provoke the inclination to fall back upon traditional political orientations – particularly attitudes favoring strong authoritative leadership. In recent years, even the suggestion of such a crisis has provoked mass reactions which indicate that the new pragmatic and nonemotional orientations do not provide sufficient psychological reassurances to allow Germans to cast off the legacy of their political traditions.

All this shows how critical are learning processes that may increase or diminish the congruence between political system and political culture – the political socialization process which will be discussed in Chapter Five. It also emphasizes the importance to the stable development and the maintenance of the system of efficient performances, by its input and output structures. To the extent that these structures successfully mediate between the citizen preoccupied with his private needs and fears and the public authorities confronted with conflicting demands outside as well as inside German society, the political system will become more entrenched not only in the pragmatic values but the emotional loyalty of the population. In foreign affairs this means providing assurances of security, against war and Communist threats, and obtaining gains without serious risks. In domestic affairs it means reconciling demands for the satisfaction of diverse interests, tied to traditional as well as modern social values, with demands for harmony and economic security.

CHAPTER V

Political Socialization

POLITICAL SOCIALIZATION involves (1) the establishment and development of attitudes toward political objects and relationships, (2) learning to accept or reject political roles and norms, and (3) the acquisition of negative or positive attitudes toward the incumbents of such roles and their activities. In Germany, as in other countries, the beliefs, emotions, and values which shape political perceptions and expectations are subject to a continuous and cumulative learning process which begins for each individual in childhood and ends only with death. This process may be conditioned by exposure to explicit and implicit political communications and by direct and indirect involvement in political activities. It may also be influenced by latent learning experiences which can establish, reinforce, and alter images of who does and should play specific political roles and what kind of behavior is fitting and proper for each of them. Over time the aggregative product of such political socialization will give form to the political culture and reflect the extent to which particular patterns are being maintained or changed.

In a heterogeneous society such as that of Western Germany political socialization is complex and involves numerous agents. The extent of their influence on relevant learning processes may vary considerably with the age, social background, and proximity to the political system of any individual. Preadult training for political roles may be so profound as to make later socializing experiences relatively unimportant. On the other hand, political orientations acquired in childhood and adolescence may be modified decisively during adulthood as a result of highly salient changes in the individual's social environment. Such resocialization may be caused by sudden traumatic experiences, as by the profound upheavals which Germans witnessed during the 1930's and 1940's. But it may also be the result of a more gradual accumulation of salient informational cues calling for new attitudinal and behavioral patterns. Political resocialization has particular relevance in contemporary Germany's evolving political culture. Whether prevailing patterns will persist or not depends on the degree to which the fundamental political orientations of the present adult population are and will remain susceptible to change and on the extent to which these attitudes will in turn influence the outlook and behavior of new citizens.

Political participation can change political beliefs, emotion, and values. Germans who are involved and active in politics are in the present transitional period apt to be more easily resocialized than those who are largely passive participants. They are not only more intensively exposed to a large variety of political communications and new learning experiences but they also tend to be more sensitive to them and correspondingly more likely to modify their outlooks.

This educative function of active participation in politics is evident in many of the younger leaders of the Federal Republic. Among the "new men of power" adaptability to a highly dynamic political environment and acceptance of opportunities to profit from learning experiences in a modernizing society have been particularly pronounced as compared to the mass of largely inactive political actors whose sociopolitical horizon is more limited and whose interpersonal relations and communications are more restricted. In this chapter we will focus principally on the political socialization of the masses which are only peripherally involved in the operation of the system; a discussion of the minority of leading participating actors will follow in Chapter VI.

The ongoing process through which children and adults in the Federal Republic acquire political orientations and are recruited into various political roles bears the marks of the disjointed development of German social and political structures since 1945 and the unsettled character of the political culture. It reflects the gap between persistent traditions and new patterns resulting from postwar socioeconomic and political changes and mirrors the discontinuities which exist today between various structures of political socialization. There is no integrated network of interlocking socialization structures to facilitate, from childhood onward, the cumulative development of generally homogeneous political orientations. By contrast, in the United States, Britain, and Norway, the family, schools, churches, civic and occupational associations, and political parties provide closely integrated and harmonious socialization patterns which serve to induct the citizen into time-honored political roles and reconcile the norms of various subcultures with those legitimating the existence of the regime and the national community. The result is a relatively good fit among the orientations of various political actors and a congruence between the supportive political culture and the operation of the political system. And since the political socialization and recruitment functions are dispersed among a variety of integrated structures, the load on any one of them does not strain its ability to perform its particular task.[1]

The trend in postwar Germany toward an increasingly pluralistic society with many variegated structures has not been accompanied by the equally rapid growth of mutually reinforcing structures for political socialization with common integrative ideological reference symbols — such as Hitler and his Third Reich provided. The loss of the charismatic leader and the sudden termination of the extensive interdependence among political socialization agents was not succeeded by a new form of integration. Drastic socioeconomic changes and sharp discontinuities between Nazi and post-Nazi political norms and role structures led instead to the development of heterogeneous socializing agents. Though the profound subcultural cleavages which blocked collaboration and continuity

[1] Obviously there are exceptions to these generalizations, such as the gap between socialization processes in lower-class Negro families and those in the dominant white culture in the United States. Even in this instance, however, other socializing agents — such as the schools, the churches, and the mass media — reduce such discontinuity and harmonize subcultural roles and norms with those of the generally prevailing political culture.

before Hitler did not re-emerge, the changes and discontinuities produced obstacles of a different sort which today complicate the integration of the pertinent structures.

Many of these obstacles have been mentioned in preceding chapters – the rootlessness of German society, the absence of a strong sense of political community, and the lack of positive affect for the present regime and its practices; the prevailing cleavages between the perceptions of private and public roles and goals, and the unresolved tensions arising from a lack of congruence between traditional and modern elements in society and polity. These factors tend to obscure rather than clarify the relevance of political communications and learning experiences for many Germans, in the course of their political socialization. Attitudinal and behavioral cues provided by uncoordinated and competing socializing agents complicate their efforts to get a clear picture of what is and what ought to be happening in politics, what is expected from them and what they may expect from other political actors, and their endeavors to reconcile the various roles and attitudes which, manifestly or latently, are projected into politics.

German children and adults are accordingly often confronted with confusing informational cues about political objects and conflicting demands for conformity with manifest or latent political norms. To escape anxiety-producing inner conflicts or conflicts with the group with which they most closely identify, they are likely to disregard potential socializing influences which are not congruent with their own principal beliefs, emotions, and values, and with those of their primary reference groups. Thus, insofar as diverse political communications and learning experiences are perceived as competitive rather than complementary, they tend to complicate the integration of the political socialization process in the Federal Republic and the maintenance of congruence between private and public roles and norms.

POLITICAL SOCIALIZATION THROUGH THE FAMILY

Learning experiences in the home and informational cues transmitted through family members appear to be of exceptional significance to the political socialization process in contemporary Germany. The tightly knit nuclear family which has evolved over the last two decades is today the most important reference group for shaping politically relevant preadult and adult attitude and behavior patterns. It is not only the primary socioeconomic planning and decisionmaking unit for most Germans but, more important, the family largely monopolizes their affective loyalties. The consequent emotional encapsulation of the family, cutting it off from its social environment, has hindered integration between political socialization through the home and other agents. The bonds which provide for strong family solidarity are missing from other social relations, and political objects cannot begin to command the supportive orientations mustered by the home.

The trend toward the objective secularization of the German family has not been accompanied by a corresponding transformation of subjective role and norm perceptions relating this essentially traditionalist structure to a modern social environment. With its strong affective ties, ascriptive membership, and diffuse roles, the family represents the most powerful particularist element in a setting characterized by the proliferation of affectively neutral, achievement oriented, and functionally specific roles and norms. Predispositions toward political objects learned in the home and reinforced by the churches and tradition-oriented government structures and rules – for example, the Federal Ministry for Youth and Family Affairs and legislation "for the protection of the family" – appear to be discontinuous with the socializing agents which stress the modern orientations of a pluralist society and its political system. And there are indications that this gap is being maintained, if not widened, by the ambivalence of prevailing social norms and the inability of authoritative political structures to resolve them.

The family's influence on political socialization is indicated by the extent to which its members share the same opinions, vote in the same way, and depend on each other for informational cues to structure their political perceptions. A 1961 study of German university students found that those who revealed the greatest political involvement and positive support for the present system usually came from families in which political issues aroused interest and discussion. On the other hand, politically uninterested or "disengaged" students usually came from families which never discussed politics or whose members were alienated from the system.

According to a 1965 mass opinion survey, politics is never talked about in one out of four German families; 29 per cent of the women and 33 per cent of the men in a 1960 survey claimed that they never discussed their voting intentions with anyone. However, 60 per cent of the women and 48 per cent of the men testified that they talked about such matters with members of their immediate family – and usually with no one else. (See Table V.3 on page 146.) Insofar as members of the former group lived with their families, keeping silent appears to be largely designed to avoid controversy in the home and thus preserve family harmony, Discussion – mostly with the spouse – seems to be mainly to establish or confirm a common family political orientation without much argument. Profound differences of political opinion within the family seem to be rare because fundamental agreement is generally assumed. Only 4 per cent of the respondents in the 1965 survey cited above thought that their own political views differed significantly from those of other members of their family – a belief substantiated by various studies.

The strength of family solidarity in political orientations is also reflected by poll data which show no significant generational differences between the political opinions of Germans whose formative learning experiences took place before 1945 and younger ones who know about this period only from hearsay. Such data also indicate that in the privacy of their homes German parents, belonging to the older generation, will share their memories of the past with their children – though they may not tell all. But since these memories are for the most part negative, such intergenerational discussions serve mainly to justify or, excuse the older generation's political behavior in the previous era, rather than to glorify the past. Most German youngsters do not blame their parents for following Hitler and share their inclination to forget what happened.

Strong partisan loyalties to a political party play only a comparatively minor role in family socialization except insofar as they reinforce the solidarity of family members. Many families have followed a "unit rule" in casting ballots in elections. Thus voting patterns show that "Christian Democratic families" prevail among the farmers in the Roman Catholic regions of Southern Germany and "Social Democratic families" among the industrial workers in the urban areas of the Protestant North. But the sharp political discontinuities of the past and the blandness of contemporary partisan allegiances militate against the development of strongly rooted party loyalties in most homes. Continuity in a family's partisan identifications over several generations – common in the United States – is rare in Germany, except among loyal followers of the Social Democratic Party. The Nazi hiatus and the determination of postwar party leaders to make a "new beginning" allowed for little continuity. Relatively few of the party leaders of the Federal Republic can lay claim to descent from a long line of politicians or membership in the same party as their fathers and grandfathers.

Learning experiences in the home involving explicitly nonpolitical roles and standards of behavior may implicitly shape political perceptions and expectations to the extent that they are projected into political relationships. The strategic position of the family in the socialization process and the average German's low sense of conscious political involvement and participation suggest that such latent political socialization may be of considerable significance for the development of relevant cultural patterns. But although in an objective sense family relationships appear to have undergone changes in the last two decades, there is little evidence to suggest that these produced closer subjective integration between socialization for family roles and learning to play the political roles associated by the constitution with the present democratic regime.

Germans who grew up during these two decades seem to reject traditional rules of learning which demanded discipline and obedience more emphatically than their elders, but on the whole they share the latter's perceptions of "proper" family roles and norms. Indeed, there is considerable evidence which suggests that equality between husbands and wives and participation of children in family decisions has become quite prevalent. Thus Almond and Verba's 1959 survey of Germans over eighteen indicated that by far the largest proportion of those who recalled that they could contradict their parents and join in family decisionmaking were then under 25 years of age. However, this pattern appears to be as yet far more pronounced in the families of a minority of relatively highly educated, urbanized young Germans than among the population in general.

The political socialization of German women – a majority of the electorate – takes place in an intramural family setting that is self-contained and largely monopolizes their affective loyalties. They may significantly contribute to the family income and enjoy legal equality with their husbands, but the roles which most seem to consider of primary importance are the traditional ones of housewives and mothers. These roles assign major responsibility for the preservation of family solidarity and demand that the women adopt attitudinal and behavioral patterns consonant with their perceived task of guarding the family harmony. It leads even unmarried women to support all measures which seem to protect the home and to oppose all which appear to threaten the family's unity. These assumed obligations impose demands on German women which they feel they can fulfill adequately only at the expense of public social roles and encourage them to live for the family but apart from the polity. The women's attentiveness to communications emanating from outside the home and their involvement in extra-family affairs is correspondingly restricted insofar as these are not perceived as directly pertinent to their family duties. In contrast, American and British women tend to feel a much greater obligation to participate in public affairs and to assume active political roles.

At the same time female authority within the home has evidently increased, and is reinforced by the solidification and encapsulation of the family unit. This represents a change in family authority patterns which contrast sharply with the hierarchic paternalism which prevailed in the past and remains important in other areas of German society. Although both men and women ostensibly adhere to social norms upholding the predominance of the male outside the home, within it the authority of the wife and mother has subtly risen. Insofar as this pattern is likely to be maintained or even strengthened, it may represent a potentially important factor affecting the patterns of the political culture, particularly in latent, preadult political socialization.

TABLE V.1 *Young Germans' Principal Confidant, 1953, 1964 (Mass Opinion Data for Youths 15–25 in Rounded-off Percentages)*

	1953	*1964*
Mother	34	31
Father	9	7
Both parents	15	33
Friends	21	21
Spouse	8	12
Relatives	5	10
Others	8	8
Total	100	122 [a]

[a] Totals exceed 100 per cent because multiple mentions were permitted. Absolute numbers not available.

Source: EMNID Institut, "Jugend 1964" cited in Bundesministerium für Familie und Jugend, *Bericht über die Lage der Jugend,* 1965, p. 11.

German husbands, confronted with the strains of a highly competitive existence outside the home, appear to have become correspondingly more dependent upon the psychological reassurance provided by the maternal roles assumed by their wives. Greater female authority within the home is also evident in the mother's relationship with her children. A 1965 survey of young Germans indicated that the mother or both parents, rather than the father alone, provide the principal sources of reference in preadult learning today (see Table V.1). The influence of the German mother, however, is usually exerted to discourage self-reliance in her children. A cross-national survey published a few years ago found that this pattern was much more prevalent in Germany than in Japan and Brazil and that German mothers expected their children to shift for themselves at a relatively late age – if ever.[2]

[2] See David C. McClelland, *The Achieving Society* (Princeton: Van Nostrand, 1961), p. 346.

TABLE V.2 *Adult Educational Norms, 1951–1964*
(Mass Opinion Data in Rounded-off Percentages)

Question: "What qualities should be particularly emphasized in children's education?"

Replies	*1951*	*1954*	*1957*	*1964*
Obedience and subordination	25	28	25	25
Orderliness and diligence	41	43	48	45
Independence and self-reliance	28	28	32	31
Other answers	5	4	3	1
No response	1	2	5	6
Total	100	105 [a]	113 [a]	108 [a]

[a] Totals exceed 100 per cent because multiple choices were permitted. Absolute numbers not available.
Source: EMNID Institut, *Informationen,* No. 42 (1964).

Generally, socialization within most German families seems to be based on traditional standards accentuating passive political orientations. Though members of the postwar generation may ostensibly reject such norms as obedience, subordination, orderliness, and diligence, these – rather than independence and self-reliance – are considered by most Germans to be the most important qualities to be emphasized in the training of children (see Table V.2). And two-thirds of a representative sample of young people between 15 and 25 interviewed in 1964 said that they would raise their own children in more or less the same way as they were brought up; only 22 per cent said they would do it differently.[3]

All this assumes that there may be a close relationship between what is learned in the home and basic political orientations. However, other socializing influences may inhibit or alter that of the family if their impact is strong enough to overcome the family influence. This is essentially the concept which is implied in authoritative governmental efforts to mold German political orientations.

POLITICAL SOCIALIZATION THROUGH GOVERNMENTAL STRUCTURES

The task of explicitly teaching Germans to accept and internalize roles and norms congruent with the efficient opera-

[3] See source cited in Table V.1.

tion of the political system is today a function of governmental and semigovernmental structures of political socialization. Through the schools, through political messages carried by various mass media, and through direct and indirect contacts with public officials, children and adults in the Federal Republic are continuously exposed to political communications from authoritative agents of the state. In view of the relative weakness in Germany of other structures promoting popular orientations strongly supportive of the present regime, this socializing function places a particularly heavy load on these authoritative agents. And, whereas political socialization through the family and other autonomous structures tends to be largely implicit, they are involved in very explicit efforts to influence political attitudes and behavior through indoctrination from above.

The principal object of government socialization endeavors is to assure a stable balance in the political system between domestic input demands for interest satisfaction and popular supportive orientations that will assure general acceptance of public policy outputs. Such efforts seek to assure the unquestioned legitimacy of prevailing governmental structures through a popular sense of identification with the regime and political community that transcends mere acquiescence and involves strong positive values and emotions.

Given a pluralistic society and a transitional political culture, these endeavors to institutionalize the operational features of a relatively new political system, without strong traditional roots, depend on a legitimating ideology. The function of such an ideology is to extract from the citizenry not only respect, but loyalty toward regime and community. It must provide authoritative norms and symbolic reference points which allow the governors to present the output of the political system as in the collective interest, rather than in the selfish interest of a few. The principles which it embodies must be taken for granted if the legitimating ideology is to provide voluntary compliance with the rules laid down by the decisionmakers and general acceptance of an inevitably unequal distribution of political roles and outputs. Last, but by no means least, the legitimating ideology must be internalized in sufficient breadth and depth to assure a reservoir of firm popular support for the regime to draw upon should extraordinary demands strain the output capacity of the political system.

The legitimating ideology propagated by governmental socializing agents in Germany is represented by the principles of representative democracy embodied in the Basic Law. We have touched upon the ambiguities contained in this instrument of government and on popular attitudes which complicate efforts to provide legitimacy for the regime and the political community it established. Official efforts to overcome these obstacles focus on the theme that the Federal Republic is a "democratic" state. It is this quality which is said to make its regime a "better" one than any other in German history and to demonstrate its superiority over the Nazi dictatorship and the Communist one in East Germany.

An enormous amount has been said and written in recent years about "Education for Democracy in Germany," the title of a compendium on the subject.[4] The frequent theme is that the primary objective must be to develop a new sense of political maturity, responsibility, and active participation among Germans of all ranks and ages. However, authoritative efforts to create popular orientations which German leaders consider necessary for the efficient operation of the political system tend to emphasize passive mass support more than active mass participation and to incorporate traditional paternalistic norms of authority relationships in the state. Thus manifest and latent political socialization in the schools and the armed forces and political communications from the governmental elites stress the legitimacy of prevalent role relationships rather than the mass recruitment of citizens into active political roles. Apart from endeavoring to impress upon children and adults the democratic citizen's obligation to exercise his franchise to vote, authoritative political socialization from above concentrates on the establishment and reinforcement of mass orientations that are expected to provide respect and affect for the

[4] Walter Stahl (ed.), *Education for Democracy in West Germany* (New York: Praeger, 1961). This is an excellent collection of essays and also contains a most useful summary of periodical literature on the subject.

new state and ready compliance with the decisions of its leaders.

The authoritative decisionmakers who direct these efforts to give popular legitimacy to the present system feel that lasting supportive orientations cannot be expected to develop spontaneously in a political culture which lacks strong democratic foundations. Throughout German society, potentially destabilizing influences are still believed to have an important, if mostly latent, effect on attitude formation. Comprehensive, massive, and explicit governmental intervention in the ongoing process of political socialization is therefore considered essential. In this view, the transformation of cultural patterns which is thought necessary if Germans are to embrace a legitimating democratic ideology requires first that "a body of social knowledge and modes of behavior capable of sustaining a democratic polity be developed." [5] Essentially, what the German émigré psychologist Kurt Lewin wrote about German "cultural reconstruction" in 1943 seems to these re-educators to remain valid today: Germans must be taught democratic orientations "in those conceptual terms in which they are accustomed to think." [6] In short, since democratic attitudes necessary to sustain the present political system cannot be expected to develop from below they must be shaped more or less paternalistically by authoritative leaders from above.

Educators, military men, and other officials concerned with authoritative political education efforts in the Federal Republic speak of the need for *Staatsbürgerliche Erziehung,* citizenship training, to counteract on the one hand the prevailing mood of privatization and pragmatic materialism and on the other the tendency toward affective "depersonalization" of life outside the family. Such citizenship training connotes to them something more comprehensive than civic education in the United States or *éducation civique* in France. It encompasses not merely *Staatsbürgerkunde,* learning about the institutions of the state, but also the acquisition of *Staatsgefühl,* affect for the state, and *Staatsbewusstsein,* a sense of identification with

[5] "Training Instructors for Teaching Social Studies," a report published by the Akademie für politische Bildung in April, 1960 and reprinted in Stahl, *ibid.,* pp. 75 f.

[6] From "*Resolving Social Conflicts:* Selected Papers in Group Dynamics," reprinted in Stahl, *op. cit.,* p. 277.

the state. Much of the German literature on authoritative political socialization emphasizes that a citizenship training program which will firmly establish and reinforce popular legitimacy of the institutional roles and norms of the present state must focus on its ethical function as the supreme source of norms in a pluralist society. Reflecting the persistence of traditional Hegelian political philosophy, leading educators and government officials maintain that even though the form of the German state may have changed, the "proper" role relationships and standards of political behavior for its citizens remain essentially the same as in the past. The state which, in the words of a leading political scientist, "imposes on children and youths a duty to be instructed," is believed to retain a position of pre-eminence in society, and political socialization efforts from above seek to impress this upon the citizens of the Federal Republic.[7]

In accordance with these precepts, authoritative political socialization particularly stresses what are declared to be the ethical imperatives of the citizen's responsibility toward the political community, on respect for law, and on the obligation to support authoritative leaders. In a representative democracy people are said not only to enjoy greater freedom and interest satisfaction than under any other regime, but also a greater moral obligation to obey their elected leaders voluntarily. Democratic ideology, anti-Nazism, and anti-Communism in German citizenship education thus are employed to forge a popular supportive consensus which will lighten the domestic demand on the political system and increase its supportive foundations in the political culture.

A large variety of governmental and semigovernmental agents participate in political socialization both directly and indirectly, and the form and content of the political communications which serve this function vary a good deal according to the source and the intended audience. The formal distribution of political authority under the federal system provides for the sharing of control over citizenship training

[7] See Theodor Eschenburg, *Staat und Gesellschaft in Deutschland,* 5th ed. (Stuttgart: Curt E. Schwab, 1965), p. 452, and numerous publications sponsored by the federal *Bundeszentrale für Heimatsdienst and Bundeszentrale für politische Bildung.*

between the central government and those of the ten constituent Länder.

Preadult political education in the schools is under the formal control of the Länder, for the Basic Law assigns to them exclusive jurisdiction over the educational system. But the central government also takes a hand, both directly and indirectly, particularly after most German youths leave school at the ages of 14 or 15. Thus the 1965 Federal Youth Program for Germans under 25, administered by the Federal Ministry for Family and Youth Affairs, budgeted almost 13 million DM for direct political education, 7.5 million for grants to various youth organizations explicitly or implicitly involved in citizenship training, and six million for the participation of young Germans in international youth activities. The central government also directs an extensive program in the armed forces designed to make the *Bundeswehr* a "school for citizenship." All young German males are subject to the draft, and recruits and other members of the armed forces are given instruction by military officers which is supposed to give them the "psychological armament" considered necessary for good "citizen soldiers." [8]

It is mainly the central government which directs adult political socialization from above. Though federal in form, the actual operation of the German political system and, more particularly, the downward flow of political communications, focuses public attention on informational cues provided by national agents of political socialization. Formally and informally, explicitly and implicitly, intentionally and unintentionally, leading officials of the national government act as political educators. They influence the ongoing learning process by focusing attention on some role and norm perceptions and images, and expectations relating to political objects, and diverting it from others, and by providing the public with evaluative cues or withholding them. Implicitly, such political education is provided continuously, as in other countries, by what the incumbents of governmental roles appear to be doing, how attentive they appear to be to demands for public

[8] See Stahl, *op. cit.*, pp. 203–230 and Eric Waldman, *The Goose Step Is Verboten: The German Army Today* (New York: The Free Press, 1964).

policy decisions, and how they make and enforce their authoritative rulings. Beyond this, German governmental agents of political socialization – especially those associated with the executive branch of the federal government – engage in rather extensive explicit efforts intended to give legitimacy to regime and political community.

Such efforts involve above all the mass communication structures through which political information from above is transmitted to the general public. Indeed, under Article Five of the Basic Law, government authorities are enjoined from monopolizing these media or imposing a censorship on them; and no newspapers and few periodicals are openly controlled by government authorities. Although all radio and television networks are publicly owned, they are organized as public corporations under the jurisdiction of the Länder and supervised by autonomous boards chosen to represent a balance of the major political and socioeconomic interest groups supporting the regime. Several efforts by the central government to increase its formal control have been unsuccessful, and both personnel and programs are bound by law to a "nonpartisan" position. But as the Federal Constitutional Court has pointed out, these structures are more than mere media for mass communication because they can influence public opinion to a significant extent. In fact, they reinforce authoritative efforts to legitimate the prevailing political order by broadcasting programs which are either explicitly designed to mold broad supportive orientations for the regime or implicitly provide the public with selected information structuring its image of "political reality."

Various agencies of the executive branch of the federal government make extensive use of these and other political communication structures to get their socializing "messages" to the public. They not only command more extensive and intensive attention than competing sources of political information, but they also control important indirect means to influence the political socialization process. As in the United States, press releases, intentional "leaks" to dependable journalists, and interviews with government leaders are widely employed to influence the general public and particular nongovernmental groups and opinion leaders. A generously financed Federal Press and Information Office, controlled by the federal chancellor, has the task of "explaining" government policies and "correcting" political information provided by other sources. It received 78 million DM in the 1961 federal budget, another 13 million were placed at the disposal of the chancellor "to use at his discretion" for similar purposes, and 7 million were budgeted "to enlighten the public about national defense problems."

Other less clearly identified large amounts are annually appropriated to various federal agencies for their "information programs" and for generous subsidies to various journals and other publications, to semiautonomous academies for political education, to institutes for citizenship training, and to conferences organized by groups supporting the present political order. In addition to the Federal Youth Plan, support for semigovernmental citizenship education is openly provided through the Federal Office for Political Education and the Federal Ministry for All-German Questions and more covertly through other federal agencies.[9] The federal executive has also had a hand in the allocation of large sums to the major parties for "political education" activities. Since these parties have a strong stake in the preservation of the present system, such activities in effect serve to promote the legitimacy of the regime.

In addition to these positive efforts to influence popular orientations, authoritative governmental agents use negative sanctions to suppress political communications which they consider inimical to the regime and its claim to legitimacy. Sometimes with the help of the courts, at other times by bypassing them, both the federal and Länder governments employ the criminal code and administrative regulations to prevent or punish the dissemination of information considered detrimental to the security of the state and the maintenance of "public morals." Such efforts have been directed in par-

[9] See, *inter alia,* Thomas Ellwein, *Das Regierungssystem der Bundesrepublik Deutschland,* 1st ed. (Köln-Opladen: Westdeutscher Verlag, 1963), p. 46 ff.

ticular against Communist "subversive" activities, but they have also been applied to radical right-wing groups and less obvious alleged opponents of the regime.

The most notorious attempt to impose a covert type of censorship on nongovernmental sources of political information occurred in 1962 when, on the initiative of the Federal Minister of Defense Franz Josef Strauss, an effort was made to prosecute the editors and publishers of *Der Spiegel* for printing portions of a classified military document. The prominence of the journal and the drastic methods which were employed to curb it aroused considerable public criticism, and in the end the Federal Supreme Court quashed the indictment. However, in a number of less conspicuous cases governmental agencies appear to have been more successful in curbing the flow of political information which they believed to threaten the authority of the state and its official agents.

The pending new criminal code may make it more difficult to apply legal restrictions on the freedom of the press, but less overt forms of government control over socializing communications are likely to persist. For example, as the editors of a journal of the opposition Free Democratic Party found in 1967, the federal government may refuse to continue financial support of publications considered too critical of the ruling political leadership. And in the view of the dominant governmental elites certain restrictions on the free flow of political information from "antidemocratic" sources are unavoidable if the new regime is to become firmly established in the political culture.

POLITICAL SOCIALIZATION THROUGH THE SCHOOLS

To German leaders concerned with the educational system's function in preadult political socialization, manifest and latent citizenship education in the classroom seems critical to the institutionalizing of the new regime and political community. Indeed, in former times explicit and implicit learning experiences in German schools strongly affected the basic political orientations of incoming citizens. But though all formal education is today still under the direct or indirect control of governmental authorities, the function of the schools in providing explicit political socialization from above is no longer as significant as in the past – and as educators and political leaders who today seek to reshape the German political culture wish it still was.

Preadult political socialization in the schools of the Federal Republic is considerably more diversified than in countries with a more highly centralized, uniformly structured educational system, such as the Soviet Union, France, and Britain. Although the various ministries of culture of the Länder cooperate in drawing up general recommendations suggesting what should be included in civic education courses, the quality and quantity of such instructions vary considerably from Land to Land and school to school. The political complexion of a Land government, the party affiliations and personal preferences of the minister of culture and his educational administrators, the strength of regional and local traditions, and the relative power of various groups who seek to influence educational policies, provide for considerable diversity. So does the fact that the educational system as a whole is divided horizontally between denominational and nondenominational schools, and vertically by the sharp distinction between basic education for the masses and higher education for the future elites. Almost all the comparatively few students who complete the university preparatory curriculum are exposed to civic education courses, some compulsory and others voluntary. However the 80 per cent or more of German children whose formal education ends after eight or nine years usually receive only very limited, elementary political training in school.

This heterogeneity of the German educational system, combined with other factors, has complicated authoritative efforts from above to provide adequate training for democratic citizenship in the schools. As we noted earlier, the educational system remains one of the strongest bastions of traditionalism in German society and this is reflected in the reluctance of German educators to assign political education a major place in the curriculum. School administrators are inclined to agree with most students and parents that other subjects are more important in equipping future citizens for adult roles and therefore downgrade the importance of explicit citizenship education courses for the training of teachers and students. Children in the people's schools are considered too immature and too much in need of intensive instruction in "basic" learning skills to allow much time for political education during the 30 to 36 hours they spend in class each week. Adolescent youths who receive a more specialized education in secondary schools are expected to concentrate on primary subjects rather than on "supplementary" courses in politics, to which only about two hours a week are allotted. In the smaller schools the shortage of teachers resulted in such courses being assigned to overworked instructors who have little interest in the subject and the "loading" of qualified teachers with other instructional duties.

There is also a widespread reluctance on the part of teachers to assume the task. As civil servants they shy away from responsibilities which might lay them open to charges of violating written and unwritten norms demanding political "nonpartisanship" in the performance of their duties. Moreover, those who are old enough to have been involved in the Nazi regime are not particularly eager to expose themselves to student criticism in discussing past events which in any case they would prefer to forget – like the rest of their generation. Teaching citizenship courses to them undermines the traditional basis of the German teacher's authority, the assumption that instruction consists of passing on his superior knowledge to inexperienced youngsters. Such presumed superiority cannot be asserted when teachers are asked to repudiate their own political past before their students or to consent to less "mature" instructors doing so in citizenship education courses. A political education program which, according to those who want it to transform the political culture, "has to be conducted . . . without, yes even despite the 'old ones,'"[10] appears to many teachers a threat to intergenerational harmony in German society and to the sensitive relationship between school and home. According to teachers who had to contend with parents who vehemently objected to what their children were taught about the recent past, instructing children that

[10] Stahl, *op. cit.*, p. 295.

their elders were guilty of political errors of commission and omission, is viewed as at least an implicit attack on the solidarity of the family. In smaller communities such reactions place teachers and school administrators under strong pressure to find reasons for evading instructions to delve deeply and critically into the "unresolved" Nazi past.

Explicit political education is thus neglected in many German schools to a far greater extent than official authoritative decrees would lead one to believe. Moreover – particularly in the denominational primary schools – civic instruction is not an integral component of the socialization of students for adult roles. Taught as a subject which appears to most students to have little direct relevance to their future tasks, it reinforces the prevalent sharp distinctions between private and public affairs and between family and state, instead of overcoming them.

The usual highly formalized instruction in current history and civic education courses discourages student participation and involvement and reinforces the prevailing emphasis on the formal, institutional aspects of politics and citizenship responsibilities. Teachers who frequently feel incompetent to explain Nazism to their students, because they themselves are unsure about the "proper" relationship between citizen and state and consider political life under a democratic form of government far from perfect, have obvious difficulties in arousing much interest or establishing strong convictions. They will stress the citizen's legal obligations to the state and its legitimate leaders, but largely by "neutral," descriptive instruction which is devoid of a meaningful interpretation of "the facts." This may give students some knowledge of the formal aspects of the political system and even a sense of evaluative competence about its performance, but not a feeling of identification and loyalty toward the regime. In short, prevailing orientations toward state, political authority, and political roles are maintained rather than modified by present political instructions in the German schools.[11]

[11] Almond and Verba's sample of Germans over 18 years of age revealed that in 1959 the proportion of those who remembered that "a lot" of time was given to current events in school was greater among the generation

Postwar reforms introduced into the educational system by authoritative directives from above are also supposed to provide implicit preadult training in "democratic citizenship" through latent political socialization. In school, German children are to learn to be self-reliant, responsible, and freely participating citizens, and toward this end efforts have been made to modernize the traditional authority relationship between teachers and students. Certain data suggest that these endeavors appear, in one respect at least, to have met with considerable success. Almond and Verba's 1959 survey of German adults indicates that the proportion who remembered disagreeing with their teachers and feeling free to participate in classroom discussions was significantly greater among those between 18 and 25 than among their elders – particularly individuals who had gone to high school.[12]

But although young Germans educated in the postwar era may have learned to be more independent than past generations by insisting on their private rights and opinions, it is neither clear that this is to be attributed to the particular influence of the school nor that it reflects the development of the system-supportive orientations sought by authoritative leaders. The evidence suggests that in contemporary preadult political socialization the latent influences in the home stress-

---

educated under the Nazi regime than young German adults exposed to political education courses in later years. At about the same time a survey of students at Frankfurt University – representing a group which had received a great deal more such instruction than the average German child and youth today – showed that although between 81 and 87 per cent had taken some social science or civic education courses before coming to a university, most of these students had not found these courses particularly interesting. The instructors bored them and the subject matter seemed unimportant. Though on the whole these students seemed more interested in politics than those who had not taken such courses, they appeared to be no better informed and no more interested in participating in political activities than the rest. The investigators concluded that, apart from reinforcing traditional, formalistic orientations toward the state, explicit citizenship training had failed to give the students a sense of competence for playing active roles in German politics. See Jürgen Habermas, *et al.*, *Student und Politik* (Neuwied: Luchterband Verlag, 1961), pp. 267–275.

[12] Calculated from Almond and Verba data, partially reported in *The Civic Culture* (Boston: Little, Brown, 1964), pp. 336–339.

ing privatization and social isolation serve as obstacles to learning participant public roles and acquiring civic pride in political institutions. Not only is there a lack of congruence and balance between the private values which the child learns in the home and the public virtues which the school is supposed to teach him, but an essentially paternalistic educational system is poorly adapted to provide integration between the two. While on the one hand the educational structures teach the child social roles which are to make him a "good" citizen, on the other they in fact increase the distance between the individual and the community.

What and how German children are presently taught in school seems to reflect and reinforce the ambivalent mixture of individualism and conformism and traditionalism and modernity, which characterizes prevailing cultural patterns in general. Apart from explicit civic education courses, most school activities emphasize private rather than public pursuits and roles. General education courses in German literature and religion, for example, stress the importance of inner contemplation (*Innerlichkeit*) and family solidarity, and instruction in more specialized subjects focuses on the acquisition of information rather than social skills. Whereas in American schools children are encouraged to learn other-directed social roles by constant practice in interpersonal relationships and thus to become sensitive to the expectations of others, German students are taught to concentrate on pursuits which isolate them from each other. They are trained to do their best in the occupation for which the school equips them, and they learn to avoid the risks of innovation or conspicuous deviancy. They are taught that a formal code of social obligations toward others must be honored for the sake of communal harmony, but they also learn to believe that such public responsibilities can be discharged by individual rather than collective action.

In sum, latent political socialization in the school tends to produce a person who minds his own rather than the community's interests, who strives to assert his individuality in solitary or family activities rather than by participation in public affairs, and who chooses to follow what seem to him safe, traditional pursuits rather than to strike out in new directions.[13]

INFORMAL INTERMEDIARY AGENTS OF POLITICAL SOCIALIZATION

Political interaction between ordinary Germans is principally confined to indirect contacts provided by *formal* secondary structures. Their orientations toward political objects are influenced by informational and interpretive cues provided by the elites who control the flow of political communications between society and polity; informal contacts outside the immediate family, which might supplement or even bypass such channels, appear to be unimportant. Frank exchanges of political opinions between friends, neighbors, and coworkers are unusual and of far less significance for political socialization than in the United States. Most Germans, and especially most German women, do not care to discuss their voting intentions outside the home (see Table V.3).

TABLE V.3 *Discussion of Voting Intentions, 1960 (Mass Opinion Data in Rounded-off Percentages)*

Conversation partner	*Total*	*Men*	*Women*
Family members	54	48	60
None	31	33	29
Friends	12	15	9
Work group associates	8	12	5
Total	105 [a]	108 [a]	103 [a]

[a] Totals exceed 100 per cent because multiple responses were permitted. Absolute numbers not available.

Source: Viggo Graf Blücher, *Der Prozess der Meinungsbildung: dargestellt im Beispiel der Bundestagswahl 1961* (Bielefeld: EMNID, 1962), p. 72.

No doubt, such reticence relates directly to still vivid memories of life under a totalitarian dictatorship. In part it seems to reflect the prevailing climate of political apathy, mutual distrust, and insistence on formal social harmony. This mood is particularly strong among those Germans who believe their

[13] See David C. McClelland, *op. cit.*, pp. 197–200, 242; Ralf Dahrendorf, *Gesellschaft und Freiheit* (Munich: Piper, 1961), pp. 284–287; and "Was aber bleibt, stiften die Lehrer," *Welt der Literatur,* January 21, 1965, p. 36.

views deviate from "respectable" attitudes in their social environment. In part, too, such reticence appears to be based on the average German's diffidence toward authoritative political "experts" and his corresponding contempt for the opinion of those do not seem to him to command such prestige – which means most of his peers.

The opportunities for such frank, informal, face-to-face discussions are not what they used to be. The extent of geographic mobility and urbanization has all but destroyed closely knit neighborhood units and other informal social groups which in the past contributed to political socialization. Except in small towns and villages few Germans still go to the local inn after working hours for leisurely political discussion with old acquaintances around the *Stammtisch;* most stay at home listening to the radio or watching television. In the cities neighbors are more or less strangers to each other and are not given to exchanging political opinions. Various studies have found that the more urban a German's social environment the more likely he is to keep his opinions to himself or within the family, and the less likely he is to discuss them with his neighbors.

Similarly, the modernization of German economic life has reduced opportunities for frank and informal discussions at work. The impersonal climate of vast factories and offices does not encourage the average employee to talk politics, especially when he believes his superiors disapprove. The lower his educational and income status the less likely is he to risk disagreement with his boss or even to feel qualified to discuss politics at work. The proportion of the low income group who feel themselves competent to do so is not only a great deal smaller than among higher income, better educated Germans, as Almond and Verba found in their 1959 cross-national study, but significantly lower than among those in similar occupations and of similar background in Britain and the United States. Though Germans may subjectively identify themselves with the collective interests of their occupational group, they tend to do so on the basis of cues from their formal leaders rather than as a result of informal discussions outside the home.

THE INDEPENDENT MASS MEDIA

Almond and Verba found that their 1959 sample of German adults relied far more heavily on newspapers and periodicals for following public affairs than respondents in the other four countries which were studied. According to a 1963 survey, 92 per cent of some 44 million German adults read a newspaper at least once a week and more than 80 per cent read one daily.[14] On the face of it, more than 1,600 newspapers with a combined circulation of approximately 21 million copies and about twice that many readers seems a strategic structure intermediate between family and governmental agents in socialization. To the extent that they are in a position to function as "gate-keepers" and interpreters in the flow of political communications, independent German publishers and editors appear to have it in their power to reinforce, modify, and integrate socializing influences from other sources.

The importance of the press before and under Hitler seemed at first to promise that it would also play a major part in the formation of political opinions after his fall. On the basis of this assumption the Western military governments strongly encouraged the development of "democratic" newspapers and periodicals, free from control by parties, interest groups, and government authorities. Most of the large German dailies owe their existence to the financial and political support which they received from the military governments in the early postwar years. However, the nationwide influence of the independent press on political socialization is today neither as great as some Germans would wish it to be nor as powerful as others fear it is.

The fact that about 40 per cent of the German press is today controlled by Axel Springer, a conservative and, some would

[14] The data on which the following discussion is based are drawn chiefly from the following: *Statistisches Jahrbuch 1964;* Elisabeth Noelle and Erich Peter Neumann, *Jahrbuch der öffentlichen Meinung 1958–64;* Bundesministerium für Familie und Jugend, *Jugendbericht 1965,* Institut für Publizistik der freien Universität Berlin, *Die Deutsche Presse* (Berlin, 1961); DIVO Institut, *Der westdeutsche Markt in Zahlen* (1962); and Karl W. Deutsch and Lewis J. Edinger, *Germany Rejoins the Powers* (Stanford: Stanford University Press, 1959), pp. 113–117, and the sources cited there.

say, nationalist publisher, has led German intellectuals and student leaders to conjure up the specter of the Hugenberg newspaper empire which supported Hitler in the 1930's. However, such analogies overlook that the political influence of the press today is a great deal weaker than it was in those days.

About two-thirds of the contemporary dailies are local editions of regional newspapers, and only three or four at best have a significant supraregional clientele (see Table V.4). No longer directly supported by political parties and interest groups, German newspapers have become primarily commercial enterprises and they feature items intended to attract a wide range of readers in the regional and local advertising markets of an affluent society. According to a 1964 survey, the daily paper for seven out of ten adult Germans was such a local-regional publication, whereas only one in twelve read such supraregional dailies as Springer's *Die Welt,* the *Frankfurter*

TABLE V.4 *Leading German Newspapers, 1965*

Paper	*Paid circulation (in 1,000 copies)*	*Sphere of influence*	*Nature of readership*
Bild-Zeitung	3,834	nationwide	mass public
Westdeutsche Allgemeine	434	Northwest Germany	mass public
Hamburger Morgendpost	336	Hamburg metropolitan area	mass public
Hamburger Abendblatt	319	Hamburg metropolitan area	mass public
Rheinische Post	283	Northwest Germany	mass public
Die Welt	254	Northwest Germany	elite-mass public
Frankfurter Allgemeine	251	nationwide	elite public
Westfälische Rundschau	231	Northern Rhineland	mass public
Neue Ruhr-Zeitung	228	Northern Rhineland	mass public
Kölner Stadtanzeiger	223	Cologne metropolitan area	mass public
Süddeutsche Zeitung	214	Southwest Germany	elite-mass public

Sources: Walter H. Mallory (ed.), *Political Handbook of the World* (New York, 1965); Institut für Publizistik, *Die deutsche Presse* (Berlin, 1961).

Allgemeine Zeitung, and the *Süddeutsche Zeitung.* The latter are primarily elite publications which, in 1964, were read daily by about half the persons holding leading positions and by more than half of those in the top income groups. Springer's *Bild-Zeitung,* the only popular daily with truly nationwide circulation, is a tabloid which devotes relatively little space to political matters that do not lend themselves to sensational headlines.

Survey research results indicate that for most Germans the daily newspaper is not a major source of information about political developments. In 1955 three out of four adults in one survey said they always read the local news in their papers, but less than half turned to them for news about national politics and only one out of three for news about international politics.

Still, most Germans are *comparatively* well informed about national political issues, as Almond and Verba found in their cross-national survey. If they do not get much information from their daily newspapers, where then do they get it? More and more, it seems, from the news programs carried by the radio and television networks. Practically every home contains at least one radio and every other one a television set. These provide the average German with sources of political information which he considers more "neutral," trustworthy, and extensive than the independent press.

According to a 1955 survey 64 per cent of German adults listened to a radio newscast at least once a day, and, according to a 1964 study of young Germans between 15 and 25 years of age, 40 per cent of the respondents relied primarily on the radio and 41 per cent on television to shape their images of their political world. The daily newspaper was singled out by only 34 per cent as a prime source of information, political conversations with friends by only 15 per cent, and with family members a mere 12 per cent.[15] Insofar as we may take such data as representative of the general adult population, it seems that radio and television are an alternative and preferred source of political perceptions and expectations. Though this is also true in the United States – another country without a

[15] The total exceeds 100 per cent because respondents were permitted to name more than one source.

national press such as that in Britain and France — Germany, radio and television are not controlled by independent newspapers and other commercial enterprises. Insofar as political information is nationwide and general in appeal and penetrates the passive apathy of the average German, it is provided to a large extent by formal communications media which serve authoritative political socialization efforts much more directly than in this country.

The independent periodical press may be more significant in political socialization than the dailies because it provides more explicit interpretive cues for its readers. Journals devoted primarily to political subjects do not have a mass readership, but more than three-fourths of German adults read one or more of the entertainment and religious weeklies that contain some tendentious political material (see Table V.5). The highly popular entertainment weeklies, like the independent newspapers, are commercial enterprises which base their appeal on features designed to attract as many customers as possible for their advertisers. Since competition between them is intense, these entertainment weeklies strive to scoop each other with sensational political items likely to attract both readers and advertisers. Catering to the assumed taste of their mass public, they combine spicy "inside" accounts of the "secret" lives of royalty and movie stars with political *exposés*, interviews, and commentaries which tend to focus on alleged dramatic shortcomings in the system — such as factional fights and bribery scandals — rather than on its more mundane aspects. Consequently, where they influence popular images of "political reality," these weeklies often present a rather unfavorable picture of the system's operation to their readers.

With a reported current circulation of well over 800,000 the controversial *Der Spiegel* is a highly successful mixture, commercially, of a lively political periodical and an entertainment weekly. Read by the German elites as well as the politically interested mass public, it represents a unique venture in independent German journalism which no other journal has been able to emulate. Modeled after *Time* magazine, *Der Spiegel* includes cultural features which appeal to a well educated readership that despises the illustrated mass weeklies,

TABLE V.5 *Major Periodicals with Political Content*

Periodicals	*1961 circulation (in 1,000 copies)*	*Percentage of adult population reading periodical,* 1963	*Sponsorship*
Entertainment weeklies			
Stern	1,339	36	Independent commercial
Quick	1,440	25	Independent commercial
Revue	1,154	21	Independent commercial
Religious weeklies			
Neue Bildpost	351	n.a.	Catholic Church
Christ und Welt	129	n.a.	Protestant Church
Sonntagsblatt	130	n.a.	Protestant Church
Allgemeine Sonntagszeitung	25	n.a.	Catholic Church
Political weeklies and monthlies			
Der Spiegel	404	12	Independent commercial
Die Zeit	92	n.a.	Independent commercial
Rheinischer Merkur	67	n.a.	Christian Democratic Union (CDU)
Vorwärts	60	n.a.	Social Democratic Party (SPD)
Bayern Kurier	25	n.a.	Christian Social Union (CSU)
Der Monat	25	n.a.	Independent Commercial
Frankfurter Hefte	6	n.a.	Independent Commercial
Aussenpolitik	3	n.a.	Independent
Europa-Archiv	3	n.a.	German Foreign Policy Association

Sources: Institut für Publizistik, *Die deutsche Presse* (Berlin, 1961); Noelle and Neumann, *op. cit.*, p. 93.

but it focuses on national and international political developments. Its frequently sharp and biting attacks on alleged shortcomings in the German political system have earned it a reputation as the most outspoken critic of the regime, though on the whole it supports the present form of government. Although prominent political leaders and government officials fear and hate the periodical as a disruptive element in German political life, to those who delight in its often savage criticism it seems to perform a vital educational function in a political system which they consider far from perfect.

Der Spiegel undoubtedly exercises some influence on the attitudes of the politically interested minority in the Federal Republic, but to what extent its revelations and criticisms strengthen or weaken elite and mass support for the regime is hard to say. It can be argued that the periodical has been instrumental in preventing or correcting political practices which threatened to weaken the regime and, in that sense, has performed a supportive function. However, it may also be true that its harsh criticism of inevitable shortcomings in the operation of the present political system encourages cynical, if not hostile, attitudes which counter official and quasi-official efforts to give legitimacy to the regime. In any case, *Der Spiegel* is far too contentious a journal to be considered a major integrative element in political socialization.

Almost all German newspapers claim to be politically "independent" or "nonpartisan" but they are not so viewed by most readers, who identify them with one or another of the major political parties and with special interest groups seeking to propagandize the public. Distrust of the press as an objective source of political communications has apparently been fed by attacks upon "irresponsible" publications by German opinion leaders, including some of the most prominent editors and publishers. Journals and newspapers constantly denounce each other as creatures of one political faction or another and as mouthpieces for individuals and groups that exploit the freedom of the press for their own selfish interests. In recent years, for example, the newspapers of Axel Springer have been engaged in a bitter dispute with journalists and writers who insist that Springer seeks to establish absolute control over all nongovernmental media of mass communication. Though they claim that he is a threat to the survival of German democracy, the Springer papers maintain that their opponents are left-wing intellectuals who seek to undermine free enterprise capitalism. Public officials have frequently denounced criticism of their conduct in the press as attacks upon the authority of the state and insisted that in the Federal Republic "published opinion" (*veröffentliche Meinung*) distorts rather than articulates "public opinion" (*öffentliche Meinung*). Former Chancellor Adenauer provided an example when, in defending his government's actions against the magazine in 1962, he labeled *Der Spiegel* a subversive publication.

In countries where the freedom of the press has stronger traditions and where journalists are more highly respected, such charges and countercharges may be accepted as part of the game of politics. But in Germany they tend to neutralize such influence as an independent press might exercise as an integrative structure in political socialization and to give correspondingly greater weight to communication sources which command greater trust and respect.

On the whole the press has supported the present regime and its roles and norms, but it has done little to promote mass participation and interest in politics. On occasion the press has taken up policy issues that involved the private interests of large sections of the general public and has mobilized mass opinion briefly. In 1964, for example, a campaign by Springer's *Bild-Zeitung* compelled the federal government to rescind an increase in the telephone rates. The *Der Spiegel* affair attracted considerable attention, mainly because it provoked extensive protests by leading newspapers and periodicals against an alleged violation of the freedom of the press. However, 31 per cent of the respondents in a mass opinion survey which followed the arrest of the *Spiegel* editors held that the federal government had acted correctly and only 22 per cent thought it had not, while 43 per cent were undecided.

Generally the press is more a medium for transmitting elite communications to the nonelites than an autonomous agent of political socialization in its own right. Insofar as a few leading dailies and periodicals are such agents, their influence appears to be restricted to that relatively small, well educated minority which is interested in political inputs as well as outputs and participates in politics to a considerably greater extent than the overwhelming majority of Germans.

The preceding observation appears also to apply to the influence of politically engaged artists and academicians. It may well be, as some observers have suggested, that the German political culture is undergoing subtle changes under their intellectual leadership, but at present the evidence is inconclusive. Indeed a number of internationally prominent German writers and university professors, belonging to the postwar generation, have taken it upon themselves to teach their countrymen the roles of responsible and participating democratic citizens — these efforts may have a positive cumulative effect, particularly on well educated young Germans. Their lectures are well attended, their books seem to be popular, and their plays are frequently performed. But on the whole the political lessons preached by a Günter Grass, Uwe Johnson, Hans Magnus Enzensberger, and Rudolf Hochhuth — to name a few — seem not to have made a very strong, positive impression on either the dominant political elites or on ordinary Germans. Other intellectuals, journalists, and political leaders are apt to denounce and ridicule these writers for their alleged "holier-than-thou" moralism, their supposed radical "nihilism," and their "political naïveté." They may grant them the jester's privilege of *Narrenfreiheit* or, if they take them more seriously, demand they leave political matters to the "experts." As for the unusual nonelite citizen who may be familiar with such writings, their effect on him appears to be the very contrary of what these reformers desire. According to one German observer:

> . . . the literature intended to disquiet has the opposite effect and helps to ease the minds of the contemporary Philistines who like to think that all the guilt for the bad state of things belongs with the neighbor, the boss, the government, current events, NATO, the atom bomb, the devil or even with a malevolent God, but is certainly not found in himself. . . .[16]

ASSOCIATIONAL INTERMEDIARY AGENTS OF POLITICAL SOCIALIZATION

As input structures of interest articulation and aggregation, formal, nongovernmental associations play an important part

[16] Johannes Gaitanides, "A Word on the Impotence of German Literature," in Stahl, *Education for Democracy in West Germany, op. cit.*, p. 350. See also Klaus Bölling, *Republic in Suspense* (New York: Praeger, 1965), pp. 347–348, and, for a contrary view, Karl W. Deutsch, "The German Republic Today . . . and Tomorrow," in Roy C. Macridis and Robert E. Ward (eds.), *Modern Political Systems: Europe* (Englewood Cliffs, N.J.: Prentice-Hall, 1963), pp. 392–394.

in the German political system, but their function in political socialization appears to be far less significant.

They participate in the process with varying degrees of intensity. First, internal communications within the various interest associations and political parties involve explicit and implicit educational activities designed to provide the directing elites with disciplined membership support in their efforts to influence government authorities. Insofar as the leaders succeed in educating the membership to identify with their goals and methods there may be obvious political socialization; insofar as the hierarchic structure of many of these formal groups promotes submissive orientations among lower functionaries and ordinary members, latent political socialization may encourage passive attitudes at the bottom and a sense of independence at the top. Second, most interest associations and political parties in Germany engage in "informational activities," directed toward the nonmember public, which seek to establish a climate of mass opinion favorable to their objectives. Such efforts may involve manifest political socialization as when sections of the general public come to adopt as their own the political orientations which are offered. They may also involve latent political socialization, as when economic or religious norms propagated by such groups are accepted and projected in turn upon political objects.

German economic associations and political parties devote extensive efforts to both internal and external educational activities. Depending on their resources, the size of their "target audience," and the contentiousness of their objectives, the leaders may invest much effort and money in endeavors to establish supportive orientations. For example, business and trade union organizations sponsor periodicals, news letters, and conferences designed to further the political education of their membership, and they seek to influence the general public indirectly through the mass media, civic organizations, and political parties which they support. The major parties engage in similar activities — particularly at election time — but because their appeal is directed toward a broader clientele their political socialization efforts are correspondingly more diffuse than those of the various interest associations. As parties of interest aggregation in a pluralist society they have increasingly sacrificed appeals in depth to appeals in breadth and particularistic membership integration to a universalistic solicitation of votes.

These activities may have a cumulative effect on mass political orientations and legitimate, to a greater extent than is presently the case, the part which such nongovernmental structures in fact play in the political system. As of now, however, most Germans appear to have no interest in mass appeals focusing principally on policy differences which do not command a great deal of support beyond the minority who are directly involved in a given issue. As we have seen, interest group and political party conflicts are still widely looked upon as destabilizing elements in the state, and if they come to the attention of the ordinary German his reaction is more likely to be negative than positive. While the interest associations and political parties may no longer be associated with bitterly antagonistic subcultural groups, their part in political socialization is also no longer as great as it was in the past.

Only one socializing structure, intervening between family and government, appears to have a really significant effect on mass attitudes toward political objects; and this one is not only divided within itself but exerts an influence which is more or less incongruent with the secularization of German society and polity. As we saw earlier, organized religion is a major force in German politics, and both major churches — but especially the Roman Catholic — explicitly and implicitly provide their members with cues relating to their political role and norm perceptions. As the recognized guardians of morality and respectability, they reinforce traditional "Christian" orientations which on the one hand extend into the privacy of the family and on the other spill over into public affairs. Through religious instruction in the schools and in church, the mass media (see Table V.5 above), and numerous ties to other important governmental and nongovernmental structures, the two principal churches sustain the most important ideological subcultures in the Federal Republic, and the religious cleavage between them.

The outward evidence of the churches' socializing influence

is the mass voting patterns which follow religious lines more than other socioeconomic characteristics. Latent political socialization through the churches is less evident but possibly even more significant. The Roman Catholic Church, traditionally hierarchic, provides its parishioners with role and norm perceptions which accentuate obedience to authoritative direction from above, as well as with an opportunity to obtain psychological release from a burdensome past. The Lutheran Church makes less explicit efforts to socialize its members and places greater emphasis on their self-development, but implicitly its teachings tend to promote an inward-oriented individualism which encourages privatization and passivity in public affairs by "the little man."

POLITICAL STABILITY AND CULTURAL CHANGE

One of the fundamental issues of German politics is how to reconcile political stability with cultural change. The present political system originated in a shotgun marriage between a people who had just emerged from a totalitarian system and a democratic regime more or less imposed upon them. Such a union can grow into a stable and durable relationship, provided it comes to rest on more than popular acquiescence and proves adaptable enough to accommodate severe strains on the bonds which link citizens and regime. In this sense the marriage vows, "to love, honor, and obey, for richer or for poorer, in good times and in bad," apply to the political relationship.

The question whether the people of Western Germany will learn to embrace the roles and behavioral standards associated with the new regime is crucial for its survival. Therefore, in the last analysis, the future of German politics depends heavily on political socialization processes. The present patterns of political culture provide no assurance that the ties between the German people and their democratic regime are as yet solid enough to assure its continued existence, particularly under less favorable conditions than now prevail. The basic issue is whether the political socialization of children as well as adults in contemporary Germany will gradually yield cultural patterns that lend firm support to a democratic form of government, or whether the persistence of present patterns — or their transformation – may force structural changes in the political system which, in effect, would radically alter its present form.

The adaptation of German cultural patterns to the principles and processes of a well functioning democracy involves three related aspects of political socialization in a changing setting. First, the process must establish a good fit between the functions which people believe to be performed by political structures and actors, and the functions which they want them to perform. Second, political socialization must facilitate a smooth adjustment between the operation of the political system and the operation of other subsystems in German society and between what are considered private concerns and public issues. Third, the learning process must provide for congruence between persistent traditional cultural patterns and new ones produced by socioeconomic and political modernization in a dynamic environment.

These vital aspects of the socialization function confront every political system operating in a transitional political culture, and, explicitly or implicitly, most books and articles on German politics touch upon them. But all too often they are considered primarily as reflecting the purely instrumental capacity of leading actors and formal institutions to process input demands into policy outputs to the satisfaction of the German voters. Without deprecating the importance of leadership behavior and institutional factors, we should not overlook the less conspicuous long-term socialization. Individual leaders will come and go, elections may now favor one party and now another, and the distribution of power within and between governmental structures is likely to fluctuate. But these phenomena are transitory when compared to the basic evolution of mass cultural patterns and the form, content, and cumulative effect of the process through which Germans today acquire their general political orientations and are inducted into political roles.

The present socialization process in Germany is complicated by the sharp structural discontinuities of recent decades and the consequent ambiguity of political attitudes. Every stable political system, whatever its form, requires a firmly established but adaptable political culture which is maintained by integrated socializing structures that transmit congruent orientations from generation to generation and from society to polity. In such systems the destabilizing effect of socioeconomic change is counterbalanced by the proliferation of learning experiences and of agents that provide for the extension of feelings of solidarity, trust, and sociability to groups larger than the immediate family. In postwar Germany, however, these features have been conspicuously missing from the socialization process. Their absence is a characteristic of a transitional society which is correspondingly subject to greater latent political instability and therefore to countervailing governmental measures designed to maintain stability, to promote cultural unity, and to give legitimacy to the prevailing political order.

Without well established cultural traditions sustaining a democratic system, the preservation and extension of a stable democracy in Germany imposes specific tasks on the political socialization process. It must (1) establish firm mass beliefs that such a regime will *endure,* (2) promote evaluative convictions that it provides the most *effective* structures for achieving individual and collective interests, and (3) evoke intensive emotional support based on the feeling that the regime is indeed a *genuine* democracy and not a mere facade for the rule of an unrepresentative minority. The foundations for meeting the second condition already seem to exist in the Federal Republic, but the bases for satisfying the first and third requisites are more tenuous. Although mass and elite opinion reflects a general, affectively neutral sense of satisfaction with the system's instrumental performance, political socialization has yet to overcome the lack of profound emotional support as evidenced in the widespread skepticism about the authenticity of German democracy and the permanence of the regime. The development of comprehensive popular beliefs, emotions, and values, however, seems to require far greater congruence between socializing structures than presently exists and far greater harmony between the disparate roles and norm perceptions which these structures provide.[17]

As we have shown in this chapter, the principal agents of

[17] See Harry Eckstein, "A Theory of Stable Democracy," in *Division and Cohesion in Democracy* (Princeton: Princeton University Press, 1966), pp. 225–288.

manifest and latent political socialization in contemporary Germany are not bound together by a solid chain of interlocking, mutually reinforcing role and norm perceptions. Insofar as these agents are functionally specific, universalistic modern structures, their influence on the political learning process does not appear intensive enough at present to provide continuity in mass political socialization. Insofar as they are functionally diffuse, particularistic traditional structures, their influence, on the other hand, seems so intensive that it works against such integration. For this reason, the gap between family political socialization and governmental socialization efforts may appear to represent a potential source of political instability, as long as intervening structures do not facilitate greater congruence.

The norms and role structures of the new democratic regime rest on the principles of an open, pluralist society and active citizenship involvement in political life. But the socialization in most German homes – endorsed by organized religion – is largely detached from the political system and discontinuous with civic education efforts from above. The latter emphasize private virtues such as minding one's own business and being loyal to the family, the former public virtues such as political participation and loyalty to state and country.

These cleavages result from the unusual aspects of postwar modernization in Germany, which increased rather than diminished the influence of home and church as socializing agents in a transitional culture. Initially their primacy may have helped to maintain domestic stability, but today such influences reinforce traditional orientation patterns militating against changes in the political culture. They sustain a general disinclination to become involved in political life and a low sense of civic competence, aggravate the tensions and ambiguities of an era of transition, and hinder the integration of private and public standards of conduct. Such orientations, should they persevere, might at the very least extend the period of cultural transition indefinitely; at worst they might lead to an open confrontation between state and family, which present religious and political leaders in the Federal Republic are determined to avoid.

Under present conditions of economic prosperity and political stability, the lack of integrated collaborating structures of political socialization does not loom as a clear and present danger to the regime. Given time and a continuation of favorable environmental conditions such a network may gradually develop and facilitate the establishment of greater congruence between the mass political culture and the structures of the democratic system. In most respects, circumstances seem favorable to the persistence and extension of German democracy, according to various indices suggested by students of political development. Political life is well ordered, public authorities are respected, and governmental rulings are readily obeyed. An affluent people appear to be contented with the lives they live, and their political attitudes, on the whole, are homogeneous. Mass and elite opinion patterns indicate considerable adaptability to changing conditions, and, at the same time, resilience to destabilizing, sudden shifts of political emotions. Subcultural cleavages appear to be neither very profound nor to pose a major obstacle to the development of a legitimating consensus behind the present regime. Thus the cumulative effect of general satisfaction with the system's performance and a gradual habituation to its roles and structures may help to overcome ambiguities, doubts, and tensions produced by the rapid transition from a totalitarian to a pluralistic society.

But this will need time, perhaps a great deal of time. Historical evidence suggests that it takes at least twenty-five and as much as a hundred years for gradual, cumulative learning experiences to produce lasting changes in the attitudes of a large number of people.[18] For a country such as Germany, which has undergone many major political transformations in less than a century, the period of transition may last a long time. The questions are whether the dynamics of internal and external demands on the system will allow that much time and whether political stability can be assured in the interval without more intensive governmental intervention in political socialization. At present, pressures to alter political socialization

[18] See Karl W. Deutsch and Richard L. Merritt, "Effects of National and International Images," in Herbert C. Kelman (ed.), *International Behavior: A Social-Psychological Analysis* (New York: 1965), p. 171.

patterns are not very intense; relevant structures function well enough to provide stability, if not affective support, for the form of the political system. But conditions which would increase the demand load on the system – such as sustained threats to the physical or economic security of the Federal Republic – would call for more intensive supportive orientations. The prevailing socialization patterns give no assurance that such support would be readily forthcoming or could easily be mobilized.

The dynamics of domestic and international developments are likely to modify present socialization patterns sooner or later. Such changes may develop gradually and spontaneously, but they may also be forced by more intensive authoritative measures from above, particularly if prevailing patterns prove increasingly incongruent with efforts to reconcile political stability, cultural change, and the preservation of the regime. One way or another changing patterns must involve the relationship between home and polity, for the characteristic of a modern political system is a political socialization process that penetrates society to its lowest unit and introduces supportive citizenship orientation into family socialization. The "opening-up" of the German family may be delayed, but it appears unavoidable if the present system is to rest upon firm foundations. The compartmentalization of private and public roles and standards, the attendant lack of mass commitment to participation in politics, and the withholding of affective identification with the regime and political community are, in this sense, destabilizing for the democratic system.

Greater mass participation, coupled with a more profound commitment, might give more stability to the regime if accompanied by greater integration among socializing structures and a wider distribution of the socializing load.

Such a development might promote the recruitment of larger numbers of German citizens as active participants in a democratic system, strengthen intermediary socializing structures, and provide a greater sense of identification with regime and community than exists at present. However, more intensive mass participation in the political input process without greater commitment to its present form might undermine political stability, as it did before Hitler came to power, and government socialization efforts might rebound and lead to increased mass alienation from the system. The latter possibility haunts the dreams of many German leaders today. This may explain their reluctance to push for greater government efforts to promote more intensive mass involvement in politics and their inclination to rely instead on evolutionary processes to establish a "democratic civic culture."

CHAPTER VI

Participants in Politics

ALL GERMANS are involved in politics. Authoritative rulings by public officials require children to go to school and adults to pay taxes, shopkeepers to observe legal closing hours, and young men to serve in the armed forces. Political participation, however, denotes a more limited and voluntary form of involvement focusing on the making, rather than the consequences, of public policy. Participant roles are associated with input activities directed toward the satisfaction of domestic political demands and with the conversion of such demands by authoritative governmental agents into system outputs.

Disparities in the extent of political participation and influence exist in every political system but the forms which they assume in present-day Germany reflect a particular mixture between formal institutional arrangements and political culture patterns. The interaction between constitutional, legal norms and political orientations has produced a rather polarized participation structure which provides for many, variegated roles, but assigns most of these to comparatively few actors. About one-fourth of the population – mostly young people – do not have any participant roles, and most of the rest only one, that of the voter. On the other hand, a relatively small minority of political actors are not only intensively involved and influential in public affairs but often play a number of roles simultaneously. A federal minister, for example, is not only a voter, but also a cabinet member and a parliamentary deputy, and usually plays a prominent political role in his party and in other nongovernmental organizations.

This division between single- and multiple-role participants and between a very large passive majority and a very small active, influential minority reflects the persistence of certain German cultural traditions as well as the influence of new socioeconomic and political structures. The functional task specializations and concomitant status stratifications of an advanced industrial society have altered, but not eliminated, traditional hierarchic distribution of political power in Germany, and the fusion of the old and the new is expressed in the patterns of political recruitment, participation, and influence.

These patterns conform more closely to the European model of elitist democracy than to that of American egalitarian democracy.[1] That is, a small policy-bearing stratum of politically relevant and active elite participants play the game according to more or less agreed upon rules and tend to settle differences over the application and interpretation of these rules among themselves, rather than by appealing to the general public to arbitrate. They are supported and protected in these key roles by cultural norms, legal arrangements, and an intervening stratum of second-string players, all of which mediate between elites and mass publics. The bulk of the citizenry neither does nor wants to interfere with these rules, not knowing them in all their complexities, but accepts the situation because it seems to meet popular role and goal expectations.

Though the affective symbols of deference associated with the crown in the democratic monarchies of Europe are lacking, traditional respect for the agents of the state and political experts and evaluative satisfaction with policy outputs have sufficed in Germany to lend mass support to the nonegalitarian, participation structure. Thus, formally joined under the public authority's legitimating umbrella, all the major elites directly or indirectly derive their representative and control functions in the political system from the legal sanctions bestowed upon them in the name of the state. Political elites may also need a popular mandate, but other groups, such as religious and administrative leaders, do not.

[1] For a discussion of the distinction see Seymour Martin Lipset, "The Value Patterns of Democracy: A Case Study in Comparative Analysis," *American Sociological Review,* XXVIII (August, 1963), 528 ff.

As we recognized earlier, the deliberate intention of the founding fathers of the present regime was to limit general citizenship participation in politics and to establish representative structures which would place the continuous operation of the political system in the hands of relatively few key actors. The development of these structures has more or less followed this design, in part because they appeared well suited to provide political stability in an era of rapid environmental changes, in part because they proved congruent with prevailing perceptions of the "proper" distribution of role assignments. Also, as we have seen, most Germans feel that political participation is something to be left to "experts," professional players who are well versed in the rules of the game and highly skilled in its performance. They accept their limited and intermittent role assignments in the participation structure and agree that there is no room for amateurs in the political arena, nor for actors who violate the rules of the game.

The stress on political "know-how" enhances the authority of the incumbents of formal positions of leadership and inhibits the development of grass roots support for nonprofessional civic action groups. The emphasis on "legitimate" role behavior supports the formal exclusion of alleged subversives from participation in politics – Communists, for example – and encourages extremely strict rules of conduct governing those who do participate, particularly in positions of public trust. Whereas Americans have traditionally shown a good deal of tolerance toward politicians who accept gifts from petitioners for special favors, in Germany even minor infractions of traditional rules against bribery of public officials are likely to cause an uproar and may spell the political death of the accused. In return for far-reaching autonomy from popular control, civil servants and government leaders, party officials and interest group functionaries, are expected to exercise their public mandates honestly, responsibly, and efficiently.

THE VOTER'S ROLE

Every three out of four years local, state (Länder), and federal elections provide practically all adult Germans with opportunities to become active in politics, and on the average

TABLE VI.1 *Participants in Political Inputs*

	Approximate % of population	*Extent of collective participation*	*Extent of collective national influence*
Eligible voters	70	intermittent	low
Voters in:			
federal elections	60	intermittent	low
state elections	49	intermittent	low
local elections	45–60	intermittent	low
Attend meetings on public affairs	9	intermittent	medium-low
Active in politics	3	mostly part-time	medium-low
Members of political groups	3	mostly part-time	medium-low
Members of parties	2	mostly part-time	medium-low
Members of local and district councils	0.4	mostly part-time	medium
Members of state and federal legislatures	0.003	mostly full-time	medium-high
National elites	0.001	mostly full-time	high

Sources: Data calculated from various election and opinion poll statistics, especially those reported in Wolfgang Hartenstein and Klaus Liepelt, "Party Members and Party Voters in West Germany," *Acta Sociologica,* VI, 1–2 (1962), Table 1, and Erwin Faul (ed.), *Wahlen und Wähler in Westdeutschland* (Villingen: Ring Verlag, 1960). National elites calculated from positional inventory reported in Lewis J. Edinger, "Post-Totalitarian Leadership," *American Political Science Review,* LIV (1960), pp. 62–63, Table 1.

between 60 and 90 per cent of them are thus intermittently recruited into participant roles (see Table VI.1). Though in most instances the ostensible object is the choice of local and Land officials, in fact even nonfederal elections tend to have national import. There are no by-elections for offices that fall vacant between regular elections, as in the United States and Britain, or plebiscites as in the Weimar Republic; local and regional elections are therefore considered of correspondingly greater significance as interim tests of the popularity of national parties and their leaders. The latter are apt to devote a great deal more effort to winning them and the communications media are likely to attribute greater weight to the outcome than the actual importance of the offices at stake seem to justify.

Although elections thus provide Germans with an opportunity to articulate their political preferences, they are of limited significance for the recruitment of governmental leaders. The voters have only an indirect and not necessarily decisive voice in selecting their formal governors. In the first place election laws provide that half – in some Länder all – the parliamentary deputies are to be chosen through a system of proportional representation which compels the voter to cast his ballot for a party list rather than a particular candidate. Thus, in federal elections for the Bundestag, the lower house of parliament, every voter may cast two ballots, one for a local constituency candidate and one for a party. Accordingly, only half the Bundestag deputies owe their seats to a direct choice of the voters, as in the United States and Britain. The rest owe them to having been placed high enough on their party's Land list by party leaders to be elected by a system of proportional representation which equitably apportions seats among these lists in accordance with the results of the nationwide vote for a party. In the second place, in federal parliamentary elections and most Land diet elections the candidates of parties which fail to secure 5 per cent of the votes obtain no seats at all, and those who voted for them thus have no voice whatever in deciding who is to govern. Finally, under the prevailing parliamentary form of government, the ultimate choice of the legislative and executive leadership rests nominally in the hands of the elected deputies – in fact with the leaders of the dominant majorities.[2]

In short, German voters may indicate their preference for one party or another, but they do not directly choose their authoritative decisionmakers as Americans and Frenchmen elect their presidents. When their ballots fail to yield a clear plurality or majority supporting one particular leader or set of leaders – as has been the case in most postwar German elections – the composition of the government will be decided by negotiations between more influential participants. The final product of such negotiations may be a coalition government rather different in nature from what the voters intended, if not expected.

[2] The direct popular election of mayors in southern Germany represents an exception to this practice.

The consistently high turnout of voters in federal elections — and, to a lesser extent, in Land and local elections — indicates that this form of citizenship participation in politics is practically universal in the Federal Republic. As various studies of German elections have indicated, such a turnout provides two important elements for the stable operation of the political system. In the first place, there is no substantial reservoir of qualified actors who ordinarily do not vote but might be recruited into such participant roles by a dramatic event and/or leader, as in the early 1930's. Beyond the relatively limited and gradual influx of new voters, the present high rate of turnout excludes the possibility of sudden political changes produced by increased electoral participation. Though the direction of voters' preferences may change, the extent of participation lends stability to the political system.

Second, present voting patterns — particularly in federal elections — suggest that electoral participation on the whole is a function of neither intense political involvement nor social background. Whereas in the past increased turnout reflected greater mass involvement in election outcomes, most Germans vote today not so much because they expect to give effect to demands for public policy decisions but because they consider it their duty. When they want to press claims upon the policymakers, Germans rely more heavily on other structures of interest articulation, such as formal pressure groups with direct access to governmental authorities. And whereas in the United States and other countries turnout tends to vary a good deal with socioeconomic background, particularly age, sex, education, religion, income, and place of residence, in Germany this background may influence party preferences but electoral participation hardly at all.

Cultural patterns and structural arrangements thus interact, to producing a self-fulfilling prophecy. For most Germans voting represents a very low commitment to a political input role, and electoral arrangements and outcomes tend to confirm their belief that voting provides them with relatively little influence over public policymaking. Whatever their social status or level of education, this political input role gives them no particular pleasure since they attach little importance to it.

Consequently, policymakers usually feel free to "interpret" their electoral mandates pretty freely. Lower-class, poorly educated voters are inclined to consider voting a somewhat futile exercise in citizenship and are not motivated, as are their French neighbors, to persuade policymakers that it should be more than that. Upper middle class and better educated Germans tend to encourage such beliefs since they are disposed to be contemptuous or afraid of the mass electorate and to consider the average voter irresponsible, unpredictable, and a potential threat to the established order. Even those who in theory support the principles of popular democracy remember that the radical right-wing and left-wing parties in the Weimar Republic profited from these principles and received the support of millions of lower class voters who were dissatisfied with the regime. Almond and Verba learned in their 1959 survey that although members of the upper social strata tended to be better informed and more interested in politics than the average German, they also were particularly critical of the influence of elections on policymaking. Traditionalist conservatives prefer to keep the masses completely out of "affairs of state," and liberal democrats believe that mass participation needs to be carefully controlled, at least until the present regime has gained stronger roots among the general public.

Such attitudes, expressed in political behavior, lend a different meaning to frequent official claims that the high turnout in German elections proves that popular democracy has been established in the Federal Republic. They also help explain the extremely low rate of voluntary participation in other political roles and the far-reaching autonomy of key participants in the political system.[3]

[3] The above discussion owes much to a large number of studies of German voting behavior, including Gabriel Almond and Sidney Verba, *The Civic Culture* (Boston: Little, Brown, 1964), Chaps. 5 and 6; Erwin Scheuch and Rudolf Wildenmann (eds.), *Zur Soziologie der Wahl* (Köln-Opladen: Westdeutscher Verlag, 1966); Erwin Faul (ed.), *Wahlen und Wähler in West Deutschland* (Villingen: Ring Verlag, 1960); Viggo Graf Blücher, *Der Prozess der Meinungsbildung* (Bielefeld: EMNID, 1962); and Renate Mayntz, "Citizenship Participation in Germany: Nature and Extent," unpublished paper, Fifth World Congress of the International Political Science Association, Paris, 1961.

MIDDLE-RANGE PARTICIPANTS

Less than 10 per cent of Germans participate in politics through multiple input roles. Most of these are middle-range participants who link the rather inactive mass to the top policymaking stratum but their political involvement is sporadic.

Generally speaking, these middle-range participants are intermittently recruited into more active political roles through occupational positions and/or organizational affiliations relating to specific input activities, such as participation in political meetings (see Table VI.1). As in the United States, only a very small proportion of the adult population belongs to a political party (in contrast to England, Italy, and some other European countries). Most middle-range participants in Germany are members of compulsory or voluntary mass interests associations organized primarily for nonpolitical purposes but sporadically involved in input activities. Thus about 12 per cent of German adults are members of formal occupational associations, and a disproportionate number of middle-range participants are recruited from the most extensively organized socioeconomic groups – businessmen, farmers, skilled industrial workers, and professional men. These are almost always men, usually middle-aged, and, except for trade union members, usually belong to the better educated, higher income groups.

These middle-range participants exert relatively little direct influence on public policymaking. For the most part they constitute the largely inactive reserve forces of various mass organizations which at certain times and for particular issues are mobilized by their leaders to lend quantitative support to political input demands. Rank-and-file party members will be called upon at election time to help solicit votes and funds. The leaders of refugee organizations and trade unions occasionally summon their followers to demonstrate their political strength and solidarity in mass demonstrations, and those of farm, religious, and business associations every so often ask their members to press their local parliamentary deputy to support or oppose a particular piece of legislation.

A small minority of upper middle-range participants plays

more active and, sometimes, more influential roles in political input processes. They usually hold one or more positions in governmental and/or nongovernmental offices that involve the articulation or aggregation of demands for public policy decisions or the recruitment of top decisionmakers. They may be party officials or civil servants whose occupational tasks include such activities, but they may also be interest group functionaries, clergymen, or journalists who primarily devote themselves to nonpolitical matters.

Like the rank-and-file middle-range participants, but to a more significant extent, these actors perform a strategic function in the German political system. Essentially they play the intervening roles which link leaders to followers, governors to governed, and balance claims from below with controls from above. Insofar as they facilitate reciprocal, two-way political communications between the bottom and top strata of the participation structure, they help to maintain congruence between claims and supports within the system in general and in various political subsystems in particular. A clergyman or journalist, for example, may not only justify and explain the policymakers' actions to his mass public, but may also give voice to inarticulate mass opinion on political issues. Similarly a middle-range party or government official or interest group functionary may not only serve as an instrument of control for the top leadership, but may also communicate "upstairs" attitudes, which he learns from his contacts with the general citizenry.

All told, middle-range participants are only intermittently and peripherally involved in public policymaking processes. For the most part they are content to leave running the system to their formal leaders. Grass-roots participation by the rank-and-file members of the numerous organized groups involved in German political life is generally nominal and inactive, and usually does not provide a particularly strong bond of emotional association between leaders and followers, or much control from below. Upper middle-range participants may be more continuously and deeply involved in politics but highly formalized and hierarchic structures severely restrict their opportunities to influence input and rulemaking processes. Such patterns permit the key participants at the top to have a great deal of autonomy, but they also represent potential weaknesses in the present regime.

The integration and efficient operation of interest articulation and aggregation processes, intervening between society and authoritative policymaking structures in the polity, depends on the degree to which relevant channels of political communication from below are kept open. Lack of responsiveness at the top to mass demands from the bottom may hinder, if not prevent, the development of firm popular support for the regime and threatens its stability in a crisis.

It is for this reason that the middle-range participants are vital to the operation of the political system. Relatively few in number, they carry a correspondingly heavy load as actors intervening between the unorganized citizenry and the policymaking leaders. German cultural patterns and organizational forms tend to assign control rather than representative functions to middle-range participants; but the maintenance of the regime requires that they be free to speak as well as to listen and that they be sensitive to opinion from below as well as above. At present this two-way interaction seems inadequately understood not only by the general public and its leaders, but by many of the middle-range participants themselves.

THE POLICY-BEARING STRATUM

A few thousand elected and appointed, coopted and anointed leaders are the policybearing stratum in the political influence and participation structure. As national and subnational decisionmakers, in various areas of public life, they play key participant roles in the making of authoritative policy decisions affecting the general population. Some wield political power on the basis of formal governmental positions, others on the strength of special skills, financial resources, or mass support. Some are widely known and stand bathed in the spotlight of public prominence, others are active behind the scenes. Together they form the political top class, influential elites who not only have a great deal more "inside information" about the operation of the system than the nonelite majority, but who can do a great deal more to mold domestic input demands and influence the processes through which such claims are converted into policy outputs.

The members of this policybearing stratum can be divided into two groups of political actors. First are the *manifest political leaders* occupying influential positions that involve continuous participation in political activities. Second are the *latent political leaders,* holding positions in the system which call for only intermittent participation in public policymaking but which involve considerable potential influence.

Manifest political leaders participate in input and rulemaking processes by virtue of their formal constitutional and paraconstitutional positions in governmental and party structures. Most obviously, they include members of the *governmental elite,* key executive and legislative leaders such as the federal chancellor, the heads of Länder governments, mayors, and leading members of federal, state, and local parliamentary bodies. In addition to these incumbents of mostly elective positions, manifest leaders include members of the *administrative elite,* key officials in the civil service, the military, and the judiciary, who exercise influence over public policymaking in an official advisory or direct rulemaking capacity. Most of the decrees and laws promulgated by the formal government decisionmakers are in fact drafted by appointed, rather than elected, key officials, and their application is likely to involve interpretive rulings by members of the administrative elite in federal, state, or local governments. Thus, German judges, like their American counterparts, may make public policy in deciding which rules should be applied, how, and to whom.

Last, but by no means least, manifest political leaders include the paraconstitutional *political party elites.* Under Article 21 of the Basic Law, political parties "participate in the formation of the political will of the people," which in effect formally invests their leading spokesmen with major participant roles in the system. Strengthened in recent years by legislation, court decisions, and political practices, this unique constitutional provision places the major party leaders in strategic positions as mediators between the governmental and administrative elites on the one hand, and the ostensibly nonpolitical elites and mass public on the other. To an extent unprecedented in German history, party leaders today control the recruitment and performance of the former and the political influence exercised by the latter. And although one set of party leaders may dominate the executive branch of the federal government, the constitutional division of power between executive and legislature and between federal and land authorities has allowed others to participate in public policy-making. For instance, Christian Democratic leaders controlled the national government from 1949 to 1966, but the leaders of the Social Democratic opposition often exercised a parliamentary veto power both in the Bundestag and – through control of a number of Länder governments – in the Bundesrat, the upper house of the federal legislature. Similarly, in both major parties regional and Länder leaders, without formal positions in national executive or legislative bodies, have frequently played key roles in federal politics.

Latent political leaders exercise influence over public policy-making on the strength of positions in ostensibly nonpolitical structures which intermittently involve them in political input processes. For example, formal legal provisions or more informal arrangements compel or permit interest group spokesmen to play political roles, though their primary function may be to attend to the economic or religious needs of their members. Mass support, financial resources, professional expertise, or a formally recognized position of moral or intellectual leadership in German society provide latent political leaders with the means for exerting greater or lesser influence upon the decisions of the manifest leaders when these decisions involve their particular interests.

The political power of these leaders is far more balanced today than under previous German regimes, and the interests they represent are far more diversified. Protestant and Roman Catholic religious leaders, employer and trade union elites, and spokesmen for agricultural and industrial interests may and do enter the political arena to press competing demands upon governmental, administrative, or party officials. Leaders of veterans' and professional groups, refugee organizations and trade associations, contend for access to and influence over authoritative decisionmakers in the state, and mass media leaders and university professors may play important participant roles as purveyors and interpreters of political communications influencing elite as well as nonelite attitudes and behavior.

The diversification and balance of these latent political leaders are due to the heterogeneous elements included in major interest groups. For instance, the major employers' organizations have as members importers and exporters, coal mine owners as well as producers of heating oil; these groups may collaborate on some political issues but compete for favorable government decisions on many others. Professional interests may unite university professors on matters affecting their status as civil servants, but their partisan sympathies for one political party or another will place them in contending camps at other times.

Whether they are manifest or latent political leaders, most key participants are primarily involved in local and regional affairs, as in the United States. Probably no more than a thousand play truly national political roles focusing on policymaking at the federal level. The unusually polycentric character of the Federal Republic does not mean that its political system does not incorporate such roles, but that its national leaders are geographically more dispersed than those of most modern industrial nations. They include not only key government and administrative officials in Bonn, but also heads of the Länder governments, judges of the chief federal courts in Munich and Karlsruhe, and directors of the federal bank in Frankfurt. National political roles are played by regional party leaders in Mainz and Kiel, as well as by economic leaders who make their headquarters in Düsseldorf, Cologne, or Hamburg. Federal policies are influenced by Roman Catholic and Protestant bishops, university professors, and mass media leaders scattered throughout the country, and by key officials of interest associations who rarely come to Bonn.

Excellent communications facilities and strong associational ties give these leaders easy access to each other and to their respective mass clienteles and allow them to participate in national affairs as effectively as if they were all concentrated in one capital city (see Table VI.2). Even more important, the development of German political life since the establishment of the Federal Republic has focused increasing attention on national policymaking and consequently has drawn leading participants deeper into federal politics.

Indirectly the renationalization of German politics results

TABLE VI.2 *Direct Contacts Between German Leaders, 1967*

	Percentage
Leaders personally acquainted with	
a high functionary of a business association	96
one or more deputies of federal parliament	94
a high official of a federal ministry	93
a leading scholar	92
a deputy of Land parliament	91
leading journalists	90
a high trade union functionary	84
a leading member of the clergy	79
federal deputy in own constituency	70
a high-ranking military officer	68

Source: Interview data from a study of a representative cross-section of German leaders, reported in Erwin Scheuch, "Sichtbare und unsichtbare Macht," *Die Zeit,* November 28, 1967, p. 3.

mainly from the reconcentration of an economic system once again dominated by a few giant industrial, commercial, and banking empires. The re-emergence of powerful, national business leaders has been accompanied by the consolidation of competing economic elites, especially farm and trade union leaders. More directly, two political factors have promoted the importance of national leadership roles.

The Federal Republic's intensive involvement in international affairs and the exceptional significance of extrasocietal inputs into its political society have established intimate links between domestic and foreign affairs and between internal and external demands for authoritative policy decisions. In contrast to the United States, almost all questions of national policy involve foreign policy questions. Leading participants in the political system are compelled to contend with such national problems as the Federal Republic's relations with France, the United States, and the Soviet Union, and its policies regarding NATO and German reunification. The country's dependency on foreign trade and its involvement in European economic integration have led business and farm leaders to play national roles that permit them to influence relevant federal legislation and treaties. The question of Germany's relations with its Communist neighbors has drawn refugee leaders, Protestant bishops, and university professors into the national political arena. In short, the recognition that international affairs have a significant bearing on a broad range of domestic problems has led diverse elite members to seek national political roles involving participation in foreign policy-making.

A second reason for the nationalization of elite political participation is that the authoritative distribution of public benefits and obligations is done primarily by federal agents. Increasingly, the mobilization, allocation, and control of German human and physical resources have, in fact if not in form, been placed in the hands of the incumbents of national political positions, and consequently key participants either occupy such positions or seek access to them. Ambitious politicians, for example, have been willing to forego secure and influential offices in local and Länder governments for even secondary leadership positions in the federal cabinet and legislature. The annual appropriations of vast federal sums as social welfare and subsidies to various economic groups have focused the efforts of interest group leaders on appropriate national executive and legislative organs. Federal legislation regulating wages and hours concerns business and trade union leaders, Roman Catholic bishops take a keen interest in national laws for the protection of family life and public morals, and university professors lobby for federal aid to education. Thus in domestic as in foreign policy, political participation in national roles has become decisive to key actors in the political system.

LEADERSHIP RECRUITMENT

The rules and processes of postwar leadership recruitment support the average German's belief that he and his kind are largely excluded from key participant positions in the political system. Entry into the policybearing stratum may have become more open in recent decades, but old as well as new admission standards impose restrictions which are a good deal more severe than those in the United States. For example, although Article 33 of the Basic Law provides that "every German shall be equally eligible for public office," it qualifies this right by adding that he must possess the necessary "aptitude, qualifications, and professional achievements." Traditional and modern criteria select manifest and latent political leaders of similar social backgrounds – not shared by the mass of citizenry.

In some respects the social background of the contemporary leadership is more representative of the general population than formerly. As indicated in Tables VI.3 and VI.4, elite members are now recruited proportionately from various geographic regions of the Federal Republic, whereas before 1933 the areas now under Communist control were overrepresented, and the Nazi leadership included a disproportionate number of North Germans. Similarly, the present political class reflects the general urbanization of the population and the diminishing importance of rural areas and small towns.[4]

But in other respects the social background of elite members differs sharply from that of the general citizenry, as it does in other industrialized societies. Most of the German leaders come from upper class and upper middle class families willing and able to let their sons spend a decade or more acquiring a secondary and, often, a university education in preparation for elite careers. As in the past, Protestants predominate among them, though the two major religious groups are now closely balanced in the population. Women outnumber men in Germany, but top participant positions remain for all practical purposes a male prerogative.

As in the United States and the Soviet Union, government and party leaders are somewhat more representative of the general population. Among them and some of the leaders of nonbusiness associations – notably trade union leaders – individuals of lower middle class background, persons without a university education, and Roman Catholics are more common than in other elite groups.

[4] See also Wolfgang Zapf, *Wandlungen der deutschen Elite: Ein Zirkulationsmodell deutscher Führungsgruppen 1919–1961* (Munich: Piper, 1965); Wolfgang Zapf (ed.), *Beiträge zur Analyse der deutschen Oberschicht* (Munich: Piper, 1965); Lewis J. Edinger, "Continuity and Change in the Background of German Decision-Makers," *Western Political Quarterly*, XIV (March, 1961), 17–36; Karl W. Deutsch and Lewis J. Edinger, *Germany Rejoins the Powers* (Stanford: Stanford University Press, 1959), pp. 60–141; Karl W. Deutsch, *et al., France, Germany, and the Western Alliance* (New York: Scribner, 1967), pp. 120–121; and anonymous, "Die 'Clique' an der Spitze," *Die Zeit*, December 27, 1966, p. 15.

TABLE VI.3 *A Profile of German Elites, 1964 (Figures Are Rounded-off Percentages)*

Elite position	*Politics*	*Public administration*	*Business*	*Nonbusiness associations*	*Mass media*	*University professors*	*All elites*
N	38	30	36	27	21	21	173
Number of years in position							
1–3	8	23	0	11	24	0	10
3–5	13	17	8	15	19	19	15
5–10	32	13	11	33	14	14	20
10–15	24	10	33	26	13	29	23
More than 15	24	17	30	11	19	38	25
n.a.	0	20	8	4	10	0	7
Total	101	100	100	100	99	100	100
Proportion males	100	100	97	96	95	100	98
Age distribution							
Over 60	27	30	39	40	23	48	34
50–60	34	40	50	30	29	38	38
40–49	32	7	6	11	29	5	15
Under 40	8	3	3	11	14	9	8
n.a.	—	20	3	7	5	0	6
Total	101	100	101	99	100	100	101
Religious affiliation							
Protestant	45	47	58	33	60	68	50
Roman Catholic	42	27	19	30	21	14	28
Other and none	6	0	14	23	9	14	10
n.a.	8	27	8	15	10	5	13
Total	101	101	99	101	100	101	101
Social class background							
Upper	21	30	33	7	33	57	29
Upper middle	29	27	36	15	29	24	27
Lower middle	26	13	19	56	19	10	24
Lower	3	0	0	4	0	0	1
n.a.	21	30	11	19	19	10	19
Total	100	100	99	101	100	101	100
Educational background							
University	71	57	61	41	81	95	66
Secondary only	21	27	28	33	14	5	23
Primary only	5	0	8	22	0	0	6
n.a.	3	17	3	4	5	0	5
Total	100	101	100	100	100	100	100

TABLE VI.3 *(Continued)*

Elite position	*Poli-tics*	*Public admin-istration*	*Busi-ness*	*Non-business associa-tions*	*Mass media*	*Uni-versity pro-fessors*	*All elites*
N	38	30	36	27	21	21	173
Size of birthplace							
Under 20,000	37	23	16	52	14	15	27
20,000–100,000	26	17	19	11	5	5	16
100,001–500,000	8	27	31	15	14	43	22
Over 500,000	29	10	33	15	48	38	28
n.a.	0	23	3	7	19	0	8
Total	100	100	102	100	100	101	101
Region of birth							
West Germany	42	23	30	37	10	28	30
South Germany	23	20	14	22	10	24	19
North Germany	8	17	19	19	14	14	15
Central and East Germany (including Berlin)	19	20	20	11	47	24	22
Outside 1919 Germany	8	0	14	7	5	10	8
n.a.	—	20	3	4	14	0	6
Total	100	100	100	100	100	100	100

Source: Data drawn from a reputational-positional selection of 173 German leaders interviewed in 1964 under the auspices of the Yale University Arms Control and Disarmament Project. See Karl W. Deutsch, Lewis J. Edinger, Roy C. Macridis, Richard Merritt, and Helga Voss-Eckermann, *French and German Elite Responses* (New Haven: Yale Political Data Library, 1966).

TABLE VI.4 *Background of German Cabinet Members, 1890–1960 (Percentages)*

Classification	*Empire*	*Weimar Republic*	*Third Reich*	*Federal Republic*
Political affiliation				
Party member	38.1	81.8	75.8	100.0
None indicated	61.9	18.2	24.2	—
Total	100.0	100.0	100.0	100.0
Religious affiliation				
Protestant	13.2	27.9	45.5	54.5
Roman Catholic	13.2	25.4	9.1	38.6
Other (Jews, etc.)	1.3	15.7	—	—
None indicated	72.3	31.1	45.5	6.8
Total	100.0	100.1	100.1	99.9

TABLE VI.4 (*Continued*)

Classification	*Empire*	*Weimar Republic*	*Third Reich*	*Federal Republic*
Occupational background [a] (nonpolitical)				
civil service	64.5	48.4	48.4	27.2
Law	40.7	31.1	15.2	21.9
Business	1.3	16.4	27.3	21.9
Professional military	16.9	7.4	18.2	—
Teaching	5.2	12.3	12.1	9.1
Journalism	1.3	19.7	9.1	4.5
Engineering	—	—	9.1	11.4
Educational background				
Primary (to 14 yrs.)	1.3	12.3	3.0	9.0
Secondary (to 18 yrs.)	21.1	12.4	21.2	11.4
University	59.2	70.4	75.8	79.5
Not indicated	18.4	4.9	—	—
Total	100.0	100.0	100.0	99.9
Military experience				
Indicated	34.2	27.1	72.8	70.4
None indicated	65.8	72.9	27.2	29.6
Total	100.0	100.0	100.0	100.0
Father's occupation				
Civil service	23.6	4.9	12.1	20.4
Business	10.4	18.9	18.2	22.3
Worker, artisan	1.3	11.5	3.0	18.2
Professional military	9.1	4.9	12.1	9.1
Law	18.4	1.6	—	6.8
Teaching	—	3.3	6.1	6.8
Large landowner	18.4	6.6	12.1	9.1
Political party leader	2.6	—	—	2.3
Misc. salaried employees	4.0	2.4	—	6.8
Small farmers	—	0.8	3.0	4.5
Medicine and clergy	3.9	3.3	3.0	—
Not ascertained	24.9	44.2	24.2	13.6
Size of birthplace				
Under 20,000	56.6	55.7	42.4	27.3
20,000–100,000	15.6	22.1	24.2	34.1
Over 100,000	21.6	18.9	18.2	38.6
Not available	6.2	3.3	15.2	—
Total	100.0	100.0	100.0	100.0
Geographic origin				
Territory of Federal Republic:				
Northern Germany	3.9	12.3	9.1	6.8

TABLE VI.4 (*Continued*)

Classification	*Empire*	*Weimar Republic*	*Third Reich*	*Federal Republic*
Southern Germany	14.4	23.9	33.4	27.2
Western Germany	14.5	26.2	18.2	43.2
Central and Eastern Germany (incl. Berlin)	63.2	34.6	24.2	22.6
Abroad	2.6	3.0	12.1	—
Not indicated	—	—	3.0	—
Total	98.6	100.0	100.0	99.8

[a] Since one person may have engaged in several occupations during his career, the columns are nonadditive.

Sources: For 1890–1945 data, Maxwell E. Knight, *The German Executive 1890–1933* (Stanford: Stanford University Press, 1952) (some data corrected with assistance of author); for 1949–1960 data, Hannelore Schmidt, "Die deutsche Exekutive 1949–1960," *European Journal of Sociology,* IV, no. 1, 168–176 (some data recalculated).

The age and length of tenure of the incumbents of key political positions suggest that age, too, restricts access. Hitler was only 43 when he came to power, and the average age of the incoming Nazi elite was under 50; but in part perhaps for just this reason traditional criteria emphasizing "maturity" seem to prevail once more in leadership recruitment.

The great majority of the present leaders are over 50, and many are a good deal older than that. The reluctance of former Chancellor Adenauer to yield his place to a man in his sixties as he was nearing 90 is an extreme example, but, when mandatory retirement rules do not compel their withdrawal, German leaders are generally loath to give way to younger men and cling to their positions with the general approval of the public. Traditionally, an aspirant to a leadership role in German politics is expected to gain extensive experience by a long apprenticeship in some lesser position – and the radicalism of the "young" Nazi elite seemed to confirm the validity of the cultural norm that sobriety and political wisdom come only with advanced age.

There are indications that with the post-Nazi generations emergence this outlook may be slowly changing, but for the present a man under 50 or even 40 remains a novelty among

German leaders. The average age of the federal Bundestag and cabinet members in 1963, for example, was in the mid-fifties and of the deputies of the Land diets 66 per cent were over 50 and 34 per cent over 60. On the other hand, only 15 per cent of the Bundestag members elected in 1965 were under 40 years of age.

Although such elite characteristics reflect the persistence of certain traditional ascriptive criteria in German leadership recruitment, in most other respects modern achievement standards have become increasingly important. Key participants are no longer largely scions of aristocratic families or members of a military caste, as in the Hohenzollern Empire, nor must they give proof of their "racial" and ideological purity, as in Nazi Germany. They are neither graduates of a few select, elite schools and universities – as is still largely the case in Britain and France – nor products of an elite military organization like the Prussian officer corps. Informal cliques formed by common socializing experiences during the Nazi period, or even earlier, may exist here and there, but there is little evidence that they are of any significance in present elite recruitment.

For the most part the top leaders have entered the policy-bearing stratum by following more or less rigid career lines (within their functional specialty), which culminated in a vertical or lateral move into a key participant role. That is, they may have worked their way to the top in a political party or the civil service, but they may also have come to play an influential role after having attained prominence outside the political system, for instance in business, education, or religion. Either way, occupational skills and/or formal associational ties have tended to be of primary importance.

Generally speaking, the more sharply defined the specific function of a leadership position in contemporary Germany the more important, too, are the possession of expert skills in gaining entry into the political class. For instance, Chancellor Erhard owed his position to his reputation as the economic architect of postwar recovery, rather than to his extremely limited experience as a party leader. Berthold Beitz, general manager of the Krupp industrial empire, and Hermann Abs, chairman of the board of the *Deutsche Bank,* are outstanding examples of highly successful business managers who obtained political influence through personal achievements in the economic system. In contrast, the political power of Josef Frings, Roman Catholic Cardinal of Cologne, has rested not so much on functionally specific skills as on his position in the hierarchy of a traditional, functionally diffuse religious organization.

A large proportion of the top policybearing stratum consists of experts who acquired, over many years, the specific occupational skills which gained them access to an elite position. Thus, 44 per cent of the administrative elite of the sample in Table VI.2 were government servants before Hitler and 69 per cent during his regime. Among business leaders, at least 22 per cent had held important economic posts before 1933 and 58 per cent had done so during the Nazi regime. Thirty-eight per cent of university professors had held similar positions in the Weimar Republic and 71 per cent under Hitler. Altogether at most only one-fourth of the elite leaders had less than a dozen years of occupational experience behind them.

In contrast to the general population, key participants are always members of at least one and often several organizations involved in political input activities, some of them manifestly political and partisan and others ostensibly nonpolitical and nonpartisan. For example, 7 out of 10 of the national leaders in Table VI.2 belonged to a major political party, close to half were members of a nonpartisan civic organization, 4 out of 10 belonged to a formal occupational association, and 1 out of 10 to a special religious organization of one of the major churches. In the highly organized German political system, the man with few or no specific technical skills which allow him to get to the top and stay there requires the mass and/or elite support provided by such formal associational ties. His influence is based on the size of such political capital. He may be able to do without mass support, particularly if he holds a nonelective position, but rare indeed is the leader who exercises political influence without some benevolent sponsorship from other top stratum members.

Organizational ties are most important in the recruitment

of key government leaders, particularly ties to a major political party. Since the fall of the Nazi regime political parties have increasingly displaced other structures as avenues of vertical entry into the manifest political leadership, whereas lateral moves from top positions in the latent political elites have diminished. Party membership, rather than specific occupational skills, has become a chief criterion for ministerial posts (see Table VI.3) and frequently for key administrative positions. Thus, all the political leaders and three-fourths of the top civil servants in the 1964 sample in Table VI.2 were members of one of the three political parties represented in the Bundestag. Most of them, moreover, also belonged to one or more economic, civic, religious, or professional organization, underscoring the importance of multiple associational ties in the policybearing stratum.

Most present government and party leaders owe their positions to the political hiatus created by the sudden disappearance of the Nazi elite. The older ones usually had belonged to a political party during the Weimar Republic, some had been major opponents of the Nazi regime, but most had neither strongly opposed nor supported the totalitarian system. When this system collapsed in 1945 they joined the parties permitted by the occupation powers and quickly assumed leadership positions in them; these sooner or later provided entry into key government offices. Thus, three-fourths of the political leaders in Table VI.2 had been party members since the end of the war and all of them since the establishment of the Federal Republic. Younger men who did not play prominent political roles at the start rose rapidly from the upper middle stratum of the participant hierarchy, as did the Christian Socialist leader Franz Josef Strauss and the Social Democratic leader Willy Brandt.

Upward mobility through the parties is no longer as easy and rapid as in the early years of political reconstruction, but this pattern of recruiting the political elite has become quite firmly institutionalized. Nonprofessional politicians, still common in the United States, or government leaders without party ties, as in the Fifth French Republic, are extremely rare in Germany today. The up and coming political leaders are all party men recruited either from the lower ranks or, less often, from the civil service or interest associations.

ELITE INTEGRATION AND PLURALISM

Perhaps the most dramatic and, possibly, most profound transformation in German politics has taken place at the level of the policybearing stratum. Elite attitudes and relations bear witness to a fundamental, if diffuse, leadership consensus endorsing the legitimacy of the new political order.[5] The deep subcultural and socioeconomic cleavages of the past have certainly not entirely disappeared but the reciprocal trust and voluntary cooperation which prevails today among German leaders is without precedent in recent German history.

In sharp contrast to the climate of distrust, apathy, and ambivalence which we observed at the level of mass political culture, elite opinion and behavior patterns manifest a high degree of agreement on the legitimate rules of the political game and a strong sense of satisfaction with the operation of the new political system. Greater participation and involvement seem also to have provided German leaders with a greater sense of identification with the present regime, one that transcends partisan, occupational, and socioeconomic distinctions, and generational differences in socialization experiences.

The contemporary political class is composed of three political generations. The first consists of leaders past 60 who have witnessed five regimes – counting the postwar occupation – and the collapse of three of them. Many of them were among the founding fathers of the present political system and look upon their handiwork as a great, innovating achievement; but their beliefs and values are for the most part rooted in the pre-1945 past.

Inclined to look backward rather than forward, these senior leaders endorse the present regime primarily because it represents to them a vast improvement over its predecessors. They are more closely identified with traditional subcultural divi-

[5] Portions of the following discussion are based on a study of German elite opinion discussed more fully in Lewis J. Edinger, *Patterns of German Elite Opinion* (New Haven: 1965). (Condensed in Deutsch, *et al., France, Germany, and the Western Alliance,* Chaps. 8–13.)

sions than their juniors in the political class and more deeply attached to corresponding social and political orientations. If they are devout Roman Catholics, for instance, they place a high value on the authority of the churches in German life, and if they are trade union leaders or businessmen they are likely to view contemporary affairs as still the old battles between "working-class" and "capitalists." However, not only are death and retirement slowly removing these men from the political arena, but to most of them their ideological commitments to the past do not seem inconsistent with their general endorsement of the prevailing order and a harmonious relationship with leaders of a different persuasion. Just because they are convinced that traditional cultural and class distinctions persist, they tend to be all the more anxious to maintain social and political tranquility through the formal, structural arrangements provided by the new regime.

The dominant political generation – those German leaders now in their fifties – is a link between the past and the future. Representing the politically most interested and the most prosperous age group in contemporary Germany, they identify the new order with their own and their country's postwar achievements. Old enough to have experienced the turmoil of the Weimar Republic and the totalitarian rule of Hitler as adults, they are determined to prevent a recurrence of these traumatic events; at the same time their involvement in postwar reconstruction has given them a strong stake in the preservation and stability of the prevailing political system. Many have held their present elite positions for a decade or more and under present conditions are likely to retain them for at least another. They thus helped to give form to the existing order, but will also exert a decisive influence on its future development because of their domination over leadership recruitment and policymaking processes.

The members of this transitional political generation are generally less closely identified with the old subcultural cleavages and ideologies than their elders and less strongly attached to the preservation of traditional roles and norms in politics. They are correspondingly more sensitive to changed environmental conditions, particularly in international affairs, and more amenable to adapting themselves to new political situations. The present federal chancellor, Kurt-Georg Kiesinger, is a typical representative of this transitional generation. Too young to have been involved in the politics of the Weimar Republic, he had sought to promote his career objectives as a member of the Nazi party from 1933 to 1945 and as a leader of the Christian Democratic Union after 1945. Sober, undogmatic, and a highly skilled manager, Kiesinger has shown himself to be extremely flexible in playing a variety of roles in post-Nazi German politics; as chancellor he has succeeded in making himself and his policies acceptable to very broad elite alignments in Germany and abroad.

A third political generation is composed of the men who have recently begun to enter the policybearing stratum. Prominent in the political parties and the mass media, they are typified by such men as the Christian Democratic Bundestag leader Rainer Barzel, and his Social Democratic counterpart Helmut Schmidt. All under 50, the older ones usually had fought in World War II, whereas the younger ones were still children in Nazi days. Oriented far more to the future than to the past, these incoming leaders are relatively indifferent to traditions and subcultural identifications and have little difficulty in finding a common ground in politics. They share a flexible, unromantic outlook and speak the same pragmatic language, which greatly facilitates communications and cooperation among them. Most of them are university graduates and frequently boast a doctoral title; they are extremely well informed about political issues, usually specialize in some functional skill, and display a high degree of confidence about their ability to deal with whatever demands may confront their country in coming years. Firm ideological commitments seem to these young leaders not only anachronistic, but a handicap to their careers and to the efficient operation of the political system.

Usually impersonal, suave, and highly skilled in managerial functions, these ascending leaders are the products of the postwar socializing experiences and well suited to the contemporary climate of mass political culture. Their political style conforms to the emphasis on sobriety and harmony among the population, and their managerial roles correspond to the average Germans' administratively oriented view of politics. As they move into key participant positions their influence is bound to increase, but the flexibility of their views and conduct makes it difficult to predict what the consequences will be.

Judging by their expressed opinions, the ascending leaders accept the prevailing political system but do not consider either present structures or policies sacrosanct. Some German intellectuals have voiced fears that the rise of a "faceless" managerial class will work against the development of democracy in German and lead to the substitution of administrative rule for mass participation. Other observers, however, believe that these are the very men to institutionalize a rational and stable democratic system and establish a firm congruence between regime and political culture.

Rather different political socialization experiences thus have not given rise to intraelite generation conflict – a very common destabilizing phenomenon in transitional cultures and new regimes. At the same time, the social homogeneity of the political class appears to have contributed significantly to a basic similarity of political beliefs and values among otherwise heterogeneous occupational and subcultural leadership groups. Present elite recruitment patterns suggest that this fundamental elite consensus supporting the present regime is self-perpetuating, barring a major political upheaval, for in all groups the dominant leaders have taken great care to groom as their successors men more or less like them in background and political opinions.

Elite interaction in Germany has moved in the direction of a "polyarchic" form as a new, balanced pluralism between distinct, "functionally specific" leadership groups has taken the place of the authoritative rule by a single, "functionally diffuse" political elite of Nazi Germany. Governmental decisions are today usually the products of a complex, but orderly and stable bargaining between diverse groups of key participants.[6] At the local, Land, and federal levels, these negoti-

[6] A recent comparison of contemporary political systems placed the Federal Republic among the most polyarchic, just behind Norway, Luxembourg, and Ireland and ahead of the United States, Britain, and other

ate with each other and with third parties the distribution of public benefits and obligations, and policy outputs tend to take the form of some sort of compromise arrangement according to the issue involved and the alignment of forces. Legislative as well as administrative governmental outputs flow from interelite negotiations between federal and Land authorities, between interest group and party functionaries, and between parliamentary and executive leaders.

Although the openly political constitutional and paraconstitutional elites possess the formal authority to make the final choice between courses of action, they cannot ignore the wishes of influential "veto groups" representing latent political elites and usually try to accommodate them. Chancellor Adenauer's great political power was ostensibly based on his rather autocratic use of his formal position, but equally important was his immense skill in balancing countervailing elite demands and preventing the formation of strong elite alignments hostile to him. His rivals and his successor had to learn through painful experience that to be effective no German political leader can afford to slight other key participants in the system even though he may command extensive mass support among the voters.[7]

This balanced interdependence of elites in the Federal Republic is regulated by a complex web of formal and informal structural relationships, to be examined more closely in subsequent chapters. In part it is based on traditional arrangements which antedate the present regime, in part it is the consequence of the post-Nazi reorganization of German socioeconomic and political relations.

The important point is that these arrangements express and

---

modern democracies. See Arthur Banks and Phillip M. Gregg, "Grouping Political Systems: Q Factor Analysis of a Cross Political Survey," *American Behavioral Scientist, IX* (November, 1965), 5, Table 2. For a discussion of the term "polyarchy" see Robert Dahl, *A Preface to Democratic Theory* (Chicago: University of Chicago Press, 1956), pp. 63–84. See, also, Rolf Dahrendorf, *Class and Conflict in Industrial Society* (Stanford: Stanford University Press, 1959), pp. 304–317.

[7] See, for example, my *Kurt Schumacher: A Study in Personality and Political Behavior* (Stanford: Stanford University Press, 1965), particularly Chap. 8.

reinforce broad elite support for political structures which combine traditional and modern features. Subcultural leadership groups which formerly were alienated from the regime – for example socialists during the Empire and military and administrative leaders during the Weimar Republic – identify themselves today with the prevailing system and its preservation.

No influential group of participants advocates major changes in a regime which generally conforms to its views of proper role assignments and political responsibilities, accommodates both traditional and modern elite values, and seems to most German leaders singularly successful in adapting itself smoothly to changing environmental conditions. German leaders neither expect nor want a strong man at the helm of the state dictating to them what they may or may not do in their particular sphere of activity. They are on the whole quite content with political arrangements which protect their interests and satisfy their values, though few leaders are unreservedly enthusiastic in their support of the system. Businessmen complain that labor leaders have too much influence and vice versa; civil servants object to "partisan meddling" by party leaders and these in turn lash out against the alleged influence of the "bureaucrats"; federal leaders fret that the states have too much power while Land leaders insist that they have too little. Such complaints are all too familiar to Americans – the "others" always seem to wield too much power in public affairs – but they are not expressions of bitter hostility toward the regime or challenges to its legitimacy.

The norms of elite political culture allow all "legitimate" key actors some influence in public policymaking – provided they are willing to abide by them – and largely exclude the nonelite. In theory, mass participation may be sanctioned by German leaders, but in fact most place little trust in the political acumen of the masses and consider it quite enough if the electorate intermittently expresses its preferences at the polls.

Whether they are leaders of the government or the opposition, interest group functionaries or university professors, the members of the political class are correspondingly far more "participant-oriented" in political orientations than the average German. They consider it necessary and proper that they should possess a great deal more influence over the input and rulemaking processes than the rest of their countrymen because they believe themselves and their fellow elite members far better qualified and competent to deal with such matters. Such self-confidence ties German leaders all the more closely to a system which provides them with far-reaching autonomy from the nonelites and helps explain their commitment to the system's preservation. In Gaullist France, by contrast, a greater sense of nonparticipation in policymaking among political leaders has produced greater alienation from the system.

Elite opinion in the Federal Republic is today essentially conservative and wary of major political changes in either domestic or foreign policy. What has been achieved in the years of socioeconomic and political reconstruction is to be preserved, and unavoidable adjustments to new conditions are to be gradual and cautious, such as reforms of the educational system. Key participants in politics, like other Germans, tend to put a high premium on domestic harmony, cooperation, and compromise, and they are united in their determination to prevent the revival of radical extremist movements which might threaten political stability. Basic differences over the form and nature of the political order and the scope of the political community are no longer considered relevant issues, subcultural and social cleavages are believed to be of minor importance, and present world conditions appear to pose no serious threats to internal or external security. Early reunification seems to most of these leaders a desirable, but not very likely, development, and nationalism holds no appeal for them. They have no longing for the restoration of a powerful German state but generally favor the gradual integration of the Federal Republic into a Western European political community closely associated with the United States. They do not want a national nuclear force and are quite content to depend on their NATO allies to help safeguard their country against aggression.

In short, elite opinion does not differ radically from mass opinion in its evaluative, generally unemotional perception of the realities and objectives of German politics, but it is more deeply committed to the maintenance of the postwar order. This may be the greatest strength of the regime and may prove to be the key to its institutionalization in the political culture.

POLITICAL PARTICIPATION AND POLITICAL STABILITY

The prevailing participation structure and processes seem well embedded in the German political system. Following upon a period of drastic socioeconomic and political reconstruction, they have provided orderly, unspectacular relationships between governors and governed and produced policy outputs that have on the whole satisfied both the more and the less influential citizens. The nonelite masses have been content to remain on the sidelines and to leave running the system to those assumed to know what needs to be done and how to do it. The elites, protected as well as controlled by their agreement on the basic rules of the game, have enjoyed a good deal of autonomy in pursuing their various objectives. As the principal agents connecting a pluralist society to its political structures, they have explicitly and implicitly provided the masses with norms legitimating and supporting the present order and have achieved a balance between tradition and modernity, continuity and change.

Present political socialization and recruitment patterns suggest that the contemporary distribution of participant roles is unlikely to undergo major changes in the foreseeable future. Whether these role assignments will continue to conform to the structural arrangements identified with the present regime is another question. The exceptional emphasis which German leaders place on the importance of the formal legal rules governing interelite and elite-mass relationships appears to reflect a belief that these arrangements still seem tentative to many citizens and may still undergo major modifications. They are relatively new, and memories of sudden drastic transformations of former German political structures maintain doubts even among key participants as to the permanence of the present ones.

Indeed, critics insist that changes are necessary either because they consider the present arrangements too democratic or not democratic enough. In the view of some articulate conservative traditionalists, German political leaders are too sensitive to mass opinion and the wishes of special interest groups. In their opinion the state and community would be better served by a more authoritarian form of government, such as de Gaulle's Fifth Republic. On the other hand, proponents of a more egalitarian democracy assert that the leaders ignore the electorate's wishes far too much and deliberately discourage greater mass participation in politics. Whereas the traditionalists claim that there is more than enough democracy already, the egalitarians see present trends leading to the restoration of an autocratic government under the aegis of a new oligarchic "establishment" composed of the dominant party, administrative, and interest group leaders.

Neither group speaks for a significant portion of elite or mass opinion. But, as a number of observers have noted, the present more or less bipolar participation structure rests on role perceptions and assignments which leave a wide gap between the political commitments of the involved and uninvolved actors. If for any reason their interests and values should diverge more sharply than they do now, the elites identified with the present regime might find themselves challenged by a counterelite with mass support.

However, there is abundant historical evidence demonstrating that even considerable mass disaffection need not seriously menace the political order as long as there is unity among the dominant groups. In this sense the stability of a regime is primarily due to elite cohesion and agreement on basic rules and policy objectives. This appears to be the case in the Federal Republic today.

The question is: Can this basic elite consensus be maintained? Given the present mix in the German political culture and the pluralism of functionally specific elites, this depends mainly on two factors. First, the rules of the game must be flexible enough to accommodate the values and interests of diverse elites and their mass clienteles. Second, the rules must be adaptable to changing conditions in the domestic and international environment. And since the making and changing of these rules are essentially a function of governmental leadership, continuing political stability demands that this leadership be responsive to elite demands and be accepted as the ultimate agent of legitimate and binding authoritative decisions.

For the past two decades these problems have not loomed very large. Political and economic recovery have favored elite cooperation, and the new political structures have functioned extremely well in facilitating elite integration. But though the prevailing political recruitment and participation patterns have seemed well able to maintain political stability under existing conditions, they include a conservative bias which excludes from the policybearing stratum individuals and groups who differ in background and attitude from those now dominant. Elites committed to the preservation of the status quo are usually not especially receptive to innovations or to aspiring leaders who deviate from their own values. In the years to come, however, the dynamics of the intrasocietal and extrasocietal environment may confront German policymakers with the need for decisions which might strain elite consensus. Elite cleavages and recruitment processes which exclude ambitious political activists from policymaking because they lack the "proper" qualifications might alienate key groups from a regime which needs their support if it is to survive without fundamental structural changes that could transform it entirely.

CHAPTER VII

Organized Interest Groups

IN THE German Federal Republic the flow of domestic input demands into the political system reflects the highly formalized patterns of polyarchic elitism and mass passivity. Efforts to promote or prevent particular decisions by governmental leaders are conditioned by (1) the norms of the contemporary political culture and regime which emphasize hierarchic, orderly procedures and stable, harmonious relationships between governors and governed, (2) structural components of the political system which limit active participation to comparatively few actors, and (3) the political objectives, power, and style of behavior of the pluralist elites bargaining over the authoritative distribution of public benefits and obligations.

Interest articulation is controlled by a number of formal and functional restrictive elements.[1] First, access to the "right" people is limited in Germany by the sheer size and complexity of the political system and the diversity of competing claims for authoritative action. In this respect the situation is no different from that in other highly industrialized and functionally differentiated mass societies. Second, prevailing political rules legitimate only carefully regulated and formalized

[1] Interest articulation is the political process through which individuals and groups make overt demands for the satisfaction of their values by the authoritative decisionmakers in a community or state. According to the nature and intensity of their claims, their perception of political alignments, and the access channels which appear available to them, people will tend to choose those means of interest articulation which seem most convenient and most likely to obtain the desired results.

access channels for citizen claims to governmental decision-makers. Anomic and spontaneous forms of interest articulation are sanctioned neither by the norms of the political culture nor by the constitutional and legal provisions of the regime. The ordinary citizen may express his claims directly through his vote, administrative and judicial channels, and personal appeals to his political leaders. Some well placed persons may in addition command more informal modes of access, such as family connections or friends in high places. But especially in the national political arena, such associations no longer carry the weight they did under former German regimes and still do in other countries.

Insofar as citizens of the Federal Republic believe they can do anything at all to influence authoritative leaders, they tend to look upon organized interest groups as particularly effective channels of access and influence – a view which is reflected in the popular image of the alleged power of these groups in contemporary German politics.[2]

The day-to-day flow of domestic input demands is for the most part channeled through these formal structures of interest articulation. By law and by custom this is the explicit function of the vast number of institutions which largely control political communications between individual value claimants and authoritative value allocators. Some are governmental structures, others are semigovernmental or nongovernmental; some serve to articulate diffuse and general interests, others are concerned with specific and particular claims. Ostensibly, all have a representative function, but frequently the various clienteles exercise little or no control over their official spokesmen. The extent of the latter's influence in the councils of government and among the general public may be based on their formal political position, on evidence of mass support, on normative criteria endorsing the "proper" representation of elements considered important in German society, or any combination of these. Some interest group leaders speak for per-

[2] In their 1959 five-nation study, Almond and Verba found that about twice as many German respondents singled out interest associations as a means of influencing their government as Americans, Englishmen, Italians, and Mexicans. The previously cited 1964 study of German elite opinion revealed similar perceptions among their leaders.

sons whom they only nominally represent and who may not even belong to their organizations. Compulsory organizational membership or a high degree of voluntary interest group homogeneity allows others to claim solid backing from their clients.

A detailed description and analysis of the entire complex network of interest organizations in the Federal Republic would take up the remainder of this volume. It will suffice to confine our discussion primarily to the input process at the national level of the political system and to the most important institutional and associational structures involved in it. In general the patterns which prevail in national politics are duplicated at lower levels of the system by analogous interacting governmental and nongovernmental structures.

Organized interest groups in local and Land politics, like those in federal politics, endeavor to influence policy outputs by the following methods: (1) assuring themselves of ready access to key points in the authoritative decisionmaking structures through the recruitment, placement, and sponsorship of party leaders and public officials sympathetic to their claims; (2) allocating effective authority to those political positions which are most accessible to them; and (3) having their goals and methods accepted by influential veto groups and, less frequently, the general public.

How these methods are specifically employed may vary a good deal from group to group and issue to issue. In some cases such activities may be carefully shielded from public view, in others interest group leaders may openly try to mobilize mass opinion in order to bring pressure to bear on elected officials or to replace them. Governmental and quasi-governmental institutional groups are likely to invoke their formal legal authority to promote their own interests, as in disputes between one ministry and another or between leaders of the executive branch and the legislature. Nongovernmental groups, on the other hand, rely more on lobbying and public relations activities. In short, many of these patterns resemble similar activities in the United States, but this should not lead us to overlook distinct structural and functional differences which influence and are influenced by the particular characteristics of the German political system and culture.

LÄNDER GOVERNMENTS AS INTEREST GROUPS

As in the United States, sectional and local interests in Germany are articulated through numerous governmental and nongovernmental structures. Parliamentary deputies in the federal and state legislatures demand benefits for their constituencies. National and regional organizations, such as the League of German Cities (*Deutscher Städtetag*), seek to promote the interests of urban and rural communities. The most powerful and influential representatives of sectional interests are the ten Länder governments, in their relations with each other and with the central government. The federal organization of the German governmental system provides the institutional framework for such input activities and diverse and permanent regional interests the source.

On issues which the Basic Law places within the exclusive jurisdiction of the Länder – particularly control over education, radio and television, the police, and local governments – their governments confront each other as the heads of semi-sovereign entities with frequently divergent regional and subregional interests. Take the question of the distribution of federal funds to the states, for example. The governments of Länder with large populations seek a per capita distribution, those of the rich states which contribute a disproportionate share of the taxes flowing into the federal treasury strive to recapture as much as possible for their own use, while those of the relatively small and poor Länder ask for more than they have put in or can claim on the basis of population. Diverse regional interests are evident in interstate negotiations to coordinate local government and educational procedures. The objectives of governments of Länder with a predominantly Protestant population tended to vary from those which have largely a Roman Catholic clientele, and the governments of heavily urbanized, industrialized states have pursued different goals from those where agricultural interests remain important.

The interest articulation function of the Länder governments in their relations with the central government is of even greater importance to German political processes. The Basic Law provides them with many opportunities for making demands upon federal authorities, particularly in the broad area of concurrent jurisdiction over fiscal and social welfare matters. Highly formalized legal arrangements, designed to facilitate as well as regulate this input process, furnish the Länder governments with several access channels, of which the Bundesrat is the most important. Theoretically this upper house of the federal parliament is not a Land institution or a collegial agency of the states, but an organ of the federal government. In practice, however, it is the primary instrument for promoting the states' individual and collective interests relative to the *Bund*.[3]

The Bundesrat is one of the most powerful upper chambers in the world and "the only one . . . which is in effect a continuous congress of state (Land) ministers who vote in accordance with the instructions of their government."[4] Each Land, as we mentioned earlier, controls a number of votes more or less in proportion to its population, and these are cast as a unit as directed by the Land governments.[5] A principal consequence of this arrangement is that it helps to structure a unified expression of Land interests in negotiations between state and federal (Bund) organs. The federal executive is required by the constitution to submit all its legislative drafts to the upper chamber before they go to the lower house, and most bills passed by the latter need to be approved by the former.[6] In addition, the Bundesrat must approve all federal executive ordinances which have the force of law, and it commands considerable veto powers in disputes between Bund and Länder, between the two houses of the federal legislature, and between the lower house and the federal executive.

Every Land government maintains an office and staff in the national capital to facilitate its formal relations with the central government and its more informal lobbying activities. These quasi-embassies are headed by quasi-ambassadors from

[3] Elmer Plischke, *Contemporary Government of Germany* (Boston: Houghton Mifflin, 1961), p. 76.

[4] Arnold J. Heidenheimer, *The Governments of Germany*, rev. ed. (New York: Crowell, 1966), p. 137.

[5] For the distribution of the seats allocated to each Land see Table II.1, p. 14.

[6] Either by a simple plurality or, in the case of constitutional amendments and certain other major pieces of legislation, by a two-thirds majority. See also Chapter IX.

the state governments who are often members of these governments and their chief spokesmen in the Bundesrat. As such they enjoy ready access to key federal officials and usually can obtain an ear receptive to their demands. Moreover, as representatives of the upper chamber, Länder ministers have the formal right to address the Bundestag or any of its committees and to make known their interests in a pending piece of legislation.

In view of the Bundesrat's powers, the demands of its controlling majority are frequently anticipated and rarely overridden by the federal executive and lower house leaders. The interests of the Länder governments are invariably taken into account when a law or ordinance is drafted and often need not even be made explicit – an unspoken threat of possible rejection in the upper house may suffice. In cases where a bill is defeated in the Bundesrat, a conference committee of delegates from both chambers (*Vermittelungsausschuss*) affords the Länder leaders another opportunity to state their claims, a procedure which almost invariably leads to a compromise solution.

Since the establishment of the Federal Republic control over at least a plurality, if not a two-thirds majority (necessary for constitutional amendments), of the votes wielded by the Länder governments in the Bundesrat has involved a continuous struggle between the major political parties, extending into state politics. However, neither the governing parties at the federal level nor the opposition has ever been able to depend on a durable, favorable alignment. Länder elections and changing governmental coalitions have led to realignments, and, in any case, party loyalties have often proved less important than the promotion of regional interests and states rights. Thus the articulation of more or less constant Länder interests has at times found members of the same party aligned on opposing sides and state government leaders of parties opposed to each other in the Bundestag forming a united front in the Bundesrat or a Land government. More frequently, the nature of the bargaining process among Länder governments, and between state and federal representatives, has made party labels relatively unimportant.

Negotiations involving Länder interests are conducted almost entirely out of the public view and far from partisan strife by committees of civil servants of the various governments. For the most part they deal with complex, but politically mundane or entirely nonpartisan, issues which the government leaders are content to leave to the bureaucratic experts to settle. Although at times the political skill and experience of a Land or federal minister may prove decisive on major issues, party channels are only one element, and not necessarily the most important, in these largely bureaucratic negotiations.[7] Expected or actual election outcomes seldom impinge upon these bargaining processes, and the rare deadlocks have invariably been due to the introduction of some basic political question, such as the relative constitutional powers of federal and Länder governments. In these instances, party channels and alignments repeatedly have proved unable to settle the matter and the disputants have had to call upon the electorate or the Federal Constitutional Court to arbitrate.

A notable example was the 1962 controversy over Chancellor Adenauer's efforts to establish a federal television station in competition with those of the Länder. A majority of the Land governments considered this a major challenge to their constitutional rights, the issue went to the Constitutional Court, and its verdict sustained their claims. In 1958, on the other hand, the Court supported the interests of the federal government against the efforts of several Länder governments to bypass the federal parliament and hold popular plebiscites on the politically potent issue of German atomic rearmament.[8]

Thus, as interest articulation and aggregation structures the Länder governments play a major part in national input processes, and neither the activities of the political parties nor those of federal institutions can be fully explained without considering this factor. Structures that were initially artificial and

[7] Otto Kirchheimer, "Germany: The Vanishing Opposition" in Robert A. Dahl (ed.), *Political Opposition in Western Democracies* (New Haven: Yale University Press, 1966), p. 252.

[8] See Gerard Braunthal, "Direct and Representative Democracy in West Germany: The Atomic Armament Issue," *Canadian Journal of Economics and Political Science,* XXVI (August, 1959), 313–323, and, by the same author, "Federalism and the Party System in Germany: The Broadcasting Controversy," *Journal of Politics,* XXIV (August, 1962), 545–561.

imposed by foreign military governments have assumed a function which has significantly influenced German political patterns.

It may be that these formal input channels have become sufficiently institutionalized in the political system to remain a permanent feature, but for various reasons this seems rather questionable. First, in the last analysis federal institutions not only have the upper hand in accepting or rejecting the demands of the Länder governments, but the nationalization of economic and political life weakens the Länder governments' ability to promote purely regional interests. Second, other input structures are becoming more important due to a trend toward greater functional specialization and less diffuse particularism in the representation of organized interests. Last, the climate of German opinion does not favor the further development, or even the maintenance, of the Länder governments' input function. In the view of most Germans the state's power to promote local and sectional interests has been excessive and interferes with the efficient operation of the national political system. Surveys of mass and elite opinion indicate considerable sentiment for a reduction of the influence of the Länder governments and general expectation that the central government will sooner or later achieve this end.[9]

INTEREST ASSOCIATIONS

German interest associations are more or less functionally specific, nongovernmental organizations. Whereas the Länder governments are diffuse, interest articulation structures repre-

[9] Mass opinion polls show that about two-thirds of adult Germans want a greater shift of power to the federal government, including 80 per cent of the most highly educated. (See EMNID, *Informationen,* No. 8, 1964.) A 1964 study of elite opinion revealed that more than half the respondents expected the federal government to wield more power vis à vis the Länder in the future and only a third expected the relationship to remain unchanged. See Lewis J. Edinger, *Patterns of German Elite Opinion* (New Haven: Yale University Political Data Library, 1965), p. 41. However, sentiment for the complete abolition of the Länder has abated. In mass opinion surveys it dropped from 49 per cent in 1952 to 24 per cent in 1960. (See Noelle-Neumann, *Jahrbuch 1958–1964,* p. 458.) Most German leaders appear to be convinced that in essence the present federal system will persist. (Edinger, *ibid.,* p. 42.)

senting the diverse demands of numerous heterogeneous groups, interest associations endeavor to defend and promote the special political goals of particular social, economic, and cultural elements in the population. And although the major political parties are primarily electoral organizations seeking broad mass support in order to gain general and direct control of governmental decisionmaking organs, interest associations have more limited objectives and clienteles. They intermittently strive to influence public policymaking, but only on certain issues and primarily on behalf of the ostensibly nonpartisan interests of their members.

The nature of these input structures and their position in the political system reflect the singular mixture of traditional and modern elements which we have marked as a chief characteristic of contemporary German politics. Traditionally, German interest associations are more inclusive, more tightly organized, and occupy a more privileged position in public life than their American counterparts. In fact, if not in name, some of the most important among them antedate the present regime and political parties, and represent cultural and organizational continuity in a society which in other respects has been marked by sharp discontinuities. On the one hand, lingering traditional identifications with status, class, and occupational groups, dating back to the Industrial Revolution and beyond, still influence the orientations and activities of such interest associations as the League of German Artisans. On the other hand, the postwar modernization of German society is reflected in the nonideological perspectives of an increasing number of interest group leaders and members and in the proliferation of associations preoccupied with pragmatic, bread-and-butter issues.

Though only a minority of the citizens of the Federal Republic belongs to such associations, there are thousands of large and small interest organizations, many with overlapping memberships, including at least 1,800 national associations. Though the Basic Law does not explicitly recognize them as formal political input structures, it grants all citizens the right to organize and join such groups, provided they are not in conflict with the criminal code or "directed against the constitutional order or the concept of international understanding."[10]

Some of these associational structures are specifically established by law, in accordance with traditional practices, to represent certain common interests. Prime examples are the occupational "chambers" (*Kammern*) which have their roots in the corporate guilds of the Middle Ages. Unlike the American chambers of commerce, these are nonautonomous institutions of public law which exercise compulsory jurisdiction over their members and are supposed to link all major segments of the economy to the political system. Most independent producers engaged in agriculture, commerce, and manufacturing, as well as members of the so-called "free professions" – such as self-employed physicians and lawyers – must belong to appropriate local chambers which determine and enforce rules of occupational standards and conduct. As such they not only function as interest associations, but exercise derivative governmental functions over their members.

These multiple economic and political functions give considerable weight to the demands of the chambers since their semiconstitutional position makes them one of the most important associational structures providing for an orderly relationship between the economic and the political system. For purposes of coordination and common interest articulation, the local chambers in most Länder form regional groupings; their national organizations in turn are supposed to defend and promote the interests of the constituent chambers at the federal level of government.

Other associations involved in politics may be more freely organized, disbanded, and joined. These include traditional institutional groups explicitly endorsed and supported by the state, particularly the churches, as well as a host of *Verbände* and *Vereine* for the promotion of material or nonmaterial interests. Some of these are multipurpose, comprehensive organizations performing various functions and pursuing numerous goals, others are primarily single purpose associations. Reli-

[10] For a listing of the most important national associations, see the annual *Taschenbuch des öffentlichen Lebens* and *Taschenbuch der Spitzenorganisationen* (Bonn: Festland Verlag).

gious associations, for example, minister not only to the sacred needs of their members, but engage in numerous secular activities in the fields of social welfare and education as well as politics. Major business and labor groups are concerned with social and political matters in addition to strictly economic questions. On the other hand, the associations of pensioners (*Sozialrentner*) and "war victims" represent single purpose organizations formed to promote exclusively transitory, specific demands.

Although these voluntary associations lack the formal legal authority which the occupational chambers wield over their members, they are for this very reason also more autonomous from authoritative governmental agencies. At the same time, most of them are far less closely tied to the political parties than German interest associations of the past. Consequently, they usually enjoy unprecedented freedom of action and flexibility in furthering their political interests as ostensibly nonpartisan input structures.

The effectiveness of all these associations varies a good deal with the extent of their homogeneity, financial strength, and access to political decisionmakers and mass publics. Sometimes a relatively small and weak organization may achieve its objectives by an intensive publicity campaign, a particular, fortuitous combination of circumstances, or an ad hoc alliance with more powerful groups.[11] On the whole, however, the greatest political influence is wielded by the large national interest associations. Formal and informal channels provide their spokesmen with direct access to key party and government leaders and to vast financial resources, and control over extensive political communications media permit them to exercise a direct or indirect influence over public opinion.

Numerous laws and administrative regulations give formal sanction and encouragement to the long established practice of direct contacts between interest associations and administrative agencies. In all the Länder, representatives of the major

[11] In 1954, for example, a touch-and-go election campaign in Bavaria afforded the state's teachers' association an exceptional opportunity to obtain commitments from a party coalition that subsequently won control of the Land government. See Thomas Ellwein, *Das Regierungssystem der Bundesrepublik Deutschland* (Köln-Opladen: Westdeutscher Verlag, 1st ed. 1963), pp. 57 ff.

associations can articulate their demands through various consultative bodies attached to government agencies.[12] Interest group spokesmen are ex officio members of the supervisory boards of the Länders' radio and television stations. In the federal government, the administrative procedures of all principal ministries stipulate that appropriate spokesmen for the so-called "peak associations" (*Spitzenverbände*) must be consulted during the drafting of a government bill. Interest articulation is further facilitated by ministerial advisory councils of nongovernmental experts representing these national organizations. And under the German system of administrative courts, interest association lawyers usually represent or advise individual claimants against the state. In key cases involving decisions which affect the collective interests of their clientele, the interest associations are in effect the real claimants.

The consequences of these formal arrangements are twofold. First, they encourage behind the scenes bargaining and accommodation between governmental and associational functionaries. Such practices have long been accepted by both sides on the grounds that direct negotiation between experts – before an issue reaches the politically responsible decisionmakers – facilitates the processing of interest group demands outside the public arena of partisan controversy.

In the second place, these arrangements induce individual claimants to depend on their associational representatives to obtain satisfaction for their demands and compel the various member organizations of federal peak associations to rely on interest elites who have direct access to the administrative elites. Here, too, the formal justification is that such procedures provide efficient and stable input processes. The intended object is to prevent the inundation of governmental agencies by individual and group demands and to provide for their aggregation and adaptation before they are fed into the authoritative conversion process.[13]

[12] In Baden-Württemberg, for example, a 1962 law stipulated that representatives of the churches, trade unions, and major agricultural, industrial, and trade associations were to be included in a Land planning council. See Thomas Ellwein, "Die Machtstruktur in Westdeutschland," *Die neue Gesellschaft,* XII (September/October, 1965), 855 ff.

[13] As a perceptive observer has noted, such procedures constitute "an

A second, complementary set of input channels for the articulation of associational interests has been shaped by the strategic aggregative and governmental functions which the major political parties have assumed in the new political order. Because decisive political power is concentrated in the hands of a relatively small number of competing party leaders, interest group elites have sought to influence party elites who, for their part, endeavor to obtain associational endorsement for their efforts to attract support from diverse elements in the pluralist society. The former accordingly enhance their influence by demonstrating their direct and indirect ability to recruit votes for the parties that meet their claims, the latter by satisfying the demands of the interest elites they consider most effective in this respect.

The specific methods employed by interest association leaders to exert influence on party leaders, who – directly or indirectly – play key decisionmaking roles in authoritative government structures, vary a good deal from group to group and situation to situation and frequently are obscure. Mass opinion in Germany is more critical and suspicious of such activities than it is in the United States, and deliberate efforts to conceal them are correspondingly greater.

In general, it appears that efforts to exert influence take the following forms: (1) attempts to obtain direct representation in government and party elites; (2) attempts to gain access to these elites through formal and informal, direct and indirect contacts; (3) attempts to provide these elites with selective information and opinions which, on the strength of their substantive content and/or prestigious authorship may influence their decisions in a desired direction (e.g., newspaper editorials and "expert" memoranda supporting interest group objectives); and (4) offers to furnish votes, publicity, and financial support to key political leaders who give promise of supporting associational interests, and threats to employ these means against those who oppose these interests.

---

especially clear instance in which entirely formal considerations can increase the power of federated groups and their key functionaries and thus have a major effect on the structure of organized interests." Reinhard Bendix, *Nation Building and Citizenship* (New York: Wiley, 1964), p. 133.

By American standards, the efforts of German interest associations to obtain direct representation in governmental decisionmaking bodies has been highly successful. The heads of the various ministries dealing with matters of concern to specific peak associations have repeatedly been recruited from their ranks, usually identify themselves with their interests, and defend the claims of their clients in the councils of government.[14] Direct interest group representation has been even more conspicuous in the legislatures. Many Bundestag deputies have been overtly or covertly associated with interest associations and have defended their claims in the lower house of the federal parliament. Between 1953 and 1958, for instance, 35 per cent of the 243 deputies of the majority party – the Christian Democrats – were directly affiliated with interest associations, mostly business groups. Among the 151 deputies of the opposition Social Democrats, 24 per cent were openly linked with interest groups, in most cases (84 per cent) to trade unions.[15] Such representation has been particularly pronounced in the Bundestag committees where most of the legislative work takes place. Through committee assignments, party leaders have enabled various interest groups to be particularly well represented in those committees which handle bills of concern to them. Most of the parliamentary maneuvering and bargaining between interest association spokesmen takes place behind the closed doors of these committees and in the intraparty "study groups" (*Arbeitsgemeinschaften*) consisting of committee representatives.

Lobbying by interest association is at least as prevalent as it is in the United States. More than 300 national organizations have offices in Bonn to provide close contacts between their headquarters and government and party agencies. In Germany professional lobbyists are not required to list their names and sponsors in public registers, but they also do not play as im-

[14] Within the last decade, for example, two of the Federal Ministers for Refugee Affairs had previously been leaders of major refugee associations; two successive top administrative officials (*Staatssekretäre*) of the Ministry of Agriculture were recruited from farm associations (one of them becoming the head of a major agricultural organization upon his retirement).

[15] See Viola Gräfin von Bethusy-Huc, *Die Soziologie wirtschaftspolitischer Entscheidungen* (Wiesbaden: Steiner, 1962), p. 127.

portant a role as in the United States; significant negotiations almost always involve direct contacts between the respective elites. "In national politics, as within the political parties and the pressure groups," an American observer has written, "one has the impression of a pattern of political discussion in which a few giants speak from the heights of government ministries, the central party organs, and the *Spitzenverbände*." [16]

From 1949 to 1963 Chancellor Adenauer legitimized a pattern of direct interelite negotiations which now appears to have become institutionalized throughout the German political system. He maintained close contacts with all major interest association leaders and frequently permitted them to bypass formal access channels. Reportedly, top interest group representatives who sought quick results did not bother with ministers and parliamentary committees, but went straight to the chancellor's office. Adenauer's personal style of politics and his great political authority encouraged such an approach, and, if it suited him, it produced the desired results for the petitioners.

Adenauer's successor, Ludwig Erhard, appears to have been both a less accessible and a less sought-after decisionmaker. Under his government other channels came to be more important in the relationship between interest group and political elites. Numerous coordinating committees and adjunct organizations of the associations and parties throughout the Federal Republic have this function. Particularly at election time, political leaders, seeking financial contributions and votes from the associations and interest group leaders with specific policy claims, use these and more informal structures for bargaining purposes. Such negotiations can yield considerable concessions to the interest associations, especially when election outcomes are considered critical and uncertain by the party leaders. They may obtain safe seats for their parliamentary spokesmen, assurances of representation in the next government, and pre-election "gifts" (*Wahlgeschenke*) from the incumbent rulemakers. At the same time there are limits to what they can demand, and pre-election "deals" are probably not as common

[16] Gabriel A. Almond, "The Politics of German Business" (The RAND Corporation, Santa Monica, Calif., 1955), reprinted in Hans Speier and W. Phillips Davison (eds.), *West German Leadership and Foreign Policy* (Evanston, Ill.: Row, Peterson, 1957), pp. 195–241.

in the Federal Republic as in the United States. For one thing, German political parties are not quite as dependent on financial support from interest group sponsors as their American counterparts because they have substantial incomes from other sources, as we shall see. For another, German public opinion as a whole is less tolerant about such arrangements. Insistent interest group demands may prove to be self-defeating if a party becomes too closely identified with associational claims and consequently loses the electoral support it needs to satisfy them.

THE BIG FIVE

As we saw in Chapter I, religious and economic values are basic sources of group identification and competition in the Federal Republic. Translated into organized interest inputs, these values are reflected in the pre-eminence of five major associational constellations: the two major churches, and the national associations of agriculture, business, and labor. These input structures stand astride the system's boundaries and link its internal components to powerful nonpolitical institutions in German society. In the case of the religious associations, effective interest articulation rests largely on the strength of their identification with subcultural affective loyalties and those ethical norms which have mass appeal. In the case of the major economic associations, it depends largely – though not entirely – on the strength of common objectives based on evaluative instrumental and pragmatic orientations toward the state and its functions.

The far-reaching actual or potential influence of governmental outputs on their interests gives the leader of these major associational groupings a strong incentive to participate in political input processes. At the same time the extent of their manifest and latent political power induces government, party, and administrative elites to pay particular attention to these group demands.

RELIGIOUS ASSOCIATIONS

Constitutional and legal arrangements and political alignments give both the Roman Catholic and Protestant churches extensive opportunities to function as interest articulation structures, particularly in the areas of cultural policies (*Kulturpolitik*) and social policies (*Sozialpolitik*). As we have seen, their privileged positions as very special institutions of public law and the prestige they command in public life allow the churches to promote their interests by direct representation in governmental bodies and by indirect influence on political decisionmakers.

In Bavaria, representatives of the churches are ex officio members of the upper house of the Land diet, and in all the Länder constitutional provisions and/or special agreements assign to the clergy formal participant roles in politics. At the federal level of government, both major churches are represented by quasi-ambassadorial representatives in Bonn who convey their wishes to governmental agencies, whereas in small towns and rural areas local clergymen perform a similar function in a more informal manner. Clerical political interests are also articulated by formal resolutions and memoranda of the governing bodies of the churches, pastoral letters and sermons, and the religious press.

More indirectly, the religious elites promote their political interests through an elaborate network of contacts with political elites. Clerical as well as lay leaders play prominent participant roles in the major parties and occupy political offices in legislative and executive bodies. And a host of church-affiliated, associational interest groups, educational institutions, and mass media of political communication provide both clergymen and lay leaders with indirect means of exercising political influence.

Formally, the two major churches participate in public life on a basis of absolute parity. In fact, however, the Roman Catholic Church has been politically far more active, outspoken, and influential than the Protestant. Its spokesmen have supported "Christian" political leaders who endorse Roman Catholic cultural and social interests – especially in the field of education – and lay leaders of church-affiliated interest associations have sought to realize Catholic principles through political action. Devout Catholics, who are far more numerous than practicing Protestants, frequently belong to at least one of these associations. There are special organizations for Catholic businessmen, artisans and workers, Catholic men and Catholic women, and Catholic parents and Catholic youths. All these, though ostensibly nonpartisan, are committed to civic action on behalf of the church. "Catholic Academies" and study groups hold conferences for political and opinion leaders, and the large Catholic press offers political directions to its readers.[17]

In the opinion of most German observers the Catholic religious elite has used its various sources of political influence with great effectiveness, particularly in rural areas where it commands a large and loyal following. Of late, however, voting patterns have suggested that either the church's influence over important sections of the German electorate may be diminishing, or that it is moving toward a policy of greater balance between the major parties – perhaps both.

Although heretofore official Catholic support has usually gone to the Christian Democrats, efforts of the Social Democrats to neutralize, if not overcome, the church's opposition to a party which has foresworn its former anticlerical policies, seem to have borne some fruit. Roman Catholic leaders in Lower Saxony were delighted when in 1965 the Social Democrats formed a coalition government with the Christian Democrats in order to conclude the first formal postwar agreement between a Land and the Church in the field of education. A trend toward less intimate ties with and consequent dependence on a single party would conform to the developing patterns of polyarchic pluralism in German politics, mentioned earlier, which are also evident in the emerging relationship between other interest associations and the major parties.

The Protestant "Evangelical Church in Germany," EKD, is a confederation of twenty-seven autonomous provincial churches (*Landeskirchen*) which nominally include those in the predominantly Protestant, Communist German Democratic Republic. Locally and regionally, the member churches and their lay associations often wield considerable influence, but in national politics Protestant religious leaders have found it difficult to agree on common political action.

[17] See Chapter V, pp. 123–164, above.

The orthodox Lutheran clergy in general has favored a traditional policy of minimal explicit involvement in partisan politics; a more active minority has been divided particularly by differences over defense and foreign policy issues. Moreover, the church's efforts to maintain some ties with the German Protestants living under Communist rule have induced its leaders to avoid political commitments which might sever the few remaining bonds. But on occasions when the Evangelical Church as a whole has taken a united stand, its voice has commanded considerable attention in West Germany.

In March, 1966, for instance, the governing Synod of the EKD endorsed a memorandum which called for a more flexible government policy of accommodation with the East European Communist countries, a subject which has heretofore been tabu in official circles. Despite bitter opposition by the refugee associations, the authority of the collective leadership of the Evangelical Church undoubtedly contributed significantly to making the subject a matter of legitimate public discussion and, ultimately, to opening a new phase in German foreign policy.

Individual clerical and secular leaders of the Evangelical Church have played more active roles both inside and outside the political parties. More than their Catholic counterparts, they have collaborated with political groups and governments of different complexions. Protestant ministers and lay leaders are to be found among the Christian Democrats, Social Democrats, and Free Democrats, and Protestant interest associations have tended to be less explicitly partisan than the Catholic in pursuing their political objectives. "Evangelical Academies" have brought together representatives from different areas of public life in conferences devoted to discussions of political issues considered of concern to Protestants, such as the maintenance of close relations with their coreligionists in the German Democratic Republic and the conclusive renunciation of nuclear armaments for their Federal Republic.

AGRICULTURAL ASSOCIATIONS

The powerful political influence exercised by the so-called "Green Front" of agricultural associations owes a great deal to the traditional socioeconomic homogeneity and "in-group" sentiments of German farmers. As one of their leaders pointed out a few years ago, organized agriculture can compensate for its relative numerical and financial inferiority to and isolation from the largest economic interest associations by its exceptional unity and qualitative strength.[18] Most of the roughly three million large and small independent agricultural proprietors are members of the German Farmers' League (*Deutscher Bauernverband*), the League of Agricultural Chambers (*Verband der Landwirtschaftskammern*), and the *Raifeisenverband,* a producers' cooperative association with extensive holdings. Unlike their American counterparts, German farmers are united in complementary rather than competitive associations which represent not only common economic objectives, but a shared social outlook based on the traditional image of a corporate agricultural estate (*Bauernstand*). In an increasingly industrialized society, the small farmers who own most of the land and live in comparative social isolation are strongly committed to the aggressive efforts of their leaders to defend agricultural interests against the competing claims of organized business and labor and importers of foreign farm products.

The "Green Front" has shown a remarkable ability to extract tax concessions, guaranteed prices, and generous subsidies for its clients from government leaders in both the Bund and the Länder. In part, this has been due to a widespread belief – particularly among the more conservative parties – that everything possible must be done to preserve the traditional pastoral virtues associated with rural life. But more pragmatic political considerations have been equally important. Farm leaders command a loyal following whose votes carry exceptional weight at election time, and they have been highly skillful in exploiting this strength in pressing their demands upon party and government elites.

In line with the conservative outlook of most German farmers, the national agricultural lobby has concentrated its efforts on leaders of the Christian Democratic Union and the smaller

[18] "Wir sind tatsächlich eine Macht!" Interview with Edmund Rehwinkel, President of the German Farmers' League in *Der Spiegel,* December 23, 1966, p. 28.

Free Democratic Party and on administrative officials in the executive branch of the federal government. In the Bundestag, about 10 per cent of the deputies of the two parties have been farmers and representatives of farm associations who have vigorously defended and promoted agricultural interests in party caucuses and relevant legislative committees. In addition, political influence has been effectively exercised through contacts in the Ministry of Agriculture, as well as directly to the federal chancellor, enabling farm leaders to gain far-reaching concessions from governmental leaders, particularly in the annual legislative package known as the "Green Plan." [19]

However, future developments are likely to weaken organized agriculture's political influence in the long run. Under a European Common Market agreement, French, Italian, and Dutch farm products will be admitted without tariff restrictions as of 1968, and subsidies to German farmers will have to be gradually reduced. It has been estimated that as much as one-third of the farmers will be unable to survive Common Market competition and will have to move into other occupations. In that case the agricultural sector will be reduced to at most 3 per cent of the labor force, and the voting strength of the farmers will suffer corresponding losses.

German farm leaders are not inclined to accept these developments without a bitter fight to maintain the publicly supported high cost agricultural "estate." Some, in fact, have already sought to bring more intense pressure to bear upon governmental leaders by threatening to throw their support to right-wing extremist groups. But, if present trends continue, agricultural spokesmen are likely to find it increasingly difficult to wring concessions from the dominant political leadership in Germany. The unwillingness of nonagricultural groups to absorb the cost of hidden farm subsidies in the form of taxes and guaranteed agricultural prices has been mounting and is

[19] During the Adenauer administration organized agriculture scored a major triumph with the Agricultural Act of 1955, which provided for generous government assistance to the farmers on the grounds that they had not gained commensurate advantages from postwar economic recovery. Under Erhard, President Rehwinkel of the Farmers' League obtained a promise of long-term public assistance for his clients to enable them to adjust to competitive conditions in the European Economic Community.

likely to grow if general prosperity seems to be threatened by the "cuddling" of a diminishing minority of small farmers. The predominantly export oriented patterns of the German economy have already presented governmental leaders with difficult, but inescapable, choices between the claims of agricultural and nonagricultural interests which of late they have tended to resolve in favor of the latter.

EMPLOYERS' ASSOCIATIONS

Big business, tightly organized into national interest associations and dominated by a few men, was the most powerful private interest group in pre-Nazi Germany and played a prominent part in mobilizing the Nazi economy for war. After 1945, the allied occupation powers sought to diminish the concentration of West German business establishments, but such measures proved to be temporary, and with postwar recovery big business regained its pre-eminent position in both economic and political life.

However, due to the increased function specialization and internationalization of the West German economy, the homogeneity of the big business associations is today more a matter of form than fact. At the same time, however, institutional arrangements and the structure of the German economic system provide greater mutual cooperation among German businessmen than is found among their American counterparts, particularly in the key industrial sectors dominated by a few giant concerns.

The collective political interests of the German business community are formally represented by all-inclusive employers' associations organized along regional and functional lines. Every employer of more than two or three workers is a member of local and regional chambers of industry and trade, as well as of specific occupational associations, which in turn are organized into federated groups. Nationally these organizations are united in various peak associations – such as the Federal Association of German Bankers – which employ a full-time staff to look after the interests of their constituent members. At the apex of all these groups stands a triumvirate of federated peak associations whose leaders serve as the formal spokesmen for the political demands of the business community as a whole.

The Diet of German Industry and Commerce (*Deutscher Industrie- und Handelstag,* DIHT), the national peak association of the chambers of industry and trade, is the least involved in federal politics. It does some lobbying and public relations work on behalf of its rather amorphous business clientele and occasionally lends its unofficial support to candidates of the conservative parties. The Federation of German Employers' Associations (*Bundesvereinigung der deutschen Arbeitgeberverbände,* BDA) is a more active group, particularly as a national spokesman for business on political issues relating to labor and social issues. As a counterpart to the peak trade union associations, it seeks to promote the political interests of employers through lobbying and public relations work.

The third member of this triumvirate, the Federation of German Industry (*Bundesverband der deutschen Industrie,* BDI), is first among formal equals in political activity and influence. Its membership is restricted to 39 affiliated national federations representing all branches of German industry and, through them, 98 per cent of German industrial concerns.[20] The BDI devotes a considerable proportion of its budget to publicity work designed to create a favorable climate of elite and mass opinion for its political aims and to mobilize support for its demands upon government leaders. Generous financial contributions to the conservative parties and close personal contacts with their leaders have enabled BDI spokesmen to exercise a considerable influence on government economic policies and, to a lesser extent, on the recruitment of political leaders.[21]

Although these three peak associations cling to their independence and sometimes even feud with each other, they

[20] The American National Association of Manufacturers, in comparison, represents only 6 per cent of manufacturing concerns in the United States.

[21] See Gerard Braunthal, *The Federation of German Industry in Politics* (Ithaca: Cornell University Press, 1965), pp. 26–61 and *passim;* Taylor Cole, "Functional Representation in the German Federal Republic," *Midwest Journal of Political Science,* II (August, 1958), 256–277; and Ronald F. Bunn, "The Federation of German Employers' Associations: A Political Interest Group," *Western Political Quarterly,* XIII (September, 1960), 652–659.

generally cooperate in articulating broad business interests. Overlapping membership in the respective decisionmaking organs and a diffuse identity of employers' interests relative to competing groups facilitate constant contacts. The presidents and general managers of the BDI and BDA sit as observers at one another's board meetings, and both peak associations jointly sponsor the Institute of German Industry (*Deutsches Industrieinstitut*) which provides their members with political information. Further links are provided by a number of coordinating committees. Moreover, some of the most important members of the three groups maintain constant informal contact through various business clubs and "luncheon groups." [22] A Joint Committee of German Trade and Industry (*Gemeinschaftsausschuss der deutschen gewerblichen Wirtschaft*), which includes all major employer groups, has not been particularly successful in its stated purpose of achieving a common front among diverse interests, but it has proved useful as a forum for discussion. A more common form of collaboration are ad hoc functional alliances between constituent associations, as between exporters and shipowners on behalf of foreign trade legislation.

Like the national farmers' associations, business associations command neither enough electoral strength nor sufficiently broad public support to mobilize large voting power behind their demands. Moreover, due to the heterogeneity of German business interests, peak employer associations lack the unity of the "Green Front" and some of the smaller professional associations. Although constituent business associations have frequently and successfully been able to use contacts with the government and administrative elites to push their demands, joint efforts have largely been confined to maintaining a diffuse political climate favorable to business in general. Thus, all three peak business associations have opposed government

[22] See Braunthal, *op. cit.*, p. 29. Perhaps the most important of these informal groups is a "super club" in Düsseldorf, limited to a few hundred of the most important West German business executives. Reportedly "the decisions made around its tables play a major role in West German industry and, indeed the entire economic life of West Germany." See Philip Shabecoff, "When the Waiter Brings Coffee, Germans Talk Turkey," *The New York Times*, January 21, 1966.

controls of private enterprise and have fought for authoritative rules favorable to large business establishments, such as the right to determine common prices and assign markets. But even on fairly general pieces of economic legislation, such as the Cartel Law of 1957, German business associations have found it difficult to achieve agreement.

Business associations have used various routes of access to legislators and members of the executive to press their demands and defend their interests. Estimates of the number of Bundestag deputies directly or indirectly representing such groups have varied widely. Roughly, 20 per cent of the parliamentarians in the lower chamber have been business managers, independent entrepreneurs, and functionaries of employer associations – almost all of them members of the conservative parties, and about two-thirds of them representing industry. Most have been relatively small fish; comparatively few important business leaders have sought election, despite constant urgings by their fellows and by conservative political leaders for more prestigious employer representation in parliament.[23] However, business has found its legislative friends to be numerous and helpful, both in their roles as "experts" in various committees and party "study groups," and as lobbyists and contacts in its relations with the executive branch.

More important, business association spokesmen have been able to transmit their demands directly to the chancellor – especially in Adenauer's days – and to key ministers through formal and informal channels. At a lower level of the executive branch, formal institutional arrangements combined with a patronage system, said to be more extensive than in the time of the Weimar Republic, have facilitated access to the public administration.[24] Finally, extensive, interlocking role relationships between party, governmental, and business elites have

[23] In addressing the 1963 meeting of the German Chamber of Industry and Commerce, for example, Chancellor Adenauer asserted that leading businessmen should sit in the Bundestag and expressed his regret that far too few seemed willing to assume direct responsibility for the affairs of state. See "Bestandsaufnahme in Politik und Wirtschaft," *Bulletin der Bundesregierung,* February 16, 1963, no. 23, p. 291.

[24] Braunthal, *op. cit.,* p. 224.

provided for continuous informal contacts between these leadership groups.

None of this, however, means that big business as a whole or big industry in particular constitutes a dominant power elite, as we emphasized in Chapter VI. Not only are countervailing governmental and nongovernmental elements too strong to make this possible, but the contemporary business elite lacks the characteristics which led its predecessors to seek such a position in the state. It is more divided along competitive and specialized functional lines, it is in many respects more internationalized, and – particularly in the case of its younger members – is far less deeply committed to distinctive socioeconomic and political orientations dividing it from other groups in the new pluralist society.

With the passing of the traditional, patriarchic owner-entrepreneurs – such as the Krupps – and their replacement by managerial executives, a new outlook has emerged. It rejects a special class "ethos" and political "calling" for business leaders in favor of pragmatic, consumer-oriented attitudes toward both domestic and international political questions. On the one hand, there is a far greater readiness than formerly to bargain directly with the so-called "social partners" (*Sozialpartner*), representing employee groups, without involving authoritative governmental structures. On the other, there is a far greater willingness to rely on administrative and party leaders to provide governmental economic policies which further business interests on behalf of a "social market economy" (*Soziale Marktwirtschaft*). The new type of German business leader feels that he lacks both the time and skill to devote himself very much to politics. As he sees it, it is his task to make money for himself and his clients, that of the political leaders to assure the maintenance of stable conditions which provide favorable domestic and international conditions for the pursuit of profits.

ORGANIZED LABOR

The fact that organized labor represents only about one-third of German employees – about the same proposition as in the United States and Britain — and that an expanding trade union membership has not kept pace with the expansion of the labor force, has led many observers to underestimate its political power.[25] Actually, the numerical strength of organized labor is both relatively and absolutely greater than under previous regimes and, for the first time in German history, trade union leaders exercise a degree of influence on authoritative rulemaking processes which effectively rivals that of other associational interest group elites.

Although organized labor lacks the homogeneity of the agricultural "Green Front" and perhaps even the more limited degree of unity among the all-inclusive artisans' and employers' associations, numerically it represents by far the largest occupational interest alignment. And at election time numbers count. German trade union members do not invariably vote as their leaders tell them to, but they do so more than do their counterparts in the United States.

Strong organizational bonds and extensive mass media provide trade union leaders with powerful means to influence their members' views. In addition, labor's spokesmen command vast financial resources — including income from banks, publishing houses, insurance companies, and breweries — which they use to promote their political demands. Moreover, the trade unions' strength in the particularly densely organized key industrial sectors and in public administration provides them with a qualitative influence over economic and political activities which vastly exceeds their numerical strength among the population in general. Finally, like other elite groups, labor leaders have access to political decisionmakers through the major political parties and through direct representation in numerous governmental and semigovernmental bodies.

The formalization of German interest articulation structures in effect makes trade union functionaries the legitimate spokesmen for employees' interests in general, whether organized or not. These arrangements assume that unorganized

[25] In the early years of the Federal Republic close to half the employees were trade union members, but rising prosperity and the mass recruitment of women and foreign workers into the economy reduced the relative strength of organized labor, particularly among the expanding group of low-skilled, salaried service employees.

labor shares the economic interests of trade union members and benefits from the political gains of their leaders, as in the areas of social security and wage and hour legislation or in employer-employee disputes before the special "labor courts." Such role assignments represent one more aspect of constitutional and legal provisions designed to assure orderly and stable relationships among key participants in the German political system.

The trade union movement takes in three major peak associations which, between them, include today about 21 per cent of salaried employees (*Angestellte*), 41 per cent of wage earners (*Arbeiter*), and 99 per cent of career civil servants (*Beamte*).[26] The largest is the German Confederation of Trade Unions (*Deutscher Gewerkschaftsbund*). With some 6.5 million members (1964), the DGB is not only the principal wage earner organization, but also the largest of salaried employees and the second largest of civil servants. The first group, however, constitutes as much as 79 per cent of the membership, whereas the other two represent merely 12 and 9 per cent, respectively. Organized into 16 largely autonomous national industrial unions (*Industriegewerkschaften*), the DGB is thus primarily an association of manual workers rather than white-collar employees.

Two rival peak associations have sought to organize the latter, maintaining that they have separate outlooks and interests. The German Salaried Employees Union (*Deutsche Angestelltengewerkschaft*) split off from the DGB in 1949 in the hope that traditional status distinctions between white-collar employees and blue-collared "proletarians" would make it the principal representative of the former. However, most German salaried employees prefer to remain unorganized – particularly the growing number of low-skilled women in service trades – so that the 475,000 members of the DAG represented in 1964 only 8 per cent of them; 13 per cent belonged to DGB unions. The German Federation of Civil Servants (*Deutscher Beamtenbund*) has been more successful in competing with

[26] These and other figures on trade union membership are derived from information reported in the *Statistische Jahrbuch für die Bundesrepublik Deutschlands, 1965* and Noelle-Neumann, *Jahrbuch der öffentlichen Meinung 1958–1964,* p. 4.

the DGB for the allegiances of the almost totally organized civil servants, which in Germany includes teachers and university professors. In 1964, the 692,000 members of the DBB represented 53 per cent of German civil servants, whereas 43 per cent preferred to cast their lot with the DGB.

In pursuing their political objectives German trade union leaders employ a variety of means to influence public opinion and government leaders. Relying on the support of a disciplined and loyal mass following they have on occasion resorted to carefully arranged demonstrations to articulate their demands. Another weapon in their arsenal has been their constitutionally guaranteed right to call strikes – including "political" strikes. Rarely applied, this weapon has more often been employed as a threat to extract concessions from government leaders. In 1951, for example, in the face of a strike threat by the DGB leadership, Chancellor Adenauer yielded and assured passage of a "codetermination law" giving labor a voice in the management of the iron, steel, and coal industries. More recently, in July, 1966, the threat of a strike by the Ruhr coal miners induced government leaders to arrange a wage settlement underwritten by public subsidies to the mine owners. At other times, however, the strike threat has proven not only ineffective, but a source for widespread public criticism directed against the trade union leaders. Consequently, these have preferred to achieve their ends by less dramatic and conspicuous means.

Labor leaders command many channels of direct and indirect access to political decisionmakers, which enable them to promote their clients' interests out of the public view. They are directly represented in numerous governmental advisory bodies and supervisory councils, they have their spokesmen in the executive and legislative organs of the federal and the Land governments, and they have a voice in the leadership councils of both of the major parties.

Since the establishment of the Federal Republic, about two out of five Bundestag deputies have been trade union members – mostly of DGB unions – and about one out of ten trade union functionaries. Although by far the largest number have been deputies of the Social Democratic Party, the Christian

Democrats also have a labor wing that has averaged approximately one-sixth of its deputies and as much as half the trade union functionaries in the lower chamber. Like other interest association representatives, these friends of organized labor in both major parties have been its spokesmen in parliamentary committees and intraparty councils. At times deputies from both sides of the aisle have formed bipartisan alliances to promote the passage of legislation desired by the unions or to fight against bills opposed by them.

Even more important, parliamentary deputies and administrative leaders affiliated with the trade unions have served as their emissaries to the executive branch. The Federal Minister of Labor has invariably been a trade union man and the unionized civil service has maintained a close relationship with its interest spokesmen in and out of parliament. Additional contacts between labor and government leaders have been provided through the Federal Social Insurance System – jointly administered by government, trade union, and business association functionaries – and through trade union representatives in the labor courts that formally adjudicate employer-employee disputes.

Organized labor's position in the political system and the essential aim of its political activities is today a matter of some controversy among its leaders. One wing of the Federation of Labor believes that the present regime incorporates strong antidemocratic and antilabor elements, which must be militantly opposed by trade unions. Such views are strongly influenced by surviving class conscious orientations and bitter memories of past labor disunity, conflicts, and defeats. Many of the old-timers in the DGB, who fought labor's battles before Hitler and were harshly persecuted under his rule, have not forgotten the part which the enemies of labor played in the destruction of the Weimar Republic and during the Nazi regime. Led today by Otto Brenner, chief of the Metal Workers – the largest union in the world and the richest in the Federation – they see labor as a distinct political subculture with little influence over authoritative policymaking in the Federal Republic. These trade union leaders feel that the principal task of the German labor movement is to fight unitedly for greater social, economic, and political democracy against the "reactionary" groups which, from their point of view, exercise a vast and growing influence in Germany.

Though emphatically anti-Communist, this militant wing of the labor movement has tended to favor a more neutralist foreign policy and greater tolerance of deviant left-wing groups than most German leaders, on the grounds that both would promote a more democratic form of government. It led the fight against rearmament, fearing that a new German army would strengthen antidemocratic elements in the Federal Republic, and for similar reasons vehemently opposed legislation granting the federal government "emergency powers" in times of crisis. Initially associated closely with the leadership of the Social Democratic Party, the militant wing in recent years has sharply disagreed with the SPD elite's efforts to win greater public support by a more moderate policy of cooperation with groups which the militants consider reactionary.

Other union leaders emphatically endorse the present political system and maintain that it is in labor's best interest to have a basically harmonious relationship with other organized groups in state and society. These include the leaders of the Civil Service and Salaried Employees unions, as well as mostly younger DGB functionaries, who look upon the labor movement as an integral part of interest group structures in a pluralist industrial society. As head of the Building Trade Federation in the DGB, as well as a prominent Social Democratic deputy in the Bundestag, Georg Leber had been the principal spokesman for this group until he became Minister of Transport in a national coalition government formed by the Christian Democrats and the Social Democrats in 1966.

A policy which seems to their opponents in the DGB opportunistic and shortsighted appears to these reformers pragmatic and realistic. Strongly influenced by contacts with American trade unionists, they consider the traditional continental European labor movement's activities unsuited for contemporary German conditions. They believe that organized labor's political activities should focus on bread-and-butter issues and feel confident that they can participate in political input processes to satisfy their clients' claims for economic and social benefits. This new type of German trade union leader is more interested in influencing government budget allotments and tax policies than in promoting class-conscious labor solidarity, and more in bargaining with government decision-makers than in fighting them. He is willing to join employers' associations in opposing the demands of farm groups and religious associations in promoting social welfare legislation.

Though the power of the Metal Workers and the strength of ideological traditions has remained strong enough to slow the patterns of change in the labor movement, even the more militant German trade union leaders appear to be adapting themselves to the new style of interest articulation and political bargaining among polyarchic elites. A conspicuous sign of a new course was the DGB Program of 1963. It dropped former demands for the socialization of key industries and opted instead for the expansion of private economic enterprises and public social welfare services.

Organized labor's political interests are increasingly shaped by the fact that it no longer represents an underprivileged social stratum but one of the most affluent employee groups in the world. Trade union leaders who manage vast economic enterprises and who participate extensively in the management of public and private enterprises share business group interests in the maintenance of economic prosperity; as representatives of labor, they have an equal interest in government measures to sustain full employment and promote German industrial growth. At the same time, traditional principles of national and international working class solidarity simply obscure conflicting interests among unions in competing industries.

In short, present trends indicate that organized labor is acquiring political goals which are transforming German trade unions into the type of functionally specific employee associations found in the United States.

INTEREST ARTICULATION AND POLITICS

The structure and style of interest articulation have a very important bearing on the development and operation of a political system. Such input processes affect the boundaries and relationships between political and nonpolitical sectors in a society, as well as the patterns of interaction among the political system's component structures. When these are more clearly defined, understood, and accepted by the participating actors, consequent political role perceptions and behavior patterns are likely to lend stability to a regime. On the other hand, if the input structures linking society and polity are diffuse and obscure, and seem neither legitimate nor satisfactory to the participants, the political order is likely to be unstable and open to major alterations.[27] By these standards the requisites for the prevailing regime's preservation certainly exist in Germany and appear to be growing stronger; whether domestic input structures that function well enough under present circumstances are also equal to a heavier and more intense flow of demands remains to be seen.

The highly formalized patterns of organized interest representations in the Federal Republic facilitate orderly input processes. The reciprocal flow of political communications between interest group clienteles, their legitimate spokesmen, and authoritative decisionmakers is relatively unambiguous, and relevant roles are clearly understood. The rules and practices of interest articulation generally concern manifest, specific, and instrumental issues; bargaining and compromise are correspondingly easier than in a system in which latent pressures, diffuse issues, and emotion charged attitudes strain political consensus.

However, carefully regulated and organized patterns of interest articulation are not by themselves guarantors of political stability. The essentially hierarchic and bureaucratic character of German interest group structures implies the possibility that they may not prove sufficiently responsive to changing conditions and demands to serve as efficient input agents for the political system. Functionally, specific interest groups which are highly inflexible and uncompromising in their goals and activities may hinder rather than facilitate the free flow of input claims into the system and their aggregation and processing of such demands by political parties and govern-

27 See Gabriel Almond and G. Bingham Powell, Jr., *Comparative Politics* (Boston: Little, Brown, 1966), chap. 4.

mental agencies. In such an event, they are likely to be displaced or absorbed by other structures, with a consequent loss of autonomy, or the blocking of established channels for the articulation of political interests might lead to mass alienation from the prevailing system and widespread hostility toward its leaders. If the dominant political leadership either will not or cannot rectify the situation because it fails to perceive it clearly or lacks the ability to make the necessary adjustments, the consequences may lead to drastic alterations in the entire system.

Present trends reflect continuing reciprocal adaptation between organized input structures and other elements of the German political system which thus far has helped to institutionalize its component elements. Though traditional patterns of interest articulation still strongly influence the relationships among interest group elites, political elites, and mass public, the associational input structures have also been adjusting to socioeconomic and political conditions which are very different from those which shaped their functions under previous German regimes.

One characteristic of the modernization of German associational interest groups has been their increasing autonomy and functional specialization. For example, the failure of an incipient "Christian" trade union movement indicates the detachment of occupational associations from diffuse subcultural loyalties. Waning ideological bonds between interest organizations and political parties point in a similar direction. And within the major peak associations divergent function interests have promoted the autonomy of the constituent groups. For the sake of at least nominal unity, multiple cross-pressures arising from pluralist interests must be accommodated at the cost of restricting and diluting the areas for common political action.[28]

[28] Functional interest alignments between constituent member groups of different peak associations weaken the cohesion of the more diffuse organizations. Thus, agricultural and industrial groups seeking protection against foreign imports have formed coalitions against business and trade union groups opposing such restrictions, and employer and employee associations in one industrial branch have cooperated in promoting their common interests against those of similar groups identified with another industry.

A second and related development is the increasing importance of specialized, single-purpose economic associations with relatively limited political objectives. These may lack the numerical strength and financial resources of the larger groups, but their restricted goals enhance their solidarity and protect them against enfeebling cross-pressures. For instance, the relatively small professional associations of teachers, physicians, and artisans have effectively united supporters of various parties and religious groups to promote common occupational demands. The same holds true for such larger single-purpose groups as the associations of pensioners and war victims. Political leaders find it easier to aggregate and satisfy their limited material claims than more extensive and diffuse demands advanced by competing mass organizations.

A third feature of the evolution of German interest articulation structures has been the increasingly harmonious relationship among the ostensibly nonpolitical elites, and between these and the political leaders. As noted earlier, bargaining and mutual accommodation have become the prevalent pattern of interaction in the polyarchic system which has developed in the Federal Republic, and the modern trend toward the functional specialization of participant roles appears to have had a great deal to do with facilitating stable and balanced interelite relations.

German interest group elites may command extensive means to influence political decisionmakers, but they are constrained in the demands they can make and the means they can employ. There are the formalized "rules of the game," reinforced cultural norms that place the interests of state and community above those of "special interests" and establish governmental leaders as the legitimate arbitrators among competing demands. There are also cross-cutting political allegiances which may override role identifications with competing associational

---

Those large peak associations whose members identify themselves with numerous collectivities — religious groups, political parties, as well as occupational associations — are increasingly being weakened by cross-pressures. Even the still relatively high solidarity in the agricultural associations is slowly being undermined as an increasing number of their members are becoming part-time farmers or absentee farm owners.

interests and induce the supporters of one party or another to disregard such identifications in favor of partisan ones. And there is a pluralism of competing elites involved in political input processes, which disperses rather than concentrates the power of organized interests over public policymaking.

These constraints on the bargaining power of interest associations allow German political leaders to aggregate and balance their demands in the name of "larger" interests and to avoid commitments that would simply make them the instruments of any particular association or interest group coalition. Their control over the rulemaking function in the political system and the far-reaching intrusion of the public sector into the private spheres of the social and economic system provide the political elites with considerable powers to curb interest group demands.

The trend toward a system of two major aggregative parties in the Federal Republic has been both a cause and an effect of a shift in the direction of organized interest inputs from administrative to party channels and a loosening of the bonds between particular associations and particular parties. With the opening up of the parties to multi-interest representation has gone a tendency on the part of the associations toward less explicit partisan commitments and shifting allegiances. That is, trade unions, churches, and business groups find it less to their advantage to be identified with only one party or group of political leaders because the party system limits the alternatives open to them. Simultaneously, the competition of plural interests has tended to favor neutralization of the civil service and to reduce to secondary importance efforts to exert direct influence on the government bureaucracy.

At the same time, the increasing amorphousness of the parties and their electoral support provides a strong and determined interest association or a coalition with opportunities to exploit intraparty cleavages. As shown in a number of recent cases, when inter- or intraparty solidarity and discipline are high and specific party objectives conflict with interest group goals, the ability of the latter to achieve their ends is likely to be relatively low. On the other hand, when party unity and party coalitions are weak or interest group demands do not clash with the objectives of party leaders, even a relatively weak association has a good chance of obtaining satisfaction if its claims are not opposed by stronger competitive organizations.[29]

On the whole, therefore, a well functioning, orderly, and balanced network of interest articulation structures seems to be thoroughly integrated into the new German political system. According to their leading spokesmen, the various associations represent positive and constructive elements in a democratic state and perform an essential function as intermediaries between the mass public and its authoritative leaders. However, such assertions are not shared by most citizens of the Federal Republic, especially when they are made by the spokesmen of organizations believed to have excessive influence in public affairs (see Table VII.1).

TABLE VII.1 *Mass Perception of Influence of Interest Groups, 1962 (Sample of Adult Population in Rounded-off Percentages)*

	Have too much influence	*Have too little influence*	*Have just about enough influence*	*No opinion*	*Total*
Protestant clergy	8	25	47	20	100
Roman Catholic clergy	46	12	28	14	100
Trade unions	37	18	28	17	100
Bankers and big businessmen	59	11	12	18	100
Farm organizations	32	25	23	20	100
Refugee organizations	26	21	31	22	100

Source: EMNID, *Informationen,* July, 1962.

Such distrust extends well beyond the general public into the ranks of prominent German opinion leaders, particularly journalists and university professors. In their view, the restraints on the power of the interest associations are too few,

[29] See, for example, Sigmund Chabbrowski, "Alle gegen Einen: Der Kampf der Verbände um die grünen Millionen," *Die Zeit,* May 17, 1963, which describes in fascinating detail a battle between agricultural and other interest associations over farm subsidies. Also, Bethusy-Huc, *Die Soziologie wirtschaftspolitischer Entscheidungen, op. cit.,* and Otto Stammer, *et al., Verbände und Gesetzgebung* (Köln-Opladen: Westdeutscher Verlag, 1965).

and the opportunities to thrive at the expense of the public treasury too many. In the opinion of these critics the present situation is a serious threat to the interests of the community, which some identify as those of the state and others as those of the general public. Either way, the responsible political leaders are accused of having shirked their responsibilities. Some critics look to the civil service to curb the power of the interest associations, others to the political parties. Generally, the alternatives to what many describe as a state governed by special interest groups (*Verbändestaat*) are said to be either a system dominated by the bureaucracy (*Verwaltungsstaat*) or one controlled by the political parties (*Parteienstaat*). Such "either-or" solutions seem to reflect a still widespread unwillingness to recognize or accept the possibility of a more or less balanced pluralist system.

Under these conditions one of the major tasks confronting German political leaders is to demonstrate their ability to maintain a stable relationship between nongovernmental input structures and authoritative output structures. If they follow the example of the French Fifth Republic and earlier German regimes, they will seek the solution in a bureaucratic "administrative state." If they adhere to the American and British pattern, they will strive to achieve it primarily through the political parties.

CHAPTER VIII

The Party System

THE KEYSTONE of the present political order in Germany is a competitive party system providing for government by party elites.[1] The conditions requisite for such a system were the exception rather than the rule under past German regimes and it therefore lacks the strong historical-cultural roots which

[1] A competitive party system depends first on free and open electoral contests which provide the voters with periodic opportunities to express their preferences for various parties and their candidates for public offices. Second, it requires generally accepted, orderly procedures which (1) permit the victors to assume control over authoritative rulemaking structures in the community and (2) assure the losers that they will continue to have legitimate opportunities to seek and obtain such power in the future. In this sense, a party system is not competitive if opposition parties are barred from coming to power by legitimate means, and parties are not competitive unless they can participate in elections with a reasonable expectation of achieving complete or partial control over public policymaking.

These and other propositions incorporated in this chapter are derived from a large number of studies, but particularly the following: Sigmund Neumann, "Toward a Comparative Study of Political Parties," in Neumann (ed.), *Modern Political Parties* (Chicago: University of Chicago Press, 1956), pp. 395–421; Joseph A. Schlesinger, "Political Party Organization," in James E. March (ed.), *Handbook of Organization* (Chicago: Rand, McNally, 1965), pp. 765–797; Frank Sorauf, *Political Parties in the American System* (Boston: Little, Brown, 1964); Joseph LaPalombara and Myron Weiner (eds.), *Political Parties and Political Development* (Princeton: Princeton University Press, 1966); Harry Eckstein and David E. Apter (eds.) *Comparative Politics* (New York: Free Press of Glencoe, 1963), pp. 247–286; Robert E. Dahl (ed.), *Political Opposition in Western Democracies* (New Haven: Yale University Press, 1966); and Lester E. Seligman, "Political Parties and the Requirements of Political Leadership," in Lewis J. Edinger (ed.), *Political Leadership in Industrialized Societies* (New York: Wiley, 1967), pp. 294–315.

sustain its operation in such countries as the United States and Britain.

Under the autocratic Hohenzollern regime, political parties were for the most part excluded from authoritative rulemaking processes in the state. The Weimar regime introduced representative government through political parties but an unstable multiparty system contributed significantly to its destruction. Persistent ideological and interest group cleavages in German society also kept the numerous parties deeply divided; their inability to achieve a basic consensus on rules governing the operation of a competitive party system helped powerful groups opposed to such a system to weaken and, ultimately, to destroy it. The party system of the Third Reich of course was neither pluralist nor competitive, but coterminous with the totalitarian system. The monopolistic Nazi party was not an autonomous organization for popular representation, but was designed to serve Hitler as an instrument of mass mobilization and dictatorial control.

The contemporary German party system offers a sharp contrast to these earlier patterns. First, the fractionalized multiparty system of the pre-Nazi era and the one-party system of the Third Reich have been replaced by a system dominated by two major parties (see Table VIII.1). These are (1) the CDU/CSU, the Christian Democratic Union (*Christlich Demokratische Union*), and its Bavarian affiliate, the Christian Social Union (*Christlich Soziale Union*), and (2) the SPD, the German Social Democratic Party (*Sozialdemokratische Partei Deutschlands*). Their combined strength in the federal Bundestag grew from 67 per cent in 1949 to over 90 per cent in 1965, accompanied by equivalent gains for the two parties in Land and local legislative bodies.

Of the seven smaller parties represented in the first Bundestag only one, the Free Democratic Party (*Freie Demokratische Partei*), has thus far managed to survive the trend toward a two party system. However, the future of the FDP as a competitive national party appears most uncertain. All its present federal deputies owe their seats to positions on their party list rather than to election in single member districts (see Table VIII.1); the possibility that the two major parties may agree to

TABLE VIII.1 *Party Strength in Federal Elections, 1961, 1965*

Party	*Distribution of votes*				*Distribution of Bundestag seats*					
	Total (in millions)		*Percentage*		*Total*		*From single member districts*		*From party lists*	
	1961	*1965*	*1961*	*1965*	*1961*	*1965*	*1961*	*1965*	*1961*	*1965*
CDU/CSU	14.3	15.5	45.4	47.6	242	245	156	154	86	91
SPD	11.4	12.8	36.2	39.3	190	202	91	94	99	108
FDP	4.0	3.1	12.8	9.5	67	49	—	—	67	49
Others	1.9	1.2	5.6	3.6	—	—	—	—	—	—
Total	31.6	32.6	100	100	499	496	247	248	252	248

Source: Bulletin der Bundesregierung, October 15, 1965, p. 1351.

abolish the prevailing system of modified proportional representation threatens to exclude the FDP and other minor parties from the Bundestag.[2]

A second and closely related innovation of the present party system is the strategic position of the CDU and SPD as key integrative structures for the general coordination of input and output functions in the political system. For the first time in German history, the major political parties have achieved relative autonomy from specific subcultural interest groups on the one hand and from organs of the state on the other. This has permitted them to function as effective mediating agents between the state and society and to reduce the influence of other governmental and nongovernmental political structures in public policymaking.

The effective boundaries between state and society and the patterns of political competition and collaboration in the pluralistic society of contemporary Germany are consequently determined, for the most part, by two sets of interdependent relationships. One of these consists of the vertical and horizontal ties between party structures and other components of the political system, such as the electorate, interest associations, and governmental agencies. The other involves the relationship between the parties and, more specifically, the interaction between the leaders of the CDU/CSU and the SPD. In the last two decades both sets of relationships have been shaped by continuous mutual adaptation, reflecting changing as well as persistent cultural values and a dynamic environment that influence the development of political structures and functions in a transitional society.

THE CHRISTIAN DEMOCRATIC UNION

The pre-eminent position of the Christian Democratic Union in post-Nazi Germany and its uninterrupted dominance over the federal government have profoundly influenced the development of the political system. Voting patterns, interest group and elite alignments, and the trend toward a two party system have been shaped primarily by the party's policies and actions, while these, in turn, have reflected the CDU's response

[2] See p. 169 above.

to the domestic and international environmental conditions influencing German politics.

The CDU bears little resemblance to past German parties and to mass membership parties in other European countries. Essentially it is a relatively amorphous alliance of quite heterogeneous groups, united by a common desire to control public policymaking. In some ways the Union resembles American electoral parties and in some other Christian Democratic parties in Europe and Latin America; but it also embodies features which distinguish the German political culture and system from those of other countries. The party counts among its members and leaders representatives of the Roman Catholic Church as well as prominent Protestants; it has a right wing with close ties to conservative business and agricultural interests and a left wing associated with the trade unions. It includes spokesmen for the expellees and refugees from areas under Communist control and groups representing the interests of various occupational and socioeconomic subsectors of German society.

The decentralized organizational structure of the CDU reflects the autonomy of its constituent groups and their resistance to efforts to create a more thoroughly integrated national organization. The highest party organ is the federal executive committee, a rather unwieldy body of some sixty members. It includes (1) the federal chairman and his four deputies — elected by the annual party congress — as well as (2) the leaders of the party's sixteen Land organizations, (3) its principal governmental and legislative representatives, and (4) the leaders of various special interest groups within the CDU. Since 1967, the party also has had a general secretary, who is supposed to coordinate the activities of its component groups and thus strengthen the cohesiveness of the national organization. It was indicative of the real distribution of power in the party that the position was filled by a federal minister, designated by the party's chairman and chancellor, who retained his public office.

In fact, the CDU elite consists of leaders whose power is based primarily on sources other than their formal positions in the national party organization. Most of them occupy key public offices in federal or Land governments and legislatures, providing them with direct links to key elites, interest groups, and voting blocs outside the party. With the exception of but a brief period, the party chairmanship has always been held by the federal chancellor, whose power in the CDU has been based more on his governmental than his party office. The same has been true for the federal ministers, legislative leaders, and Land government chieftains of the CDU. Other leaders have wielded influence in the party on the strength of their associations with important nongovernmental pressure groups and interest clienteles.

The strong regional and local roots of the CDU are reflected in the power wielded by the leaders of the constituent Land organizations and the autonomous Bavarian affiliate of the party, the CSU. As with the major American parties, the federal system has encouraged subnational CDU chieftains to assert their independence. Local and sectional interests have often led them to defy the wishes of CDU members of the federal government in forming coalitions with other parties or voting in the upper house, the Bundesrat. The selection of CDU candidates for the lower house of the federal legislature, the Bundestag, rests with state and local party leaders who, on occasion, have deliberately rejected the recommendations of its federal officeholders, including the chancellor. Even Adenauer, despite his great prestige in the CDU, was singularly unsuccessful in obtaining the nomination of candidates of his choice, and failed to obtain support for his repeated proposals for a national list of candidates selected by the federal leadership.

The CDU has a relatively small membership in voting strength (in 1967 about 400,000, or approximately 3 per cent of its electorate), and in this respect more closely resembles American electoral parties than such European mass membership parties as the Italian Christian Democratic party. Rank-and-file CDU members participate, on the whole, only sporadically in party activities—mostly at election time—and only about 7 per cent of the Union's income in 1965 was derived from membership dues. Accordingly, the party depends all the more heavily on other sources for financial and mass support.

In part, such resources have been provided through national

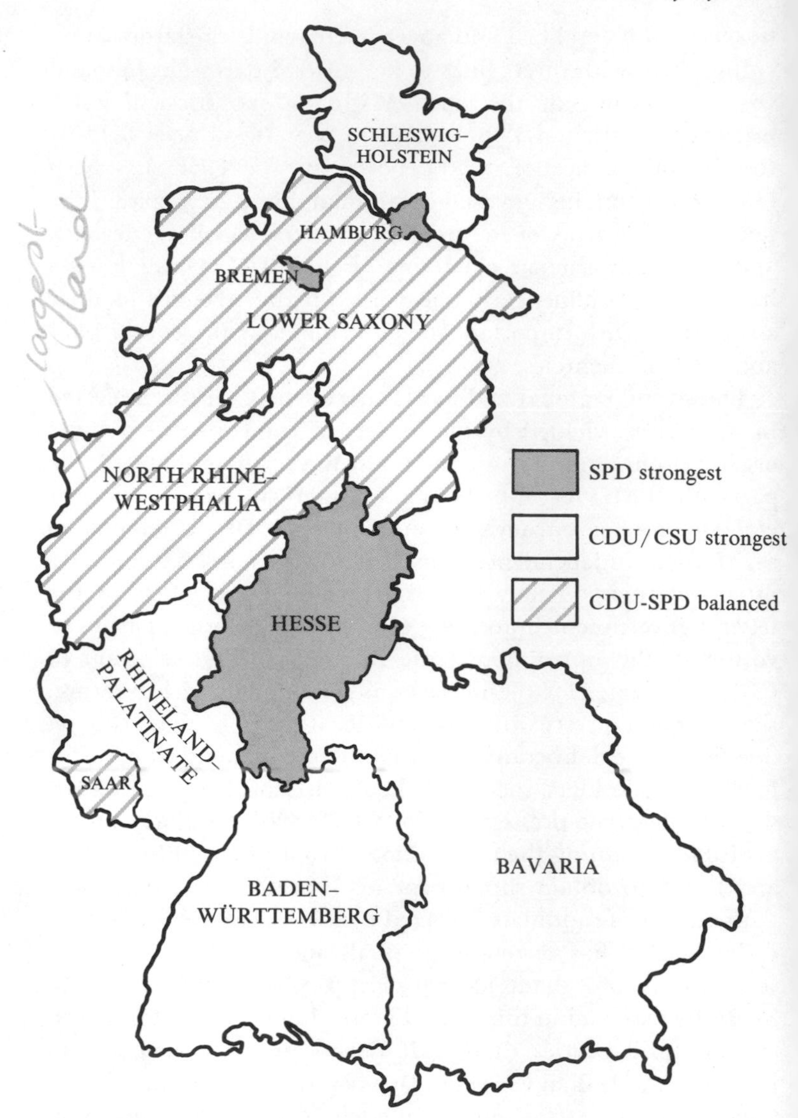

FIGURE VIII.1 *Strength of Major Parties, 1965 Federal Election, by Länder*

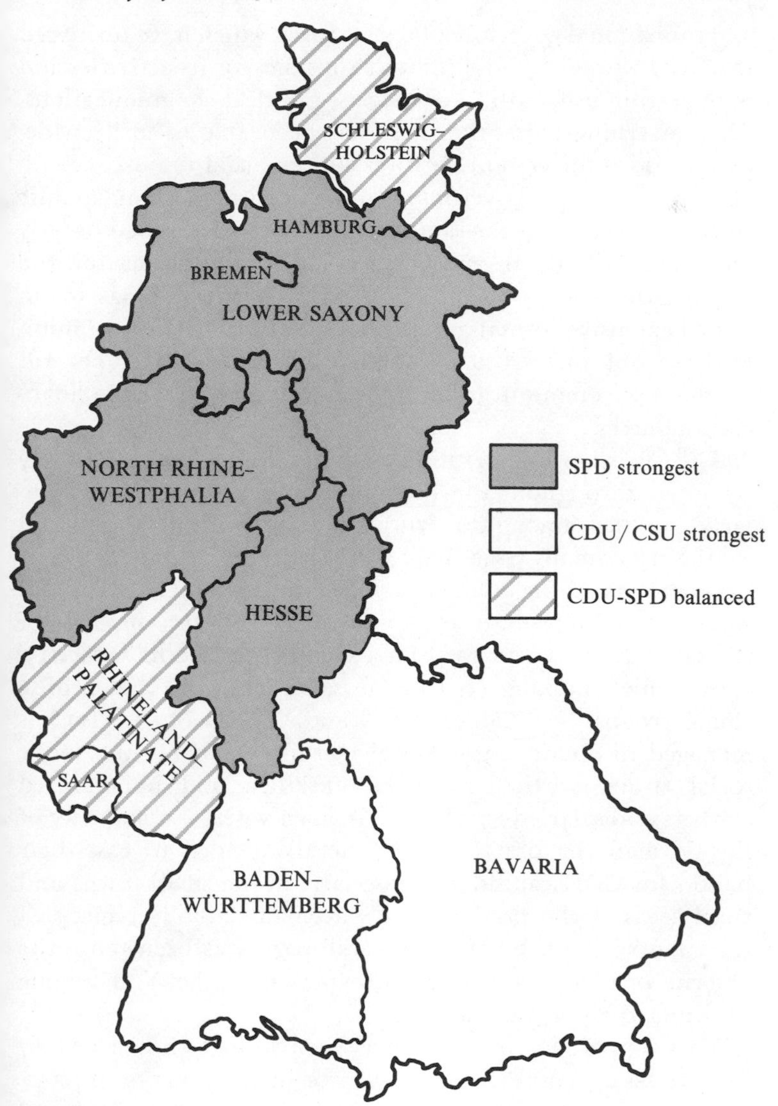

FIGURE VIII. 2 *Strength of Major Parties, State Diet Elections, 1963-1966*

and subnational governmental structures, which have furnished the CDU with direct and indirect subsidies for its activities and with gratuitous facilities for its mass political communications. As a governing party the CDU has been able to make widespread use of the communication and financial resources available to the federal government for its educational and public relations services. At the same time, the CDU has relied heavily on nongovernmental mass media and organizations for the mobilization of mass support. For this purpose it has maintained extensive formal and informal ties to key elites, opinion leaders, and interest associations who command important channels of communication to the public and/or sizable financial resources.

The Christian Democratic Union has been supported widely by voters throughout the Federal Republic, but it is particularly popular among the rural electorate of northern and southern Germany (see Table VIII.2 and electoral maps). It has commanded the adherence of devout Roman Catholics and conservative Protestants, of most farmers, and of a majority of the best educated and wealthiest elements in German society, such as high ranking civil servants, businessmen, and professional groups (see Tables VIII.3 and VIII.4). But it also has managed to obtain a great deal of support among the lower social strata, particularly from unskilled and unorganized workers and salaried employees. Women voters — a majority of the German electorate — have generally tended to cast their ballots for CDU candidates, especially in the small towns and rural areas of the predominantly Roman Catholic regions of the country. And, by and large, the party has been more the favorite of older groups, which experienced the Nazi regime as adults, than of younger voters.

Mass support for the CDU has been strongly influenced by its success in winning the allegiance of most major interest associations and key elite groups. Business and agricultural organizations have been attracted by its conservative economic policies and, among religious organizations, especially those affiliated with the Roman Catholic Church have favored the Union and its candidates. Most of the publishers and editors of German newspapers and periodicals have tended to support

Region	Land	Proportion of 1961 population	Party strength in 1965, federal election total					Party strength in state diet elections, 1964–1967					
			CDU/CSU	SPD	FDP	Others	Total	CDU/CSU	SPD	FDP	Others	Total	
North Germany	Schleswig-Holstein	5	48	39	9	4	100	46	39	6	9[a]	100	1967
	Hamburg	3	38	48	9	5	100	30	59	7	4	100	1966
	Lower Saxony	12	46	40	11	4	101	42	43	7	9	101	1967
	Bremen	1	34	49	18	6	101	30	46	11	13	100	1967
West Germany	North Rhine-Westphalia	30	47	43	8	3	101	43	50	7	b	100	1966
	Hesse	9	38	46	12	5	101	26	51	10	12	99	1966
	Saarland	2	47	40	7	5	99	43	41	8	8	100	1965
	Rhineland Palatinate	6	49	37	10	4	100	47	37	8	8[a]	100	1967
South Germany	Baden-Württemberg	15	50	33	13	4	100	46	37	13	3[a]	99	1964
	Bavaria	18	57	33	7	4	101	48	36	5	11	100	1966
Total Federal Republic (excluding Berlin)		101	48	39	10	3	100	40	44	8	8[a]	100	1964–67

[a] Mostly National Democratic Party.
[b] Less than 1 per cent.
Sources: Calculated from data in *Bulletin der Bundesregierung*, 1964–1967, and Deutsches Industrieinstitut, *Analyse der Wahl zum 5. Deutschen Bundestag* (September, 1965).

TABLE VIII.3 *Distribution of Party Preferences, 1964 (in rounded-off percentages)*

	Proportion of adult population, 1961	Preferences expressed in opinion poll, 1964					
		CDU/CSU	SPD	FDP	Others	None indicated	Total
Total	100	34	34	6	2	24	100
men	46	30	41	7	2	20	100
women	54	38	28	5	2	27	100
Age cohorts							
born before 1933	72	35	32	6	2	25	100
born after 1933	28	34	38	4	1	23	100
Religious identification							
Protestants	51	28	39	8	2	23	100
Roman Catholics	45	45	26	4	1	24	100
others or none	4	20	46	3	4	27	100
Educational level							
primary (8 years)	82	31	38	4	2	25	100
secondary (9–10 years)	13	46	20	13	1	20	100
higher (including university)	5	43	20	16	1	20	100

Occupations							
industrial and agricultural workers	50	22	50	2	2	24	100
salaried employees	23	37	29	9	1	24	100
civil servants and other government employees	7	49	27	7	1	16	100
self-employed and professions	12	40	19	12	2	27	100
independent farmers	9	62	7	14	2	15	100
Income level (monthly)[a]							
under 400 DM	17	48	46	4	4	—	102
400–799 DM	61	40	50	5	5	—	100
over 800 DM	22	57	30	14	1	—	102

[a] Income of principal earner in household as a proportion of all respondents reporting income in survey. (For total adult population, 1963 income.)

Sources: Noelle and Neumann, *Jahrbuch der öffentlichen Meinung, 1958–1964,* pp. 3ff. EMNID, *Informationen,* Nos. 13 and 26 (1964).

TABLE VIII.4 *Trends in Party Preferences, by Occupations, 1949–1965 (data in rounded-off percentages)*

	CDU/CSU			*SPD*			*Others*		
	1949	*1953*	*1965*	*1949*	*1953*	*1965*	*1949*	*1953*	*1965*
Industrial and agricultural workers	21	38	30	37	37	52	41	26	3
Salaried employees (including civil servants)	39	52	43	18	16	29	43	22	7
Self-employed (including professions)	44	55	40	14	11	19	42	34	17
Independent farmers	45	61	62	14	5	7	41	34	9

Sources: Data for 1949 and 1953 represent proportion of voters casting ballots. (Reported in Faul, *Wahlen und Wähler in Deutschland,* p. 209.) Data for 1965 represent proportion of respondents in pre-election survey reporting preferences. (Reported in IFAS release, September 17, 1965.)

the CDU, as have most of the leaders of artisan, refugee, professional, and salaried employee organizations. Among government employees, many top civil service and military leaders sympathize with the party and, frequently, are members of the CDU.

During the first decades of postwar political reconstruction, the CDU rapidly outdistanced its rivals for control over the new political system, especially the SPD. Under the strong and skillful leadership of its first chancellor and federal chairman, Konrad Adenauer, it managed to establish itself as a popular electoral party appealing to broad sectors of German society, and proved exceedingly effective in responding to the prevailing political environment inside and outside Germany. After winning a popular plurality in the first federal election in 1949, the CDU in 1953 became the first party in German history to gain an absolute parliamentary majority in a free national election; further gains in 1957 gave the Union a majority of the popular vote as well.[3]

These cumulative electoral victories were the product of strategies and tactics which very effectively combined traditional and modern elements in German society and politics. The goal of the men and women who established in 1945 the local and regional groups, which subsequently merged into the CDU, had been a new type of German party. Surviving members of pre-Nazi conservative and sectarian parties, trade union leaders, and representatives of the major churches and business interests, they wanted to overcome the political cleavages of the past by forming a nonsectarian "Christian" union, committed to a democratic form of government and identified with no particular social stratum, subculture, or political philosophy. The product was a political formula which proved to be ideally suited to the political climate of post-Nazi Germany. It combined broadly gauged policies diffuse enough to attract extensive elite and mass support with carefully balanced governmental outputs by the CDU's public officeholders, which satisfied the values and demands of very heterogeneous groups. The CDU's political formula incorporated a judicious mixture

[3] Under the prevailing system of proportional representation, a parliamentary majority did not require a majority of the popular vote.

of secular material aspirations, middle class values, and sacred Christian moral norms. It provided assurances that the CDU would meet demands for modernizing innovations without sacrificing cherished cultural traditions, and it fused popular demands for security and stability through strong governmental leadership with demands for freedom from governmental intervention in the "private" affairs of the citizen.

The diffuse policy proposals and more specific governmental activities of the CDU have allowed former Nazis as well as anti-Nazis, democratic pluralists as well as traditionalist proponents of a corporate order, to consider it their party. It has managed with its socioeconomic policies to satisfy adherents of "free enterprise capitalism" as well as supporters of a "Christian socialist" welfare state. But its new political formula also has required the party and its leaders to be highly flexible in strategies and tactics in order to maintain equilibrium among the diverse CDU supporters. To work effectively, the CDU formula must provide for a broad supportive consensus in the political community at large, resting upon a balance between diverse voting blocs, interest associations, and elite groups outside the party. At the same time, it necessitates an equilibrium among contending factions within the CDU, involving mutual tolerance and shared belief that Christian Democratic control over governmental structures requires intraparty unity and compromise.[4]

During its evolution the Christian Democratic Union developed various practices designed to maintain the requisite external and internal balance. The selection of CDU candidates for elective and appointive offices in the government and party has been carefully regulated by a so-called *Proporz* arrangement, under which every major group supporting the party is granted some form of representation. CDU-sponsored policy outputs at various levels of authoritative decisionmaking usually have been produced by extensive bargaining and logrolling among relevant interest groups and their spokesmen within the party. As the dominant party in the federal government and

[4] See Peter H. Merkl, "Equilibrium, Structures of Interest and Leadership: Adenauer's Survival as Chancellor," *American Political Science Review*, LVI (September, 1962), 634–650.

many of the Länder, the CDU in this respect has been in a more advantageous position than its rivals, for it has been able not only to propose but to dispose of various policy demands to the satisfaction of the claimants.

CDU leaders thus have been faced constantly with the exceedingly complex task of maintaining a stable coalition among interdependent, but shifting group alignments inside and outside the party. The pluralist character of German politics and the decentralized structure of their party demand considerable political skills and personal authority of leaders who wish to serve successfully as brokers between competing factions. To play this role effectively, a national or subnational CDU chieftain must not allow himself to become too closely identified with any specific group, and yet must satisfy the demands of particular clienteles among voters and interest associations. His style of leadership must make him appear to be a conciliator and moderator among various claimants for a voice in CDU policymaking. He may not seem to give preferential treatment to any party faction and must present himself to the general public as a statesman above the disputes inherent in the CDU and its political formula.

During the 1950's, Chancellor Adenauer and other CDU leaders belonging to the founding generation of the present regime were extremely effective as arbitrators. But even before Adenauer reluctantly surrendered the chancellorship in 1963 and the party chairmanship in 1965 – at the age of eighty-nine – the equilibrium of forces that had sustained the CDU's dominance in German politics had begun to weaken. With the end of the era of socioeconomic and political reconstruction and the emergence of a new generation of highly ambitious leaders, it became apparent that the party's political formula could also create serious strains and tensions. Moreover, though Adenauer had accustomed the country and the Union to a firm balancing hand at the helm, he had failed to provide for intraparty procedures which would allow the choice of a successor commanding equal authority under altered political conditions.

A brief but bitter battle for control of the CDU in the mid-1960's brought to the surface centrifugal forces in the structure and appeal of the party. It became apparent that its amorphous structure and diffuse policy commitments did not provide the CDU with the cohesive strength of less open and more cohesive mass membership parties. Various factions could not readily agree on the nature and extent of adaptive processes demanded by new environmental conditions and on the choice of a party leader who could be trusted to execute them. Altered political circumstances made it more difficult than formerly to maintain the public image of the CDU as a party which provided balanced interest satisfaction and efficient governmental leadership. In foreign affairs the easing of cold war tensions in Central Europe led to conflicting demands within and outside the CDU for corresponding adjustments in its policies. In domestic affairs a slowdown in economic expansion also created new problems for a party which had accustomed Germans to ever greater prosperity during its long rule. More intense cross-pressures for new fiscal and social welfare measures intensified intraparty friction as competing interest groups among supporters of the CDU sought to safeguard what they had gained under its sponsorship. As the leading governing party the Union was faced with the need to accommodate the demands of Germany's allies as well as to provide for the protection of the national economy by measures likely to displease its friends abroad and at home.[5]

Chancellor Ludwig Erhard, Adenauer's successor as leader of the CDU and its brittle coalition with the Free Democrats, was unable to maintain the reassuring image of strong, authoritative leadership which the CDU had provided under his predecessor. His attempt to act as a plebiscitary "people's chancellor" helped the CDU to win the 1965 election, but the popularity of the self-proclaimed architect of the "economic miracles" of the 1950's proved to be fleeting and he was unable to check increasing factionalism in the party. During his three years in office (1963–66), Erhard was exposed to constant public criticism from spokesmen of the Social Democratic opposition as well as leaders of the CDU – particularly Adenauer – who

[5] In particular, it became evident that the failure of the CDU to develop a comprehensive modern economic program to meet such exigencies also made it more difficult for its leaders to find common and popularly acceptable criteria for maintaining a balance between these input demands and the output capabilities of the German political system.

called him inept and weak and ultimately helped to bring about Erhard's downfall.

It became evident that no major group or leader in the CDU was strong enough to take over control of the party without unleashing centrifugal forces that might bring about its disintegration. Gerhard Schröder, Erhard's foreign minister, was too closely identified with the Protestant North German wing of the Union and with the pro-American "Atlanticists" to be acceptable to the Roman Catholics and pro-Gaullist South German wing. Schröder's supporters, for their part, opposed the Bavarian CSU leader Franz Joseph Strauss, as a ruthless politician catering to nationalist and antidemocratic sentiments. The CDU Bundestag leader, Rainer Barzel, came from East Germany but was a Catholic and at different times had belonged to both the left and right wings of the party. He was looked upon, however, as too much of an unprincipled opportunist to become a trusted mediator among the contending factions.

The Christian Democratic elite realized, though, that its public disputes were doing its members more harm than good, because they threatened to deprive the CDU of its long leadership of the federal government. A compromise was achieved by giving the chancellorship and, subsequently, the chairmanship of the CDU to Georg Kiesinger, a regional leader who was not too closely identified with any faction. Although he had been a member of the Nazi party throughout the Hitler era, he had since shown himself to be a loyal supporter of the new political order and its leading party, first as one of Adenauer's parliamentary lieutenants and then as Minister-President of Baden-Württemberg.

Kiesinger seemed an ideal compromise candidate. He symbolized the CDU's appeal to former Nazis as well as anti-Nazis and to popular sentiments that favored burying the past entirely. He was identified with a pro-American as well as pro-French policy and therefore was expected to be acceptable to both of Germany's principal allies. The new chancellor had on the one hand not incurred the enmity of powerful groups in the CDU, and on the other did not appear to possess the popularity and organizational strength to impose his will on them;

Schröder, Strauss, and Barzel readily agreed to serve under him.

A second and potentially far more significant decision of the CDU leadership was to terminate the long, but often stormy national alliance with the conservative Free Democrats and form a "grand coalition" with the SPD, the principal opposition party since the establishment of the Federal Republic. Though neither of the two major parties had sufficient parliamentary support to rule alone, together they now commanded overwhelming strength. With barely 10 per cent of the Bundestag deputies, the reluctant new opposition party, the FDP, displayed little desire for a battle with the CDU-SPD juggernaut. Instead it sought to demonstrate its capacity to form a new alliance with either of the two major parties in the hope that the grand coalition would soon disintegrate and thus place the FDP in a better bargaining position.

The CDU leaders, however, apparently were determined to maintain the grand coalition, at least until the 1969 national election. It gave them an opportunity to remain in power without having to contend with the challenge of a powerful opposition party during a difficult period of readjustment. In the name of national unity, the Social Democrats were invited to share responsibility for unavoidable, but potentially unpopular decisions facing the federal government as more or less equal partners. The CDU leadership apparently gambled that the next federal election would give them either an absolute majority or, at least, a plurality sufficient to dominate any national coalition. But whatever the outcome of the new alignment, it clearly marked the end of the postwar phase of competitive German party politics and the beginning of a new era of close cooperation between the two major parties.

THE SOCIAL DEMOCRATIC PARTY

The SPD is a far more homogeneous party than the CDU, and its organization a great deal more integrated and centralized. Staffed by a vast army of paid and unpaid functionaries, it encompasses a tightly woven structural net extending from the national party headquarters through twenty district organizations to some 8,000 local branches. The focus of decision-making power is the presidium of the SPD national executive committee, consisting of the party chairman, deputy chairman, treasurer, and a few coopted members of the party executive. The executive committee itself is composed of about thirty of the leading public officeholders and organizational functionaries of the SPD, including its principal parliamentary leaders, who meet about once a month and are elected by the biannual congress of delegates from the regional organizations.

In contrast to the CDU elite, the national leadership of the SPD has consistently displayed high collegial unity and wielded broad authority over the activities of the entire party. Though subnational Social Democratic leaders on occasion have defied the wishes of the central leadership on matters of regional and local politics, the formal decisions of the presidium and executive committee generally are accepted as binding by all party members. Neither the SPD Bundestag delegation nor the national party congress has ever openly repudiated the actions of these highest party organs.

On the whole, the Social Democratic Party has shown great internal solidarity. Disagreements among its top leaders are not aired in public, as in the CDU, and rarely leak to the outside. Hallowed rules of party discipline require that factional disputes be settled within the family; majority decisions are considered binding and dissenters are expected to submit to them in at least an outward display of unanimity or resign from the party. A member who violates these norms by voicing on the outside his disagreement with official party policies invites punitive sanctions which may range from public censure to expulsion from the SPD. Opponents of the party leadership who have been unwilling to resign their membership have been careful to confine their criticism to intraparty discussions or, more rarely, publish their views anonymously.

The SPD has by far the largest membership of all German parties. In 1967 it included more than 700,000 men and women, roughly 7 per cent of its voters, whereas only about 3 per cent of the electorate and about an equal proportion of CDU supporters belonged to the party of their choice. The size of the SPD membership has remained fairly constant over the years. Most Social Democrats were recruited into the party at an early age – usually through their families, party affiliated youth groups, and trade unions — and come from the lower social strata and income groups. Whereas CDU members are for the most part independent farmers, professional people, and businessmen, those of the SPD are primarily industrial workers, low-ranking civil servants, and other salaried employees.[6]

The party organization represents a major source of strength for the Social Democratic leadership. It provides the SPD elite with vital links to the rank-and-file membership and the party's electorate, as well as to key political participants who belong to the party, such as trade union leaders and public officials at all levels of government. Thanks to its large organization, the SPD is also far less dependent on outside financial resources and political communications media than the CDU and minor parties. Most of its income is derived from membership dues and business enterprises owned or controlled by the party — such as large publishing houses — rather than from government and interest group subsidies.[7] And the size and devotion of its membership allow the SPD to depend upon the unpaid services of thousands of volunteers for turning out the vote at election time.

In spite of, and, in part, because of, its greater social homogeneity and organizational strength, the Social Democratic Party has had a great deal more difficulty in adapting itself as successfully to the political environment of postwar Germany than has the CDU. The SPD is a much older party, with deeply rooted traditions reaching back more than a century. As the prototype of a disciplined mass membership party of subcultural integration, it had mobilized a large and loyal following during the Hohenzollern and Weimar eras to promote the socioeconomic and political interests of the German industrial workers on the basis of a democratic, Marxist ideology. But, though it was long the largest party in Germany, the SPD had

[6] See Ulf Preuss, "Von der Arbeiterpartei zur Volkspartei," *Die neue Gesellschaft,* 13 (September/October, 1966), 371–385.

[7] According to some estimates the SPD in 1965 received about 26 per cent of its reported income from membership dues (the CDU 7 per cent, the FDP 4 per cent), 32 per cent from governmental sources (the CDU 35 per cent, the FDP 25 per cent), and 32 per cent from other sources (the CDU 58 per cent, the FDP 71 per cent). See *Der Spiegel,* April 25, 1966 and Deutsches Industrieinstitut, *Berichte des deutschen Industrieinstituts zur Politik,* I (October, 1967), 11.

been unable to command the allegiances of more than about a third of the electorate. Until the "grand coalition" of 1966, it had participated in no national government since 1930 and for no more than fifty months in its entire history. Under the Hohenzollern regime the party never had a minister, and, though it was the principal founder and supporter of the Weimar Republic, the governing coalitions that it had formed off and on with nonsocialist and antisocialist parties had allowed the SPD little freedom of action. The Nazi regime suppressed the party in 1933 and killed or severely persecuted most of its leaders. When the SPD was re-established in 1945, it sought to assume at long last control of the political system, but could not muster the necessary support and for seventeen years remained the principal opposition party in the new Federal Republic.

The Social Democratic drive for power suffered a major setback at the outset, when the party's branches in the Soviet occupied zone were compelled to amalgamate with the Communist Party to form the Socialist Unity Party. Outlawed in those parts of Germany where it had enjoyed particularly strong support in the past, the party was forced to concentrate its efforts upon the Western portions, where it had never been as popular. Initially, strong leadership and a strong organization seemed to give the SPD a decided advantage over its major rival, the CDU, but it was unable to adapt its national policies and strategy with equal facility to the prevailing political environment. Traumatic memories of past defeats and Nazi suppression and deeply rooted in-group traditions prevented the Social Democrats from turning their back upon the past and adjusting to political conditions which made radically different demands upon the party.

In this respect the organizational strength of the SPD also proved to be a severe handicap for the party's efforts to compete with the CDU. Most of the old-timers who reassembled under its banners in 1945 and reconstituted the party organization were not particularly amenable to transforming the SPD into an externally oriented "catch-all" party similar to the CDU. To be a Social Democrat was for them an article of faith rather than a matter of instrumental utility, a conviction which had been strongly reinforced by Nazi persecution. New adherents were expected to give proof of equal devotion and dedicated service to the party, its leaders, and its principles by men who considered the SPD more a community of true believers than an instrument for gaining public office.

Second, the party's appeal for nationwide support proved to be particularly unsuited to the political climate of post-Nazi Germany. Kurt Schumacher, its dynamic leader from 1945 to 1952, committed the SPD to a course of action which repelled rather than attracted voters and elites. Although he called for a "new beginning," which would transform the SPD from a working class movement into a popular reform party, the strategy he adopted to achieve governmental power increasingly isolated the SPD from contemporary political opinion. An ailing cripple who had languished for more than a decade in a Nazi concentration camp, he sought to correct what he considered past errors of commission and omission by following policies which made the party appear more nationalist and radical than it was. The "lessons of the past" demanded, in Schumacher's view, that the Social Democrats wage a militant, patriotic, and class oriented battle for power on behalf of the German masses and refuse to collaborate with "reactionary" groups, which were held responsible for the Nazi regime and were considered unregenerated proponents of authoritarianism. Schumacher insisted that the SPD alone was competent to undertake the political reconstruction of Germany, because it was the only truly democratic and patriotic force in the country. He attacked with equal vehemence the "clerical-capitalist" alliance forged by the CDU, the Communist "stooges" of the Soviet Union, and the Western occupation powers.

Schumacher's course, which survived his death in 1952 for a number of years, failed to have the intended mass appeal. In fact, it helped the CDU to forge an alliance against the SPD which effectively blocked its bid for power. For most West Germans the Social Democratic Party remained a "Marxist," working class movement, less respectable than the CDU and not nearly as competent in satisfying their demands for security, harmony, and authoritative leadership in an age of anxiety.

Cumulative electoral defeats gradually weakened the power

of the old-line organization men in the SPD and brought to the fore a new generation of leaders determined to modernize the party. Headed by Willy Brandt, the popular Lord Mayor of West Berlin, they were for the most part public officeholders who wanted the SPD to emulate the political formula of the CDU without losing the organizational strength of a disciplined mass membership party. Mostly men in their thirties and forties, they insisted that the SPD be more pragmatic in its efforts to displace the CDU as the leading party and that it employ similar strategies and tactics. They considered the Schumacher course too negative and sterile and most of the traditional Social Democratic principles and practices more of a hindrance than a help in competition with the CDU. Highly sensitive to foreign and domestic opinion outside the SPD, the new leaders looked upon the solidarity of the party organization as merely a means for mobilizing greater mass support, rather than an end in itself, and maintained that the party had to become more outward oriented and flexible in its program and actions.

Beginning in the late 1950's, the SPD developed a new public profile which was intended by its leaders to make it more attractive to the voters and elites of the Federal Republic. Following the example of the CDU elite, the Social Democratic leadership relied heavily on opinion surveys and modern public relations methods to find ways of overcoming the suspicions of Germans who supported other parties primarily because they considered the SPD less trustworthy.

In 1959, the tightly knit Brandt team obtained the adoption of a new basic party program, which proclaimed that the SPD was a democratic, anti-Communist, and progressive reform party and no longer a working class movement. Asking for the support and trust of all Germans who wanted liberty, security, and social justice, the "Godesberg Program" discarded past demands for the socialization of basic industries and embraced "free competition and free entrepreneurial initiative," along with Keynesian economic policies. It abandoned the party's former opposition to German rearmament – atomic and conventional – and gave support to the new military establishment; it substituted a call for a harmonious "partnership" between the SPD and the churches for previous attacks on "clerical" influence in German politics.

In words familiar to Americans, the major opposition party told the German voters that it was "time for a change" in the federal government: the SPD leaders could do everything those of the CDU could do, only better. The Social Democrats dropped their neutralist stance, no longer objected to military expenditures, and gave wholehearted support to the NATO alliance. They claimed to be just as anti-Communist as the governing party, every bit as devoted to European integration, and even more deeply attached to close friendship with the United States. The party invited the support of powerful interest groups which previously had backed the CDU, such as the refugee associations, and a delegation of its leaders called on the pope to demonstrate their party's changed attitude toward the Catholic Church. The SPD declared that a new papal encyclical, "Mater et Magistra," was in full agreement with its own social reform policies; its government leaders in Lower Saxony promoted a treaty with the church which met its demands for sectarian schools. The SPD's deputy chairman, Herbert Wehner, a former Communist and atheist, preached in a Lutheran church and Protestant ministers and lay leaders were given prominent positions in the party.

At the same time, the SPD greatly toned down its criticism of the CDU and indicated its willingness to form a national coalition similar to those which already prevailed in a number of the Länder governments. Insofar as it was still prepared to represent the major opposition party as an alternative governing party, the SPD sought to make its criticism of CDU policies appear to be constructive and designed to strengthen domestic harmony and political stability. It claimed that it could give the country more effective and united leadership than the divided CDU-FDP alliance, and cited the accomplishments of Social Democratic local and Land governments as proof that the party was fully competent to promote and protect the values and interests of the entire German people. The 1965 election manifesto of the SPD was all but indistinguishable from that of the CDU in its diffuse appeal for the support of the voters (see Table VIII.5). In effect, the choice before the elec-

TABLE VIII.5 *CDU and SPD Election Manifestos, 1965*

	CDU: governing party	*SPD: opposition party*
General appeal	The CDU asks "all Germans" to trust it once again to look after their interests. It is "a party of cooperation and balance" and "a modern party in a modern society" that is "unencumbered by outworn ideologies and . . . prejudices."	The SPD wants "to win the trust of the men and women of our country." "In all matters of the national interest the responsible political elements in our country must stand together. . . ."
	The CDU "can point to great achievements and success in the past; its gaze is directed toward the future." "What the CDU has achieved can only be made secure by the CDU."	"Thanks to the joint efforts of all, the structure of the German Federal Republic is a solid one, her economy prospers." But "complacency, egoism, lack of foresight and want of leadership imperil achievements and hinder further progress." "If our country is to hold its own in this world of drastic changes, all energies and capacities inherent in our people must be mobilized and directed toward new goals and fresh elements must be introduced into the government." "The Federal Republic must progress more rapidly. We shall meet the challenge of making up for the neglect of past years."
Foreign policy	"The CDU considers its duty the re-establishment of national German unity, the construction of a just order for Europe, and the securing of world peace." It fights for "freedom and self-determination for all Germans . . . in one state." "Pending reunification, it claims the exclusive right of the Federal	"To maintain peace, freedom, and security is the supreme law for every German government." ". . . [W]e shall promote every reasonable measure to diminish tensions." "Basic law and conscience oblige everyone to strive without letup for Germany's reunification." ". . . [S]elf-determination and the

TABLE VIII.5 *CDU and SPD Election Manifestos, 1965 (Cont.)*

	CDU: governing party	*SPD: opposition party*
Foreign policy (*Cont.*)	Republic to represent all of Germany." "The CDU seeks a durable world peace" based on "respect for international law by all, human rights for all, and an end to all coercive domination." "The CDU is against the cold war. It seeks reconciliation of Germany with her eastern neighbors."	right to domicile are inalienable rights. . . . We shall energetically demand those rights." "The federal government must see to it that the [Atlantic] alliance grows closer and stronger." "European unification serves world peace and prosperity. Therefore, we shall accept every initiative and advance every foreign suggestion which aim at strengthening and enlarging the European communities." "We recommend the increase of relations between the Federal Republic and the countries of Eastern Europe."
Domestic policy	"Our times call for a modern social policy." The CDU "will keep our currency stable, improve our standard of living," and "enable everyone to receive a fair share of increasing affluence." 	The SPD seeks "stability of currency and economic order, constant and sound expansion of the economy, property and independence for all. . . ." "Neither shall we interfere with business decisions nor shall we infringe upon private property." The SPD "guarantees social security for all," favors economic competition, wage scale autonomy for employee and employers organizations; it wants to help the middle classes, agriculture, the aged, widows, and orphans, as well as war victims, refugees, and the family. Its program "does not contemplate a tax increase."

Source: Slightly edited translations from William G. Andrews (ed.), *European Political Institutions,* 2nd ed. (Princeton, N.J.: Van Nostrand, 1966), pp. 151–152, 198–205.

torate was reduced to one of two sets of party leaders, rather than significantly different policy proposals or ideological principles.

Though the Social Democrats made gains in 1965, the CDU retained its plurality. But within a few months the SPD won a resounding victory in North Rhine-Westphalia, the largest Land of the Federal Republic, which set the stage for its entry into the national government a short time later. The disintegration of the CDU-FDP coalition in 1966 gave the Social Democratic leadership the alternative of a partnership with either of the former allies; it chose the CDU on the grounds that a coalition with the Free Democrats would rest on too fragile a foundation to survive for long.

The Grand Coalition brought together the ex-Nazi Kiesinger with the former anti-Nazi exiles Brandt and Wehner, and SPD trade union leaders with CDU business leaders. According to the SPD leadership, it was a major achievement for their party and a logical and necessary move toward a Social Democratic national government. As a more or less equal partner in the new alignment, the SPD at long last would be able to demonstrate its capacity to rule Germany and reap the rewards in future elections. A truly democratic regime based on stable government by alternating majority parties would become the normal pattern in Germany as in the United States and Britain. Critical voices asserted, however, that the Social Democratic leadership in fact had weakened the development of German democracy by joining forces with the CDU elite and would be unlikely to reap even tactical advantages from a shortsighted "opportunistic" decision.

It remained to be seen who was right. However, the new course of the SPD apparently had helped to transform it into a more viable competitor of the CDU. Whereas in 1957 the CDU had obtained 18 per cent more votes than the SPD, in 1965 this lead had been reduced to half that proportion.[8] The Social Democrats had picked up strength among Roman Catholics, salaried employees, professional men, and urban voters (see Table VIII.6). In 1967, they governed 44 of the 56 largest

[8] See Tables VIII.1, VIII.2, VIII.3, and the electoral maps on pp. 238–246.

TABLE VIII.6 *CDU and SPD Gains in Single Member Districts, 1965 Federal Election (in rounded-off percentages)*

	CDU	*SPD*
Large urban districts (60)	3	9
Urban districts (27)	2	10
Semiurban districts (50)	5	8
Mixed urban-rural districts (39)	6	7
Rural districts (72)	6	7
Average gain in all districts (248)	5	8

Source: Dietrich Rollmann, "Ist die CDU noch modern?" *Die Zeit,* January 11, 1966.

cities and held their own with the CDU in the government of the Länder. And, though the party thus far has failed to win substantial support among the middle and upper income groups, it seems to have measurably reduced their opposition to Social Democratic rule.

Business leaders have welcomed the new Social Democratic economic policies and have reacted most favorably to the policies of Karl Schiller, the SPD economic minister in the Kiesinger government. Key civil servants and military men no longer consider an SPD government a threat to the interests of the state, most mass media and interest group leaders have applauded the new SPD-CDU alignment in national politics, and the Roman Catholic hierarchy has adopted a more neutral position between the two parties.

New policies and tactics alone, however, do not explain the increased respect and cooperation commanded by the Social Democratic Party among top participants in the political system. They have been made persuasive and convincing by a new type of Social Democratic leadership, which fits more closely than its predecessors into the pluralist elite culture of contemporary Germany.

Top positions in the SPD, as in other elite groups, have increasingly been taken over by highly skilled managers and functional specialists recruited on the basis of expertise and educational achievements from the middle and even the upper social strata. Many of them university educated, they have found it a great deal easier than did the old-line organizational functionaries to achieve an understanding with leaders of the CDU, the civil service, and the major interest associations. A member of the new generation of Social Democratic leaders is less concerned with presenting himself to the party as a good "proletarian" than with his public image as a statesman, and is less interested in selfless service to the organization than in advancing his personal ambitions for public office. He prides himself on his pragmatism and is likely to show greater facility in bargaining with kindred elite members for political advantage than gaining and holding the affections and devoted loyalty of less sophisticated party members.

In short, the transformation of the SPD has involved adaptive changes in its leadership which, here too, has brought to the fore new men of power – recruited on the basis of modern achievement rather than traditional ascriptive criteria – who perceive politics as a game of skill among qualified experts and the public more as consumers than as producers of public policy under a democratic regime.

Continuing changes in the position of the SPD in German politics suggest far-reaching consequences for the party system and other interdependent structures in the polity. Whether the present adaptive processes will permit the SPD to overcome some serious difficulties and duplicate the successes of the CDU without inheriting its problems remains to be seen. Much will depend on the ability of the SPD leaders to wed the cohesiveness of a disciplined mass membership party with the more diffuse appeal of an electoral party.

To obtain at least plurality support among the present German electorate, the SPD will have to expand its appeal to lower income groups and, at the same time, gain more adherents among the middle and upper income strata. To retain the organizational strength and in-group solidarity of a mass membership party, however, such efforts must not exceed the capacity of the party's middle-range functionaries and rank-and-file members to tolerate policies and tactics designed to obtain more support outside the party.

Whether the strategy adopted by the SPD leadership to manage these tasks will succeed is by no means certain. The results of Land elections following the formation of the Grand Coalition indicated that it had not gained greater mass support for the SPD and probably even cost it votes. This, in turn, made it more difficult for the reformist leadership to justify its policies in the face of considerable opposition among the politically most active members and sympathizers of the party. Many of the old-timers in the SPD have not taken kindly to the wholesale abandonment of Social Democratic traditions, though their loyalty to the party and their deeply ingrained sense of party discipline has induced them to go along with the leadership. Some of the younger Social Democratic activists, however, especially university students, have been more vocal in expressing their dissatisfaction with "unprincipled" leaders who are said to collaborate all too closely with the "reactionary" forces of the CDU. And, since the SPD leadership does not want to lose the support of the most highly politicized and educated among the younger generation, it may very well feel constrained in moving not quite as far and as fast as the CDU elite in adapting its policies to the demands of elite and electoral groups outside the party.

GOVERNMENT BY PARTY ELITES

The principles and practices of party government in contemporary Germany allow a relatively small group of party leaders extensive control over political processes. Formal legal arrangements devised by the CDU and SPD elites over the past two decades have, in this respect, strongly influenced the interdependent relationship between the party system and other components of the political system.

In such well established democracies as the United States and Britain an uninterrupted and gradual development of governmental institutions has decisively affected the evolution of the party system, but sharp discontinuities between regimes reversed the process in Germany. Here, as in postwar France, Italy, Japan, and the Communist countries, the formation of the party system preceded the establishment of a new regime and had correspondingly greater influence in shaping new patterns of government.

After the collapse of the Third Reich the CDU and SPD quickly emerged as the organizational instruments of the principal architects of a new political order. Party leaders relatively uncompromised by past associations with the totalitarian regime were sought out and encouraged by the foreign occupation powers to fill the vacuum left by the elimination of the former political elites and were able to consolidate their preeminent position with the permission – often indeed with the blessings – of the Western military governments. With the exception of the religious leadership, the remnants of the old elite groups for the most part were prevented from taking a leading part in political reconstruction by socioeconomic disorganization and allied regulations. And of the four parties sanctioned by the occupation authorities, neither the Free Democrats nor the Communists proved viable competitors of the CDU and SPD in obtaining mass support and positions of political power.

During the postwar social and political realignment the Christian Democratic and Social Democratic leaders had a head start over other elite groups, which permitted them to lay the foundations of a new political order before the establishment of the Federal Republic in 1949. By the time the occupation authorities called upon German political leaders to create a new state in Western Germany, the two major parties had already achieved sufficient strength to dominate the proceedings of the constituent assembly and jointly forge a regime designed to formalize their control over the political system.

In general, government by party elites has been promoted by the diffuse rather than distinct separation of formal governmental functions between national and subnational organs and executive and legislative structures. More specifically, Article 21 of the Basic Law has provided the principal parties with many opportunities to maintain and expand their dominant position. As we noticed earlier, it assigns to parties supporting the regime – and to them alone – paraconstitutional status as intermediaries between citizenry and government.[9] This unique modification of the classical principles of representative democracy has been hailed by its principal beneficiaries as one of the strongest pillars of the new regime.

According to CDU and SPD leaders, the institutionalization

[9] See pp. 175–176 above.

of a smoothly functioning and stable democratic order requires such an explicit, formal sanction for the activities of "legitimate" political parties because of past experiences and present cultural patterns. Article 21 is said to reconcile traditional German political orientations toward public authorities with the principles of democratic party government, and prevailing perceptions of the "general interest" with the operation of a competitive party system in a pluralist society.

On the strength of Article 21, the new party system and the dominant position of the CDU and SPD have been formally reinforced by numerous laws, administrative regulations, and judicial decisions, which have curbed the political ambitions of other associations. The Communist Party and a right wing party were outlawed in the 1950's as illegitimate, "antidemocratic" organizations; the formation of new political groups and parties has been restrained by strict rules which provide that such organizations must be democratic in their objectives and structure; and the political activities of interest associations have been limited by legal restrictions on their efforts to influence public policymaking by penetrating or bypassing the political parties.

At the same time, Article 21 has enabled the CDU and SPD elites to derive many benefits from their formalized position in the political system. It has provided them with free and extensive use of publicly owned media of political communication as spokesmen for the government or major opposition party and allowed them to draw upon the public treasury to help finance their activities both directly and indirectly.

Until the practice was curbed by the Constitutional Court in 1966, the parties in the Bundestag and a number of Land legislatures granted themselves annual appropriations for "political education," which were not shared by other parties. In 1967, a new law limited such subsidies from the public treasury to expenditures for election campaigns and stipulated that they should be distributed on the basis of 2.50 DM per vote received by a party (about $1 in current purchasing power). Hereafter, parties which are not represented in the outgoing legislature are also to receive such subsidies, provided their internal organization conforms to "democratic principles" and they receive at least 2.5 per cent of the vote.[10]

Though its importance for the development of the German party system can easily be overrated, the electoral system sponsored by the CDU and SPD undoubtedly has helped to promote their dominant position and the trend toward a two-party system. Regulations governing nomination and electoral procedures have made it increasingly difficult for candidates of smaller parties to run and be elected to public office, particularly in federal elections. To appear on the ballot a candidate must first be formally nominated by a "legitimate" party, which, in effect, requires the approval of its leaders. If he should be elected to the Bundestag he may not take his seat unless his party has obtained at least three direct mandates or 5 per cent of the votes cast; similar restrictive provisions curb minor party representation in the Land legislatures.

The rules of legislative organization and procedure in the various German parliaments also tend to enhance the political power of the two major parties and, more particularly, that of their leaders. Under the Standing Orders of the Bundestag, all key legislative posts and all committee assignments are reserved for members of properly constituted Parliamentary Parties (*Fraktionen*) and distributed by the leaders in proportion to their party's strength in the chamber. A deputy will thus be excluded from the most important rulemaking activities of the Bundestag if his party's delegation consists of fewer than fifteen legislators or the leaders blackball him. Such arrangements tend to discourage interest groups from supporting minor party or independent candidates and to strengthen party discipline and cohesion. A deputy who is expelled or resigns from his Parliamentary Party does not lose his seat, but for all practical purposes he is powerless to serve his constituents and unlikely to be re-elected. It is therefore not surprising that few Bundestag deputies have ever quit their *Fraktion* and

[10] Article 21 also requires the parties to give public account of the sources of their funds. However, under the new law, they need not specify the names of individuals who donate less than 20,000 DM or those of associations contributing less than 200,000 DM.

that these have invariably joined another Parliamentary Party.

In the last analysis, however, the present pre-eminence of the two largest political parties rests formally upon constitutional arrangements that place the recruitment of governmental leaders and control over public policymaking in the hands of party elites commanding majority support in German legislatures.

The party leaders who drafted the Basic Law and the constitutions of the Länder endeavored to establish a representative form of government in which the interplay between ruling and opposition parties in German politics would be regulated through institutional arrangements that separated as well as fused the functions of the executive and the legislature. Striving for a judicious balance between the principal policymaking structures in a representative democracy, they sought to make the executive less dependent upon a legislative majority than it would be under a parliamentary system, such as the British, but more so than under a presidential system, such as that of the United States. In this way they hoped to avoid the sort of governmental instability which plagued the Weimar Republic and other regimes with fractionalized multiparty systems and bitterly divided legislative majorities. At the same time, carefully designed and extensively elaborated constitutional arrangements were to assure the control of the executive by the parliamentary representatives of a majority of the electorate and thus prevent the re-emergence of autocratic governments responsible neither to the legislature in general nor to the parties represented in it in particular.

Following the precedence of the Länder constitutions, the Basic Law of the Federal Republic stipulates that the chief of the government, the federal chancellor, is to be chosen by and responsible to the popularly elected lower chamber of the federal parliament, the Bundestag. The constitution makers, however, gave the chancellor substantial powers, by which they intended to assure strong and stable governmental leadership under a fractionalized multiparty system, rather than a two party system. He was to be the principal policymaker in the state, who could, if need be, govern temporarily even without the approval of a deeply divided majority of the Bundestag—

provided he had the backing of the federal president and the Bundesrat representing the Länder governments. Like the Land minister-presidents, the chancellor cannot be impeached or formally forced to resign unless the popularly elected chamber chooses a successor under a unique constitutional provision calling for a "positive vote of no confidence" in the incumbent. Should a hostile majority of the deputies refuse to support him, yet be so divided that it cannot agree on a replacement, the head of the government may appeal to the court of last resort. He may dissolve the recalcitrant legislature and let the electorate decide between him and his parliamentary opponents.[11]

His formal powers allow the federal chancellor primary and almost exclusive authority over the formulation of governmental policies and the activities of his subordinates and advisers. He alone is constitutionally responsible to the Bundestag for the actions of his government; that chamber has no legal right to pass on the composition of his cabinet or to force the dismissal of his ministers. Formally, the chancellor may appoint or remove them as he sees fit, control the federal bureaucracy subject only to civil service regulations, and exercise considerable discretion in the distribution of public funds and the application of the laws passed by the legislative branch. Although the Bundestag ordinarily must approve his major policy proposals and budgetary requests, his is the power to initiate practically all legislation and to use to the fullest the right to issue administrative regulations under powers granted to the federal government by the laws and constitution of the Federal Republic. The federal chancellor may legally withhold information requested by the Bundestag, ignore its wishes and expressions of disapproval, and veto budgetary appropriations that exceed his requests.

These formidable executive powers do not, however, free a German chancellor from the need for majority support in a legislature tightly controlled by political parties and their leaders. He can neither claim a formal direct mandate from the voters — like chief executives in the United States and the Presi-

[11] A federal chancellor needs the consent of the federal president for dissolution; the head of a Land government may order new elections on his own authority.

dent in the Fifth French Republic — nor can he rely on such traditional sources of authority as are bestowed upon "Her Majesty's Prime Minister" by the British Crown. A federal chancellor, like the minister-presidents of the Länder, must rely correspondingly more heavily on his political skills to forge and maintain stable parliamentary alignments behind his government and its policies. Formally, he need not belong to a political party or even be a member of parliament; in fact, the requisites of majority government in postwar Germany have not only required him to be both, but to be the leader of one of the two major parties, and, as such, of an even broader alignment extending to other parties and elite groups outside parliament.

Practically all national and subnational postwar German governments have been coalitions forged and sustained by the leaders of interparty and intraparty elite alignments inside and outside the legislature. Even when one of the major parties has managed to claim an absolute parliamentary majority, its leaders usually have sought to expand its supportive base by taking other parties into the government. Such coalitions have not followed a consistent pattern throughout the Federal Republic because national party leaders usually have been unable to dictate the composition of subnational governments. As a result, parties opposed to each other at the federal level have formed coalitions in the Länder and parties opposed to each other in one Land have governed together in another.[12]

Another fact worth noting is the practice of de facto coalitions between government and opposition parties. Thus, though the Social Democrats were not represented in the federal gov-

[12] In 1965, the CDU controlled the national government with the support of the FDP, and the SPD represented the parliamentary opposition. But in the Land of Lower Saxony the CDU and SPD formed a coalition, whereas the FDP was in opposition. A year later, the national CDU-FDP alliance broke up and the CDU and SPD joined to form a new federal coalition government and the FDP became the sole opposition in the Bundestag. At the same time, however, the Social Democrats and Free Democrats in the Federal Republic's largest Land, North Rhine-Westphalia, formed a new coalition which left the Christian Democrats as the opposition in the state diet. In the Land Württemberg-Baden, on the other hand, the leaders of the CDU decided to emulate the federal coalition with the SPD and ended their alliance with the FDP.

ernment between 1949 and 1966, their control of a number of Länder governments gave them sufficient strength in the Bundesrat to induce the governing Christian Democrats and the Free Democrats to seek their support for measures requiring a two-thirds majority for passage through the upper house. In the same period the governing parties and the formal opposition frequently cooperated to push measures through the lower house and to elect high federal officials, such as the federal president and judges of the Constitutional Court. A large number of the decisions made by either or both chambers of the federal parliament resulted from informal agreements between the leaders of the formally opposing major parties, which were particularly important when the governing coalition was internally divided.[13]

These patterns of cooperation and competition between CDU, SPD, and minor parties have allowed a relatively small group of party leaders – rather than the voters or their parliamentary representatives – to determine who should govern and for how long. No chancellor has resigned because his party was defeated at the polls, but both Adenauer and Erhard were compelled to leave office because they lost the support of the dominant party leaders in the Bundestag – including those of their own party. The constructive vote of no confidence has been used only twice to remove the chief of a government – in 1956 and 1966 in North Rhine-Westphalia – and no federal chancellor or Land minister-president has sought to dissolve a legislature that would no longer support him.[14]

In federal and subnational politics, party government has produced several rather different styles of executive leadership.

[13] Thus the Codetermination Law of 1951, which granted German labor a voice in the management of certain industries, the 1953 Reparations Agreement with Israel, or the 1965 law extending the statute of limitation on the prosecution of Nazi crimes, could not have passed without a de facto coalition between leaders of the CDU and the opposition SPD.

[14] When a majority of the Bundestag asked Chancellor Erhard, in October, 1966, to seek a vote of confidence which he was bound to lose, he declined to be a party to what he termed a "show trial." His defeat would have permitted Erhard to ask the federal president to dissolve the legislature under Article 68 of the Basic Law, but he preferred to resign in favor of a successor supported by a parliamentary coalition of CDU and SPD leaders.

One, particularly associated with Chancellor Adenauer, has made the parties in an executive centered coalition primarily the governing leader's instruments. Another and more prevalent style has tended to make the government and its formal leader the instrument of party elites inside and outside the legislature.

Adenauer's highly personal style of "Chancellor Democracy" was rather paternalistic and, to the proponents of a more liberal form of parliamentary government, it seemed too autocratic and arbitrary. However, it conformed to German traditions of strong executive authority in the state and even won the grudging approval of many of Adenauer's political opponents.

Adenauer managed to establish and maintain a tight rein over the activities of the federal government by skillfully combining his roles as chief of the executive branch, chairman of the CDU, and leader of an interparty parliamentary coalition. Formally distinct, these roles, as well as those of Adenauer's principal lieutenants, in practice became all but indistinguishable.[15] Most major policy decisions were made by Adenauer alone or in consultation with a small "kitchen cabinet" of his most trusted ministers, key civil servants, and parliamentary deputies; the regular cabinet, the Bundestag, national CDU organs, and the electorate ratified rather than determined government policy. Relying heavily on the services of his administrative assistants in the chancellor's office, Adenauer was the supreme arbitrator between the legislative and administrative elites and between party and interest group leaders.

Under Adenauer's successor, Chancellor Ludwig Erhard, much of the decisionmaking power shifted to party leaders in the Länder and the federal parliament. Erhard's more passive style of executive leadership in some respects resembled that of American presidents who defer to party leaders in the congress and the states; in others the style frequently adapted by the

[15] In fact, they became indistinguishable even in a more formal sense. Thus, when one of Adenauer's administrative assistants was hailed into court and charged with taking bribes, the chancellor gained his acquittal with the argument that if the man had accepted favors, it had been in his capacity as a member of the CDU chairman's staff rather than in his capacity as a civil servant.

heads of unstable and fractionalized parliamentary governments.

By training and experience an economist rather than a political tactician, Erhard was neither willing nor able to follow in his predecessor's footsteps. Instead he tended to apply his strong faith in economic laissez-faire processes to transactions in the political market place as well and heavily relied on the spontaneous evolution of a consensus to produce a political equilibrium. Erhard therefore permitted contending groups within his government and the country at large to have far greater autonomy in promoting their interests and negotiating agreements without the intercession of the chief of the federal government.[16]

The Erhard style of party government, however, proved unsuited to the prevailing patterns of the political culture and to the evolving processes of elite alignment. Erhard lacked the prestige and the skill which had allowed Adenauer to resist or vitiate the cross-pressures of competing demands and control factions in his ruling coalition. He appeared unable to curb interest group claims and factional disputes within his government and party and incapable of providing the country with the strong, authoritative leadership expected by most Germans. Erhard's fate was sealed when he could no longer coordinate the processes of majority government and completely lost control over the CDU elite.

Party government under Chancellor Kiesinger, Erhard's successor, seems to follow the patterns of collegial leadership which have become increasingly prevalent in German politics. Constrained in the exercise of his formal powers by the need to maintain stability among the multiple elite alignments encompassed by the Grand Coalition of the CDU and SPD, the chancellor has sought to play the role of a discreet mediator. Kiesinger has not been as free as Adenauer in the choice of his ministers or in the determination of governmental policies; both the composition of his cabinet and the rulemaking proc-

16 It was quite characteristic of Erhard's style of leadership that he allowed Adenauer to remain national chairman of the CDU for some time and finally assumed the position only with considerable reluctance.

esses of the coalition have had to satisfy the need for collegial unity among powerful party leaders and the part of the chancellor has come more to resemble that of a board chairman who is first among equals.

In contrast to the Erhard era, the inclusion of all the major party leaders in one government once again has shifted the focus of decisionmaking to the executive branch. Though the parliamentary leadership has sought to assert its autonomy at times, in effect the policies adopted by the party elites represented in the grand coalition are assured passage through the Bundestag.

POLITICAL INTEGRATION AND THE PARTY SYSTEM

Essentially, political parties are organizations whose purpose it is to affect processes in a political system which could be carried on without them. The stability and popular acceptance of a pluralist party system depends largely on ingrained mass and elite attitudes, which perceive its principal components as structures essential for the exercise of majority rule as well as the protection of minority interests. Thus, in countries with well established two party systems — such as the United States and Britain — the major parties are generally considered the prime avenues of access to authoritative policymaking structures and the principal links between governmental and nongovernmental agents in the state. In contemporary France, on the other hand, the supporters of the Gaullist regime look upon the parties as more of a hindrance than a help for the efficient operation of the political system.

In Germany the origin and nature of a system with still tenuous roots in the political culture have placed a major responsibility for the institutionalization of party government and competition upon its supportive parties. Under the rules they have sponsored and promoted, any viable party must have broad support if it wants to control the making of public policy; but if the present party system is to last, the parties committed to its maintenance must provide jointly for the integration of groups and individuals into the larger political system. Formal arrangements regulating the electoral and governmental functions of the parties are not enough. The legitimation of the prevailing political order demands that it rest upon a cohesive mass consensus which extends beyond electoral support for either or both of the major parties and encompasses profound acceptance of the integrative functions of the party system as such.

This task places a particularly heavy load upon the two principal parties, the CDU and SPD; it requires them to assume many functions which in the past were performed by other political structures and which might be so again if the parties should fail to perform them. At the same time, however, the integrative capacities of the CDU and SPD are not unlimited, so that their leaders are compelled to establish an order of priorities in party goals and functions. In order to achieve a balance between what they believe needs to be done and what can be done to facilitate the engineering of political consent in a transitional society, the dominant party elites accordingly have chosen to accentuate certain objectives and tasks at the expense of others.

In the view of most CDU and SPD leaders, the ambivalent political orientations and dynamic situational factors which confront their efforts to legitimate party government and competition require them to be highly pragmatic in matching the integrative functions of the major parties with their integrative capabilities. They consider harmonious interaction between the two parties crucial for the stability and maintenance of the regime and have therefore subordinated intraparty competition to the need for fundamental cooperation between the CDU and SPD. Second, they consider the preservation of extensive evaluative support for the party system of greater immediate importance than the development of intensive emotional attachments to the parties and their separate goals. Third, they believe that the integrative functions of the major parties require a high degree of flexibility in responding to external pressures, rather than consistent commitments to the doctrinal principles of party members.

Their common stake in the institutionalization of the prevailing regime has led the two major parties to collaborate closely in political socialization efforts designed to "sell" it to the German people. Keenly sensitive to the tenuousness of public support for the system, the CDU and SPD elites have jointly sought to present and interpret policy issues in terms of solutions obtainable only through the major political parties and their leaders. They have joined forces to establish by work and deed that the present political order is indispensable for responsible and responsive government and the efficient resolution of group conflicts in a modern pluralist society. Collaboratively they have sought to demonstrate that the party system provides an efficient and necessary linkage between state and society, between rulers and ruled, and between formally dispersed centers of governmental authority in the Federal Republic.

As political recruitment structures, the CDU and SPD have sought to draw the participants in German politics into roles defined through the party system. At the level of the mass public these endeavors primarily have taken the form of competitive efforts to mobilize extensive electoral support for the parties' candidates for public office through their own organizations and those of allied interest associations. The integrative function of the voting process at times may have been obscured by the dramatic content of hotly fought electoral contests. But, on the whole, the massive endorsement of the two major parties by German voters seems to indicate that most of these accept such intermittent participant roles that give legitimacy to the prevailing party system.

The relatively low rate of sustained mass participation and past cleavages among political activists makes the fact that the two major parties have become the principal structures for the recruitment and interaction of most middle-range and, above all, top-range political actors, seem to speak well for the integrative activities of the CDU and SPD. Both the formal organization of the political order and the prevailing political climate have encouraged these actors to adopt roles which tie them closely to the party system. On the one hand, relatively open party recruitment structures have replaced those which formerly restricted political participation on the basis of social origin or religion. On the other hand, whereas the tangible benefits of party membership are more widely distributed than under former German regimes, a more tolerant political climate has greatly reduced the risks involved.

As we have seen, interest associations and nonpolitical elites have come to look upon the major parties as effective, if not exclusive, channels of access to governmental decisionmakers. And for the manifest political elites, and those who aspire to join their ranks, membership in the CDU or SPD has become pretty much a practical, if not a legal necessity, since these parties effectively control the selection of most key public officials.

As we also remarked earlier, most of the elected and administrative leaders of the Federal Republic are members of the major parties and, frequently, achieved their elite position through such membership.[17] The leading role of the CDU and SPD in postwar political reconstruction shaped these recruitment patterns and they have since been reinforced by the evolving structures of party government and the norms of an increasingly achievement oriented, functionally specific society.

Today the major parties offer many benefits to Germans who aspire to a political career and possess the necessary functional skills. Opportunities for upward social and economic mobility into highly paid and prestigious positions of public authority are available through both the CDU and SPD. Both, moreover, provide their leading members with protection against loss of income and status. The competitive risks of a political career no longer involve threats to life and liberty under the present system, and they are cushioned by party membership benefits which greatly soften defeat in an election. A leading Christian Democrat or Social Democrat can face the loss of public office with relative equanimity, since he can usually fall back upon some other position which provides not only income and status, but frequently a chance to make a comeback. Multiple officeholding is very prevalent among the leaders of both major parties, and CDU and SPD candidates who fail to win an elective public post frequently are compensated for their efforts with a prominent position in the party organization or government

[17] See pp. 185–186 above. In view of the decline of the FDP, the figures cited there fail to indicate what appears to be an even greater concentration of CDU and SPD members among the present political elites.

administration. Alternatively, they may find prestigious, lucrative posts awaiting them in interest associations or business enterprises which value their political experiences and connections or wish to reward them for past services. Or they may simply return to positions which they temporarily abandoned to pursue political ambitions.[18]

Consequently, neither the "hankering for the spoils of government by impatient politicians" [19] nor the fear of grievous income and status deprivation are serious divisive elements among more active participants in contemporary party politics. Provided he plays the game according to the rules and roles agreed upon by the major parties, a German who chooses to follow a political career may not achieve spectacular gains, but also he risks very little. Multiple officeholding and hierarchic structures in the CDU and SPD may have restricted rapid advancement, but they have not to any significant extent led politically ambitious men to seek alternative routes to the top. Stable recruitment patterns probably have diverted some potential aspirants for public offices into nonpolitical careers holding out more immediate rewards. Others, however, have found the tangible and intangible benefits available through the major parties adequate compensation for placing their functional skills at the disposal of the CDU or SPD.

Interest aggregation is another major integrative function that has been performed both jointly and separately by the two leading German parties. Like the political recruitment processes, it is closely related to their governmental activities and derivative of their authoritative policymaking functions. Through interest aggregation, diverse input claims flowing

[18] For instance, many legislators are also local party functionaries and public officials. Lateral movements between elective and appointive positions in the federal and Land governments have been frequent, particularly among SPD functionaries. Civil servants, including teachers, judges, and military men, may freely engage in political activities and when elected to a public office need only take temporary leaves, which protect their seniority and pension rights. University professors, who are civil servants in Germany, have continued to teach and draw their salaries while simultaneously serving as federal deputies in the Bundestag.

[19] Otto Kirchheimer, "Germany: The Vanishing Opposition" in Robert A. Dahl, *Political Opposition in Western Democracies* (New Haven: Yale University Press, 1966), p. 251.

into the political system from society are assimilated, balanced, and fused into more general policy proposals for submission to the relevant decisionmakers, be they voters at election time or governmental leaders in executive and legislative offices.

Of course, the major parties themselves also articulate specific interests, and there are other aggregative structures in the political system. On the one hand, both the CDU and the SPD themselves express demands based on the particular values of their leaders and members. On the other hand, numerous other nongovernmental and governmental agents also combine and coordinate specific claims regarding the authoritative distribution of public benefits and obligations in the political system. The aggregation of political demands is one of the functions of the "peak" interest associations, as we have seen, as well as of such minor "protest" parties as the radical National Democratic Party. In Germany, as in the United States, governmental agencies serve as aggregative structures in the name of the "national interest" and the "public welfare" of the political community.[20] And, under the constitutional principles of majoritarian government, the formal rules of the present regime assign legislative organs a leading part in the performance of aggregative processes in the state. Thus, the elective and lawmaking responsibilities of national and subnational parliamentary bodies involve deputies representing particular interest clienteles and constituencies in constant bargaining negotiations with each other, as well as with the members of nonlegislative structures inside and outside the government.

The key integrative function of the party system is reflected by the large extent to which these aggregative processes are today manifestly or latently controlled by the major parties. The new principles and practices of party government and competition have provided the CDU and SPD with both the opportunities and the incentives to intervene at strategic points in the flow of exchange transactions between policy claimants and policymakers in the marketplace of German

[20] A government bill submitted to the Bundestag, Bundesrat, or a Land parliament is usually the product of extensive preliminary negotiations among relevant interest groups and administrative agencies.

politics. Between them, they control not only the selection of the governmental decisionmakers but major routes of access to authoritative decisionmaking sites in the state. At the same time their competition for mass and elite support has led the two parties to seek the extensive aggregation of interests through services promised or rendered to voters and organized pressure groups.

The reciprocal adaptive patterns promoted by the present party system have produced an unprecedented bargaining style in German politics, which altogether appears to have promoted public consensus and acceptance of the new regime. In this respect the accommodation of very broad political interests and values by the major parties has helped significantly to lend balance to the political system and to provide for the reconciliation of competing demands. At the same time, however, the engineering of extensive support through the party system has also created problems which complicate and limit the integrative functions of CDU and SPD. These problems relate above all to the creation of a more intensive legitimating consensus for the regime and, generally speaking, are the direct result of the relatively recent but drastic transformation of the German political system and the principal goals and functions of its major parties.

PROBLEMS OF INTENSIVE INTEGRATION

As the keystone of the present political order, the party system is confronted with "system maintenance" responsibilities that in older and more solidly established systems are either not as important or more extensively shared by other structures. The legitimation of a regime based upon a competitive party system involves in Germany more than the establishment of formal, rational rules and procedures for the performance of instrumental functions through the parties. It requires particularly that the two parties most closely associated with establishment and operation of the present system perform political socialization and communication functions which promote popular emotional allegiance to the new regime and political community, as well as to the principles of a competitive party system. That is, the major parties must serve as structures for the intensive integration of Germans into the political system by (1) mobilizing affective mass support for the regime which transcends partisan loyalties, (2) directing the expression of political sentiments into legitimate channels, and (3) transforming such sentiments into generalized feelings of overarching emotional identification with the prevailing political order.

Thus far, the German party system has demonstrated a very limited capacity in this respect. True, only a relatively small proportion of the citizens of the Federal Republic have expressed outright feelings of alienation from the political system by supporting groups and publications highly critical of the regime and its leading parties. On the "left," such sentiments have been articulated primarily through highly vocal, but relatively tiny and amorphous organizations of university students and intellectuals. On the "right," they have found greater expression through minor nationalist parties and periodicals, but these, too, have not been able to obtain much mass support. Though the most recent of such groups, the National Democratic Party (*National Demokratische Partei* or NDP), has obtained about 8 per cent of the votes in a number of Land elections, until now it has produced neither the leadership nor the cohesive strength which might make it a clear and present danger to the regime and its major supportive parties.

Like the short-lived Poujadist movement in postwar France, the NDP essentially has served to provide waning socioeconomic elements in Germany – especially small Protestant farmers, businessmen, and artisans – with an outlet for their fears of status and income deprivation. It has functioned as an aggregative protest party, especially since the formation of the Grand Coalition brought the Social Democrats into the national government. But though the membership and leadership of the NDP includes many former Nazis and its demagogic appeal is reminiscent of the nationalistic and authoritarian Hitler movement, present conditions do not appear to promise it similar successes. Basically it is a traditionalist and reactionary party, which is likely to remain a marginal political group, particularly if one or both of the major parties manages to accommodate the expressive needs and intangible value preferences of its inconstant supporters. The picture might change if a major economic crisis should transform more widespread, but now latent antagonism toward the CDU and SPD into overt manifestations of popular hostility.[21]

Evidently, however, the CDU and SPD have not been able to overcome prevailing feelings of affective neutrality toward the regime and party system. Thus, although the prevailing blandness of partisan sentiment and the limited mass involvement in political input processes may facilitate dispassionate bargaining among the policymaking elites, they also appear to reflect the ordinary German's sense of emotional aloofness and lack of positive system affect.

Voting and other forms of political participation through the party system may attach the citizens emotionally to a regime, even when, as in Germany, voting is perceived as a "duty" and is believed to have little influence on the choice of governmental leaders and policies.[22] Mass support for the major parties in Germany, however, seems largely to exclude such emotional investments and to rest for the most part on purely pragmatic considerations of evaluative expediency and qualified acquiescence — even among the small minority of party members.[23] Neither collaboration nor competition between the CDU and SPD has as yet produced a more profound affective consensus of civic loyalties, based on cohesive sentiments of communal identification and popular trust and confidence in the expressive as well as instrumental functions of a democratic party system.[24]

Cultural patterns and other contextual factors undoubtedly have made it difficult for the major parties to overcome this reserve and break through the emotional barriers which have divided Germans from the political system. As we have seen,

[21] It has been estimated that perhaps as much as 15 per cent of German adults are a potential source of support for right-wing parties. In this connection see p. 110 above.

[22] This is perhaps the most obvious explanation for elections in such authoritarian and totalitarian regimes as Nazi Germany. See Richard Rose and Harve Mossawir, "Voting and Elections," *Political Studies*, XV (June, 1967), 174–201.

[23] See Gabriel Almond and Sidney Verba, *The Civic Culture* (Boston: Little, Brown, 1964), pp. 131 ff. and 141.

[24] German opinion surveys have consistently indicated strong distrust toward the major parties and their ability to provide both representative and effective governmental leadership.

the legacy of the past has created a good deal of resistance to efforts to attach them more intimately to the regime, especially through its party system. There are memories of divisive and destabilizing party conflicts in the Weimar era and of searing integrative experiences under the totalitarian rule of the Nazi party. There is a lack of congruence between the principles of a pluralist democracy and the authoritarian monistic traditions of the German political culture. Political parties which are committed to support the former and reject the latter are confronted by demands for strong, authoritative leadership which will guarantee harmony and stability in the state. The tolerance for sustained political controversy and the expression of legitimate dissent which are needed to sustain a competitive party system, and the requisite balance between affective communal cohesion and partisan cleavages over policy issues have not yet been achieved.

For their part, the major parties have found it difficult to invoke emotional responses by dramatizing their activities. In this connection, the deliberate efforts of the CDU and SPD elites to "rationalize" postwar German politics evidently have prevented them from promoting more profound civic attachments to the regime and its party system. On foreign policy issues, they have tended to mute appeals to patriotic emotions and often have slighted popular sentiments in response to international developments over which German leaders have had little or no control. More generally, endeavors to establish an extensive consensus of evaluative support for the system apparently have weakened efforts to extract emotional loyalties through symbolic leadership and the performance of expressive functions by the system supporting parties.

It seems that extensive changes in the nature and primary goals of the major political parties have reduced their ability to function as structures of intensive integration. For the trend toward a two-party system and the concomitant evolution of the CDU and SPD strategies and tactics have tended to maintain, if not to widen, the emotional distance between Germans and the political system. To the extent that the two parties have become primarily electoral organizations for the recruitment of governmental policymakers, they appear to have become increasingly remote, quasi-official structures in the eyes of many citizens of the Federal Republic, even including some of their own members. And to the extent that their interest aggregating functions for the most part have involved negotiations with the large, organized pressure groups and their governmental functions bargaining among policymaking elites, this sense of remoteness seems to have increased.

The development of a competitive party system which might mobilize and maintain affective allegiances to the regime may at least have been delayed by prevailing patterns. As the policies of the CDU and SPD more and more have come to resemble each other and collaboration between their leaders has become more intimate, the differences between the two parties also have become too obscure to allow them to mobilize much emotional support for the on-going system. The party elites' competitive bids for the allegiances of "floating voters" without strong partisan preferences have tended to weaken sentiments of party loyalty among more constant supporters and to alienate political activists in the CDU and SPD, who are more concerned about ideological principles. And party leaders seeking to balance their promises and their performances, their representative functions and their governmental functions, have seemed to many Germans all too opportunistic, self-serving, and shifty to warrant much affective support for themselves, their party, and the regime.

PARTY SYSTEM AND POLITICAL SYSTEM

The development of the German party system has suggested to many observers that it increasingly resembles that of the United States. Indeed, there appear to be many similarities. Differences between and within the two major parties revolve around relatively superficial policy questions, rather than irreconcilable political philosophies, and competition for control over public policymaking is tempered by basic agreement on the rules of the game. In Germany, as in the United States, the party system provides a common national focus for political communications, orientations, and relationships under a federal form of government, and furnishes structures for the recruitment of political participants and their integration into the political system. The major parties aggregate political input demands and control their conversion into authoritative policy outputs through their participation in governmental functions. The party system has encouraged a bargaining style of politics, especially among German elites, and has served as a stabilizing and consensus building element in a pluralist society, on the strength of its conflict management functions. The resolution of political differences through compromise solutions is reflected in tactical coalitions between and within the major parties, as well as by alignments across party lines between representatives of contending interest groups.

Such analogies, however, can easily obscure significant differences between the German and American party systems. Social class and religious identifications still are far more important in German than in American party politics, whereas the German party system is not influenced by the pressure of ethnic and racial cleavages. Sectional differences are less important in the Federal Republic when they do not overlap with religious alignments. Party loyalties among voters and political leaders are more profound, though not to the same extent as in the British two party system.

More generally, party politics in the advanced industrial societies of the United States and Germany reflect differences in the structural features of the two political systems, as well as differences in political culture patterns and other environmental factors. Thus, although the party systems in the two countries appear to perform many similar functions, they are distinguished not only by different antecedents but by differences in the types of demands with which they must deal and in the way in which such demands are handled through party structures.

As we saw at the beginning of this chapter, the constitutional norms of the present regime call for a party system which, in principle, gives the voters a meaningful choice between alternative sets of governmental leaders. In fact, however, neither the leading political actors nor most German voters thus far have been willing to institute a truly competitive party system providing for alternating party governments and a constant public confrontation between the "ins" and the "outs."

Electoral contests for public office frequently have had considerably less influence on the composition of governing majorities and their policy outputs than postelectoral negotiations among the dominant elite groups.

Over the last decade, the leaders of the CDU and SPD have been inclined to avoid rather than seek decisive confrontations between government and opposition parties because they have considered it more important, first, to institutionalize the legitimacy of a comparatively new regime and its supporting party system. Thus far, however, the formal and informal procedures which they have followed in this respect have done little to instill in the nonelites a sense of participation in political input processes and a sense of confidence in the policy outputs of democratic party government. Insofar as the new party system has gained legitimacy in Germany, it appears to have done so because of, rather than in spite of, "subject oriented" popular attitudes, and through the instrumentalities of the state rather than on the strength of the autonomy of the party system. Most Germans have still to be convinced that the political functions claimed for the present party system by its principal leaders could not be performed just as well, if not more efficiently, by other structures.

All this suggests that, by emphasizing political harmony rather than partisan diversity and political stability rather than conflict, the leaders of the major German parties may be running the risk of making the party system appear superfluous, or as no more than an extension of authoritative governmental structures. For parties, as we have said, are not absolutely necessary for the efficient operation of a political system. They are essentially multifunctional organizations designed to perform tasks which might otherwise be assumed by other structures, such as private interest associations and governmental recruitment and policymaking agencies. Moreover, since their capacity to exercise manifold political functions is restrained by the resources that parties can command or mobilize, parties are compelled to accept limitations on their ability to influence political developments. Unless they are willing to permit important systemic functions to go entirely neglected, they must allow nonparty structures to share, if not monopolize, control over political input and output processes.

In the German party system these problems have been aggravated by particular environmental circumstances. First, ambivalent political culture patterns have greatly complicated the efforts of the principal party leaders to gauge and anticipate shifting currents of political opinion and deny them the advantages of firmly established popular attitudes supporting the regime. Second, the party leaders have been compelled to give constant proof of their ability to deal efficiently not only with the problems of a complex, modern industrial society, but with critical issues arising out of the highly dynamic environment for German politics. Third, the structural and geographic dispersion of decisionmaking sites in the political system has complicated the creation of a cohesive party system which serves to nationalize political attitudes and relationships in a pluralistic, polycentric society.

The leaders of the CDU and SPD have sought to stay on top of these problems by emphasizing some party functions and delegating, or simply leaving the performance of others primarily to nonparty structures. They have considered it necessary, above all, to devote a great deal of effort to asserting party control over strategic decisionmaking processes affecting national politics and to guarding this power against the encroachment of actual or potential rivals. This has involved protecting the governmental activities of the major parties against the intrusion of executive, legislative, and judicial organs of the state. Also, it has involved defending their nongovernmental functions against the efforts of interest associations, other parties, and civic groups to bypass or displace the major parties as political input structures. Consequently, the principal party leaders have tended to place greater stress on their political communications with other elite groups than on keeping open direct communication channels from the electorate, on the recruitment functions of the party system rather than on its socializing functions, and on its policymaking functions rather than its representative functions.

Whether the course chosen by the CDU and SPD elites will

lead in time to the establishment of a stable and smoothly functioning competitive two party system remains to be seen. The gloomy prognostications of some observers to the contrary, "catch-all" parties may be particularly well suited for the political integration of a society such as that of Germany, provided that the present collaborative relationship between the CDU and SPD proves to be a transitional stage on the road to a viable multiparty system. It seems that much depends on the ability of these parties to establish a sense of public trust in their activities by recruiting governmental leaders and providing policy outputs which will serve to identify the party system with the satisfaction of the tangible as well as intangible goals of most Germans. A great deal may depend on their ability to attach the citizens of the Federal Republic more intimately to the regime by directing and controlling integrative functions which these parties cannot perform by themselves. And, finally, the parties' leaders will have to manage the difficult feat of achieving a balance between (1) preserving internal organizational cohesion and (2) adapting their goals and performance to external pressures on the party system in particular and the political system in general.

CHAPTER IX

Governmental Processes

POLITICS IN GERMANY, as elsewhere, focuses on the authoritative distribution of public benefits and binding obligations through governmental organs which determine and enforce who is to *get* what, when, and how and who is to *do* what, when, and how. Rule-making structures convert input demands for governmental action into public policy decisions and administrative and adjudicative output structures implement and interpret the application of public policy in specific cases. In this sense, governmental processes are both outcome and source of political conflicts and bargaining; they reflect as well as produce demands upon and supports for the political system; they shape as well as conform to the formal allocation of political authority in the system.[1]

Like other components of the present German political system, those of its governmental subsystem incorporate traditional and modern features inherited from past regimes and innovative features introduced under the present one. Linked to each other and to nongovernmental structures through interdependent political functions, the organs of government involve public officials in highly complex, interlocking relationships.

[1] See Harold D. Lasswell, *Politics: Who Gets What, When, How* (New York: Meridian Books, 1958); Gabriel A. Almond and G. Bingham Powell, Jr., *Comparative Politics* (Boston: Little, Brown, 1967), pp. 128–163; David Easton, *A Systems Analysis of Political Life* (New York: Wiley, 1965); Karl W. Deutsch, *The Nerves of Government* (New York: The Free Press, 1963).

Postwar constitutional engineering sought to provide for change as well as continuity in the governmental system by superimposing new policy-making structures upon long established administrative and adjudicative structures. The framers of the Basic Law were determined above all to prevent the establishment of another totalitarian regime – Nazi or Communist – and therefore endeavored to define the boundaries of the governmental system and the responsibilities of its components as explicitly as possible. The constitution thus makes an elaborate distinction between governmental and nongovernmental political agents and disperses policy-making authority among federal and Land organs and among executive, legislative, and judicial structures. To give the new regime legitimacy and ensure its integration and efficient operation, its architects at the same time sought to counterbalance this dispersion of rule-making authority by retaining the traditional German administrative and judicial systems.

In practice, the development of the governmental system has reflected on the one hand the strong influence of relatively constant formal, legal arrangements in German politics and on the other dynamic environmental pressures. On the whole, public officials have sought to achieve a judicious balance between efforts to institutionalize the new constitutional order and efforts to adapt governmental processes to input demands for domestic and foreign policy outputs. Governmental leaders, legislators, judges, and administrators have elaborated as well as modified the Basic Law in applying it to particular situations, both through more specific regulations as well as more informal ad hoc interpretations. But they have also been compelled by constitutional and other legal norms to exercise restraint and discretion in their governmental functions. And although some German observers consider such formal curbs essential safeguards against arbitrary and irresponsible government, others argue that they impair the efficiency and flexibility of public officials.

The issue is familiar in all highly industrial mass consumption societies with democratic governments responsible for extensive regulatory and service functions. However, it is particularly significant in Germany. Extensive governmental intervention in and controls over the mobilizing and allocating of societal resources have a long tradition in that country, extending from the corporate order of the Middle Ages, through the Prussian administrative state of the eighteenth and nineteenth centuries, to the Nazi and postwar occupation regimes in more recent times. Religious and secular principles still deeply embedded in the political culture, as we have seen, sustain not only the right, but the duty of executive organs of the state to assume far-reaching responsibilities for the security and welfare of the population and the authoritative coordination of societal functions.

In the past, German governments, usually operating through interlocking executive and judicial structures, rarely hesitated to intrude into areas which in the United States have become only recently the business of "big government." Nongovernmental agents, such as the churches, were prone to rely on the state to ensure the satisfaction of their wants through public functions considered to be beyond their own capacity. Private charities were not expected to satisfy social welfare needs and Germany was the first country to adopt an extensive social security system; self-adjusting forces of a free market economy were not considered adequate to ensure economic development and stability and the growth of state-supported monopolies and cartels thus accompanied the industrial expansion of Germany in the late nineteenth and twentieth centuries.

Though the extreme form of governmental direction under the Nazi regime was succeeded in Eastern Germany by another totalitarian system, in Western Germany direct governmental controls were reduced, but by no means abandoned, after 1945. Military government and German officials closely directed social, economic, and political reconstruction and created a vast administrative apparatus to liquidate the legacy of wartime dislocation and postwar chaos. The needs of millions of refugees, widows, orphans, and crippled veterans required extensive social welfare measures; the destruction of practically every German city called for vast urban planning and home construction projects; fiscal benefits for business, designed to promote rapid economic expansion, were balanced with "equalization of burden" laws designed to permit the least privileged groups to share some of the immense profits accumulated by the principal beneficiaries of economic recovery in industry and trade.

Economic and political recovery altered but did not diminish the load of frequently competing input demands on German governmental structures and consequent output responses have involved the utilization of a sizable proportion of the country's skilled manpower and material resources in the public sector (see Table IX.1). Direct control over about 40 per cent of the gross national product (GNP) of goods and

TABLE IX.1 *The Public Sector: Government Employment, Income, and Expenditures in Major Industrial Societies, 1959*[a]

	Federal Republic	*France*	*United Kingdom*	*United States*	*Japan*
Percentage of GNP going into income of governmental agencies and public enterprises[b]	41.3[b]	40.0	41.1	27.4	44.9
Percentage of GNP going into expenditures of governmental agencies and public enterprises[b]	38.8[b]	40.1	45.3	27.9	42.3
Percentage of working age population employed by governmental agencies and public enterprises	7.15	7.82	10.61	8.14	4.49

[a] Not all public enterprises included.
[b] Including social security revenues and expenditures.
Source: Prepared from data in Bruce M. Russett, *et al., World Handbook of Political and Social Indicators* (New Haven: Yale University Press, 1964), pp. 58, 59, 63, 64, 70.

services in turn has provided governmental decision makers with far-reaching opportunities to guide the mobilization and distribution of goods and services in the private sector. Here, as in the many other areas subject to governmental controls, policy formulation and output reflect the interaction between formal procedures and the dynamics of political change in a transitional society.

POLICYMAKING

The outstanding feature of the present regime, as we have seen, is party control over its principal rule-making structures. Such control is, however, limited not only by the interplay of shifting electoral, interest group, and elite alignments but by legal restraints as well. The principles of the *Rechtsstaat,* government under law and through law, restrict as well as legitimate party government in the Federal Republic.

In national policy making numerous formal arrangements are designed to check the power of party leaders who control the executive branch of the federal government, the *Bundesregierung.* German federalism gives the state governments greater direct influence over the central government's decisions than in the United States and the constitutional powers of the national parliament make the executive branch responsible to the bicameral legislature. The Basic Law provides the Federal President with opportunities to act as a nonpartisan arbitrator between executive and legislative leaders and permits the Federal Constitutional Court to impose curbs upon party government and exercise autonomous rule-making functions. Last but not least, national policy is both directly and indirectly shaped by key administrative officials and military men in governmental and quasigovernmental agencies charged with planning and regulatory functions.

Executive rule-making authority and party government are primarily linked through the position of the federal chancellor.[2] The Basic Law calls neither for executive leadership by committee, as in Switzerland, nor for cabinet government, as in England. It stipulates that as head of the Bundesregierung the chancellor is to be its primary policy maker, less dependent upon his cabinet and the legislature than the chief of the government under a parliamentary system with collective ministerial responsibility, yet more so than under a presidential system. The chancellor alone is chosen by the lower chamber and he alone is formally accountable to the Bundestag for the

[2] See pp. 270–272, above.

policies of the executive branch. Accordingly, the federal ministers are supposed to be the chancellor's subordinates, rather than his peers, whose tenure in office automatically ends with the death, resignation, or replacement of the incumbent chancellor. Constitutionally, neither the federal president nor the parliament can compel the chancellor to include anyone in his cabinet or dismiss one of its members. His recommendations are binding on the chief of state, who has the formal power of appointment and dismissal and must sign bills and decrees submitted to him by the chancellor or one of the ministers; parliament, on the other hand, has no constitutional right either to censure a minister or to single him out for a vote of confidence.

Under the constitution and the Standing Rules of the Bundesregierung, federal ministers have primarily four policy-making roles. First, as members of the cabinet, they may participate in formulating collective decisions which the chancellor has the formal right to accept or reject. Second, they may individually advise the chancellor on policy matters, though he can ignore or overrule their recommendations. Third, they are charged with supervising and planning policy making within their ministries, provided they are not ministers without portfolio. These responsibilities may include not only preparing bills for consideration by the cabinet, Bundesrat, and Bundestag but, more directly, formulating administrative regulations and legal ordinances (*Rechtsverordnungen*) that spell out in detail the specific application of federal laws. Fourth, they have the authority to supervise policy making by subordinate officials, including Land officials responsible for administering federal laws and ministerial regulations.

The principal policy-making functions of the federal executive also identify its key ministries: Economics, Interior Affairs, Finance, Foreign Affairs, and Defense. It does not necessarily follow that the corresponding ministers will be more influential in policy making than their colleagues. Some cabinet members who have ostensibly held only a minor portfolio – such as the Social Democratic Minister for All-German Affairs in the 1966 Kiesinger cabinet, Herbert Wehner, or Chancellor Erhard's chief assistant, Minister Ludger Westrick – have in fact exercised a great deal of influence over the chancellor and their fellow ministers.

The influence of the chancellor and various ministers on the formulation of policy by the executive branch has depended primarily on the political resources, personality, experience, and skills of the incumbents and on the extent to which they have relied on subordinate officials and been subject to outside pressures. Chancellor Adenauer accommodated his policies to the demands of Germany's allies – particularly the United States – but on the strength of his formal and political powers allowed his ministers little voice in formulating these policies. The cabinet ratified rather than made decisions and the federal ministers were the chancellor's subordinates in the most literal sense of the Basic Law. Under Chancellors Erhard and Kiesinger, on the other hand, policy making has been far more subject to collegial cabinet decisions because the chief of the government has depended heavily on the advice and approval of ministers commanding powerful party and interest group support and/or exceptional managerial and technical skills.

The direct and indirect rule-making functions of the bicameral national parliament have reflected the development of constitutional principles originally designed to fuse a federal with a parliamentary form of government and to balance executive with legislative powers. The intention of the framers of the Basic Law was to give the chancellor and his Bundesregierung sufficient powers to provide efficient and stable executive leadership but to prevent executive absolutism. They therefore sought to counterbalance these powers by (1) granting the Länder governments and legislatures a voice in national policy making and supervision – principally through their representatives in the Bundesrat – and the selection of the federal president and principal judges, and (2) by giving the popularly elected lower house, the Bundestag, the right to choose the chancellor and replace him, to exercise exclusive jurisdiction over some legislation, and to exercise concurrent legislative and elective powers where Länder interests were involved. In fact, however, this intricate distribution of constitutional powers has become increasingly obscured by bureaucratic ties in the relationship between the federal and

Land governments and party ties in the relationship between the federal executive and Bundestag.

The Basic Law formally distributes the power to initiate, deliberate, and enact public policy among executive and parliamentary structures (see Chart IX.1). In practice, however, the Bundesregierung has consistently been dominant in formulating policy, the Bundesrat increasingly influential, and the Bundestag of diminishing effectiveness.

The Bundesrat's intermediary position between central and Land governmental structures on the one hand and the federal executive and Bundestag on the other has made it relatively powerful as a second chamber compared to the House of Lords or the French and Italian Senates.[3] Some observers consider it, in fact, akin to a supplementary executive structure in the national government. The intent of the framers of the Basic Law was to balance the obligation of the Länder governments to apply federal laws uniformly and faithfully with their right to control corresponding federal policy through the Bundesrat.[4] Strictly speaking, the formal rule-making powers of the Bundesrat are not as great as those of the Bundestag or those of the upper chamber of the American Congress. But the increasing size and range of concurrent federal legislation and the extent to which the central government has come to depend on the Länder for the execution of its domestic policies has actually led to an increment in the Bundesrat's policy-making functions.

Some commentators have hailed this development because, after the Nazi experience, they see it as a reassertion of traditional German federalist principles against the threat of an all-powerful national government. To them the Bundesrat is

[3] See pp. 202–203, above.

[4] In addition to the powers enumerated on p. 202, the Bundesrat must consent to the impeachment of the federal president and to the declaration of a state of legislative emergency, which allows the chancellor to govern for six months without the support of the lower house; it must agree to all measures affecting the federal structure of government (including changes of Land boundaries, the establishment of new structures for the administration of federal rulings in the Lander, and the transfer of such administrative assignments from one Land agency to another). The federal government may not take measures to compel a Land to execute its rules without the approval of the Bundesrat nor bypass Land authorities in sending instructions and agents to agencies formally under their control.

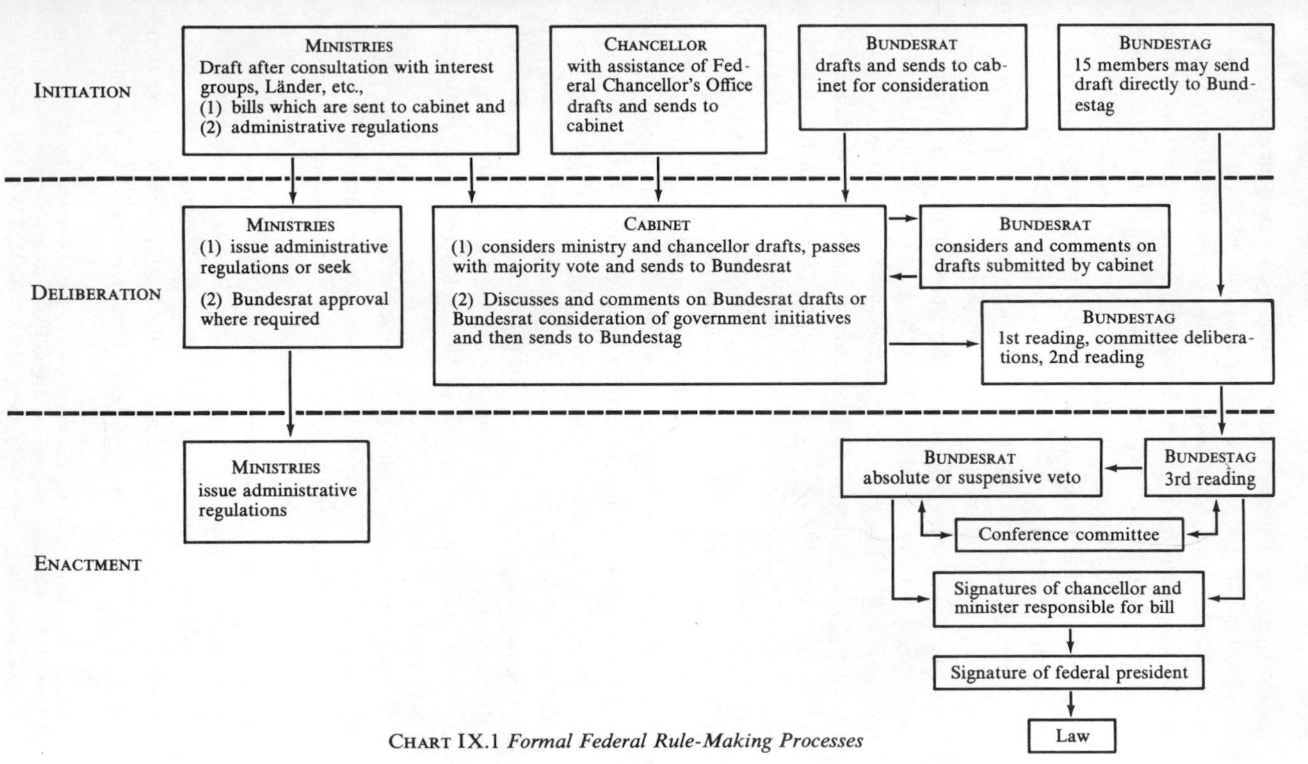

CHART IX.1 *Formal Federal Rule-Making Processes*

less subject to interest group and party pressures than the Bundesregierung and Bundestag and, therefore, more responsible and efficient in providing for the general welfare under a democratic regime. Others, however, have either denounced the Bundesrat as the expression of a federalism that hinders rather than facilitates the coordination of national governmental functions, or as an instrument of bureaucratic machinations that subvert the principles of representative party government and promote the development of executive control through an administrative state.

Such praise and criticism of the upper chamber of the federal parliament relate directly to the rather low public esteem commanded by the popularly elected lower chamber. Constitutional provisions for a parliamentary form of government establish the Bundestag as the principal policy-making structure in the Federal Republic and ostensibly provide it with rather extensive means of control over the executive. The formal powers of the only direct national representation of the German electorate are, in this respect, considerably larger than those of the present French Chamber of Deputies, though not as great as those of the American House of Representatives. As a collectivity, however, the Bundestag has in fact exercised relatively little control over the Bundesregierung and has been rather subordinate in rule-making processes, whereas individually some deputies have been highly influential in formulating national policy as members of the executive or as prominent party leaders.[5]

This pronounced imbalance between executive and legislative authority results from a combination of factors. One is the persistence of traditions that emphasize the pre-eminence and distinctiveness of the representatives of "the state" in their relationship with an assembly speaking with many voices and representing competing interests. As in the Reichstag of the Hohenzollern Empire and the Weimar Republic, the spokesmen for the executive branch symbolically confront the deputies on a dais raised several feet above the well of the chamber

[5] Gerhard Loewenberg, *Parliament in the German Political System* (Ithaca, N.Y.: Cornell University Press, 1967) and Wilhelm Hennis, "Der deutsche Bundestag 1949–1965," *Der Monat,* XVII, 215 (1966), 26–36.

and both figuratively and literally speak down to them when addressing the Bundestag. (The representatives of the Länder governments occupy a corresponding position to the left of the presiding officer.) The chancellor, ministers, and their principal administrative assistants have the constitutional right to attend not only the plenum meetings of the Bundestag but those of its committees, and like the representatives of the Bundesrat, those of the executive have the right to speak in plenum or committee sessions any time they wish to state the views of the Bundesregierung. The Bundestag, on the other hand, has no formal powers to command their appearance and to compel them to disclose information, reply to questions, or debate an issue.[6]

Second, the lower chamber labors under the same handicap as most legislatures in advanced industrial societies. That is, the complexity and size of governmental rule-making functions inhibit the effective participation of deputies lacking the expertise, information, and administrative staff available to members of the executive. Bundestag members do not command anywhere near the staff and other legislative resources available to American congressmen and no seniority system allows well-placed and secure majority and minority members of key committees to confront the executive on somewhat equal terms. These weaknesses are particularly noticeable in the all-important areas of defense and foreign policy, where Bundestag deputies frequently have been left entirely in the dark or only a small group selected by the executive has been entrusted with information.[7]

Finally, the autonomous policy-making and control functions which the constitution assigns to the Bundestag have been profoundly affected by the evolution of party government and

[6] Chancellor Adenauer would often show his contempt for the opposition deputies by either absenting himself from the chamber when they wanted him to speak or listening in silence from his floor seat as if he were just an "ordinary" deputy of the governing party. His successor, Erhard, simply replied to a question of the opposition leader with the brusque comment: "That's none of your business!"

[7] When Arab countries severed relations with the Federal Republic in 1965, on the grounds that it had supplied arms to Israel, it became known that only a few Bundestag deputies had been privy to these secret arrangements.

party alignments since 1949. The authors of the Basic Law and the Standing Orders of the Bundestag built upon nineteenth-century principles of parliamentary government and sought to prevent executive as well as legislative predominance through a system of checks and balances. They did not anticipate that in but a few years the German governmental system would make the transition from parliamentary to party government that took more than a hundred in England and that both executive and legislature would be firmly controlled by the leaders of a single governing party or a grand coalition of parties.

Unlike the American president and his cabinet, the members of the Bundesregierung are able to intervene directly in legislative affairs as leading members of the dominant majority, as well as representatives of the executive. Consequently both the policy-making agenda and the general policy-making outputs of the Bundestag for the most part have been controlled by the Bundesregierung. About 80 per cent of the bills considered by the chamber from 1949 to 1965 were initially drafted in a federal ministry and sent to the Bundestag by way of the cabinet and the Bundesrat. And whereas such executive drafts usually are passed by the Bundestag with relatively minor changes, bills introduced by one of its members – particularly if he belongs to the opposition – are unlikely to become laws without the approval of the Bundesregierung.

On the other hand, Bundestag control over the executive has not been particularly significant. The formal power of the chamber to elect and remove the chancellor in effect has been reduced to ratifying the indirect choice of the voters and the direct choice of the king-makers among the dominant party leaders. Insofar as there have been public confrontations between governing and opposition parties and between representatives of the executive and the legislature they have, increasingly, taken place outside the chamber, particularly in the press; conflicts and bargaining within the Bundestag have been confined almost entirely to the nonpublic sessions of its committees and party caucuses. Floor debates were rare even before the great coalition between the CDU and SPD made them almost meaningless as a control over the executive and usually devoid of dramatic content. Only 260 of the 429 laws passed by the Bundestag from 1961 to 1965 were even discussed in plenum sessions and then mostly in dry and highly technical platform lectures read from prepared manuscripts by committee chairmen and experts designated by the parliamentary party leaders.

The executive has tended to discourage and the Bundestag leadership has not sought frequent debates on broad policy issues; the ruling parties have considered them neither necessary nor useful for effective and responsible government. The traditions, organization, and style of German parliamentary procedures and the processes of party government provide the deputies with neither the opportunities, the skills, or even the desire to engage in such debates. The survival of the Bundesregierung is not decided by debates in the Bundestag and they do not serve to educate a general public that neither knows nor cares very much about their content. The deputies themselves — as well as their party, electors, and interest group clients — consider other parliamentary tasks far more important. Suggestions to enliven Bundestag debates have addressed themselves to form rather than substance and for the most part have come to naught.[8]

Questions and interpellations addressed to the Bundesregierung have provided the legislators with somewhat greater opportunities to exercise some open control over the executive. But the formal procedures allow for little spontaneous give-and-take. So-called "little" and "big" inquiries must be put in writing, require the signature of 15 or 30 deputies, and permit members of the government benches to carefully prepare a written or verbal reply — if they consent to answer at all. By and large these devices have been used to call attention to rather minor issues such as applying legislation and adminis-

[8] For some years, the president of the Bundestag campaigned unsuccessfully for a more intimate seating arrangement, under which government and opposition benches would face each other, as in the English House of Commons. More recently a Bundestag committee proposed that the government bench be lowered to a less domineering position, the speaker's lectern be moved closer to the center of the chamber, and deputies be required to speak without manuscripts and for no more than fifteen minutes.

trative procedures in specific instances of interest to some deputy.[9]

The introduction, in 1960, of a special, less rigid question period at the beginning of each plenary session gave some promise that the Bundestag might become a more visible and active instrument of control. The five minutes allotted to each deputy for related questions were used by the opposition Social Democrats during the Spiegel affair of 1962 to discredit the credibility and behavior of the Minister of Defense, Franz Joseph Strauss, and to force his resignation from the Adenauer government. Some time later the question hour once again permitted the SPD to compel the Minister of the Interior, Hermann Höcherl, to admit that former Nazis in the federal security services had engaged in wire-tapping activities forbidden by the Constitution. However, when the great coalition was formed the question hour also ceased to serve as an instrument of legislative supervision over the executive; the small Free Democratic opposition party proved neither willing nor able to employ it with telling force against the combined forces of the CDU and SPD.

Most of the work of the Bundestag is taken up by activities in committee sessions that are closed to the public, though secret in only the most formal sense. In contrast to the House of Commons, and more like the United States Congress, the Bundestag operates largely through 26 functional subparliaments that correspond more or less to equivalent ministries in the executive branch. But these standing committees have nowhere near the power of American congressional committees over the recruitment and actions of members of the executive or the formulation of national policy. Except for the Defense Committee – which has never used it – they do not have the formal right of investigation; for the most part they serve as clearing houses for pluralist demands which have not been accommodated in preceding bargaining sessions in the ministries, the cabinet, the Bundesrat, and the "working groups" of the parliamentary parties.[10]

[9] A deputy may, for example, ask the Minister for Postal and Communications Affairs whether he has taken any steps to install a telephone booth in some village of his constituency.

[10] See p. 211, above.

Though the work of the standing committees has annually produced far fewer laws than are enacted by the United States Congress and their contribution to general policy formulation is far less significant, Bundestag deputies complain of being overworked and overwhelmed by these responsibilities. Absenteeism, which involves a fine, is not nearly as common as among American congressmen and the legislators labor diligently in turning out ever more voluminous laws.[11] They are unwilling to approve skeletal laws that give the executive branch great leeway in interpretation and application and consider it their duty to submit drafts to meticulous consideration in committee. In part this outlook is a legacy of German parliamentary traditions which conceives highly explicit legislative codification as the principal means of popular control, especially fiscal control, over the executive. In part, too, it is based upon the deputies' belief that the resulting legislative workload and the pluralistic interest demands represented in the Bundestag can be most adequately and efficiently processed through the committee system of miniparliaments. Committee assignments have allowed both majority and minority members to look after the interests of their pressure group clients and constituents in specific policy outputs. And they have provided Bundestag deputies with opportunities to demonstrate their usefulness to their party as technical experts or parliamentary tacticians deserving not only renomination and reelection but elevation into a leading executive position in the federal government or one of the Länder.[12]

Unlike American legislatures, the Bundestag has made scant use of its constitutional power of investigation to influence policy making and control the executive. Under Article 44 of the Basic Law, special investigating committees, empowered to conduct open or secret hearings, must be established upon the motion of one-fourth of the deputies. Although this permits a

[11] Thus the register of federal legislation expanded from 896 pages in 1955 to 2,179 pages in 1965.

[12] These opportunities were extended with the establishment of parliamentary state secretaries in various federal ministries in 1966. Similar to the parliamentary undersecretaries in England, the incumbents are in effect *ministerables* undergoing an apprenticeship for higher offices. The present Lord Mayor of Berlin was previously parliamentary state secretary of the foreign ministry.

minority to initiate such investigations, these are likely to have little effect without the cooperation of the Bundesregierung and the governing parties. Legislative investigating committees not only have no more legal power than standing committees to extract information from agents of the executive, but essentially conflict with the principles of party government. The ruling majority is not inclined to support investigations which are likely to embarrass its representatives in the Bundesregierung and to challenge the legitimacy of their authority and actions, whereas the opposition can make little or no electoral use of findings which the majority can refuse to make public. Since the German system does not provide for such nonpartisan investigating bodies as the British Royal Commission, the Bundestag has, therefore, characteristically left it mostly to the courts to uncover and evaluate errors of commission and omission by the executive branch.[13]

Constitutional provisions for a dual executive allow the federal president, as chief of state, no significant policy-making functions – at least under normal conditions. He is enjoined from engaging in "partisan" activities and bound to accept the decisions of the Bundesregierung, parliament, and courts. Formally elected for a five-year term by the federal assembly (*Bundesversammlung*) – an electoral college composed of the Bundestag deputies and an equal number of representatives of the Land legislatures – the president is in fact selected by agreement among the dominant party elites and is subject to

[13] For more than a decade of its existence the Bundestag allowed its investigative powers to lie dormant. In the early 1960's, allegations in the press led the opposition Social Democrats to initiate several investigations into relatively minor matters, such as military procurement policies. In 1962, the so-called "Fibag Committee" examined allegations by *Der Spiegel* that Minister of Defense Strauss had engaged in improper dealing with a construction firm that had been awarded a contract to build military barracks. However, the committee never issued a report and the Social Democrats did not press the matter further. In 1964–65, revelations in *Die Zeit* led to an investigation into unconstitutional wire-tapping activities by the federal security service, which induced the Minister of the Interior to institute certain reforms. With the establishment of the Great Coalition in 1966 there was no longer an opposition strong enough to initiate an investigation; the public hearings on proposed "emergency laws" sponsored by the CDU and SPD in 1967 were in effect little more than an opportunity for proponents and opponents to restate already well known opinions on the subject.

party government. He must appoint the choice of the Bundestag majority for the chancellorship and cannot dismiss him; he cannot veto actions of the Bundesregierung or parliament and he must sign all legislation, decrees, letters of appointment and dismissal submitted to him by the chancellor or the minister responsible; in fact, all the president's "public acts," including his official letters, speeches, and publications formally call for the approval of the governing executive. At the same time he does not enjoy the political immunity of the British monarch; impeachment proceedings before the Constitutional Court may be initiated by a two-thirds majority in either house of parliament against a president believed to have exceeded his constitutional powers.

The incumbent therefore must be extremely circumspect in seeking more influence in policy making on the strength of his personal, rather than his formal authority. He may try to warn and admonish the official policy makers in statements designed to express or mobilize public opinion and he may attempt to exploit his constitutional right to be informed and consulted by the chancellor to influence governmental policy more covertly and directly. Experience has shown, however, that governmental leaders supported by solid parliamentary majorities will not and need not accept presidential interference and advice. Theodor Heuss, president from 1949 to 1959, was apparently quite unsuccessful in a few efforts to influence Chancellor Adenauer's policies; in his only public controversy with the Chancellor, involving the constitutionality of German rearmament, Heuss yielded to Adenauer's demand that he withdraw his legitimate request for an advisory opinion from the federal constitutional court. His successor, Heinrich Lübke, sought a more significant role with somewhat less discretion but evidently no more success. Both Chancellors Erhard and Kiesinger told him in effect to mind his formal presidential business and leave policy making to those responsible for it under the constitution.

In the opinion of some German constitutional lawyers the federal president may possess some latent powers to block or, at least, to delay policy decisions and exercise greater influence over the composition of the political executive under exceptional circumstances. As yet untested provisions of the Basic Law might conceivably allow a president so inclined to play a more independent and decisive role in a deadlock between regular policy-making structures. If the party leaders in the Bundestag and Bundesregierung should be too deeply divided to maintain majority party government the president may, at his discretion, either dissolve the lower house or support a minority government. Provided he has the agreement of the upper house, the president has the constitutional power to allow a chancellor to rule for six months by decree if a majority of the Bundestag will neither support nor replace him. Under the prevailing patterns of party government such developments are most unlikely, but the re-emergence of a more unstable multiparty system could lend greater weight to the constitutional and personal authority of an incumbent president.

POLICY IMPLEMENTATION

In the present German political system the administrative subsystem occupies a key position on the output side, corresponding to that of the party subsystem on the input side. The latter channels demands for public policies into governmental conversion structures, the former provides for the implementation of policy decisions. This picture of a functional balance between the two subsystems, however, can easily obscure differences that might prove to be decisive for the future development of the entire political system.

First, the highly differentiated governmental processes of an advanced industrial society do not necessarily require a party system, particularly a competitive one, but they do call for an elaborate administrative system.[14] Second, although the parties are today the most important, but by no means the only input structures in Germany, the implementation of public policy decisions is for all practical purposes the monopoly of administrative output structures. Third, whereas party leaders in government frequently are relatively inexperienced and transitory officeholders, more or less dependent on the assistance of administrative officials in realizing their general partisan objec-

[14] See Almond and Powell, *Comparative Politics,* pp. 157 ff.

tives, members of the career public service tend to be more secure and more skilled in performing functionally more specific tasks. Fourth, the size and complexity of governmental activities inevitably compel the ruling party leaders to delegate policy-making tasks to administrative officials. Civil servants, soldiers, and other public employees interpret the application of legislative acts and ministerial ordinances to specific cases and structure policy outputs through their planning and supervisory functions.

Finally, the German political culture makes the present form of party government depend heavily on the support of a loyal and efficient public service. Among the general public, as we have seen, administrative officials command far greater trust and respect than party politicians. They provide the average citizen not only with his most immediate contacts with the authority of the state, but with those most constant and salient regarding his perceived civic rights and obligations. His output-oriented perception and evaluation of political processes have been shaped by these day-to-day contacts with an administrative system which has proven far more durable than policy-making structures and which rests on far deeper roots in German society than the party system. Germans have learned from their history that whereas parties, governments, and regimes may come and go, they can depend upon their civil service as a relatively continuous and stable manifestation of political authority.

The prevailing formalistic approach to politics among more active and influential participants has produced a corresponding inclination to view policy issues and their resolution as "compartmentalized problems of public administration and jurisprudence." [15] Members of the governing party elites accordingly have sought to legitimate their authority largely through the administrative system rather than apart from it or even in conflict with it. Thus particularly the CDU leadership considered it more important in the period of political reconstruction to win the support of civil servants who had

[15] Edward L. Pinney, *Federalism, Bureaucracy, and Party Politics in Western Germany: The Role of the Bundestag* (Chapel Hill: University of North Carolina Press, 1963), p. 182.

served the Nazi dictatorship than to deprive the new regime of their services by an extensive purge.

The formal structure of the administrative system provides for a distribution of output functions between national and subnational agencies which corresponds essentially to procedures that were established when Germany was unified in 1871, drastically altered under the Nazi regime, and restored during the era of political reconstruction. It reflects the negative reaction of its German and foreign architects to the concentration of administrative authority they associated with both Nazi and Communist totalitarian systems and the fact that the formation of Land governments preceded the establishment of the federal government. Under the Basic Law the federal ministries exercise direct control primarily over the implementation of foreign policy, including defense and trade, and over the national communications network of railroads, waterways, and postal and telegraph services. Independent federal agencies, somewhat analogous to regulatory commissions in the United States, administer the social security and employment systems. Most other political output functions are assigned to the Länder governments and subordinate administrative structures (see Chart IX.2).

Corresponding to this constitutional distribution of administrative functions, the public service is divided into a number of interlocking but autonomous structures and interdependent but separate bureaucratic hierarchies. The federal ministerial bureaucracy is largely concentrated in Bonn and, apart from those functions subject to its immediate administrative jurisdiction, primarily plans and supervises the uniform implementation of national policies by regional and local government officials. Most civil servants are employed by either Land ministries or by county and municipal agencies subject to their regulations (see Table IX.2) and provide the average German with most of his immediate contacts with the authority of the state. Standards of employment and performance are more or less similar throughout the public service, but not always identical. Though federal regulations provide for fixed pay scales in different grades, some Land governments pay higher salaries than others and appointments and promotions to top

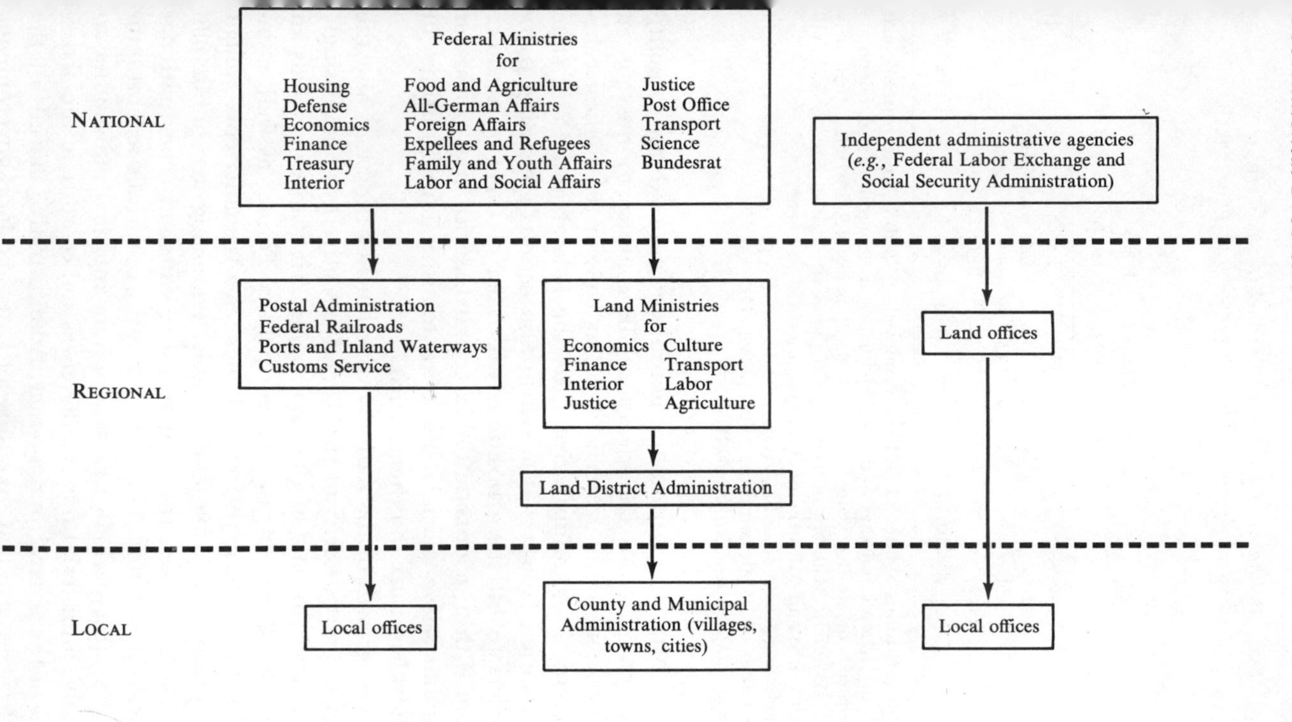

CHART IX.2 *Structure of Public Administration*

TABLE IX.2 *Public Administration Personnel in the German Federal Republic, 1965 (in rounded-off percentages)*

	Civil servants and judges	*Salaried employees*	*Wage earners*	*Total*
Federal[a]	4.3	4.8	5.2	14.3
State[b]	31.2	16.4	5.4	53.0
Local	7.6	14.5	10.4	32.5
Total	43.1	35.7	21.0	99.8
N = 1,870,613				

[a] Not including about 1.3 million employed by public enterprises – such as the federal railways and the federal postal, telegraph, and telephone service – or in the armed forces. Federal personnel included primarily employed in Ministry of Defense (56 per cent), Ministry of Finance (19 per cent), and Ministry of Transportation (10 per cent).
[b] Including teachers and university professors (28 per cent of Land and 15 per cent of public administration personnel).
Source: Statistisches Jahrbuch, 1966.

administrative positions are not infrequently subject to political and religious considerations. In contrast to the United States, the German merit system extends to the highest echelons of the administrative elite, the federal and Land state secretaries. However, the system also permits governing party leaders to fill these positions with men of their own choice from within or outside the career civil service and to transfer administrative officials out of a ministry into positions of equivalent rank in other agencies.

The growth of the national government's functions and the expanding authority of the federal executive have increasingly enhanced the role of the Bonn ministerial bureaucracy as an integrative element in German politics. Formal as well as informal procedures introduced under the Adenauer government established extensive and durable ties among key public officials and between the administrative elite and other national leadership groups. The state secretaries of various federal ministries meet periodically as a sort of informal subcabinet to resolve ministerial policy differences and coordinate the activities of the federal bureaucracy. Administrative officials of the federal government, like those of Land and local governments, sit with party and interest group representatives on the governing boards of public and semipublic corporations and together with business and trade union functionaries supervise the activities of private enterprises subject to "codetermination" laws. And, as we have previously pointed out, numerous institutionalized practices have forged close ties between the federal public service and national pressure groups, legislative bodies, and party organizations.

The federal ministerial bureaucracy also provides the principal integrative link between central and regional governmental structures. Critics of the present administrative system have asserted that the constitutional division of functions between federal and Land agencies has deprived the system of the cohesiveness and efficiency of the old Prussian civil service. But, though the national government for the most part has only supervisory powers over the field administration of its policies by Land agencies, its indirect authority has been quite adequate to ensure the uniform execution of federal laws and regulations. Discrete bureaucratic negotiations between national and subnational officials, particularly in the committees of the Bundesrat, evidently have been extremely effective in overcoming not only formal barriers, but partisan differences between the elected leaders of the federal and Land governments.

As the administrative agents of the federal government, as well as their own, the ministries in the ten Länder and their respective bureaucratic infrastructure occupy strategic intervening positions between national and local structures of policy implementation.[16] Though it has seemed to some German observers that the Land governments gradually have become little more than adjuncts of the federal government,[17] they have maintained considerably more regional administrative

[16] See G. Sawyer, "Federalism in West Germany," *Public Law,* VI (1961), 26–44; Taylor Cole, "New Dimensions in West German Federalism" in Edward L. Pinney (ed). *Comparative Politics and Political Theory* (Chapel Hill, N.C.: University of North Carolina Press, 1966), pp. 99–122; Peter H. Merkl, "Executive-Legislative Federalism in West Germany," *American Political Science Review,* LIII (1959), 732–741.

[17] See, for example, Theodore Eschenburg, *Institutionelle Sorgen in der Bundesrepublik* (Stuttgart: Curt E. Schwab, 1961), p. 225.

autonomy than one finds in such unitary states as England and France. In this sense, the German system of "administrative federalism" has served as a check upon the nationalization of the political system, particularly in those areas of public policy which the Basic Law assigns exclusively to the Länder. Educational and police administration vary a good deal from Land to Land and efforts to establish more uniform practices, for the most part, have involved bureaucratic negotiations between Land officials, with the federal government serving at best in an advisory capacity.

Regional diversification in administrative practices has also been evident in the implementation of federal laws and ordinances in various Länder. Under the Basic Law the Länder governments are charged with formal responsibility (*Rechtspflicht*) for the uniform application of federal rules within their administrative jurisdiction and are obliged to do so in good faith "as a matter of their own concern." However, Land officials have at times interpreted this obligation rather broadly and loosely. The constitutional powers of the central government are by and large too cumbersome and restrictive to be readily employed in forcing compliance with its directives in the daily routine of public administration. The Basic Law does not permit federal authorities to bypass or overrule the Land ministries without the express approval of the Bundesrat, the principal guardian of states' rights. Even then it may require a favorable decision by the Federal Constitutional Court to compel Land officials to accept federal supremacy. Lacking hierarchic authority over the Land bureaucracies and financial control over the Land ministries, the national government has relied all the more heavily on bureaucratic cooperation and negotiations for mutually acceptable policy outputs.

In contrast to this regional decentralization, the administrative system within the Länder is highly centralized. Lines of authority run from the Land governments – especially their Interior Ministries – through Land district administrations to county and municipal agencies (see Chart IX.2). In the last analysis most laws are executed by local officials directly or indirectly accountable to the Land ministries and, whereas the national government has relatively few local agents, the

Länder ministries employ many. The collection of most direct taxes, for example, rests in the hands of the Länder governments and most of the administrative functions of local authorities are strictly supervised by them.

Local governments enjoy far less autonomy than do those in the United States. Article 28 of the Basic Law grants self-governing municipalities the right to regulate their own affairs "within the limits set by law." But over the years these limits have become ever smaller while output responsibilities of local governments have grown. Local autonomy, which the American military government had sought to make the basis of a new German "grass-roots" democracy, fell victim to the inability of German villages, towns, and cities to mobilize sufficient resources to meet the demands placed upon them and to the consequent expansion of federal and Land control over their affairs. Under the so-called "financial constitution" local governments have been able to dispose at their own discretion of only about 15 per cent of tax revenues and have been compelled to rely correspondingly on funds disbursed through the Land governments. Under the federal and Land constitutions, their schools, police departments, social services, in fact practically all but local transportation and public utility services, are controlled by Länder authorities. In short, local governments in Germany today in most respects are actually administrative agencies of the Länder governments – and through these, of the national government – and most of their employees are in fact if not in form members of the Land administrative bureaucracies.

In some German towns a long tradition of civic identification and government by local notables has served to some extent as a check upon the intrusion of higher authorities. There, old patrician families, leading businessmen and artisans, and local politicians still wield some influence over the powers delegated to local governments. In all the large urban centers, however, municipal government has passed into the hands of professional administrators skilled in modern city management and bureaucratic bargaining with superior federal and Land officials. Whether they are elected or appointed, these men tend to be more interested in governmental efficiency than local autonomy and to reject parochial orientations for a broader administrative view of the problems of interurban metropolitan areas.

It is therefore not surprising that most Germans, then, see little point in becoming involved in the politics of their local governments and take little or no interest in its nonadministrative activities. For policy decisions affecting local output processes both private citizens and public officials quite realistically look elsewhere. The high proportion of mayors and other municipal functionaries in the Land parliaments suggests that these provide local interests with access to one decision-making site. It seems, however, that since the rule-making functions of the Land parliaments are rather limited, the promotion of local interests calls for the most part for negotiations with officials of the Land ministries and, to a lesser extent and more indirectly, with members of the Bundestag and the executive branch of the federal government.

The functional integration of administrative processes through bureaucratic negotiations has been facilitated by subcultural homogeneity among leading members of the career service. For the most part of upper middle class background and frequently the children of civil servants, these senior officials are university educated, trained in law, and the products of a long period of similar in-service socialization experiences. They have demonstrated a sense of cross-organizational elite cohesion that is quite exceptional in contemporary German society and transcends the particularist interests of different administrative organizations. Informal associations between top officials who served together in a pre-1945 ministry have helped to minimize friction between federal and Land agencies.[18] But probably the most important factors promoting high-level bureaucratic cooperation have been the generally accepted formalistic distinction between partisan "political activities" and nonpartisan "administrative" processes and the

[18] The success of joint federal and Land fiscal services has been attributed to the fact that most of the senior officials involved were formerly members of the unified Tax Administration under the Nazi regime. See Herbert Jacob, *German Administration since Bismarck* (New Haven: Yale University Press, 1963), p. 171. I am indebted to this study for a number of perceptive observations about past and present patterns in German administrative practices.

corresponding self-identification of senior civil servants with a "neutral" state apparatus. One federal state secretary said recently, as he was retiring from office, that the state "demands from us selflessness, nonpartisanship, and discretion" in serving its interests and is entitled to the dutiful "loyalty and dedication" of its administrative officials.[19]

All told, the fusion of new political structures with older administrative ones appears to have been highly successful. The effective incorporation of the public service into the political systems has promoted its integration and contributed significantly to the legitimation of the new regime. In sharp contrast to the era of the Weimar Republic, neither national nor regional administrators have failed to support the system loyally and their collaboration has allowed elected leaders to strengthen their authority and overcome sectional and partisan cleavages. A well functioning administrative system has probably done more to gain public acceptance of the regime than electoral processes and the party system. It has provided party government with an aura of efficiency and legality and ensured that its policies would be implemented. However, it has also made party government highly dependent upon bureaucratic procedures and associations that extend well beyond strictly administrative output functions into policy making and pressure group politics.

THE JUDICIAL SYSTEM

German jurisprudence has traditionally distinguished between universal, general, and absolute principles of justice (*Recht*) and relativist, particular, and finite principles of law (*Gesetz*). Under the prevailing rules of a democratic Rechtsstaat the courts are supposed to combine both sets of principles and to render equal justice under law. Constitutional provisions stipulate that they shall render justice on the basis of judicial interpretations of desirable or established social norms and serve the law as the principal structures of rule adjudication and legitimation.

As with the administrative subsystem, the successful fusion

[19] Speech by the retiring state secretary of the Federal Ministry for Defense, Professor Dr. Karl Carstens, reported in *Bulletin der Bundesregierung,* January 9, 1968.

of traditional and new structures and functions has made the judicial subsystem a strong source of institutional support for the present political system. The deep confidence which most Germans have in law and justice dispensed through their courts has enhanced the legitimacy of the regime and encouraged Germans to express their mutual distrust through established channels of litigation.

The autonomy and respect commanded by the judicial system reflect as well as reinforce the extensive juridification of political processes in the Federal Republic. Private citizens and organizations as well as public officials and governmental organs rely heavily on the courts for orderly and reasonable resolution of their disputes and for authoritative definitions of legitimate standards of social and political behavior. The judiciary is expected to maintain harmony among pluralist interests through adjudicative proceedings and it is trusted to ensure a just and lawful distribution of political rights and obligations between citizens and state, governmental and nongovernmental agents.

The authority of the courts as impartial arbitrators between conflicting interests is enhanced by the rule of judicial anonymity. Most courts are collegial bodies and the verdict of a majority of their members is handed down in the name of the entire bench. Individual opinions of support for and dissent from the majority decision are never made public or recorded, as in the American judicial system. In the opinion of German jurists the practice protects the courts against outside interference and reinforces the prestige of the judicial organs of the state.

Like most higher administrative officials, the judges and prosecutors in the German courts are recruited principally from the upper middle class, go through a long period of university and in-service legal training, and enjoy the job security and tenure rights of civil servants. In contrast to the American practice, German law students must decide while still in school between a career in private practice and a career in the judiciary, and most judges and state attorneys are appointed and promoted from within the career service.

National and subnational judicial structures are closely in-

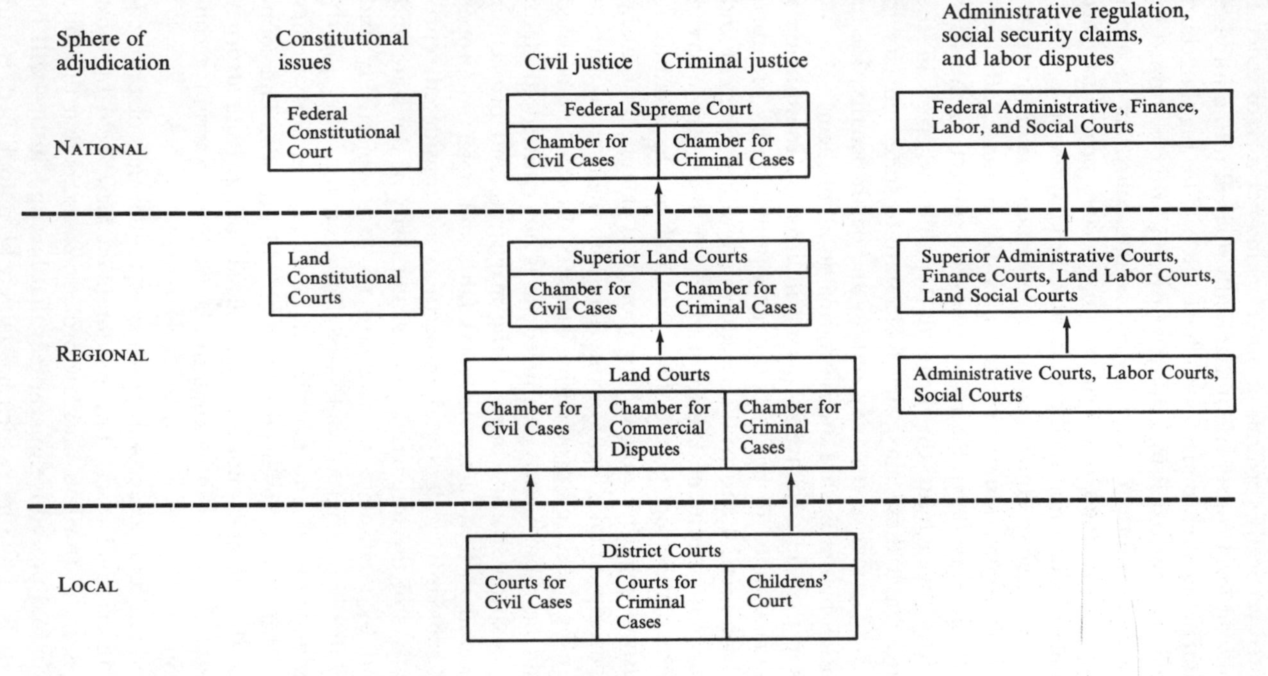

CHART IX.3 *The Court System*

tegrated vertically through an interlocking network of federal, Land, and local courts and horizontally divided into a number of functional hierarchies (see Chart IX.3). The regular court system is organized into a judicial pyramid that is topped by the Federal Supreme Court, an appellate court. As in other European countries, uniform standards and procedures are regulated by national civil and criminal codes; review proceedings before higher courts concern solely questions of interpreting their application to specific cases. For instance, offenders against nationwide traffic regulations are subject to the same penalties throughout the Federal Republic, whereas in the United States these may vary from state to state and city to city. No German court may impose the death penalty, for its abolition by the Basic Law is binding on all of them.

As in the United States, a person indicted for committing a crime is assumed to be innocent until proven guilty in court. But both pretrial and trial procedures are rather different and conform to continental European rather than Anglo-Saxon patterns. A person bound over for trial by the examining magistrate may be confined for months if it appears that he may attempt to take flight or interfere with the pretrial investigation by the state's prosecuting attorney. Even if the accused should be subsequently acquitted he is not entitled to claim compensation in the courts if the magistrate and prosecutor are found to have acted in good faith and observed proper legal standards. Judges and prosecutors are considered representatives of the impartial judicial authority of the state and bound by their office to ascertain the facts objectively and fairly in the pretrial as well as trial proceedings. They jointly examine witnesses and evidence in court to ascertain whether the criminal code has been violated by the accused. The counsel for the defense is not a public official but a private attorney whose task it is to show that the facts do not warrant a conviction.

German legal experts disagree over the fairness of proceedings in criminal cases. The predominant view, held by most judges, state attorneys, and law professors, asserts that the code of criminal procedure guarantees that law and justice will be served. Trial by jury, which has largely been abolished, is said to be more arbitrary and inefficient than prevailing procedures; jurors are believed to lack the objectivity and skill to weigh the evidence impartially. The professional jurists and lay experts who together sit in judgment in most German courts are, in this view, far more likely to ensure that justice will be done and the laws observed.

Critics of the present system, on the other hand, assert that it discriminates against the accused. Pretrial and trial procedures are said to place him at a disadvantage because neither he nor his attorney has adequate means to mount a strong defense against the evidence collected through the machinery of the state's judiciary. Particularly persons from the lower social strata, who are most frequently accused of criminal offenses, are allegedly subject to the bias of prosecutors and judges attached to conservative upper middle class norms. All too often, these critics claim, the verdict in such cases is a foregone conclusion and the sentence is based on a completely antiquated penal code.

The national system of administrative courts is organized into a second judicial pyramid composed of chambers staffed by professional and lay judges. As in France, it provides private citizens an opportunity to seek redress from the state for alleged injuries caused by the administrative actions of its officials. In contrast to the regular courts, administrative courts are thus exclusively concerned with matters of law rather than justice. They must decide whether a government agency or one of its officials acted "correctly" in performing their formal duties. The issue to be adjudicated may be whether a policeman had the right to make an arrest, or whether a teacher followed proper procedures in meting out punishment to an unruly pupil. A businessman may claim that he suffered damages through the error of a postal clerk and a worker that an injury sustained on his job was caused by the improper enforcement of governmental safety regulations.

The administrative court system also allows government agencies and officials to appeal against the decisions of superior administrative authorities which they consider to have violated established procedures. And in cases which do not involve constitutional issues, the Supreme Administrative Court may rule on disputes between Land governments, between Land and federal governments, and between various administrative agencies.

In the view of German and other European legal commentators these procedures are first of all efficient, because they allow experts in administrative law to deal with the large number of complex cases arising from the expanding service functions of government in an advanced industrial society. Second, the administrative court system is said to provide citizens with more adequate and fairer means of redress against arbitrary or negligent officials than is available in countries where administrative authorities cannot be sued without their consent.

A number of court systems that are even more specific, functionally, include the social courts that adjudicate disputes involving unemployment compensation and social security payments, finance courts concerned with disputes over governmental revenue collections, and patent courts. The system of labor courts was first introduced during the Weimar Republic through the efforts of trade unions, which considered other courts antagonistic to labor. Usually composed of an equal number of employer and employee representatives and a professional specialist, they deal with disputes involving labor relations.

The constitutional courts are postwar innovations designed to strengthen the new political order by introducing a third branch of government, coequal with the executive and legislature and authorized to overrule them on constitutional issues. The Federal Constitutional Court is solely bound by the Basic Law and may set aside the verdict of any other court, including the constitutional courts of the Länder, if it finds that such a verdict violates the federal constitution. In 1959, it threw out a decision by the Federal Supreme Court on the grounds that it violated the civil rights provisions of the federal constitution.

The constitutional courts are not, nor were they ever intended to be neutral, "nonpolitical" instruments of the state in the sense of the positivist tradition in German jurisprudence. Their judges are supposed to be nonpartisan in interpreting the constitutional principles of the prevailing order, but biased in favor of the regime. In other words, the constitutional courts and particularly the Federal Constitutional Court are quite explicitly judicial structures for legitimating and preserving the present political system.

The membership of the Federal Constitutional Court and the manner of its selection indicate its close identification with the present regime and the weight which the ruling elites attach to the functions performed by the tribunal. Half of the sixteen justices of its two senates are elected by a two-thirds majority of the Bundesrat, representing the partisan and regional interests of the Länder governments; the others are chosen by a special committee of the Bundestag dominated by the major parties. Six of the judges are always members of the career judiciary, recruited from the highest federal courts and elected for life; ten are recruited for eight-year terms from the ranks of the administrative elite, the major parties, and other leading groups in German society and have usually been reelected for much longer tenures in office. Consequently, the membership of the Constitutional Court has represented something of a balanced ticket of the polyarchic elite structure of the Federal Republic, combining "prior judicial experience, government career service, professional legal practice, academic life, and direct political experience." [20]

Since its establishment in 1951 the Court clearly has become the most important source of judicial influence in German politics and the most active and powerful tribunal in Western Europe.[21] Because no other German Court had ever commanded equal powers of constitutional review, the mere existence of the tribunal opened up an entirely unexplored field of politics and jurisprudence. Federal and Land authorities, parties and interest groups, and ordinary Germans who believe their constitutional rights to have been violated, have learned

[20] Edward McWhinney, "Judicial Restraint and the West German Constitutional Court," *Harvard Law Review,* LXXV (1961), 28. See also the text of the Federal Constitutional Court Act in James K. Pollock and John C. Lane (eds.), *Source Materials on the Government and Politics of Germany* (Ann Arbor: Wahrs Publishing Co., 1964), pp. 94 ff.

[21] See Donald P. Kommers, "The Federal Constitutional Court of West Germany," unpublished paper delivered at the 25th annual meeting of the Midwest Conference of Political Scientists, April 27–29, 1967 and Donald R. Reich, "Court, Comity, and Federalism," *Midwest Journal of Political Science,* VII (1963), 197–261.

to look to the Court and to respect its decisions. Unlike those of the Italian Constitutional Court and the Constitutional Council of the Fifth French Republic, the opinions of the German tribunal have come to carry a great deal of weight in politics and the Court has clearly established itself as the effective guardian and authoritative interpreter of the principles of the Basic Law. Of all the new institutions introduced under the present regime the Constitutional Court today is probably the least controversial and most prestigious.

Rather than enumerate and explain the complex formal responsibilities of the Court, it may be more useful to consider some of the functions it has performed. First, the tribunal has displayed a good deal of autonomy in guarding the constitutional rights of citizens of the Federal Republic against arbitrary administrative and judicial actions. Second, the Court has functioned as a mediating structure between executive and legislative organs, between federal and Land governments, and between majority and minority political factions. Some of the most important decisions in recent years have settled constitutional controversies between the federal and Land governments, whereas others have sought to restrict the power of the dominant party elites. Third, the Court has supported executive and legislative efforts to legitimate and protect the regime. By declaring the Communist Party and a neo-Nazi party unconstitutional it also served notice that a similar fate might be suffered by other "extremist" groups. Finally and more generally, the Court has gone beyond the Basic Law to establish more explicit standards for legitimate constitutional behavior.

By and large the justices of the Constitutional Court have been quite cautious in moving into an uncharted area of German jurisprudence and have taken care not to stray too far from prevailing cultural patterns. On the whole they have sought to stick very close to the letter of the Basic Law, though on occasions their interpretations have invoked alleged norms of a higher "natural law" as guidelines for the public interest. The Court has been more conservative than innovative, especially on socioeconomic and civil liberties issues, and has sought to remain above partisan controversies. At least a majority of the justices, evidently, have considered it more important to identify the Court as the community's bulwark against the demands of parties and interest groups than as a bargaining site in a pluralist society. And although some of the Court's opinions have reflected exceptional tolerance toward dissent and political diversity, in general they have tended to place far greater emphasis on the need for order, harmony, and stability.

THE MILITARY ESTABLISHMENT

Because of the importance which military men and soldierly virtues have had in German society and politics in the past, the development of the new military establishment has been watched rather closely both in Germany and abroad. German authoritarianism and nationalism have been widely identified with military dominance over policy making, whereas civilian control has been associated with democratic government at home and a peaceful foreign policy abroad. But quite apart from the fact that such correlational propositions are based on rather simplistic, incorrect assumptions–civilian control over the military was never more absolute in Germany than under Hitler – the present situation is far too different to permit facile historical analogies.

For the first time in German history the formation and consolidation of a new political system preceded the creation of a military establishment. Whereas the French philosopher Mirabeau had been able to call Prussia an army with a state and the *Reichswehr* of the Weimar Republic came to be known as a state within a state, the Federal Republic for quite a number of years was a state without an army. For an entire decade after the Nazi military machine was dissolved, there was no military establishment in Western Germany. The surviving members of the old military elite who had not been killed in Hitler's purges or in World War II were in no position to exercise any influence on political developments, and a very large majority of West Germans were emphatically opposed to rearmament. By 1955–56, when the Federal Republic began very slowly to acquire armed forces, recruiting and organization could be closely controlled by elected party leaders who were determined to create a defense establishment that could not pose any threat to the new regime.

Like most other measures taken to safeguard the new political system, the innovations that were introduced were meant to avoid assumed weaknesses of the Weimar regime. The senior officers of the Federal Defense Force (*Bundeswehr*) were carefully selected by a civilian screening committee to ensure their loyalty to the regime. Various measures were taken to create an army of "citizens in uniform" closely supervised by executive leaders responsible to the Chancellor and the Bundestag. Administrative and command functions within the Defense Ministry were divided between civilian officials and military men and all service branches were put under the control of a civilian state secretary accountable to the Defense Minister. The administration of military justice was placed almost entirely in the hands of civil servants and the prosecution and punishment of all but minor disciplinary infractions were turned over to the regular judiciary. To prevent any possibility of secret rearmament and a covert expansion of the armed forces, the annual budget and personnel strength of the Federal Defense Force were to be submitted to parliament. The Defense Committee of the Bundestag was authorized to investigate the military establishment and the Bundestag's Plenipotentiary for Military Affairs (*Wehrbeauftragte*) was to see to it that the constitutional rights of the soldier were not violated and the new reform measures properly administered.[22]

Not all of these innovations have proven to be either workable or effective. Some have been considerably modified in the name of military efficiency, such as measures to create a democratic citizens' army. Others, such as the Office of the Bundestag Plenipotentiary for Military Affairs and the supervisory powers of the Bundestag Defense Committee have turned out to be

[22] See Lewis J. Edinger, *West German Armament* (Documentary Research Division, Research Studies Institute, Air University, October, 1955), *passim;* F. Ridley, "The Parliamentary Commissioner for Military Affairs in the Federal Republic of Germany," *Political Studies,* XII (1964), 2–20; H. P. Sacher, "Controlling the New German Military Elite: The Political Roles of the Parliamentary Defense Commissioner in the Federal Republic," *Proceedings of the American Philosophical Society,* CIX (1965), 63–84; Günter Moritz, "The Administration of Justice within the Armed Forces of the German Federal Republic," *Military Law Review,* VII (1960), 1–22; Eric Waldman, *The Goose Step Is Verboten: The German Army Today* (New York: The Free Press, 1964), *passim.*

rather ineffectual. But, on the whole, most of the reforms appear to have taken root, not least because party leaders in the executive branch have vigorously asserted civilian control over the military. In 1966, Minister of Defense von Hassel did not hesitate to dismiss the commanding inspector of the Air Force who objected to certain of his policies.

As many observers have remarked, the political influence of the military in Germany today is not only lower than ever before, but probably a great deal less important than in any country with so large a military establishment. Most of the 460,000 soldiers in the armed forces (1967) are short-term conscripts with little liking for military service. The professional officers and noncommissioned officers enjoy so little public esteem that some of them feel alienated from the mainstream of German society and have joined such right-wing groups as the National Democratic Party.[23] Altogether, though, the professional military appear to be entirely loyal, if not devoted to the present regime. In fact so many officers have become supporters and even members of the CDU that its opponents have charged that the Federal Defense Force not only has been civilianized but that it has come under the control of the Christian Democratic Union.

All told, the present Federal Defense Force bears very little resemblance to the former German military establishments. All its combat forces are under NATO command and such military policy issues as logistics, strategic planning, equipment, and fiscal needs depend for the most part on the decisions of non-German policy makers. As the implementing structure for national defense policies, the Defense Force in effect performs administrative functions. With rapid advances in military technology its professional military men increasingly have become specialists and managers cooperating closely with equivalent experts in other areas of German society as well as in interallied military organizations.

Insofar as there have been any civil-military conflicts in the Federal Republic they have usually taken the form of bureaucratic frictions within the Defense Ministry. A number of gen-

[23] German soldiers may not only vote but may engage in political activities during their off-duty hours and join trade unions.

erals resigned in 1966 because they believed that civil servants in the ministry had too much influence over military procurement procedures. When the military has been accused of open interference in political policy making, the involvement has almost invariably been initiated by governing party civilian leaders wanting "expert" opinions to give force to their policy proposals. In 1961, for instance, Defense Minister Strauss made public a memorandum from the top generals of the Federal Armed Forces in order to strengthen his argument for nuclear armaments. In a less conspicuous manner, however, senior military officers, like high administrative officials, no doubt influence policy making through their advisory and planning functions.

BIG GOVERNMENT AND DEMOCRATIC GOVERNMENT

Government in any advanced industrial society is a vast and complex machinery. The men in charge are under constant pressure to guard against major breakdowns, and the cumulative effect of minor ones, by maximizing the efficiency of governmental processes. As in any other large organization, efficient performance calls for concentrated decision-making authority, extensive functional coordination, and clearly defined, enforceable rules. Consequently there is a corresponding emphasis on reducing internal frictions by stable executive leadership and hierarchic bureaucratic structures.

Responsive and representative democratic government, however, implies some governmental inefficiency. It involves dispersion of decision-making authority, open conflicts over public policies, and continuous political controversy over the accommodation of widely varying demands. Essentially, it rests on the assumption that "Pluralism of institutions, conflict patterns, groupings, and interests makes for a lively, colorful, and creative scene of political conflicts which provides an opportunity for success for every interest that is voiced." [24]

The question of how democratic government can be reconciled with efficient government is neither a new problem nor

[24] Ralf Dahrendorf, *Class and Class Conflict in Industrial Society* (Stanford: Stanford University Press, 1966), p. 317.

particularly a German one. But what may well be an unavoidable gap between democratic principles and governmental practices assumes special significance in Germany because of that country's past experience with strong autocratic and feeble democratic regimes. A number of observers of German political developments feel that the demand for efficient and extensive governmental services and the expansion of executive authority may gradually transform polyarchic party government into oligarchic administrative government.[25] Similar observations have been made about the trend of developments in other advanced industrial societies, including the United States. They gain particular force, however, when applied to the Federal Republic because German cultural patterns appear to lend greater support to administrative rule than to democratic party government.

Insofar as administrative government is associated with the old Prussian system of executive rule through an elite corps of "servants of the state," there is no danger of its restoration. The frequently cited assertion of the German sociologist Max Weber, that authority in the state is exercised not only through, but by its administrative staff, referred to the autocratic Hohenzollern regime of more than half a century ago; it has little or no relevance for the present, radically different situation. The intervening years, particularly the Nazi era, and postwar developments have profoundly altered the civil service and its position in German society and politics.

The public administration and judiciary no longer are monolithic hierarchies united by a common "ethos." Though the retention of rigid educational requirements and career patterns has preserved some of its traditional cohesiveness, conservative values, and rank consciousness, the governmental bureaucracy has by no means been immune to the forces of

[25] See, for example, Otto Kirchheimer, "Germany: The Vanishing Opposition" in Robert A. Dahl (ed.), *Political Oppositions in Western Democracies* (New Haven: Yale University Press, 1966), pp. 247–259, and Karl Jaspers, *The Future of Germany* (Chicago: University of Chicago Press, 1967). In this connection, see also the unpublished paper by Richard Rose, *Party Government vs. Administrative Government,* prepared for a conference of the Committee on Political Sociology of the International Sociological Association, in Berlin, January, 1968.

change. Functionally specific, vertical links between governmental and nongovernmental officials in a pluralist society have weakened horizontal ties within the public service. Particularly at the top, lateral movements between administrative and elective governmental positions and between public and private offices have become increasingly common. The lure of higher pay and rapid promotion in private industry has been more attractive to some of the most highly skilled functional specialists in the civil service than dedicated service to the state. The bonds of affinity between federal and Land administrative officials have been frayed with the emergence of a new generation of civil servants. Its members, just like American bureaucrats, tend to identify their interests with particular agencies and clienteles and have little use for the old ethos. The traditional distinctions between ordinary government employees (*Angestellte*) and civil servants (*Beamte*) are giving way to new differentiations based on tasks and skills. Over the opposition of the old professional generalist trained in law (*Verwaltungsjuristen*), party leaders in government have increasingly placed technocratic experts in key positions in the public service.

German civil servants, like civil servants in the United States, complain that they are overworked, underpaid, and blamed for the shortcomings of rules they did not make but are compelled to administer. They feel they are overburdened with responsibilities, allowed little autonomy, and hedged in by innumerable legal restraints. But, though they may resent it, they have learned to accept the intrusion of "partisan" interests into public administration and have become extremely cautious in sticking to the letter of their assigned responsibilities.[26]

To all appearances, the professional administrative elite has not shown any inclination to assume policy-making responsibilities claimed by party leaders in the government and has faithfully, if at times skeptically, followed their instructions. Nonetheless, the possibility that democratic government, through competing party elites, may gradually give way to a more authoritarian form of administrative government, as in

[26] For a revealing expression of these sentiments see Wilhelm Clausson, "Eine deutsche Aktendemokratie," *Die Zeit*, March 15, 1968, p. 8.

France, cannot be ruled out. The difficult problems raised by the postwar transformation of German society and the still rather frail foundations of the present regime have encouraged the use of administrative procedures for the resolution of political issues. Interlocking governmental and nongovernmental bureaucratic organs may have furthered the integration of the political system, but they have not promoted the development of autonomous structures which are requisites for a smoothly functioning democratic form of government.

The elaborate system of constitutional checks and balances provide for by the Basic Law at the present time is more a formal than a truly effective obstacle to the growth of administrative government. On the contrary, bureaucratic procedures have largely been relied upon to make the system efficient and overcome partisan and interest group cleavages. High administrative officials have had policy-making functions thrust upon them by elected leaders who have relied heavily on their cooperation in upholding the authority of party government.

This may only be a passing and even necessary phase in the modernization of German society and the legitimation of democratic party government. As we have seen, the new regime has gained popular acceptance mostly on the strength of its apparent efficiency. Its sponsors have therefore felt that they had little choice but to depend on established and respected administrative and judicial structures and on officials who had served the Nazi regime.[27] For this reason the dominant party leaders have quite deliberately encouraged and promoted the "politicization" of the higher public service and judiciary. State secretaries have either been asked to join one of the major parties or been appointed from their ranks, civil servants "on leave" are heavily represented among the deputies of the Bundestag; and a large number of administrative officials sit under different party labels in the Land parliaments.

The crucial question is who will control whom in the future

[27] An extensive "denazification" purge of the public administration and judiciary was felt by most postwar political leaders not worth the risk and cost of socioeconomic instability. Both the Western military governments and the dominant German party leaders chose rather to employ the skill and expertise of officials they could not replace to ensure the implementation of their policies. See Lewis J. Edinger, "Post-Totalitarian Leadership," *American Political Science Review,* LIV (March 1960), 58–82.

or, more broadly, whether competitive party government can surmount the cultural, socioeconomic, political pressures favoring the growth of administrative government. We cannot overlook the fact that it has been the absence of an acceptable alternative which has provided party government with popular support and that it might lose support if nonparty rule through executive authorities appears to be not only an alternative, but a more attractive solution for citizens of the Federal Republic. Conceivably, diverse interests could very well be accommodated under such a regime and a new form of bureaucratic pluralism could replace the present party system.

In short, we return to the issues in our discussion of the functions and viability of the present party system. The burden of sustaining the regime rests primarily on its major parties, which means that their leaders must be willing and able to assure representative government at some cost to efficient government.

Democratic party government demands first that the elected political leaders exercise ultimate control over the formation and implementation of policies for which they alone are responsible to the voters. They therefore have not only the right but the duty to impose these policies upon administrative officials and to take the risk of rejecting the advice of technocratic specialists.

Second, democratic party government requires avenues of access to the policy makers and lines of political communications between governors and governed that are entirely separate from the administrative system. Voters, interest groups, and nongovernmental elites must be able to voice their policy demands through parliamentary or party organs or through the press; government leaders in turn must be able to bypass administrative channels to maintain a two-way flow of communications.

Third, and perhaps most important, democratic party government demands that the public and its leaders support a competitive party system even at some cost to governmental efficiency. Alternating party governments representing distinct policy objectives and electoral contests that offer the voters meaningful choices are both the strength and the weakness of democratic systems. They strengthen confidence in democratic government when they provide the voters with a sense of participation in political processes and do not permanently exclude the representatives of large segments of the population from policy making. But they can also weaken democratic government and open the door to administrative government if they produce discontinuity and instability in policy making.

Although many of these requisites for a properly functioning system of democratic party government exist today in Germany, they are not as yet fully met. Until they are, the regime is threatened not so much by right- or left-wing radicalism as by the creeping, invisible expansion of bureaucratic processes. Thus, some of the administrative measures taken to legitimate a militant democracy and make it work efficiently might undermine the very principles on which the present regime is based.

CHAPTER X

Problems and Prospects

IN SHARP CONTRAST to the period of relatively rapid political change between 1918 and 1949, political developments in Germany over the past two decades have proceeded at a relatively slow rate. Gradual, cumulative changes are less perceptible than sudden, dramatic, and revolutionary ones and may not always be as apparent to contemporary observers as to later historians. But internal and external developments are bound to produce transformation in political structures and functions which in turn will affect the system's intra- and extrasocietal environment.

The magnitude, nature, and direction of future changes in the German political system are, however, difficult to predict. In theory, explanation and prediction involve identical processes of logical reasoning. But the historical data which may allow us to establish a causal relationship between past and present patterns are of limited use in making forecasts. Unpredictable events are likely to introduce new intervening variables between contemporary and future political attitudes and processes and to cause changes which cannot be readily anticipated when we project present trends into the future. Moreover, in contrast to the English political system, the German one is still too new to provide us with dependable indicators for predicting its adaptability to changes in the domestic and international environment.[1]

[1] For comparison, see Richard Rose, *Politics in England* (Boston: Little, Brown, 1964), pp. 242–250.

Whether the present regime can survive and become rooted in the German political culture is a crucial and troublesome issue, for what will happen in Germany and to Germany is directly related to developments in international politics and in other political systems. To pose this question is to ask whether the political system we have described and analyzed will be able to accommodate and process the load of future input demands and produce adequate policy outputs without fundamental changes in form and substance. The answer will depend on the one hand on the sources, nature, and intensity of the stimuli for political change and on the other on the potential performance capabilities of the system.[2]

The preceding chapters have posed many questions but provided few clues in this respect. They have indicated elements of continuity as well as innovation in German politics and factors which may ensure long-range stability as well as those which may cause instability. Some of these exist in other advanced industrial societies, others again are distinct and unique; some reflect the perseverance of deeply ingrained cultural traditions and others the system's susceptibility to environmental pressures; some suggest that stimuli for political change may originate within the system and others that they may be introduced from outside.

The fortunes of the post-Nazi regime have come to be closely associated with economic developments, as we have seen, and the possibility that a major economic crisis might seriously weaken, if not destroy it has been a constant concern of its supporters. The economic basis of the political system, however, appears strong enough to sustain considerable pressures. Barring a severe international economic crisis the Federal Republic is unlikely to be plagued by a major depression, such as contributed to the fall of the Weimar Republic, though short-term recessions are bound to occur.

The spectacular economic growth of the postwar era has

[2] See Gabriel A. Almond and G. Bingham Powell, Jr., *Comparative Politics: A Developmental Approach* (Boston: Little, Brown, 1966), pp. 190–212. The following "capability analysis," like other parts of this book, seeks to facilitate comparison with other political systems examined in this series by adhering closely to the conceptual framework presented in the above introductory volume.

come to an end, but projections indicate that the German currency will remain one of the strongest in the world and that the gross national product will expand at the healthy rate of about 5 per cent per annum over the next decade. Current estimates anticipate that the 1980 German per capita income will be twice as high as in 1961 and that the opening up of new markets and the diversification of industrial and capital exports will provide for continuing expansion in German trade.[3] All told, the resources and adaptive capacities of a basically sound economic system and the extractive, regulatory, and distributive capabilities of the political system appear equal to meeting future demands for affluence, material security, and large public expenditures. There is, therefore, good reason to expect that public confidence in the economic basis of the regime can be maintained.

What has been called "almost revolutionary" change in governmental economic policies since 1966[4] indicates that political authorities, especially the federal executive, will probably be increasingly active in planning and directing economic change and in regulating the extraction and distribution of economic resources. The inability or unwillingness of domestic producers to modernize their facilities on their own has already produced far-reaching governmental outputs designed to mobilize new resources by technological advances, greater industrial automation and rationalization, and eliminating inefficient producers in agriculture and mining. On the other hand, input demands from the economic system are prodding the government into greater efforts to reform a traditional educational system, which has not kept pace with the need for highly skilled functional specialists. Continued economic growth requires diplomatic negotiations which will promote foreign trade—particularly with Communist countries—and provide the German economy with abundant foreign labor and nuclear power resources. We can also anticipate additional fiscal and social welfare regulations to satisfy de-

[3] See, for example, Kurt Simon, "So werden wir 1980 leben: Eine Prognose der Wirtschaftsentwicklung," *Die Zeit,* July 26, 1966, p. 15.

[4] See David Binder, "Bonn: The Economic Miracle Is Dead," *The New York Times,* January 16, 1968.

mands for a more extensive and equitable distribution of the national income among the Länder, communities, and citizens of the Federal Republic. Elite and mass opinion are likely to accept greater governmental controls over the economy as long as these ensure an abundant flow of goods and services into German society.

The sociocultural bases of the political system are less firmly established than the economic and its capabilities for managing the problems of a transitional society are more uncertain. Social, economic, and political changes are closely related, but this does not mean that they will necessarily proceed at the same rate of speed and spontaneously yield congruent patterns of social relations and orientations. In Germany, as in postwar Japan, social change has been accelerated but it has certainly not kept pace with economic and political change.

It is here that the regime, and more particularly the dominant political elites, are faced with perhaps the most important and difficult problems of system maintenance. Though the prevailing climate of conservatism in German society has lent stability to political life, it has also maintained a wide gap between basic social structures, such as the family, and political structures and between the values of the mass culture and elite culture. Such discontinuities have protected the political system against strong input pressures for social change. But they have also accentuated the German public's detachment from the system and slowed the development of profound supportive orientations which will ensure its preservation.

Greater continuity between the social and political systems demands greater capabilities for the extraction and distribution of nonmaterial social resources than the political system has demonstrated thus far. Socialization processes will have to become more congruent and provide for a closer identification of private and public values. Present contradictions between traditional and innovative social patterns and between egalitarian and hierarchic principles will have to be reduced. Demands for communal harmony, collective security, and social stability will have to be more effectively reconciled with the individualistic, pluralistic, and competitive norms of an open democratic society.

The major stimuli for such adaptive processes between society and polity cannot be expected to come from outside the political system but will have to come from within it. That is, the requisite social and political changes will have to be promoted from above by the elites and by governmental outputs into German society. This notion, however, raises the specter of administrative government or some form of autocracy concealed behind the façade of a "guided" democracy. Therefore, if governmental efforts to strengthen a democratic regime are not to prove self-defeating they will have to be directed by political leaders who are not only responsible to the electorate but committed to a competitive system of alternating party governments and popular participation.

Political developments in the Federal Republic will no doubt continue to be profoundly influenced by extrasocietal pressures, which will test the foreign policy capabilities of the political system. As we have stressed throughout this book, German politics is distinguished by extremely close interdependence between domestic and international developments. Economic and security considerations, the reunification issue, and the West Berlin problem have emphasized the primacy of foreign affairs in relation to political inputs and outputs and helped to promote the growth of executive authority in government. The efforts of German leaders to overcome the Nazi legacy in their relations with other countries have heavily stressed the exportation of symbolic outputs designed to establish that the Federal Republic is a democratic and peace-loving country.

A number of factors suggest that the Federal Republic is likely to pursue a less self-abnegating and passive foreign policy in the future. Whereas heretofore German capabilities to win friends and influence people in other political systems were sharply restricted by an international setting that offered very limited policy choices, a changing external environment promises to extend the range of policy options available to German leaders and their ability to respond to and structure the flow of input demands from abroad.

First, anti-German sentiments are gradually waning in both Communist and non-Communist countries. The incoming generation of German policy makers will probably no longer have to labor as much as its predecessors against the weight of foreign memories of German aggressions. Second, the diminishing cold war tensions and the attendant loosening up of the Western and Communist alliance systems are reducing the weight of security considerations in the making of German foreign policy and the sense of military dependency on the United States. Third, both the transition from a bipolar to a multipolar, polycentric power alignment and a halt in the movement toward European political integration are creating a more diversified international environment for the pursuit of German foreign policy objectives. Finally, the economic resources of the political system are increasingly providing German leaders with powerful means for backing their diplomatic activities in the Communist countries and industrializing nations as well as in Western Europe and the United States.

Unless political developments within Germany or in world affairs drastically alter these environmental conditions, we may expect German leaders to explore and pursue new opportunities for strengthening the international capabilities of the political system. The chances are that they will follow a policy more independent from the United States, provided the Soviet Union does not raise new threats to the security of the Federal Republic. The present policy of "small steps" toward closer relations with the Communist countries of Europe, including the German Democratic Republic, is likely to become one of much bigger strides if it meets with success. And, once General de Gaulle no longer presides over France, the German influence in non-Communist Europe seems bound to grow stronger.

At the same time, new opportunities are also likely to create new problems for German decision makers. One will be to avoid commitments that restrain the flexibility of German foreign policy and the extraction of resources from the international environment without arousing new fears and hostilities abroad. Here an intimation of things to come may be the hesitancy of German leaders to sign the Nuclear Non-Proliferation Treaty negotiated by the United States and the Soviet Union, for fear that it would deny the Federal Republic full access to nonmilitary nuclear energy resources.

A second problem will be to find ways of balancing competing foreign policy goals and commitments. Efforts to promote reunification by isolating the German Democratic Republic and formally incorporating West Berlin in the Federal Republic may be compromised by efforts to improve relations with Communist countries. Attempts to maintain a close relationship with France may be increasingly difficult to reconcile with efforts to extract maximum benefits from the European Economic Community and from cooperation with the United States.[5]

On the whole the system appears, however, to have developed a sufficiently high responsive capability to absorb extra- and intrasocietal pressures without major structural changes. The machinery for recruiting political participants and channeling input demands into policymaking organs is highly developed and well organized, and so are the governmental structures for producing effective governmental outputs. In this respect the increasing institutionalization of polyarchic elite rule through interlocking interest group, party, and government organs and the formalistic and bureaucratic features of the regime seem to pose no major problem for its survival. They may not promote more extensive popular democracy but evidently they facilitate political compromise in a transitional culture and society.

If the autonomy of the leading political actors continues to be restrained by their sensitivity to popular as well as elite demands and by procedures which give legitimacy to their actions, the system is likely to prove adaptable to future environmental pressures. At the same time, however, responsible political leaders must be willing and able to introduce innovative and, possibly, unpopular changes which will maintain the system's viability.

[5] See Karl W. Deutsch, Lewis J. Edinger, Roy C. Macridis, and Richard L. Merritt, *France, Germany, and the Western Alliance* (New York: Scribner, 1967), pp. 119–302.

Thus far the capabilities and resources available to German political leaders have enabled them to obtain evaluative mass and elite support for the regime on the strength of its material achievements and efficient output performance. Major innovative changes in domestic or foreign policy might, however, require a greater symbolic capability to extract emotional allegiances than the system has demonstrated thus far.

Anti-Communist sentiments may have served well enough in the past to justify unpopular govermental measures and mobilize support for a militant democracy. But they may prove to be neither sufficient nor desirable ideological sustenance for a democratic regime. Should domestic or international developments intensify anti-Communist sentiment in Germany, they might increase demands for a more authoritarian form of government. On the other hand, if cold war tensions continue to abate, encouraging German elites to seek some form of accommodation with Communist countries, popular anti-Communist feelings would tend to conflict with foreign policy objectives.

As long as the system can sustain a stable and mundane political climate, low symbolic capability may not matter very much. But it could become a serious weakness should the system be confronted with input demands which strain its resources for efficient performance. The prosaic component in the German political culture has been dominant since 1945 but the romantic-idealist component has not been obliterated. Of late there have been signs that it is re-emerging, especially among university students who have no personal memories of the Nazi era and associate the present regime with crass materialism and stand-pat conservatism. Should such sentiments grow and find no outlet through the political system they might conceivably produce greater pressures from right- and left-wing extremists to change it radically.

We thus return to one of the underlying themes of this book: preserving and developing a democratic system in Germany demands not only the accumulation of material but nonmaterial "satisfaction capital." If the regime is to survive in times of adversity it cannot rest merely on negative inducements, such as the threat of legal sanctions, material deprivations, Communism, and war, but must be based on positive emotional supports anchored in the political culture. This, in the last analysis, is the greatest challenge facing the German people and their leaders in years to come. If they are to meet it they will have to learn to accept the shortcomings as well as the advantages of a pluralist democracy.

Selected Bibliography

1. General Studies on Contemporary Government and Politics

Bölling, Klaus. *Republic in Suspense* (New York: Praeger, 1965).

Bracher, Karl Dietrich. "Die zweite Demokratie in Deutschland – Von Weimar nach Bonn," in Bracher, *Deutschland zwischen Demokratie und Diktatur* (Bern: Scherz, 1964), pp. 108–137.

Deutsch, Karl W. and Lewis J. Edinger. *Germany Rejoins the Powers* (Stanford: Stanford University Press, 1959).

Ellwein, Thomas. *Das Regierungssystem der Bundesrepublik Deutschland,* 1st ed. (Köln-Opladen: Westdeutscher Verlag, 1963).

Erler, Fritz. *Democracy in Germany* (Cambridge, Mass.: Harvard University Press, 1965).

Eschenburg, Theodor. *Staat und Gesellschaft in Deutschland,* 5th ed. (Stuttgart: Curt E. Schwab, 1962).

Golay, John Ford. *The Founding of the Federal Republic of Germany.* (Chicago: University of Chicago Press, 1958).

Grosser, Alfred. *Die Bonner Demokratie* (Düsseldorf: Karl Rauch, 1960).

———. *The Federal Republic of Germany* (New York: Praeger, 1965).

Heidenheimer, Arnold J. *The Governments of Germany,* rev. ed. (New York. Crowell, 1966).

Hiscocks, Richard. *Democracy in Western Germany* (London: Oxford University Press, 1957).

———. *Germany Revived: An Appraisal of the Adenauer Era* (London: Gollancz, 1966).

Litchfield, Edward H. (ed.). *Governing Postwar Germany* (Ithaca: Cornell University Press, 1953).

McInnis, Edgar, Richard Hiscocks, and Robert Spencer. *The Shaping of Postwar Germany* (New York: Praeger, 1960).

Merkl, Peter H. *Germany: Yesterday and Tomorrow* (New York: Oxford University Press, 1964).

———. *The Origins of the West German Republic* (New York: Oxford University Press, 1965).

Plischke, Elmer. *Contemporary Government of Germany* (Boston: Houghton Mifflin, 1961).

Prittie, Terence. *Germany Divided: The Legacy of the Nazi Era* (Boston: Little, Brown, 1960).

Speier, Hans and W. Phillips Davison (eds.). *West German Leadership and Foreign Policy* (Evanston: Row, Peterson, 1957).

Stahl, Walter (ed.). *The Politics of Postwar Germany* (New York: Praeger, 1963).

Von der Gablentz, Otto Heinrich. *Die versäumte Reform: Zur Kritik der westdeutschen Politik* (Köln-Opladen: Westdeutscher Verlag, 1960).

Wildenmann, Rudolf. *Macht und Konsens als Problem der Innen und Aussenpolitik* (Frankfurt-Bonn: Athenäum, 1963).

2. Historical Background

Angell, James W. *The Recovery of Germany* (New Haven: Yale University Press, 1960).

Baumont, M., J. H. Fried, and E. Vermeil (eds.). *The Third Reich* (New York: Praeger, 1955).

Bracher, Karl Dietrich. *Die Auflösung der Weimarer Republik: Eine Studie zum Problem des Machtverfalls in der Demokratie* (Stuttgart: Ring Verlag, 1955).

———. *et al. Die nationalsozialistische Machtergreifung* (Köln: Westdeutscher Verlag, 1960).

Bullock, Allen. *Hitler: A Study in Tyranny* (New York: Harper, 1953).

Butz, O. *Modern German Political Theory* (Garden City, N.Y.: Doubleday, 1955).

Dill, Marshal. *Germany: A Modern History* (Ann Arbor: University of Michigan Press, 1961).

Fischer, Fritz. *Griff nach der Weltmacht* (Düsseldorf: Droste, 1961).

Fränkel, Ernst. "Historische Vorbelastung des deutschen Parlamentarismus," *Vierteljahreshefte für Zeitgeschichte,* VIII, 4 (1960), 323–340.

Glum, Friedrich. *Philosophen im Spiegel und Zerspiegel: Deutschlands Weg in den Nationalismus und Nationalsozialismus* (Munich: Isar Verlag, 1954).

Hallgarten, George W. *Hitler, Reichswehr und Industrie: Zur Geschichte der Jahre 1910–1933* (Frankfurt: Europäische Verlagsanstalt, 1955).

Krieger, L. *The German Idea of Freedom* (Boston: Beacon Press, 1959).

Meinecke, Friedrich. *Die deutsche Katastrophe* (Wiesbaden: E. Brockhaus, 1947).

Mohler, Armin. *Die konservative Revolution in Deutschland* (Stuttgart: F. Vorwerk, 1950).

Mosse, George L. *The Crisis of German Ideology: Intellectual Origins of the Third Reich* (New York: Grosset & Dunlap, 1964).

Neumann, Franz. *Behemoth* (New York: Harper, 1966).

Obermann, Emil. *Soldaten, Bürger, Militaristen: Militär und Demokratie in Deutschland* (Stuttgart: J. G. Cotta, 1958).

Parsons, Talcott. "Democracy and Social Structure in Pre-Nazi Germany," in *Essays in Sociological Theory,* rev. ed. (New York: The Free Press, 1954), pp. 104–123.

Peak, Helen. "Observations on the Characteristics and Distribution of German Nazis," *Psychological Monographs,* LIX, 6 (1945), 1–44.

Pinson, Koppel S. *Modern Germany: Its History and Civilization* (New York: Macmillan, 1954).

Veblen, Thorstein. *Imperial Germany and the Industrial Revolution,* rev. ed. (Ann Arbor: University of Michigan Press, 1966).

Whiteside, Andrew J. "The Nature and Origins of National Socialism," *Journal of Central European Affairs,* XVII, 1 (1957), 48–73.

3. Economic System

Arndt, Hans-Joachim. *West Germany: Politics of Non-Planning* (Syracuse, N.Y.: Syracuse University Press, 1967).

Bundesministerium für Wirtschaft. *Soziale Marktwirtschaft in Zahlen* (Bonn, 1964).

Federal Ministry of Economics. *Achievement in Figures: Results of the Work of Reconstruction in the Federal Republic of Germany, 1949–1962* (Wiesbaden, 1963).

Liesner, H. H. *The Import Dependence of Britain and West Germany* (Princeton: Princeton University Press, 1957).

Menderhausen, Horst. *Two Postwar Recoveries of the German Economy* (Amsterdam: North Holland Publishing Co., 1955).

Stolper, Wolfgang. *Germany Between East and West* (Washington, D.C.: National Planning Association, 1960).

———. "West German Development in an Expanding World Economy," *World Politics,* IX, 1 (1956), 98–117.

Wallich, Henry C. *Mainsprings of the German Revival* (New Haven: Yale University Press, 1955).

4. Culture and Society

Adorno, Theodor W., *Betriebsklima: Eine industriesoziologische Untersuchung aus dem Ruhrgebiet* (Frankfurt: Europäische Verlagsanstalt, 1955).

Bolte, Karl Martin. *Sozialer Aufstieg und Abstieg: Eine Untersuchung über Berufsprestige und Berufsmobilität* (Stuttgart: Ferdinand Enke, 1959).

Clässens, Dieter, Arno Klönne, and Armin Tschöppe. *Sozialkunde der Bundesrepublik Deutschlands* (Düsseldorf: Diederich Verlag, 1965).

Dahrendorf, Ralf. *Society and Democracy in Germany* (Garden City, N.Y.: Doubleday, 1967).

———. "Conflict and Liberty: Some Remarks on the Social Structure of German Politics," *The British Journal of Sociology,* XIV, 3 (1963), 192–211.

———. "Recent Changes in the Class Structure of European Societies," in Stephen R. Graubard (ed.), *A New Europe?* (Cambridge, Mass.: The Riverside Press, 1963), pp. 291–337.

———. "The New Germanies: Restoration, Revolution, Reconstruction," *Encounter,* XXII (1964), 50–58.

Dicks, Henry V. "Some Psychological Studies of the German Character," in T. H. Pear (ed.), *Psychological Factors of Peace and War* (New York: Philosophical Library, 1950).

"Die Bundesdeutschen," special issue of *Der Monat,* XVII, 200 (1965).

Froehner, Rolf. *Wie Stark sind die Halbstarken? Dritte Emnid Untersuchung zur Situation der deutschen Jugend* (Bielefeld: Stakelberg Verlag, 1956).

The Germans: Public Opinion Polls, 1947–1966 (Allensbach und Bonn: Verlag für Demoskopie, 1967).

Hamilton, Richard C. "Affluence and the Worker: The West German Case," *American Journal of Sociology,* LXXI, 5 (1965), 144–152.

Huebner, Theodore. *The Schools of West Germany* (New York: New York University Press, 1962).

Jaide, Walter. *Eine neue Generation?* (Munich: Juventa Verlag, 1963).

Janowitz, Morris. "Social Stratification and Mobility in West Germany," *American Journal of Sociology,* LXIV, 1 (1958), 6–24.

Lemberg, Eugene, *et al. Die Vertriebenen in Westdeutschland,* 3 vols. (Kiel: Hirt, 1959).

Lowie, Robert H. *Toward Understanding Germany.* (Chicago: University of Chicago Press, 1954).

McClelland, David C., *et al.* "Obligations to Self and Society in the United States and Germany," *Journal of Abnormal and Social Psychology,* LVI, 3 (1958), 245–255.

Noelle, Elisabeth and Gerhard Schmidtchen. "Eigentumsbildung in Arbeiternehmerhand: Sozialpolitische Projekte aus der Sicht der Bevölkerung," *Bundesarbeitsblatt,* XII (1965), 518–533.

Picht, Georg. *Die deutsche Bildungskatastrophe* (Freiburg: Walter Verlag, 1964).

Prittie, Terence. "Passing of Work-Obsessed Germany." *The New York Times Magazine,* April 21, 1963, 51–52 ff.

Reigrotzki, Erich. *Soziale Verflechtungen in der Bundesrepublik: Elemente der sozialen Teilnahme in der Kirche, Organisation und Freizeit* (Tübingen: J. C. B. Mohr, 1956).

Robinsohn, Saul B. and J. Caspar Kuhlmann. "Two Decades of Non-Reform in West German Education," *Comparative Education Review,* XI, 3 (1967), 311–330.

Schaffner, Bertram. *Father Land: A Study of Authoritarianism in the German Family* (New York: Columbia University Press, 1948).

Schelsky, Helmut. *Die skeptische Generation: Eine Soziologie der deutschen Jugend* (Düsseldorf: Diederichs Verlag, 1957).

U.S. High Commission for Germany. *The West German Educational System* (Bad Godesberg, 1953).

U.S. High Commission for Germany. *Women in West Germany* (Bad Godesberg, 1952).

5. Political Culture and Participation

Abendroth, Wolfgang. *Wirtschaft, Gesellschaft und Demokratie in der Bundesrepublik* (Frankfurt: Stimme Verlag, 1965).

Almond, Gabriel and Sidney Verba. *The Civic Culture* (Boston: Little, Brown, 1963).

Berghahn, Volker. "Right Wing Radicalism in West Germany's Younger Generation," *Journal of Central European Affairs,* XXII, 3 (1962), 317–336.

Blücher, Viggo Graf (ed.). *Der Prozess der Meinungsbildung: dargestellt am Beispiel der Bundestagswahl 1961* (Bielefeld: EMNID, 1962).

Bremme, Gabriel. *Die politische Rolle der Frau in Deutschland* (Göttingen: Vandenhoek & Ruprecht, 1956).

Bundesministerium für Familie und Jugend. *Bericht über die Bestrebungen auf dem Gebiet der Jugendhilfe* (Bonn, 1965).

Dahrendorf, Ralf. "Demokratie und Sozialstruktur in Deutschland," in Dahrendorf, *Gesellschaft und Freiheit* (Munich: Piper, 1961).

———. "Deutsche Richter: Ein Beitrag zur Soziologie der Oberschicht," in Dahrendorf, *Gesellschaft und Freiheit* (Munich: Piper, 1961).

Dohnanyl, Klaus von. "Die Verführung der Führer," *Die Neue Gesellschaft,* XII, 5 (1965), 860–863.

Edinger, Lewis J. "Continuity and Change in the Background of German Decision-Makers," *Western Political Quarterly,* XIV, 1 (1961), 17–36.

———. "Electoral Politics and Voting Behavior in Western Germany," *World Politics,* XIII, 3 (1961), 471–484.

———. "Post Totalitarian Leadership," *American Political Science Review,* LIV, 1 (1960), 58–82.

Ellwein, Thomas. "Die Machtstruktur in Westdeutschland," *Die neue Gesellschaft,* XII, 5 (1965), 852–863.

Faul, Erwin (ed.). *Wahlen und Wähler in Westdeutschland* (Villingen: Ring Verlag, 1960).

Free, Lloyd A. "Germany: The Divided Ally," in Free, *Six Allies and a Neutral* (New York: The Free Press, 1959).

Habermas, Jürgen, *et al. Student in der Politik* (Neuwied: Luchterband Verlag, 1961).

Hartenstein, Wolfgang and Gunther Schubert. *Mitlaufen oder Mitbestimmen: Untersuchung zum demokratischen Bewusstsein und zur politischen Tradition* (Frankfurt: Europäische Verlagsanstalt, 1961).

——— and Klaus Liepelt. "Party Members and Party Voters in West Germany," *Acta Sociologica,* VI, 1 (1962), 43–52.

Jaide, Walter. *Das Verhältnis der Jugend zur Politik: Empirische Untersuchungen zur politischen Anteilnahme und Meinungsbildung junger Menschen der Geburtsjahrgänge 1940–1946* (Neuwied: Luchterhand Verlag, 1964).

Knutter, Hans-Helmuth. *Ideologien des Rechtsradikalismus im Nachkriegsdeutschland* (Bonn: Röhrscheid, 1961).

Linz, Juan. "Cleavage and Consensus in West German Politics: The Early Fifties," in S. M. Lipset, and Stein Rokkan (eds.), *Party Systems and Voter Alignments: Cross-National Perspectives* (New York: The Free Press, 1967), pp. 283–316.

Scheuch, Erwin. "Führungsgruppen und Demokratie in Deutschland," *Die Neue Gesellschaft,* XIII, 5 (1966), 356–370.

——— and Rudolf Wildenmann (eds.). *Zur Soziologie der Wahl* (Köln-Opladen: Westdeutscher Verlag, 1965).

Schmidt, Hannelore. "Die deutsche Exekutive 1949–1960," *Journal of European Sociology,* IV, 1 (1963), 166–176.

Schultes, Karl. "German Politics and Political Theory," *The Political Quarterly,* XXVIII, 1 (1957), 40–48.

Stahl, Walter (ed.). *Education for Democracy in West Germany* (New York: Praeger, 1961).

Verba, Sidney. "Germany: The Remaking of Political Culture," in Lucian W. Pye and Sidney Verba (eds.), *Political Culture and Political Development* (Princeton: Princeton University Press, 1965).

Waldman, Eric. *The Goose Step Is Verboten: The German Army Today.* (New York: The Free Press, 1964).

6. Representation of Organized Interests

Almond, Gabriel. "The Political Attitudes of German Business," *World Politics,* VIII, 2 (1956), 157–186.

Bethusy-Huc, Viola Gräfin von. *Demokratie und Interessenpolitik* (Wiesbaden: Steiner, 1962).

Braunthal, Gerard. *The Federation of German Industry in Politics* (Ithaca: Cornell University Press, 1965).

Breitling, Rupert. *Die Verbände in der Bundesrepublik* (Meisenheim: Anton Hain, 1955).

Bunn, Ronald F. "Codetermination and the Federation of German Employers' Associations," *Midwest Journal of Political Science,* II, 2 (1958), 278–297.

———. "Ideology of the Federation of German Employers' Associations," *Midwest Journal of Political Science,* III, 3 (1959), 369–376.

———. "The Federation of German Employers' Associations: A Political Interest Group," *Western Political Quarterly,* XIII, 3 (1960), 652–669.

Cole, Taylor C. "Functional Representation in the German Federal Republic," *Midwest Journal of Political Science,* II, 2 (1958), 256–277.

Ellwein, Thomas. *Klerikalismus in der deutschen Politik* (Munich: Isar Verlag, 1956).

Elsner, Ilse. "Der Mythos vom Koloss: Wie mächtig ist die deutsche Arbeiterbewegung?" *Die Neue Gesellschaft,* IX, 6 (1962), 451–455.

Eschenburg, Theodor. *Herrschaft der Verbände?* (Stuttgart: Deutsche Verlagsanstalt, 1955).

Hartmann, Heinz. *Authority and Organization in German Management* (Princeton: Princeton University Press, 1959).

Hirsch-Weber, Wolfgang. *Gewerkschaften in der Politik* (Köln: Westdeutscher Verlag, 1959).

———. "Some Remarks on Interest Groups in the German Federal Republic," in Henry W. Ehrmann (ed.), *Interest Groups on Four Continents* (Pittsburgh: University of Pittsburgh Press, 1958), pp. 96–116.

Kaiser, J. H. *Die Repräsentation organisierter Interessen* (Berlin: Duncker & Humblot, 1956).

Kerr, Clark. "Collective Bargaining in Post-War Germany," *Industrial and Labor Relations Review,* V, 3 (1952), 327–332.

———. "The Trade Union Movement and the Redistribution of Power in Postwar Germany," *The Quarterly Journal of Economics,* LXXII, 3 (1957), 537–550.

Kirchheimer, Otto. "West German Trade Unions," in Hans Speier and W. Phillips Davison, *West German Leadership and Foreign Policy* (Evanston, Ill.: Row, Peterson, 1957).

Lewis, Roy and Rosemary Stewart. *The Managers: A New Examination of English, German and American Executives* (New York: Mentor Books, 1961).

McPherson, W. "Labor Relations in Post-War Germany," *Annals of the American Academy of Political and Social Science,* CCCX (1957), 55 ff.

Neunreither, Karl Heinz. "Politics and Bureaucracy in the German Bundesrat," *American Political Science Review,* LIII, 3 (1959), 713–731.

Pinney, Edward L. *Federalism, Bureaucracy, and Party Politics in Western Germany: The Role of the Bundestag* (Chapel Hill: University of North Carolina Press, 1963).

Reich, Nathan. "Germany's Labor and Economic Recovery," *Proceedings of the Academy of Political Science,* XXVII, 2 (1955), 117–133.

Ross, Arthur M. "Prosperity and Labor Relations in Europe: The Case of West Germany," *Quarterly Journal of Economics,* LXXVI, 3 (1962), 331–360.

Schuchman, A. *Codetermination, Labor's Middle War in Germany* (Washington, D.C.: Public Affairs Press, 1957).

Spiro, Herbert. *The Politics of German Codetermination* (Cambridge, Mass.: Harvard University Press, 1958).

Stammer, Otto. "Interessenverbände und Parteien," *Kölner Zeitschrift für Soziologie und Sozialpsychologie,* IX, 4 (1957), 587–605.

———, *et al. Verbände und Gesetzgebung* (Köln-Opladen: Westdeutscher Verlag, 1965).

Triesch, Günther. *Die Macht der Funktionäre.* (Düsseldorf: Karl Rauch, 1956).

Varain, Heinz Josef. *Parteien und Verbände: Eine Studie über ihren Aufbau, ihre Verflechtungen und ihr Wirken in Schleswig-Holstein 1945–1958* (Köln-Opladen: Westdeutscher Verlag, 1964).

Wells, Roger H. *The States in West German Federalism: A Study in Federal-State Relations* (New York: Bookman, 1961).

7. Party Competition and Integration

Alexander, Edgar. *Adenauer und das neue Deutschland* (Recklinghausen: Paulus Verlag, 1956).

Allemann, Fritz Rene. "Bonns verschränkte Fronten," *Der Monat,* XIII, 209 (1966), 7–15.

Barnes, Samuel H., *et al.* "The German Party System and the 1961 Federal Election," *American Political Science Review,* LVI, 4 (1962), 899–914.

Besson, Waldeman, "Regierung und Opposition in der deutschen Politik," *Politische Vierteljahresschrift,* III, 3 (1962), 225–241.

Braunthal, Gerard. "The Free Democratic Party in West German Politics," *Western Political Quarterly,* XIII, 2 (1960), 332–348.

Chalmers, Douglas A. *The Social Democratic Party of Germany: From Working Class Movement to Modern Political Party* (New Haven: Yale University Press, 1964).

Culver, Lowell W. "Land Elections in West Germany," *Western Political Quarterly,* XIV, 2 (1966), 304–336.

Deuerlein, Ernst. *CDU/CSU 1945–1957: Beiträge zur Zeitgeschichte* (Köln: Bachem, 1957).

Edinger, Lewis J. *Kurt Schumacher: A Study in Personality and Political Behavior* (Stanford: Stanford University Press, 1965).

——— and Douglas Chalmers. "Overture or Swan Song: German Social Democracy Prepares for a New Decade," *Antioch Review,* XX, 2 (1960), 163–175.

Flechtheim, Ossip K. "Die Institutionalisierung der Parteien in der Bundesrepublik," *Zeitschrift für Politik,* IX, 2 (1962), 97–110.

———. *Dokumente zur parteipolitischen Entwicklung in Deutschland seit 1945,* 6 vols. (Berlin: Dokumenten Verlag, 1963–67).

Heidenheimer, Arnold J. *Adenauer and the CDU: The Rise of the Leader and the Integration of the Party* (The Hague: Martinus Nijhoff, 1960).

———. "Federalism and the Party System," *American Political Science Review,* LII, 3 (1958), 809–828.

———. "Foreign Policy and Party Discipline in the CDU," *Parliamentary Affairs,* XIII, 1 (1959–60), 70–84.

———. "German Party Finance, the CDU," *American Political Science Review,* LI, 2 (1957), 369–385.

Heydte, Friedrich August and Karl Sacherl. *Soziologie der Deutschen Parteien* (Munich: Isar Verlag, 1955).

Hirsch-Weber, Wolfgang and Klaus Schütz. *Wähler und Gewählte: Eine Untersuchung der Bundestagswahlen 1953* (Berlin: Vahlen, 1957).

Janowitz, Morris and David R. Segal. "Social Cleavage and Party Affiliation: Germany, Great Britain and the United States," *American Journal of Sociology*, LXXII, 6 (1967), 601–618.

Johnson, Nevil. "State Finance for Political Parties in Western Germany," *Parliamentary Affairs*, XVIII, 3 (1965), 279–292.

Kaack, Heino. *Die Parteien in der Verfassungswirklichkeit der Bundesrepublik* (Bonn: Schriftenreihe der Bundeszentrale für politische Bildung, 1964).

Kaltefleiter, Wolfgang. "Wähler und Parteien in den Landtagswahlen 1961–65," *Zeitschrift für Politik*, XII, 3 (1965), 224–250.

Kirchheimer, Otto. "Germany: The Vanishing Opposition," in Robert A. Dahl (ed.), *Political Opposition in Western Democracies* (New Haven: Yale University Press, 1966), pp. 237–259.

Kitzinger, Uwe W. *German Electoral Politics* (Oxford: Clarendon Press, 1960).

Krippendorff, Ekkehart. "Das Ende des Parteienstaats?" *Der Monat*, XIV, 164 (1962), 23–27.

Lange, Max Gustav, *et al. Parteien in der Bundesrepublik: Studien zur Entwicklung der deutschen Parteien bis zur Bundestagswahl 1953* (Stuttgart: Ring Verlag, 1955).

Mayntz, Renate. "Oligarchic Problems in a German Party District," in Dwaine Marvick (ed.), *Political Decision Makers* (New York: The Free Press, 1961), pp. 138–192.

———. *Parteigruppen in der Grossstadt: Untersuchungen in einem Berliner Kreisverband der CDU* (Köln-Opladen: Westdeutscher Verlag, 1959).

Merkl, Peter H. "Comparative Study and Campaign Management: The Brandt Campaign in Western Germany," *Western Political Science Quarterly*, XV, 4 (1962), 681–705.

Neumann, Sigmund. "Germany: Changing Patterns and Lasting Problems," in Neumann (ed.), *Modern Political Parties* (Chicago: University of Chicago Press, 1956), pp. 354–392.

Pollock, James K., *et al., German Democracy at Work: A Selective Study* (Ann Arbor: University of Michigan Press, 1955).

Preuss, Ulf. "Von der Arbeiterpartei zur Volkspartei," *Die Neue Gesellschaft*, XIII, 5 (1966), 371–385.

Pulzer, P. G. J. "West Germany and the Three Party System," *Political Quarterly*, XV (1962), 681–705.

Rueckert, George L. and Wilder Crane. "CDU Deviancy in the German Bundestag," *Journal of Politics*, XXIV, 3 (1962), 477–521.

Schneider, C. J. "Political Parties and the German Basic Law of 1949," *Western Political Quarterly*, X, 3 (1957), 527–540.

Schuster, Hans. "Wohin treibt unser Parteiensystem?" *Politische Studien*, XIII, 143 (1962), 261–271.

Statistisches Bundesamt. *Die Wahl zum 4. deutschen Bundestag am 17, September 1961* (Wiesbaden, 1965).

Unklebach, Helmut, *et al. Wähler, Parteien, Parlament* (Frankfurt: Athenäum, 1965).

Weymar, Paul. *Konrad Adenauer: Die autorisierte Biographie* (Munich: Kindler, 1955).

Williams, J. E. "Federal Elections in West Germany," *World Today,* XVIII, 2 (1961), 512–518.

8. Policy Processes

Amphoux, Jean. *Le Chancelier Fédéral dans le Régime Constitutionnel de la République Fédéral d'Allemagne* (Paris: Librarie Général de Droit et de Jurisprudence, 1962).

Baade, Hans W. "Social Science Evidence and the Federal Constitutional Court of West Germany," *Journal of Politics,* XXIII, 3 (1961), 421–461.

Bracher, Karl D. "Problems of a Parliamentary Democracy in Europe," in Stephen R. Graubard (ed.), *A New Europe?* (Cambridge, Mass.: The Riverside Press, 1963), pp. 245–264.

Braunthal, Gerard. "Direct and Representative Democracy in West Germany: The Atomic Armament Issue," *Canadian Journal of Economics and Political Science,* XXVI, 3 (1959), 313–323.

———. "Federalism and the Party System in Germany: The Broadcasting Controversy," *Journal of Politics,* XXIV, 4 (1962), 545–561.

Chaput de Saintonge, R. A. A. *Public Administration in Germany* (London: Weidenfeld & Nicolson, 1961).

Cole, Taylor C. "Three Constitutional Courts: A Comparison," *American Political Science Review,* LIII, 4 (1959), 963–984.

———. "The West German Constitutional Court: An Evaluation after Six Years," *Journal of Politics,* XX, 2 (1958), 278–307.

Dechamps, Bruno. *Macht und Arbeit der Ausschüsse* (Meisenheim: Westkulturverlag, 1954).

Domes, Jürgen. *Bundesregierung und Mehrheitsfraktion: Aspekte der Verhältnisse der Fraktionen der CDU/CSU im zweiten und dritten deutschen Bundestag zum Kabinett Adenauer* (Köln-Opladen: Westdeutscher Verlag, 1964).

Grosser, Alfred. "The Evolution of European Parliaments," in Stephen R. Graubard (ed.), *A New Europe?* (Cambridge, Mass.: The Riverside Press, 1963), pp. 219–244.

Hanrieder, Wolfram F. *West German Foreign Policy 1949–1963* (Stanford: Stanford University Press, 1967).

Hennis, Wilhelm. "Der deutsche Bundestag 1949–1965," *Der Monat,* XVII, 215 (1966), 26–36.

Hughes, Christopher. "The German Federal Council," *Parliamentary Affairs,* XIII, 2 (1960), 248–255.

Jacob, Herbert. *German Administration since Bismarck* (New Haven: Yale University Press, 1963).

Johnson, Nevil. "Questions in the Bundestag," *Parliamentary Affairs,* XVI, 1 (1962–63), 22–34.

Kralewski, W. and K. Neunreither. *Oppositionelles Verhalten im ersten deutschen Bundestag 1940–1953* (Köln: Kiepenheuer & Witsch, 1963).

Leibholz, Gerhard. "The Federal Constitutional Court in Germany and the 'Southwest Case,'" *American Political Science Review,* XLVI, 3 (1952), 723–731.

Loewenberg, Gerhard. *Parliament in the German Political System* (Ithaca, N.Y.: Cornell University Press, 1966).

———. "Parliamentarianism in Western Germany: The Functioning of the Bundestag," *American Political Science Review,* LV, 1 (1961), 87–102.

McWhinney, Edward. "Judicial Restraint and the West German Constitutional Court," *Harvard Law Review,* LXXV, 1 (1961), 5 ff.

Merkl, Peter H. "Equilibrium, Structure of Interest and Leadership: Adenauer's Survival as Chancellor," *American Political Science Review,* LVI, 3 (1962), 639–650.

———. "Executive-Legislative Federalism in West Germany," *American Political Science Review,* LIII, 3 (1959), 732–741.

———. "The Financial Constitution (*Finanzverfassung*) of Western Germany," *American Journal of Comparative Law,* VI, 2 (1957), 327–340.

Neunreither, Karl Heinz. *Der Bundesrat zwischen Politik und Verwaltung* (Heidelberg: Quell & Meyer, 1959).

———. "Federalism and the West German Bureaucracy," *Political Studies,* VII, 3 (1959), 232–245.

Pinney, Edward L. *Federalism, Bureaucracy and Party Politics in Western Germany* (Chapel Hill: University of North Carolina Press, 1963).

———. "Latent and Manifest Bureaucracy in the West German Parliament: The Case of the Bundesrat," *Midwest Journal of Political Science,* VI, 2 (1962), 149–164.

Rheinstein, M. "Approach to German Law," *Indiana Law Journal,* XXXIV, 3 (1959), 546–558.

Rupp, H. G. "Judicial Review in the Federal Republic of Germany," *American Journal of Comparative Law,* IX, 1 (1960), 29–47.

Sternberger, Dolf. "Gewaltenteilungen und parlamentarische Regierung in der Bundesrepublik Deutschlands," *Politische Vierteljahreshefte,* I, 1 (1960), 23–37.

Ulrich, Junker. *Die Richtlinien Kompetenz des Bundeskanzler* (Tübingen: Mohr, 1965).

Ziller, Gebhard. *Der Bundesrat* (Frankfurt: Athenäum, 1966).

9. Policy Issues

Altmann, Rüdiger. *Das Erbe Adenauers: Eine Bilanz* (Munich: Kindler, 1963).

Bluhm, Georg. *Die Oder-Neisse-Linie in der deutschen Aussenpolitik* (Freiburg: Rombach, 1963).

Bölling, Klaus. *Republic in Suspense* (New York: Praeger, 1963).

Brandt, Gerhard. "Socio-Economic Aspects of German Rearmament," *European Journal of Sociology,* VI, 2 (1965), 294–308.

Deutsch, Karl W. and Lewis J. Edinger. "Foreign Policy of the German Federal Republic," in Roy Macridis (ed.), *Foreign Policy in World Politics,* 3rd rev. ed. (Englewood Cliffs, N.J.: Prentice-Hall, 1967).

——— and Lewis J. Edinger. "Germany Rejoins the Powers," *Yale Review,* XLIV, 1 (1959), 20–42.

——— and Lewis J. Edinger, Roy C. Macridis, and Richard L. Merrit. *France, Germany, and the Western Alliance* (New York: Scribner, 1967).

Eschenburg, Theodor. *Institutionelle Sorgen in der Bundesrepublik* (Stuttgart: Curt E. Schwab, 1961).

———. *Zur politischen Praxis in der Bundesrepublik* (Munich: Piper, 1966).

Feld, Werner. *Reunification and West German-Soviet Relations* (The Hague: Martinus Nijhoff, 1963).

Freund, Gerald. *Germany Between Two Worlds* (New York: Harcourt, Brace, 1961).

Gimbel, John. "The Spiegel Affair in Perspective," *Midwest Journal of Political Science,* IX, 3 (1965), 282–97.

Grosser, Alfred. "Germany and Europe," in C. G. Haines, *European Integration* (Baltimore: Johns Hopkins University Press, 1957), pp. 177–195.

Hartmann, Frederick H. *Germany Between East and West: The Reunification Problem* (Englewood Cliffs, N.J.: Prentice-Hall, 1965).

Jaspers, Karl. *The Future of Germany* (Chicago: University of Chicago Press, 1967).

Lewis, Flora. "Six Big 'Ifs' in Germany's Future," *The New York Times Magazine,* Nov. 18, 1962, 31 ff., 126 ff.

Neal, Fred Warner. *War, Peace and Germany* (New York: Norton, 1962).

Richardson, James L. *Germany and the Atlantic Alliance* (Cambridge, Mass.: Harvard University Press, 1966).

Richter, Hans Werner (ed.). *Bestandsaufnahme—Eine deutsche Bilanz* (Munich: Kurt Desch Verlag, 1962).

Strauss, Franz Josef. *The Grand Design* (New York: Praeger, 1965).

Von der Gablentz, Otto H. *Die versäumte Reform: Zur Kritik der westdeutschen Politik* (Köln-Opladen: Westdeutscher Verlag, 1960).

Willis, F. Roy. *France, Germany and the New Europe 1945–1963* (Stanford: Stanford University Press, 1965).

Index

UNIVERSITY LIBRARY
NOTTINGHAM